Thirst and Body Fluid Regulation

Body fluid regulation is pivotal to human health and is served by extensive clinical and preclinical science. By combining modern advances with previous findings in the field, this book presents a comprehensive treatment of major experiments, theories, and new advances in the field of body fluid regulation, thirst, and drinking. It features the main integrative brain mechanisms for fluid regulation, the development of such systems, fluid balance during heat and exercise, aging and clinical disorders, and comparative aspects of fluid regulation. The volume focuses on mammalian thirst or drinking behavior alongside relevant aspects of the physiology of fluid balance. The principal fluid compartments and their regulation by both intakes and losses are highlighted, using both human and animal studies to illustrate the main concepts.

Neil E. Rowland is Professor of Psychology at the University of Florida, USA.

T0349195

Thirst and Body Fluid Regulation

From Nephron to Neuron

Neil E. Rowland

University of Florida

CAMBRIDGE UNIVERSITY PRESS

Shaftesbury Road, Cambridge CB2 8EA, United Kingdom

One Liberty Plaza, 20th Floor, New York, NY 10006, USA

477 Williamstown Road, Port Melbourne, VIC 3207, Australia

314–321, 3rd Floor, Plot 3, Splendor Forum, Jasola District Centre, New Delhi – 110025, India

103 Penang Road, #05–06/07, Visioncrest Commercial, Singapore 238467

Cambridge University Press is part of Cambridge University Press & Assessment, a department of the University of Cambridge.

We share the University's mission to contribute to society through the pursuit of education, learning and research at the highest international levels of excellence.

www.cambridge.org
Information on this title: www.cambridge.org/9781108813822

DOI: 10.1017/9781108878166

First published 2022
First paperback edition 2022

A catalogue record for this publication is available from the British Library

ISBN   978-1-108-83991-4   Hardback
ISBN   978-1-108-81382-2   Paperback

Cambridge University Press & Assessment has no responsibility for the persistence or accuracy of URLs for external or third-party internet websites referred to in this publication and does not guarantee that any content on such websites is, or will remain, accurate or appropriate.

Contents

Contents

Figures

Preface

Recently, writing a short general article on thirst (Rowland, 2020), I became acutely aware that there is no modern or comprehensive text in the field. The comprehensive scholarship represented, for example, by A. V. Wolf's *Thirst: Physiology of the Urge to Drink and Problems of Water Lack* (1958), J. T. Fitzsimons' *The Physiology of Thirst and Sodium Appetite* (1979), B. J. Rolls and E. T. Rolls' *Thirst* (1982), or S. P. Grossman's *Thirst and Sodium Appetite: Physiological Basis* (1990) are now over 30 years old. In contrast, more recent scholarly works have been in the form of contributing author conference volumes, such as those edited by D. J. Ramsay and D. A. Booth (*Thirst: Physiological and Psychological Aspects* [1991]) or L. A. De Luca, J. V. Menani, and A. K. Johnson (*Neurobiology of Body Fluid Homeostasis: Transduction and Integration* [2019]). And while these latter are excellent resources, they lack the cohesiveness or perspective of a monograph. And so was born the idea for this book.

In the writing of this book, I realized why nobody has tried to write a comprehensive academic treatment of thirst in recent years: the body of knowledge in the field is so vast and diverse that it would be impossible to do it justice within manageable length and time limits. My aspirational model for this book was James Fitzsimons' monograph, cited above, which in a little over 500 pages was able to synthesize most of the relevant knowledge as of 1979. Today, such coverage would need 10 times the pages. I therefore recognize that there are a myriad of interesting or important facts and ideas that have not been included or fully developed in this somewhat shorter book. Some notable omissions include pharmacology of drinking and sodium appetite, each of which has a separate chapter in Fitzsimons (1979). Otherwise, many aspects of scope and/or organization are similar.

As in most areas of science, the reductionist paradigm in thirst has inevitably led to application of new technologies, especially from molecular genetics and biology. One of the aims of this book is to provide a synthesis that includes many older or foundational studies of physiology and behavior with the new neurobiology and, as relevant, to point out where there are gaps in extrapolation between these approaches. As I suggested previously, this book is not comprehensive, and I take full responsibility for both the deliberate and inadvertent omissions.

If books are a currency of civilization, then libraries and publishing houses are the banks and librarians are the custodians. I want to thank Cambridge University Press, in particular Steven Acerra, for indulging me to continue their historical ties to this field led by Fitzsimons (1979) and Rolls and Rolls (1982). Electronic collections are the present and future, and it is critically important that libraries continue to be a protected and valued repository of human knowledge. I want to thank and appreciate the countless nameless and faceless librarians, our custodians of knowledge who, during the recent COVID-19-related closure of libraries, have scanned or retrieved numerous articles I have used in writing this book: without them, this would not be.

Research scientists stand on the shoulders of their academic ancestors. My own career has been influenced directly or indirectly by many mentors and collaborators of whom I will mention just two of the most important: Stylianos Nicolaidis, my dissertation mentor at the Collège de France who got me started in the field and filled me with the enthusiasm for research, and Melvin Fregly, my longtime colleague and mentor at the University of Florida. I also want to thank Gloria Smith and Kimberly Robertson, my laboratory managers for about the first and second halves of my research career, and many graduate students without whom none of this would be possible. And most of all, thanks to my spouse, Susan Semple-Rowland, who has put up with me for over forty years, is my bicycling buddy now spanning five continents, and, academically, has introduced me to the world of online teaching.

1 Fundamentals of Thirst and Body Fluid Regulation

Life on this planet originated in the oceans. Movement of species to terrestrial habitats was possible only because elements of that aquatic legacy were internalized. This internal fluid is a fragile reservoir, and it must be preserved and frequently replenished in order to maintain vital processes. Animals have developed a warning mechanism to indicate when their internal fluid reservoirs need filling. That warning mechanism is thirst.

Thirst may be defined as inner sensation(s) that motivate organisms to seek and eventually to consume water. Thirst is an inferred motivational state, whereas drinking is an observable behavior. Much of this book will be about drinking behavior, and I will attempt to keep this distinct from statements about thirst. I will occasionally refer to fluids other than water, but, unless stated, the term *drinking* will refer to consumption of natural or pure water.

This chapter will provide some fundamental facts and theories about thirst and drinking. It is organized into four sections, most of which will be expanded upon in subsequent chapters:

- Pioneers: a brief history of the study of fluid balance and thirst
- Fluid compartments: basics of body fluid distribution and how it is measured
- Water intake: classification and measurement of water consumption
- Brain and neuroanatomy of the lamina terminalis

To streamline reading of the main text, brief descriptions of some research techniques that are commonly used in the field appear in the appendix.

1.1 Pioneers

1.1.1 Local or Dry Mouth Theories of Thirst

One of the first formal analyses of thirst was compiled in the mid-eighteenth century by Albrecht von Haller as part of a treatise on

1

physiology. The following edited passage is adapted from that text (see Fitzsimons, 1979, p. 1, for the unedited version):

Thirst is seated in the tongue, fauces, oesophagus and stomach. Whenever these parts, which are constantly moistened by mucous and saliva juices, grow dry, there arises a sense much more dangerous and intolerable than hunger. This uneasy sense continues until the proportion of diluting water in the blood restores the necessary moisture and free secretion required in the parts before mentioned.

This establishes what became known as the dry mouth theory of thirst. A later advocate of this theory was Walter Cannon, who, in his 1919 Croonian Lecture, wrote:

Water supply is maintained because we avoid, or abolish, by taking water or aqueous fluid, the disagreeable sensations which arise and torment us ... if the salivary glands, because of a lowering of the water-content of the body ... fail to pour out their watery secretion in sufficient amount and in proper quantity to keep moist the mouth and pharynx. (p. 301)

This advances von Haller's analysis insofar as reduced salivary flow is deemed a consequence of reduced body water content. Some years later, Cannon (1939) presented detailed observations supporting a dry mouth theory of thirst, including that moistening the mouth produces an immediate alleviation of thirst. He also made a prescient connection between thirst, appetite or consumption, and associative learning:

Behavior may be directed by movements to get rid of ... annoying stimulation.... On the other hand, experience may condition behavior by revealing that a certain food or drink is the cause of unanticipated delight.... It is not to be supposed that the two motivating agencies – the pang and the pleasure – are separate..., when relief from hunger or thirst is found, the (conditioned) appetite may simultaneously be satiated. (pp. 75–76)

Cannon seems to be arguing that the preconditions for thirst may be systemic, but that oral factors underlie the onset as well as the termination of thirst. Under natural circumstances, dehydration and onset of thirst occur slowly, typically over a period of minutes or hours, but the satiation or termination of thirst is rapid, typically over a period of seconds to minutes.

It is evident that humans can verbally or symbolically report thirst and its intensity, but it is only by inference that we can attribute thirst to animals. A major class of theories put forward to counter the local or dry mouth arguments considered thirst as a general or systemic sensation. The empirical evidence for these theories came largely from animal experiments. The latter provide a degree of control and reproducibility that is often difficult to achieve with humans and form the basis of most of what we know about biological mechanisms in general and thirst in particular. But systemic theories of thirst do not disprove involvement of oral factors, and studies of dehydration in humans suggest that systemic and oral causes of thirst usually coincide.

1.1.2   General or Systemic Theories of Thirst

In the early nineteenth century, Guillaume Dupuytren (cited by Rullier, 1821) demonstrated that drinking induced in experimental animals by heat exposure could be prevented by intravenous injections of water or other dilute fluids. Shortly thereafter, Thomas Latta (1832) found that the severe thirst and circulatory collapse caused by cholera was relieved by intravenous infusion of a dilute solution of sodium salts. These and other studies showed that fluid can bypass the oral cavity and still satiate thirst; thirst (or its satiation) is not an exclusively oral phenomenon.

The reverse type of experiment in which the oral cavity is moistened by drinking but water is not absorbed, a procedure often known as sham drinking, was described by Claude Bernard (1856). Bernard had earlier made his classic observations about the constancy of the milieu intérieur, which formed the basis for understanding the concept of departures from that state. He prepared a dog with a gastric cannula, dehydrated it by giving food, and then, with the cannula open, presented water. He noted:

The animal started to lap, and the water passed through the mouth ... and arrived in the stomach from where it escaped through the open cannula. In spite of wetting all the upper part of the alimentary canal, thirst was not relieved: the animal ... drank until fatigue stopped it.... Thirst is not a local sensation ... but on the contrary is the expression of a general need to restore the liquids of the economy that have suffered a loss.

The general theory of thirst received indirect support from early reports of exaggerated thirst after brain damage. Carl Nothnagel (1881) observed striking thirst starting about three hours after a man had fallen from his horse and struck his head. Stephen Paget (1897) included Nothnagel's case among nine published and five new cases of thirst (and/or hunger) after injury or disease of the brain. Since the patients all recovered, Padgett noted that the damage was probably not to the "vital centers" (i.e., the brain stem regions known to subserve vital functions such as respiration), but instead might have been more rostral. This work advanced the concept of thirst-related regions or centers in the brain and, because dry mouth did not seem to be involved in any of the cases, further supported a general or systemic theory. Hugo Wettendorff (1901) proposed that the brain was the receiving and coordinating center for neural information coming from dehydrated tissues and that all tissues, including the oropharynx, would contribute to the emergent sensation of thirst. At about the same time, in part based on his finding that injection of hypertonic NaCl caused drinking in dogs, André Mayer (1901) proposed that drinking was one counter-regulatory mechanism that protected animals from increased osmotic pressure, as well as associated changes in the circulatory system. However, since the cardiovascular centers were known to be in the hindbrain (medulla), Mayer believed that thirst would also arise from that region.

Eric Leschke (1918) found that patients to whom hypertonic NaCl was administered as a clinical treatment reported thirst. The mechanism for this effect was investigated by Alfred Gilman (1937). He injected dogs with concentrated NaCl solution and then measured serum osmotic pressure and specific gravity after 30 minutes, after which the dogs drank avidly. NaCl does not enter cells and thus caused a large rise in serum (extracellular) osmotic pressure and a decrease in specific gravity due to a shift of water from intracellular fluid (ICF) to extracellular fluid (ECF) (see Section 1.2). When dogs were injected with isosmotic urea, a solute that is freely permeable to cells, there was a smaller increase in serum osmotic pressure, and, when allowed to drink, dogs drank only about half as much as after NaCl. Thus, cellular dehydration was established as a critical stimulus to drinking. It has sometimes been referred to as intracellular or osmotic drinking, and, as subsequent human studies showed, it is associated with a sensation of thirst.

Around the turn of the twentieth century, several studies implicated the pituitary gland and/or damage to the cerebral ventricular system as causing increased urine output. Leschke (1918) made the connection that increased fluid loss via urination would produce dehydration and hence thirst and considered the cerebral integration of intake and excretion:

We have to imagine that as is the case for sensory-motor reflex arcs there exist reflexes at several levels for the regulation of water and solute metabolism, the lowest of which passes through the medulla, the next highest and most important for the regulation of all sympathetic innervation passes through the floor of the diencephalon, and the highest, alone associated with consciousness, passes through the cerebral cortex. (p. 776)

Bengt Andersson (Andersson, 1952; Andersson & McCann, 1955) was the first to show that local osmotic or electrical stimulation of the brain, and specifically the anterior hypothalamus, produced drinking or polydipsia in goats, and this ushered in a new focus on the neurology of drinking.

Cellular dehydration is not the only stimulus to drinking, or to thirst as a general sensation. Although isosmotic blood loss through hemorrhage does not always cause acute thirst (Holmes & Montgomery, 1953), possibly because of other associated traumatic events, the loss of body sodium through diuretics or sodium restriction often does cause water intake that is not associated with increased osmotic pressure. Instead, the critical factor is loss of blood volume or ECF, and the resultant drinking and thirst are called *extracellular* or *volumetric*. This led to studies combining intracellular and extracellular dehydrations and showing that the drinking produced was additive. This is the basis of a dual-depletion model of thirst (Fitzsimons, 1979), a systemic theory that is widely accepted by investigators in the field.

This short history is designed to give a flavor for the origins of many of the theoretical and procedural aspects of the modern study of drinking and thirst. More complete historical accounts may be found in Fitzsimons (1979). Within the past century or so, there have been numerous technological advances that have propelled the field, including the following:

- Stereotaxic brain surgery in small animals (Horsley-Clark apparatus)
- Improved sensitivity of assays and measures that allow use of smaller animals
- Electronic advances that allow recording from single neurons, including patch clamping
- Improved pathway tracing in the brains of experimental animals, and functional magnetic resonance imaging (fMRI) in humans
- Advent of transgenic and derivative molecular biological techniques

Some of these methods or techniques are explained briefly in the appendix.

1.2   Thirst and Water Intake: Measurement

1.2.1   Drinking

Most studies of thirst or drinking use natural water such as that from a tap or spring and suitable for human consumption. These sources may contain small and variable concentrations of dissolved ions or other materials (Section 1.2.3). Distilled or deionized water provides a more reproducible but somewhat unnatural standard. Each experiment must present water in a physical container suitable for the species under study, preferably minimizing spillage, and allow an appropriate period of time over which measurement is taken. Once this duration is established, the two key parameters are the volume consumed and the pattern or structure with which that drinking occurs. In some studies, other fluid(s) and/ or choices are presented, but the same principles apply. The water presented is normally at room or ambient temperature, but a few studies have used water temperature as an independent variable.

Gravimetric methods are accurate measures of intake. These can be made at single or discrete times by removing, weighing, and replacing the fluid container. Preferably, the container may be mounted on an electronic load cell and weighed continuously. Volumetric methods dispense the fluid from a calibrated tube or container and read the meniscus at defined intervals.

Lick analysis (in rodents) is the most common method of obtaining patterns of drinking. In this method, the animal either completes a circuit with each lick or interrupts a photobeam with its tongue. In either case, the total amount consumed in the session must be measured (by weight or volume), and, with the assumption that each lick is a constant volume, the pattern of licking may be equated to the temporal pattern of volume consumed. In some applications, animals may be asked to perform operant responses to obtain delivery of a fixed and usually small volume via a spout. The animal performs one or several licks to consume that delivery and then controls how soon it will work for the next delivery. Given that free water cannot be hoarded or otherwise saved by animals, the temporal record of responding is equivalent to the pattern of drinking.

Within this context, different species have been defined as fast or slow drinkers (Adolph, 1943; Rolls et al., 1980). Dogs and sheep are in the fast drinker category, and when they drink it usually occurs as a single large and rapid bout of sustained lapping or sucking from the fluid reservoir. The amount consumed thus seems to be established before the bout begins. In contrast, most rodents are in the slow drinker category and tend to take small amounts with each sip or lick, with variable pauses or breaks between bouts. Thus, water consumed early in a bout has the potential to generate postingestive signals that may affect drinking later in the bout. These issues are particularly important in the analysis of termination of drinking (Section 1.3).

1.2.2   Thirst

Thirst can be measured directly only in humans. The best way to do this is to use a visual analog scale, which is a line with anchors at each extreme. The question might be "How thirsty do you feel now?" with the anchors "not at all" and "very thirsty" (Rolls & Rolls, 1982). The subject then makes an appropriate mark on the line, and this can be converted into a digital score. For example, the low anchor may be 0 and the top anchor 10, so a mark exactly in the middle would receive a score of 5.0. The advantage of this method is that it can be repeated many times during a test session, during which onset and dissipation of thirst may be a key dependent variable. Because there may be individual differences in usage of the scales, it is also possible to use difference scores or other adjustment methods for the individual range used within the study. Often, other subjective ratings are obtained at the same times, using similar visual analog scales to assess dryness of the mouth, fullness of the stomach, pleasantness of actual or anticipated drinking, and other sensations.

1.2.3   The Taste of Water

Most of the water that we drink contains a small quantity of dissolved minerals or other substances that can impart a taste to the water. Brackish water contains substantial concentrations of NaCl and tastes salty. Bedouin nomads described water as either brackish or sweet (i.e., not brackish), but not tasteless. Taste buds are normally bathed in a mixed saliva from all of the major salivary glands. Overall, this is a hypotonic solution of sodium (Na^+) and potassium (K^+) salts, as well as other molecules (Humphrey & Williamson, 2001). Water consumed by mouth thus is hypotonic relative to the background or adaptation level in saliva, giving rise to a taste sensation. Salivary osmolality tends to increase with dehydration, which may enhance the contrast effect of water.

Electrophysiological recordings from gustatory nerves have reported fibers that are sensitive to water, or for which water is the best stimulus (e.g., Liljestrand & Zotterman, 1954; Shinghai, 1980). There appear to be species differences. Recordings from the chorda tympani in humans undergoing middle ear surgery showed a decline in integrated nerve activity after water rinse relative to touch or other tastant solutions (Zotterman & Diamant, 1959). On the other hand, when single cells were recorded in the nucleus of the solitary tract (NTS) of rats, the first taste relay in the brain stem, some cells were modestly excited by water, and some inhibited (Rosen et al., 2010). In the parabrachial nucleus (PBN), a pontine relay nucleus, some units were strongly excited by water and not by other tastants, thus appearing to be water specialist cells. These authors suggest that water enters taste buds via aquaporin channels, several subtypes of which are expressed in taste buds, causing cell expansion and eventual depolarization due to activation of volume-regulated anion channels. A different mechanism for water taste was proposed by Zocchi et al. (2017). Using anesthetized mice, they found that changing the solution bathing the tongue from artificial saliva to

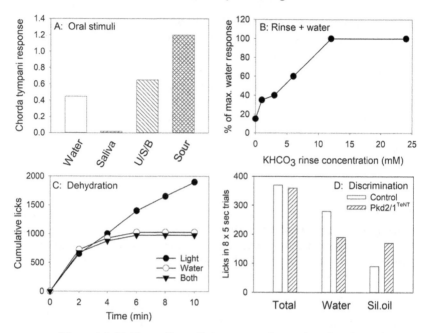

Figure 1.1 Evidence for a distinct taste of water in mice (from Zocchi et al., 2017). Panel A shows the integrated chorda tympani response to application of water, artificial saliva, an average for umami, salt, or bitter (USB), and sour (citric acid). Panel B shows the effect of prior oral rinsing with different concentrations of bicarbonate on the chorda tympani response to water. Panel C shows the number of licks in a 10-minute session by mice engineered to express channel rhodopsin 2 in taste receptor cells expressing a sour (acid) receptor, PKD2L1. The cells were activated by an optic fiber (blue light) in an empty drinking spout. Stimulation of these cells produced licking without evidence of satiation. Panel D shows that genetic silencing of PKD2 cells (Pkd2/1^{TeNT}) impaired discrimination of water from silicone oil.

water produced robust responses in the chorda tympani (Figure 1.1, panel A). Specific removal of bicarbonate from the artificial saliva abolished the response to water (panel B), whereas osmolality change alone had no effect (panel C). Using genetic knockout of the acid-sensing taste receptor shows this is critical for the normal water response (panel D).

Regardless of the sensory mechanism involved, water is known to activate cortical regions in humans, assessed by fMRI. Using artificial saliva as a control stimulus, De Araujo, Kringelbach, Rolls, and McGlone (2003) found that the taste of water activated the frontal operculum and caudal orbitofrontal cortex. A region of the middle insula was also activated by water but only when subjects were thirsty. Collectively, these studies show that water does have a distinct taste and that at least some aspects are dependent on hydration status. It follows that water samples that are hypotonic relative to saliva, but containing different dissolved ions, most likely give rise to qualitatively different water tastes, such as sweet and brackish. Unless otherwise noted, the studies cited in this text use either tap water, bottled water, or tap water that has been distilled or deionized.

1.3　Initiation, Maintenance, and Termination of Drinking

Drinking, like most behaviors, is episodic – at least for terrestrial mammals that comprise the principal focus of this text. The structural aspects, such as licking, for the most part refer to maintenance of an ongoing behavioral episode. Factors that initiate an episode and those that terminate it are critical to understanding when and how much is consumed (see Rolls et al., 1980, for an extended review). In laboratory studies using humans or animals, there is usually an experimenter-determined establishing procedure, such as a period of fluid deprivation or infusion of hypertonic NaCl. These procedures in humans increase self-reported thirst or mouth discomfort, including dryness, and when water is presented it is consumed with short latency. Comparable establishing procedures in animals elicit consumption of water. Motivation to obtain water under these conditions has been investigated less frequently but may not always yield the same thresholds or amounts as consumption-based tests (Miller et al., 1957).

The initiation of thirst implies that a threshold has been exceeded. Most of this text refers to studies in which drinking occurs under ideal laboratory conditions and a physiological threshold of fluid depletion may be the principal initiating factor. The actual threshold can be modified by many factors, including time of day (Chapter 7), the taste of water, and actual or perceived cost or danger in going to the water source. Drinking may also occur without obvious physiological depletion: Humans and many animals are opportunists, taking some water if an unexpected encounter with water arises. That said, much of the work on drinking revolves around the implicit or explicit concept of physiological threshold(s).

Once drinking has started, what determines how much is consumed and/or the length or structure of the drinking bout? It must first be appreciated that water initially enters the stomach, and from there it empties into the intestine rather slowly – often an hour or more for complete emptying – and is absorbed from various levels of the intestine

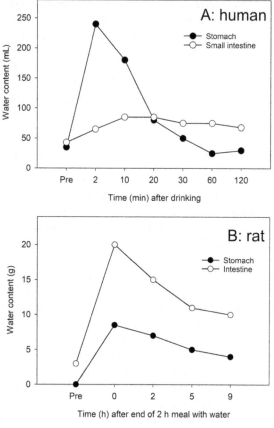

Figure 1.2 Emptying of water from the stomach. Panel A (from Mudie et al., 2014) shows successive MRI scans of overnight-fasted humans before and at various times after drinking 240 mL water. Water in the small intestine was present in multiple small (~5 mL) pockets at all times after drinking. Panel B (from Lepkovsky et al., 1957) shows the mean water content in the stomach or intestine, measured by drying the wet contents, of rats before and at various times after eating a daily 2 h meal of dry food with water available. These rats drank about 14 mL water and ate 14 g food over that 2 h access.

also relatively slowly (Figure 1.2). The drinking bout in both fast and slow drinkers terminates while most of the water is still in the stomach and only a small fraction has been absorbed into the bloodstream with consequent rehydration of dehydrated tissues. It follows that there must be preabsorptive controls to effectively predict or anticipate the eventual rehydrating effect of water consumed in a given episode. Those controls could measure water passing through the mouth (oral metering), water accumulated in or stretching the stomach (gastric controls), similar intestinal controls, or sensitive monitors in the hepatic portal region where the absorbed water will first arrive. As we will see in the following chapters, there is good evidence for each of these, but the extent to which each applies will depend on the species and the context. As a general rule, for faster rates of drinking, the more predominant metering will be at the earlier levels of the orogastrointestinal tract.

From a physiological perspective, termination of drinking will occur when the preabsorptive signals summate to a level that overrides or inhibits the dehydration signal, which in many cases remains suprathreshold at the time that drinking stops. There are several mechanisms by which this could occur, again to be discussed in Chapters 3–6 and 8–9. The broader perspective is that when we measure the amount of water consumed, we measure only one dimension of a multidimensional construct. Many studies cited in this text measure amount consumed, but some have included more detailed behavioral observations, and I will attempt to incorporate those as relevant.

Drinking is only half of the equation of maintaining fluid balance, and it is the part over which animals have voluntary control. The other half is the physiological regulation of fluid loss, an involuntary but critical aspect. Dehydrated animals reduce fluid loss, and overhydrated animals dissipate the excess fluid. Because of this complementary relationship between inputs and losses, it is not surprising that they share common elements in their control mechanisms. In particular, vasopressin (AVP) is a potent antidiuretic (i.e., water conserving) hormone, and its levels in blood are controlled by the firing rate of magnocellular neurosecretory cells in the supraoptic (SON) and paraventricular (PVN) nuclei of the hypothalamus. The activity of these cells is determined by sensory elements that also control or modulate drinking behavior. The text thus will refer extensively to AVP in addition to drinking.

1.4   The Lamina Terminalis

Arguably, the largest advance in understanding the control of drinking that has been made since the publication of Fitzsimons' (1979) magnificent monograph has been the emergence of the lamina terminalis as the principal integrative structure. Fitzsimons was able to include pioneering work from the mid-1970s pointing to the two circumventricular organs of the third cerebral ventricle – the subfornical organ (SFO) and organum vasculosum of the lamina terminalis (OVLT) – as key sites for the action of the hormone angiotensin (ANG) II. In particular, by

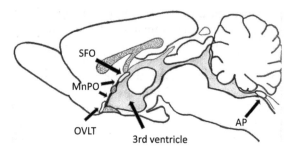

Figure 1.3 Key structures of the lamina terminalis. Shown is a schematic midsagittal diagram of a rodent brain, showing locations of the OVLT, dorsal and ventral MnPO, and SFO along the rostral wall of the third cerebral ventricle. Also shown is the area postrema in the fourth ventricle.

the mid-1970s, it was known that lesions of the SFO attenuated or abolished drinking evoked by administration of ANG II (Simpson & Routtenberg, 1975), microinjections of ANG II into various parts of the brain revealed that the OVLT was more sensitive for drinking than the SFO (Nicolaïdis & Fitzsimons, 1975), ANG II injected intracerebroventricularly (ICV) caused drinking when access to the SFO was blocked by a cream plug (Buggy et al., 1975), and lesions along the anterior wall of the third ventricle impaired drinking during hypernatremia (Andersson et al., 1975). Fitzsimons (1979, p. 300) wrote, "The OVLT or supraoptic crest ... its exact neural connections are unknown. A complicated vascular network with fenestrated capillaries which allow blood-borne molecules direct access to neurones suggests that the OVLT is a promising receptor site for the dipsogenic action of circulating angiotensin."

Functional aspects of the SFO and OVLT, as well as the median preoptic nucleus (MnPO) that lies between them (Figure 1.3), collectively also known as the lamina terminalis or anterior wall of the third cerebral ventricle, will be examined in many of the following chapters. This section is a foundation for those studies and presents aspects of structure and connectivity of the mammalian lamina terminalis.

1.4.1   Embryology and General Structure

Kiecker (2018) has reviewed the embryological origins of the circumventricular organs. In general, much less is known about the OVLT and SFO than the neurohypophysis, median eminence, and pineal gland. The fourth ventricular circumventricular organ, the area postrema

(AP), is also less studied. The OVLT, SFO, and AP are recognized as sensory circumventricular organs, with the principal function to detect or transduce hormones and other signal molecules. It should first be appreciated that these structures arise from different zones of the roof plate of the neural plate.

The OVLT derives from the midline of the anterior neural border, which later will differentiate into telencephalic structures. The SFO derives from closure of the diencephalic division of the roof plate, and the AP from closure of the hindbrain division. OVLT neurons are within a thin layer of neuroepithelium that will fold to become the lamina terminalis, under the control of various chemotropic factors. The origins of the OVLT are more closely linked to those of the median eminence and neurohypophysis than they are to the origins of the SFO.

The SFO progenitors most likely are located in the dorsal part of the neural tube at the border between the diencephalon and telencephalon, employing different developmental chemotropic factors. It appears to differentiate later than the OVLT. The hindbrain AP also originates in a distinctive manner. All of the circumventricular organs (CVOs) share permeable capillaries due to fenestrations and discontinuous tight junctions between epithelial cells. They are highly vascularized and are lined with tanycytes, which send processes into the cerebrospinal fluid (CSF). These structures thus appear to develop independently; the common features noted above are examples of homeoplasy. There is some evidence for species differences between widely different phyla, although the extent to which this is true in the mammals described in this book is debatable. That said, I will comment when apparent species differences in function may be suspected. Duvernoy and Risold (2007) made a comparative analysis (12 species) of the vascular structure of the CVOs. In general, the OVLT has both deep and superficial capillary networks, with the deep network on the ventricular side and the superficial network on the wall of the prechiasmatic cistern. These findings in regard to capillary structure were largely confirmed by Prager-Khoutorsky and Bourque (2015), who also described the intercalated glial cells including tanycytes. These authors did not find evidence for functional segregation within the OVLT, at least with respect to osmoreception.

Julien and Bayer (1990) examined the time course of cytogenesis in rat SFO and found that neurons formed in a triphasic pattern and earlier in the anterior than posterior SFO. Earlier production gives rise to cells on the periphery of the SFO, whereas later production gives rise to cells in the core regions, suggesting that the latter may be interneurons. Thus, it is not surprising that the adult SFO is a heterogeneous organ

(Coble et al., 2015; Morita & Miyata, 2012), with a few capillary loops near the surface of the ventricles, and a fine capillary network at the rostral pole. The fenestrated capillaries in this core region allow peptides and other molecules in the systemic circulation to leak into the parenchyma and engage corresponding receptors on neurons. In contrast, ependymal cells in the periphery of the SFO forming the border with the third ventricle have channels into the SFO as well as tanycytes that project from the ventricles into the SFO. These properties allow cells in the peripheral zone to respond to molecules in CSF. Functional differences among cells in the SFO of rats were evident from early Fos-mapping (see the appendix) studies to assess neuronal activation. Infusions of hypertonic NaCl induced the strongest Fos immunoreactivity (Fos-ir) in cells in the peripheral parts of the SFO, whereas infusions of ANG II or hypovolemia induced Fos-ir in the central core region (Grob et al., 2003; Oldfield et al., 1991; Rowland, 1998; Rowland et al., 1994; Smith & Day, 1995). It was apparent from these and other Fos-mapping studies (see Rowland, 1998, for review) that the number of cells exhibiting Fos-ir was related to the dose or level of the stimulus. One interpretation of this is that cells within the SFO have a range of different thresholds for activation, although there is no direct evidence in this regard.

1.4.2   Connectivity and Phenotype of Lamina Terminalis Neurons

The SFO is anatomically well defined, with a fiber tract (ventral hippocampal commissure) dorsally, the third ventricle ventrally and laterally, and all known afferent and efferent connections through its rostral pole. The volume of the SFO is 1.0 and 0.2 mm^3 in rats and mice, respectively. In contrast, the MnPO and OVLT are more ventral, are narrower, and/or have poorly defined anatomical boundaries.

Numerous studies have documented extensive interconnections of the OVLT, MnPO, and SFO and their neural connections to other brain regions (Figure 1.3). One of the first studies (Miselis, 1981) mapped the efferent connections of the SFO using anterograde tracers. Axons leave the rostral pole of the SFO and some synapse in the MnPO (also known as the nucleus medianus) and OVLT, as well as in the neurosecretory SON and PVN. Gutman et al. (1986) confirmed these connections by electrical stimulation and recording, and found that most sites were bidirectionally connected. Lind et al. (1982) described the connectivity of the CVOs in rats, using local horseradish peroxidase injections. They found extensive bidirectional connections between the SFO and OVLT, with many connections also ending in the intervening MnPO. Oldfield et al. (1991) found that the largest efferent outflow from the MnPO was to the SON, with a lesser projection to PVN and other sites such as the ventrolateral periaqueductal gray (Uschakov et al., 2009).

Grob et al. (2003) identified excitatory glutamatergic connections among the SFO, MnPO, and OVLT, as well as inhibitory GABA-ergic connections from the rim of the SFO and OVLT to MnPO. More recently, the functional roles of these connections have been investigated using selective stimulation with optogenetic techniques (see the appendix), mostly using mice. Details or functional outcomes of these studies will be given in later chapters; here, I present some basic neuroanatomical findings. The SFO has monosynaptic excitatory connections with the MnPO and OVLT. Originating SFO neurons are glutamatergic and so may be termed SFO^{GLUT}, although they co-express a number of other markers, including neuronal nitric oxide synthase (NOS), the transcription factor ETV-1, and calcium/calmodulin-dependent kinase II (CaMKII) (Oka et al., 2015). The number of SFO cells synapsing in the MnPO and OVLT are similar (Augustine et al., 2018). SFO^{GLUT} neurons also connect with the SON and PVN (Oka et al., 2016).

A non-overlapping class of cells in the SFO expresses the inhibitory transmitter GABA, with phenotypic expression of the vesicular GABA transporter (VGAT), and will be referred to as SFO^{VGAT} neurons (Oka et al., 2016). A third population of cells in the SFO appear to be glia. In addition, there are inhibitory (GABA-ergic) projections from several brain regions onto SFO^{GLUT} neurons. The largest number of these inhibitory inputs come from MnPO, about half that number from OVLT, and an intermediate number of inputs from the septal region (Augustine et al., 2018). Not shown are other afferents to this system, including from gastrointestinal or oral receptors (Zimmerman et al., 2016, 2019).

As noted above, inducing cellular dehydration by injecting hypertonic saline induces Fos-ir in structures of the lamina terminalis. In vivo and in vitro electrophysiological studies have documented the intrinsic osmosensitivity of cells along the lamina terminalis, as well as in other brain regions. The mechanisms of osmoreception and the evidence for osmoreceptors instead of or in addition to Na$^+$ is presented in Chapters 3, 4, and 8. Noda and colleagues (reviewed in Hiyama & Noda, 2016) have identified a specialized sodium channel, known as Na$_x$, that is expressed in the nuclei of the lamina terminalis of mice. This channel is expressed only in astrocytes and ependymal cells that line the ventricular surface of mice (Watanabe et al., 2006). In rats, Na$_x$ may instead be expressed in neurons of the lamina terminalis (Nehmé et al., 2012). This channel is regulated by extracellular sodium concentrations

$[Na^+_o]$ and not by voltage or osmolality, and so is a true sodium sensor. The threshold $[Na^+_o]$ for opening Na_x in vitro is 150 mM or slightly above normal physiological level in blood plasma, but it is reduced by 20–30 mM in the presence of endothelin-3, allowing its dynamic range to be within normal plasma concentrations.

Neurons of the lamina terminalis express high levels of the ANG II type 1 receptor (AT1R) (Mendelsohn et al., 1984) that is now known to be the 1A variant, at least in rodents. These receptors are expressed preferentially, and possibly exclusively, on the soma or dendrites of glutamatergic cells in these regions. Direct stimulation of this specific population of SFO cells by local application of ANG II produces reliable water intake in rats (Simpson et al., 1978). Either peripheral or central administration of ANG II induces activation of all the structures of the lamina terminalis, assessed by induced Fos-ir (see Rowland, 1998, for a review), although the phenotype of the activated cells was not determined in those studies. In addition to ANG II, other neuropeptides will diffuse into these organs and activate specific receptors (McKinley et al., 2019; Mimee et al., 2013). A subpopulation of ANG II–sensitive cells in the SFO also are glucose sensitive (Paes-Leme et al., 2018). The central core region of the SFO appears to be involved in cardiovascular responses to dehydration, whereas the peripheral zone is more directly implicated in thirst (Coble et al., 2015). These authors also review evidence that ANG II generated within the SFO plays an important role in fluid homeostasis, in addition to ANG II originating in the circulation.

1.5   Summary

This chapter has surveyed the development of concepts and experimentation in the field, marking distinct phases of initial theoretical constructs as well as behavioral and physiological inquiry. Within the past 50 years, one major focus has been on elucidating the brain structures that underlieour current concepts of drinking or thirst. In particular, the forebrain CVOs (i.e., SFO and OVLT) have intrinsic sensory properties and neural connections that appear to be pivotal in this regard. Many of the later chapters will build on this framework, mixing behavioral and mechanistic study. The next chapter is still foundational, devoted mostly to the physiology of body fluid compartments and exchanges.

2 Body Fluid Compartments, Inputs, and Outputs

Drinking is commonly defined as intentional consumption of a liquid, but more broadly it is the active translocation of water from the environment into the systemic compartment of an organism. This process requires transport of water across several selectively permeable structural barriers or membranes. Drinking is in part a consequence of continuous loss of water from the body via processes that also involve transport across membranes. Integral to these movements of water are ions or small molecules dissolved in that water. This chapter will consider the composition of the principal fluid compartments of the body and the physiological processes that regulate water and ionic movement between these compartments.

Body fluid compartments exhibit remarkable constancy in size and composition. They vary relatively little between individuals of a given species, with age, or across time of day for a given individual. They are similar across most mammalian species, and deviations of more than a few percent from these norms are life-threatening. The norms and structures used in this chapter refer to humans as well as many other terrestrial mammals. I will review other species and specializations in Chapter 11.

2.1 Fluid Compartments

2.1.1 Intracellular and Extracellular Compartments

About 60% of the body mass of humans and most mammals is fluid, with a ±10% range depending on age, sex, adiposity, and other variables. Roughly two-thirds of that fluid is located inside cells throughout the body tissues (intracellular fluid [ICF]) and one-third is located outside cells (extracellular fluid [ECF]). Some 75% of the ECF, equal to about 15% body mass, is interstitial (i.e., between cells in tissues around the body) while the remaining 25%, equal to about 5% body mass, is plasma in the bloodstream (Figure 2.1). The ECF also contains a small percentage (2–3%) of transcellular water, which includes fluid contained in

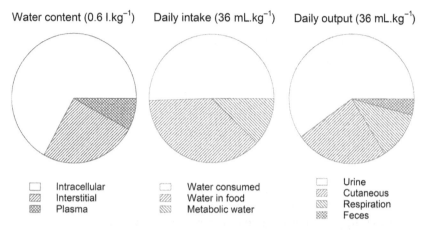

Water content (0.6 l.kg^{-1})   Daily intake (36 mL.kg^{-1})   Daily output (36 mL.kg^{-1})

☐	Intracellular	☐	Water consumed	☐	Urine
▨	Interstitial	▨	Water in food	▨	Cutaneous
▩	Plasma	◺	Metabolic water	◺	Respiration
				▩	Feces

Figure 2.1 Left: Distribution of body water content among intracellular, interstitial, and plasma compartments. Middle: Typical daily fluid intake and that derived from food. Right: Typical daily fluid loss via urine, cutaneous, respiration, and feces. Data are derived from Fitzsimons (1979), referring to a 70 kg human in a temperate climate, but here they are transformed to per kilogram body weight values.

cerebrospinal, lymphatic, and ocular compartments but is not usually considered in computation of body fluid fractions.

The ICF and ECF compartments are in a continuous but regulated process of exchanging water and dissolved substances. Cell membranes, which separate the intracellular and extracellular spaces, are impermeable to most dissolved substances but allow the relatively free exchange of water. Water flows across these membranes when there is a difference in osmotic pressure between intracellular and extracellular compartments. In contrast, the walls of capillary blood vessels allow passage of water and many small dissolved substances and constitute the region of exchange between interstitial and blood plasma compartments. The composition of plasma (not shown in Figure 2.1) is similar to interstitial fluid except that it has ~10% higher concentration of Na^+ and a number of soluble plasma proteins. The most abundant of these proteins are albumins and globulins. Non-ionized moieties in plasma, such as urea, are relatively permeable to cells and have only a minor effect on water movement.

The dissolved substances are called *osmolytes* because they generate an osmotic pressure. Osmotic pressure of a solution is proportional to the number of particles per unit volume. In a steady state, the osmotic pressure is the same inside and outside cells and there is no net flux of water across cell membranes. Osmotic pressure is reported as

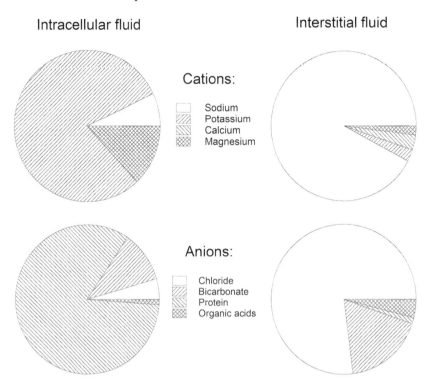

Figure 2.2 Typical distribution in humans of ions in the intracellular fluid (left) and interstitial fluid (right). The top row shows the principal cations and the bottom row shows the principal anions.

milliosmoles per kilogram of solution (mOsm/kg). Osmotic pressure in most mammals is near 300 mOsm/kg. Mammals require the osmotic pressure and ionic composition of body fluids to be maintained within narrow limits to be compatible with adequate function of their vital organs.

The principal exchangeable osmolytes are electrolytes (ions), but these differ markedly in concentration between intra- and extracellular compartments (Figure 2.2). The ECF has high concentrations of sodium (Na^+) and chloride (Cl^-) ions; cell membranes are impermeable to Na^+. NaCl is almost completely ionized in solution, and the resultant osmotic pressure is nearly (but not exactly, due to association of some particles and small contributions from other ions) twice its concentration expressed in milliequivalents (mEq/L). Thus, a 150 mmol/L or 0.15 M solution of NaCl exerts an osmotic pressure of about 300 mOsm/kg.

This is near the normal osmotic pressure of ECF and is known as isotonic.

Inside cells, the principal cation is potassium (K^+). K^+ thus contributes to osmotic pressure inside the cell, along with Cl^- and cytoplasmic proteins. The relative concentrations of Na^+ and K^+ in urine are important to consider in some conditions, but in general, K^+ does not play a major role in drinking or thirst.

The bloodstream additionally contains soluble proteins, primarily albumins and globulins. The walls of many capillary blood vessels are composed of endothelial cells separated by narrow clefts. These clefts are overlaid with a glycocalyx layer containing pores (~5 nm radius) that form a functional system for ultrafiltration. Plasma proteins have minimal ability to pass through this filter and, as a result, give rise to plasma oncotic pressure of about 28 Torr (equivalent to millimeters of mercury). Further, hydrostatic pressure is higher in the vasculature (viz., blood pressure) compared to the surrounding interstitial fluid, and it is about 20 Torr higher at the arterial compared to the venous end. Ernest Starling originally described these forces in the late nineteenth century: The forces that drive fluid from capillaries into the interstitium are capillary pressure and interstitial protein osmotic pressure, whereas forces that drive fluid from the interstitium into capillaries are plasma protein osmotic pressure and interstitial pressure. A modified equation (Levick & Michel, 2010) is that the net flow of fluid per unit time across the endothelium is a function of the total surface area multiplied by the net driving force. Formally, net driving force is equal to (capillary minus interstitial hydrostatic pressures) minus (Staverman's coefficient) × (plasma protein minus subglycocalyx oncotic pressures). The net shift of fluid in capillaries normally is outward, and that fluid is returned to the circulation via the lymphatic system.

2.1.2   Maintaining the Compartments

Because membranes have some permeability to water, it is impossible to prevent continuous loss of water from the bodies of terrestrial animals. The outputs or losses result from urination, sweating, breathing, and defecation (Figure 2.1). The 24-hour loss by volume, for a 70 kg human at neutral temperature, averages 2.5 L or 3–4% of body mass. Of this, urine (1.5 L) is the major component, followed by loss from the outer surface of the skin (0.6L), with smaller losses via exhaled breath and feces. Humans in a hot climate and/or during vigorous activity increase the loss by sweating, with rates as high as 1 L/h (see also Chapter 9). Sweat is hypotonic, usually <50 mEq/L Na^+, thereby increasing the Na^+ concentration remaining in the plasma and hence its osmolality. Absent such exceptional or occasional losses, the major output is urine, a fluid expelled after a tightly regulated filtration process in the kidneys.

To maintain body fluid content and composition within tolerable limits, these losses must be offset by intake of water and appropriate electrolytes. Up to 50% of the total daily intake of water by a normal human is either directly or indirectly (i.e., after metabolism) associated with food (Figure 2.1). The remainder of the daily fluid requirement is met by drinking. Ingested water enters the gastrointestinal tract, from which it is absorbed into plasma with a time course that is characteristic for that species (Figure 1.2). In arid environments, many animals rarely drink free water but instead derive most if not all of their water from food (Chew, 1961). Conversely, drinking free water or other fluid in excess of physiological need is often observed in water-rich environments, and this is the case for many humans today.

Foods, here defined as energy-yielding substrates, contain varying amounts of water ranging from dry grains through fruits and vegetables to soups. Some human-specific beverages such as beer and soda are usually thought of as drinks, but because they also have a net energy yield, the distinction between food and drink is not always clear-cut. This is also true for infant mammals consuming milk (Chapter 6). The water plus any minerals or salts contained in foods are used by the body in the same way as fluids that are drunk, not least because they enter through the same orogastrointestinal tract.

Much of our food is consumed episodically in the form of meals, and those are often accompanied by drinking, frequently called prandial drinking. Some drinking during meals may be for oral comfort. That prandial drink may help with swallowing and/or chasing the taste, rather than being a true physiological exigency (Chapter 7). Oral lubrication is one normal function of saliva, which is secreted under basal conditions (0.3–0.4 mL/minute) and is stimulated around tenfold by chewing or eating. Xerostomia is a syndrome of dry mouth resulting from insufficient salivary flow, and it has several etiologies. Individuals with xerostomia often use agents to restore or replace oral lubrication. In rats fed dry food, surgical removal of salivary glands produces a rapid alternation of extremely small eating and drinking bouts, the function of which is to provide necessary lubrication that is no longer provided by saliva (Kissileff, 1973).

In addition to water that is directly a component of food, macronutrients (viz., carbohydrate, fat, and protein) yield water as they undergo oxidative metabolism into usable energy. Starches yield 0.56 g water per gram of dry carbohydrate, fats 1.07 g/g, and protein 0.39 g/g. For a typical mixed dry diet, this would amount to about 0.6 g water per gram of food.

Foods contain varying amounts of salts or other materials that ultimately will need to be excreted in urine or feces, thereby losing some of the water gained from eating that food. For example, foods to which NaCl has been added require additional water to excrete that salt. Rats eating regular dry chow, which naturally contains about 1% of NaCl along with some other minerals, typically drink from 1.0 to 1.5 mL for every gram of food consumed. If extra salt is added, this water-to-food ratio rises commensurately. Modern humans eat far more NaCl than our ancestors; in some individuals, this contributes to physiologically undesirable consequences (e.g., hypertension), but it imposes a higher water requirement for everyone.

When sufficient water is unavailable to meet the minimum needed for excretion of waste products from eating dry food, the response is to eat less; this is called dehydration anorexia. It may also be viewed as a manifestation of solute avoidance (Chapters 5 and 7). It does not occur immediately but rather requires an accrued level of dehydration. This is an adaptive response to lack of water because by obtunding further solute load, it mitigates the physiological compromise of severe dehydration (Chapter 8).

For most humans in postindustrial societies, water or other fluids are available in adequate or even excessive amounts and without much cost or effort involved. But this has not always been the case. Terrestrial animals, by definition, do not live in water. Many early human settlements were near rivers or lakes, and fresh water was nearby. But humans and other animals can occupy habitats in which water is not nearby and/ or is in short supply and must be shared with other species or, in broader terms, involves effort, exposure, and possible danger. Collectively, these may be considered a cost.

An objective analysis of simulated cost and drinking was performed by Marwine and Collier (1979) using rats in a laboratory. In respects that will become evident as this book unfolds, rats and humans share many characteristics, and this study may provide an insight into the constraints on water acquisition by early man. In their study, the results of which are depicted in Figure 2.3, rats were housed individually in operant behavior chambers and were required to perform work in the form of lever presses to gain access to a water spout. Once accessed was reached, rats could drink as much as they wished, but when five minutes elapsed without recorded drinking, the spout was retracted and they had to press a lever again to gain renewed access. The number of lever presses (the simulated

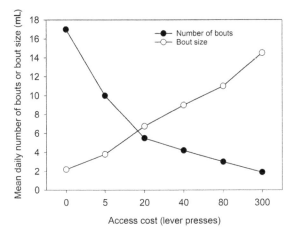

Figure 2.3 Flexibility of patterns of water consumption in rats as a function of cost to access the water (from Marwine & Collier, 1979). Shown are the mean ($N = 4$) number of drinking bouts per day and their mean size as the access cost was increased from zero (free drinking) to 300 lever presses.

cost) for access was increased in 12 steps from 1 to 300 presses, with eight days at each step. Dry food (rat chow) was freely available throughout. During the study, rats ate 9–14 mostly nocturnal meals per 24 hours, as is typical of many studies of meal patterns (Chapter 7). In contrast, the number of times the water spout was accessed declined from a mean of 17 bouts per day and mostly with meals at the lowest costs to one to two bouts per day at access costs of 80 presses or more. Rats largely compensated by a reciprocal change in the amount of water consumed in each bout, so the total daily water intake remained constant. It follows that at higher lever press access costs (e.g., two bouts per day and 10 meals), most meals were not accompanied by drinking. Thus, imposition of small costs dramatically changes drinking patterns, and this shows that prandial drinking is a pragmatic choice rather than a necessity. In contrast, total 24-hour water intake is conserved, at least within the range of cost parameters in this study.

Humans and rats are examples of slow drinkers; drinking episodes are relatively slow in terms of volume consumed per unit time and, under conducive environmental conditions, may be broken into several smaller bouts. In contrast, some animals are rapid drinkers insofar as their intake is extremely fast and occurs as a single bout (Rolls et al., 1980). This may be an adaptation to drinking when there is a risk of predation. Under adverse conditions, drinking may occur infrequently and be matched to minimum physiological needs. In contrast, under permissive conditions, drinking may and often does exceed physiological need: Indeed, much human drinking appears to be in the absence of obvious dehydration. Some authors have made the distinction between primary drinking, which is depletion based, and secondary drinking, which is need-free (Fitzsimons, 1979). The former condition is the prototypical condition in which people report thirst and animals exhibit water-motivated behavior. But thirst can also occur in the absence of clear depletion, and, conversely, drinking can occur without thirst and may under some conditions become a learned habit.

2.2   Fluid Loss

The entire body is enclosed in a more or less continuous and complex membrane that we know better as skin. Skin is largely, but not completely, impermeable and allows the internal environment to be substantially different from the outside environment. As I noted earlier, the body loses water and/or ions in three ways:

(1) Excretion: Urine forms by far the greatest loss (1.5 L/day), compared with feces. I will discuss mechanisms of urine formation by the kidney later in this chapter. Urine contains water, as well as various ions and waste products, the amount and concentrations of which can vary over wide ranges and are controlled by specific physiological mechanisms.

(2) Perspiration or sweating: Up to 20% of normal fluid loss is through the skin, about 0.6 L/day. Sweat is composed of water and various ions, with the major ones being Na^+ (at about 0.1 times its concentration in interstitial fluid or plasma), K^+ (at about 3 times its concentration in interstitial fluid or plasma), and their associated anion (Cl^-). Sweating is also used for evaporative cooling, and sweat rates are much higher during exercise or in hot climates (Chapter 9).

(3) Respiration: Expired air is saturated with water vapor at body temperature, and this almost always contains more water than inspired air, so there is a net loss at each breath. In temperate climates with normal activity, this amounts to about 0.3L/day. No ions are lost via this route.

These collective and continuous losses of water and ions must be balanced accurately with appropriate inputs. Terrestrial mammals have developed a variety of specializations to these functions (Chapter 11) that serve to economize or minimize the required inputs.

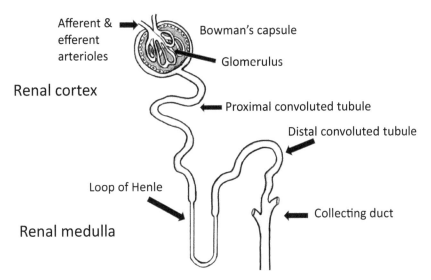

Figure 2.4 Schematic representation of a nephron. Shown are the two main zones (cortex and medulla), afferent and efferent arterioles forming a glomerulus inside Bowman's capsule, proximal and distal convoluted tubules, the intervening loop of Henle, and the collecting ducts that accumulate urine.

2.2.1 The Mammalian Kidney

Urine produced by the kidney is normally the largest contributor to fluid loss. A mammalian kidney works on a perfusion–reabsorption principle and is composed of two zones, the cortex and medulla (Figure 2.4). Stretching from cortex to medulla and back again are tubular structures called nephrons. Humans have an average of one million nephrons per kidney. The number and length of nephrons, and hence their operating characteristics, differ across mammalian species, although the basic principles remain the same.

Blood from the general circulation enters the kidneys via the renal arteries. The renal artery splits into afferent arterioles and then, for each nephron, forms a network of capillary vessels called a glomerulus inside a small spherical structure called the renal corpuscle. It is here that the perfusion part of the kidney cycle begins. It is a continuous process of ultrafiltration: Capillary blood pressure first forces extracellular fluid in plasma through the partially permeable walls. Large molecules such as proteins are too large to permeate and so stay in the blood, but all small molecules, including ions and glucose, are freely permeable. The normal glomerular filtration rate is about 120 mL per minute in healthy young adults and declines with age. In one hour, this filtration rate equates to almost twice the total volume of blood plasma; thus, it is crucial that most of the filtered fluid is recovered elsewhere in the nephron.

The initial ultrafiltrate passes into a twisting tube called the proximal convoluted tubule, which is on the cortical side of the cortex/medulla boundary. Epithelial cells that form the walls of the tubule have an inner-facing (luminal) convoluted structure or brush border that greatly increases the internal surface area of the tubule. The exterior walls of these cells contain pumps that extrude Na^+ and K^+ into the surrounding interstitial fluid and into the dense network of peritubular capillaries. This sets up a concentration gradient that allows Na^+ ions to enter the cells from the luminal side containing the ultrafiltrate of plasma. For simplicity, I will not consider additional aspects of acid/base balance. All of the filtered glucose is reabsorbed in the proximal tubule; glucosuria in untreated diabetes mellitus is due to the fact that the glucose transport capacity of the proximal tubule is exceeded. Water passively follows the glucose and ions that are pumped out of the proximal tubule.

The tubule then becomes U-shaped, forming a loop of Henle, and then enters the renal medulla as the descending limb and returns to the cortex via an ascending limb. The ascending and descending limbs of the loop are in close proximity and, along with capillary vessels (vasa recta), form a countercurrent multiplier system. The walls of the descending limb are impermeable to ions and to urea, the major nitrogenous waste product, but are highly permeable to water. In contrast, the ascending limb has an active transport mechanism to export Na^+, K^+, and Cl^- (via a Na-K-Cl cotransporter, NKCC2), as well as other cations such as calcium and magnesium. The critical aspect of this loop is that the ions (e.g., Na^+) extruded from the ascending limb surround the descending limb and provide an osmotic gradient across which water is passively extruded, thereby progressively increasing the concentration of solutes in the proximal tubule. Thus, at the start of the proximal tubule, the concentration of NaCl is close to that of plasma (300 mOsm/L), but increases typically by fourfold at the tip of the loop when 75% of the water would have been reabsorbed. The ascending tubule pumps Na^+ out, thereby decreasing its concentration below that in plasma. No water is lost in this segment, but at all places along the loop there is a sufficient concentration gradient to drive absorption of water from the proximal tubule.

The ascending limb, now entering the renal cortex, becomes the distal convoluted tubule and eventually the collecting ducts. Water can be actively reabsorbed from the last part of the tubule and collecting duct under the action of the nonapeptide hormone antidiuretic hormone (ADH), also known as vasopressin and which I will refer to as arginine vasopressin (AVP) in most of this text. AVP increases water permeability by inducing surface expression of aquaporins. The net result of this action is to decrease the volume and increase the solute concentration of urine. AVP is secreted during plasma hyperosmolarity from nerve terminals in the posterior pituitary originating from cell bodies in the supraoptic and paraventricular nuclei of the hypothalamus; this will be discussed further in Chapter 4.

Aldosterone, a steroid hormone, is secreted from the zona glomerulosa of the adrenal cortex and acts on the distal tubules and renal collecting ducts to stimulate reabsorption of Na^+ and K^+. The adrenal cortex makes and secretes several steroids, with aldosterone produced by activation of the enzyme aldosterone synthase. Several factors can activate this enzyme, including angiotensin II (ANG II), adrenocorticotropic hormone (ACTH) from the anterior pituitary gland, and increased plasma K^+. Further, stretch receptors in the atrium of the heart detect low blood pressure and directly affect the adrenal cortex. The function of this system is to retain Na^+, prevent further loss of plasma volume, and thereby restore blood pressure and ultimately ionic homeostasis. The important role of ANG peptides is recognized in the term *renin-angiotensin-aldosterone system*, but where does the renin come from? To answer that, we must return to the distal tubule and the renal corpuscle.

The afferent arteriole to the renal corpuscle is flanked by granular or juxtaglomerular cells that are in contact with the distal tubule as it ascends. These juxtaglomerular cells synthesize renin and secrete it into the blood flow when the perfusion pressure in the afferent arteriole is low. This occurs, for example, with decreased blood volume but also as a result of innervation by the sympathetic nervous system. Renin then catalyzes the splitting of a precursor peptide, angiotensinogen, in the circulation into the decapeptide ANG I, and under the action of angiotensin-converting enzyme type 1 (ACE1) to the octapeptide ANG II. Other aspects of the renin-angiotensin system, including several active peptide members (Coble, Grobe, Johnson, & Sigmund, 2015), will be examined in Chapter 5. ANG peptides have a plasma half-life of less than one minute, whereas renin has a half-life of about 20 minutes. Thus, the activity of circulating renin is the primary determinant of blood levels of ANG peptides. ANG peptides stimulate aldosterone synthesis, increase blood pressure, and stimulate drinking behavior (Chapter 5). In addition, several tissues have local renin-angiotensin systems with specific functions.

2.2.2   *Sweat Glands*

Most of the sweat produced by humans is from eccrine cells, found in particularly high concentrations on the hands and forehead. Plasma is filtered in a coiled structure within each sweat gland. Normally, sweat is hypotonic and, under the action of aldosterone, which stimulates Na^+ reabsorption, the Na^+ concentration becomes lower. Sweat rate is controlled by the opening of the sweat duct, which, in part, is controlled by sympathetic nerves originating primarily in executive thermoregulatory regions of the hypothalamus.

The rate of sweating depends on thermal load and is prominently increased during vigorous exercise and/or hot environments. One primary function of sweating is to produce cooling of the body surface by evaporation. Adolph and his colleagues (1947) performed pioneering studies in the California desert using military personnel and, among other measures for preventing dehydration, emphasized minimizing activity during the hot midday hours. Interestingly, acute thirst does not seem to be stimulated strongly by such dehydration, and it often takes many hours to fully recover fluid balance (Chapter 8).

There are two other important targets of aldosterone: the colon and the salivary glands. Action in the colon is to recover Na^+ from the lumen of the gastrointestinal tract in the face of insufficient systemic Na^+ (e.g., as in hypovolemia). The salivary glands secrete fluid, and most of that is normally swallowed and the fluid and ions recycled. The ionic composition of saliva is an adapting stimulus for taste buds and may affect taste perception (Fregly & Rowland, 1985). In species such as ruminants with high salivary rates, the aldosterone-induced salivary conservation of Na^+ in the ECF is especially important and acts as a complement to renal conservation.

2.3   Measurement of Fluid Compartments and Their Composition

Almost every chapter in this book contains descriptions of empirical studies, and these often include measurements of body fluids. While the technical details are not important to interpret the results presented, it is useful to have a general understanding of the most commonly used methods, as well as any assumptions that may be involved. In this section, I will briefly describe some measurements and how they will typically be presented in subsequent chapters. Further details or explanations of these and other methods are presented in the appendix.

Total water lost during an acute experimental procedure can be estimated from loss of body weight, and, since body fluid content is proportional to body weight, this is most often expressed as the percentage of initial weight lost over a specified period. For periods of more than a few hours, this measure is less useful because food intake may occur and influence the estimate of fluid loss.

ECF volume is an important variable in the field of thirst and drinking. Since plasma is in equilibrium with interstitial fluid, plasma volume is often used as a proxy for ECF volume. Most experimental studies of fluid balance use the indirect indices of hematocrit ratio or plasma protein concentration, either at a single time in different treatment groups or from serial blood samples within groups or subjects. The results will often be expressed as percent change in the measure relative to the control or initial condition. Given certain assumptions, this will give an estimate of the percent difference or change in plasma volume.

The concentration of ions, particularly extracellular Na^+ and K^+ and osmotic pressure, is often of interest. These can be measured by direct and sensitive chemical analyses of plasma samples. I will often report these as percent change from an initial or a control condition. The same measures may be made on urine samples, although the absolute values in urine are typically severalfold higher than in plasma.

Commonly measured hormones determined in relation to fluid balance include ANG II, AVP, and aldosterone. The first two are subject to rapid degradation, and appropriate steps must be taken during sampling to stabilize these moieties prior to analysis. These are all usually measured by sensitive and specific radioimmunoassays, and, as above, I often will express results as percent or times (fold) change or difference from a control. Determination of renin activity uses the plasma sample to generate ANG II in vitro and then measures the ANG II generated. It is usually assumed the result is a reflection of ANG II concentrations that would be generated in vivo and also may be expressed as a percent or fold change from a control condition.

Most of the assays described above require blood sampling once or at multiple times. In humans, venous blood sampling for clinical work is routine, and because of humans' large blood volume, the relatively small amounts needed for assays do not appreciably perturb the vascular system. Sampling in animals requires catheterization or acute venipuncture. The latter involves either behavioral training (e.g., in zoo animals) or acute sedation and typically a single sample. For repeated or serial samples, an indwelling sterile catheter is essential, and the animal should be adapted to any handling or physical restraint. In small animals, the volumes of blood taken can be significant relative to total blood volume. The contemporary use of mice poses particular problems because their total blood volume is only 1–2 mL, and a capillary tube sample of 50 μL is about 5% of the total, a fraction that itself will provoke physiological countermeasures.

2.4   Summary

Body water is contained in intracellular and extracellular compartments, in approximately a 2:1 ratio. The ionic concentrations are quite different between compartments, and Na^+, the predominant cation in the ECF, is of particular significance with respect to maintaining the volume of the ECF. Several specialized organs and hormones for maintaining ionic and fluid balance are described.

3   Intracellular Dehydration Thirst and Drinking

3.1   General Considerations

Natural stimuli that cause dehydration and thirst are water deprivation, physical exertion in the heat, or consumption of food with relatively low water content. These thirsts are relatively slow in onset and/or are caused by antecedent events known to the individual. But they are complex or hybrid dehydrations insofar as they have varying degrees of involvement of both intracellular and extracellular dehydrations (see Chapters 8 and 9), and they are more difficult to reproduce with precision across individuals. For these reasons, much of the early experimental analysis of drinking and thirst used pure intracellular dehydration, which can be induced rapidly and quantitatively. This precise experimental control enables study of thresholds, time course, and the homeostatic mechanisms activated to return the organism to a state of euhydration. Some studies have used human subjects, and we will start with these, but more detailed analysis has been dependent on animal studies. The sudden onset of an inferred extreme sensation of thirst in animals is not only impossible under natural circumstances but is probably an unpleasant or stressful experience added to the dehydration itself. It is remarkable that animals often do show robust drinking responses to intracellular dehydration under these adverse conditions and, although we cannot ask animals about thirst, they must be highly motivated to drink.

Intracellular dehydration is caused by accumulation or administration of hypertonic solutes restricted to or preferentially retained in the extracellular compartment. As reviewed in Chapter 2, the extracellular fluid is substantially composed of NaCl, reflecting the relative impermeability of cell membranes to Na^+. The prototypical manner of producing intracellular dehydration is to add more Na^+ (e.g., as NaCl) to the extracellular compartment. This generates an osmotic pressure gradient across cell membranes that causes water to move from the intracellular to the extracellular compartment. In an otherwise static system, this movement would occur until both intracellular fluid (ICF) and extracellular fluid

(ECF) compartments had the same osmotic pressure, at which time both would be hypertonic relative to the initial condition. Calculation of this theoretical osmotic pressure change due to a given osmotic load should use total body water (~69% body mass) rather than extracellular volume (Fitzsimons, 1961a).

Experimentally, sodium salts (e.g., NaCl) are among the most commonly used solutes to produce intracellular dehydration (both Na^+ and Cl^- will exert osmotic pressure, but I focus on the asymmetrical distribution of Na^+ between ECF and ICF). Intravenous infusions or bolus injections of hypertonic NaCl produce a very rapid increase in osmolality of plasma and interstitial fluid that is commensurate with the amount of solute injected (Fitzsimons, 1961a). If Na^+ salts are used, the responses produced could be due to transduction of either hyperosmolality or Na^+ concentration, or both. To distinguish between these possibilities, solutions of substances such as mannitol – a nonionic molecule that cannot cross cell membranes – equivalent in osmotic pressure to NaCl dose(s) are used. Injection of urea, which readily crosses cell membranes, has been used as an osmotic load that does not cause major fluid shifts between compartments.

Systemic routes of administration other than intravenous (i.v.) have been used, including gastric gavage or, in animals, the acutely painful subcutaneous (s.c.) or intraperitoneal (i.p.) routes. These routes produce identical physiological effects compared with intravenous administration, but with slightly slower onset. Some studies have produced regional osmotic stimulation, such as by intracerebral administration of volumes too small to have an appreciable systemic effect, or by infusion of small volumes into a specific artery to stimulate tissues in the vascular bed served by that vessel. Abnormally high or chronic consumption of NaCl in the diet or drinking fluid produces intracellular dehydration, but with slower time course and loss of some experimental control due to individual variability of solute intakes.

Several physiological responses are set in motion when hyperosmolarity or hypernatremia is detected. One is secretion of the antidiuretic hormone, vasopressin (AVP), discussion of which will be deferred until Chapter 4. Natriuresis must also occur to expel the osmotic load from the body, but in so doing it will lose extracellular fluid with consequent hypovolemia. Thus, after an intravenous bolus administration of hypertonic NaCl, plasma Na^+ concentrations are instantaneously increased to a dose-dependent maximum, but subsequent natriuresis causes hyperosmolality to decline and hypovolemia to emerge. For study of a purely osmotic mechanism, a handful of studies has used nephrectomy (i.e., surgical removal of both kidneys, an acute and terminal procedure) to prevent sodium excretion.

The remainder of this chapter describes studies of drinking due to intracellular dehydration in several mammalian species. Studies on the neural mechanisms of intracellular dehydration are presented in Chapter 4. Other aspects of intracellular dehydration drinking, associated with specific contexts, are treated in Chapters 6–11.

3.2   Intracellular Dehydration Drinking or Thirst in Humans

Leshke (1918) described thirst in patients administered hypertonic NaCl as part of a clinical treatment. More detailed analysis was provided by Holmes and Gregersen (1947), who infused 250–300 mL of 5% NaCl (0.83 M) over 15–20 minutes, also as part of a clinical treatment. They measured a median decrease of 70–80% in salivary flow, with dryness of the mouth including a thick or metallic mouth sensation starting after about half the load had been infused. Water was presented after the end of the infusion, and subjects drank 200–800 mL in the first few minutes. Although this intake, presumably to satiation, was insufficient to dilute the stimulus to isotonic, it caused an immediate reversal of dry mouth. Preloads of water (400–600 mL) before the NaCl infusions greatly attenuated thirst and changes in salivary flow. The authors suggested that dry mouth was critical to thirst. This study makes an important distinction between hyperosmolality, which causes development of thirst sensations, and the oral and/or early postingestive factors that reverse those sensations and terminate drinking (Rolls et al., 1980).

Wolf (1950) made the first rigorous estimate of the osmotic threshold for intracellular thirst. He gave slow intravenous infusions of NaCl solutions of varying tonicity to healthy young medical students and asked them to report when they had an "unequivocal desire to drink water." Dry or unpleasant mouth sensations were reported by all subjects. From blood measures, Wolf estimated that the thirst threshold occurred when cellular water had decreased by $1.23 \pm 0.48\%$.

Phillips et al. (1985) provided greater detail about the subjective and objective indices of intracellular dehydration thirst in healthy, young adult males. In two separate test sessions, subjects received intravenous infusion over 15 minutes of either hypertonic (0.45 M; 4.8 mL/kg or ~300 mL, given the average body mass of 70 kg) or isotonic saline. Five minutes after the infusion ended, they were given access to room temperature water for one hour. A second venous catheter was used for periodic blood samples to measure standard physiological variables, and, at these times, subjects also completed a series of visual analog scales to assess conscious sensations. Isotonic infusion produced no changes in sensations or plasma measures, and only a small amount of

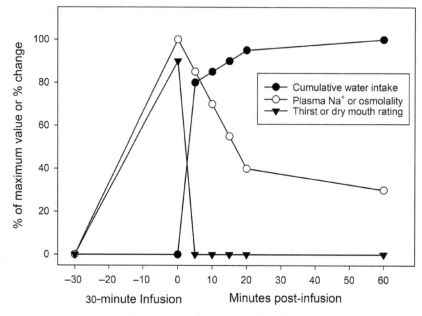

Figure 3.1 Effect of hypertonic NaCl infusion in humans. The figure displays a schematic representation, based on data in Phillips et al. 1985, of temporal changes in plasma Na$^+$ concentration, thirst, or dry mouth rating during and after i.v. infusion of 0.45 M NaCl, and cumulative water intake following the infusion. Each data point is expressed as the percentage of the maximum change during the study for that variable.

drinking. The results for hypertonic NaCl are shown in Figure 3.1. Mean water intake after hypertonic NaCl was 5.1 mL/kg (i.e., ~350 mL, just over 50% of that theoretically needed to dilute the load to isotonicity), with 80% of that occurring in the first five minutes. Ratings of thirst, prospective pleasantness of drinking water, mouth dryness, and unpleasantness of mouth taste all increased progressively and significantly during the infusion and were reversed to pre-infusion levels within five minutes of water access. In contrast, whereas plasma measures that are taken as surrogates for cellular dehydration (i.e., Na$^+$ and osmolality) increased in parallel with the subjective ratings, during the infusion they did not reverse as quickly or completely during and after drinking. Some 60% of the cellular dehydration was removed within 20 minutes of onset of drinking, but it had not fully returned to baseline even after one hour. AVP levels at the end of the infusion were elevated about twofold from baseline, and had returned to baseline after one hour of water access, but a detailed time course was not examined in this study. Hematocrit and plasma protein measures revealed that plasma volume increased during the infusions and was only partially restored after one hour. This study shows that subjects can distinguish between sensations of thirst and mouth feel, and these change with identical time courses.

Zerbe and Robertson (1983) examined thirst and AVP secretion in response to slow intravenous infusion of several different solutes, using six healthy volunteers (three male and three female). No sex differences were reported, but this is one of the first studies to include women. In separate sessions, hypertonic solutions of NaCl (5%), mannitol (20%), urea (20%), or glucose (20%) were infused for a two-hour period, plus a control session with isotonic saline. Infusion rates for 5% NaCl, mannitol, and urea were adjusted such that the rates of loading were comparable (4.6–6.1 mOsm/kg/h). No water was available, but subjects were asked to report when thirst was first experienced, as well as whether it was unequivocal. Blood was taken at regular intervals for measurement of AVP and other routine plasma parameters. After two hours, the NaCl infusion increased plasma osmolality and sodium by 5%, increased blood volume by 8%, increased AVP by fourfold, and was associated with unequivocal thirst in five of the six subjects at a mean osmolality of 3.2% above baseline (Figure 3.2). This is about double the threshold estimated by Wolf (1950) and suggests that procedural variables may influence subjective reporting. From the serial blood samples, individual regressions of plasma osmolality versus AVP were constructed. They showed high linearity within subjects but over fivefold variability between subjects. The slopes of these regressions, an index of osmotic sensitivity, ranged from 0.26 to 1.43 pg AVP/ml/mOsm/kg.

The increases in plasma osmolality after mannitol or urea infusions were comparable to those after hypertonic NaCl (Figure 3.2). Mannitol caused an increase in AVP comparable to that produced by NaCl, and the slopes of the AVP/osmolality regressions were also similar, with the same individual differences as for NaCl sensitivity. Unlike NaCl, mannitol caused a 6.2% decrease in plasma Na^+, and unequivocal thirst was reported by only three of the six subjects. Urea produced a much smaller change in AVP (<twofold) and unequivocal thirst in only one subject. Glucose caused an increase in osmolality, a decrease in AVP, and no reports of thirst. Zerbe and Robertson (1983) concluded that their results were consistent with the existence of an osmoreceptor located outside the blood–brain barrier. They attributed (without proof) the substantial individual differences in osmoregulatory sensitivity to genetic factors.

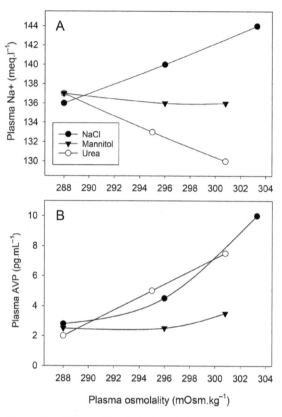

Figure 3.2 Effect of i.v. infusion in humans of various hypertonic solutions on plasma Na$^+$ concentration and AVP (from Zerbe and Robertson, 1983). The infusions were NaCl, mannitol, and urea (6.1, 4.6, and 5.8 mOsm.kg^{-1}.h^{-1}, respectively) for 2 h; data points (left to right) are pre-infusion or after 1 and 2 h.

The effect of the menstrual cycle on osmoregulation was examined by Vokes et al. (1988). In their first study, performed at five phases of the menstrual cycle, it was found that basal plasma osmolality was some 4–5 mOsm/kg higher in the follicular than the luteal phases. Plasma Na$^+$ differed by a similar 1.5% across the cycle. In their second study, five women (20–33 years of age) were infused with hypertonic NaCl (3% or 0.51 M) at 0.1 mL/kg/min for two hours; blood samples and thirst ratings were taken every 20 minutes. Key results from the early follicular (days 4–6) and late luteal (days 23–25) phases are shown in Figure 3.3; for clarity, periovulatory (days 13–15) data are omitted because they fall

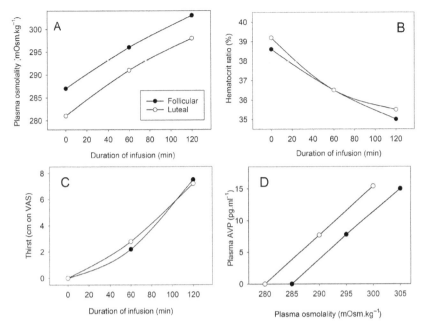

Figure 3.3 Effect of i.v. infusion of hypertonic NaCl (approx. 6 mEq. kg^{-1} over 2 h) on group mean physiological parameters and thirst ratings in women studied during follicular and luteal phases of their menstrual cycle (from Vokes et al., 1988). No water was available during the infusion.

between the other two. Plasma osmolality was increased comparably, but from a baseline differing by 6 mOsm.kg^{-1} (panel A). Volume expansion indicated by the fall in hematocrit did not differ (panel B). Thirst was stimulated comparably as a function of infusion time (panel C), as was plasma AVP (not shown); however, the relationship between plasma osmolality and AVP (panel D) showed an identical slope at the two phases, but with the aforementioned difference in basal osmolality. The relationship between thirst and osmolality (not shown) was similar to the AVP function. This is evidence that the set point for osmoregulation changes across the menstrual cycle, although the mechanism for that effect was not determined. Related studies showing changes in osmo-regulation during pregnancy will be presented in Chapter 6.

Thompson et al. (1991) examined the effects of intravenous infusion of hypertonic NaCl (0.855 M; 3 mL/kg/h for 2 h) in patients diagnosed with compulsive water drinking, patients with diabetes insipidus (DI), and healthy controls. All groups included males and females; the present discussion refers to the healthy control group; discussion of DI and compulsive drinker groups will be deferred to Chapter 10. Water was presented 15 minutes after the end of the infusion, and a two-hour drinking period was allowed. Blood was sampled and subjective thirst assessed throughout the session. Following the infusion, and similar to data in Figure 3.1, drinking caused a very rapid dissipation of thirst but a slow and partial reversal of plasma hyperosmolality or hypernatremia. In this study, it was also found that plasma AVP returned to baseline within a few minutes of the onset of drinking, in parallel with the thirst ratings and much faster than osmolality. This rapid reversal of both AVP and thirst while hyperosmolality remained well above the threshold for drinking shows that preabsorptive consequences of drinking inhibit either osmoreceptors themselves or their downstream effects. Whether such inhibition of drinking and AVP originates in the same neural system(s) cannot be determined from these data. Similar to Zerbe and Robertson (1983), Thompson et al. (1991) constructed regressions for plasma osmolality and AVP and found a similar mean but smaller range (0.21–0.43 pg AVP/mL/mOsm/kg). The design of Thompson and colleagues' study allowed for construction of individual regressions of thirst rating versus plasma osmolality; these were all linear with a twofold range of individual sensitivity.

3.3   Intracellular Dehydration Drinking in Large Mammals

Reports of private sensations are not possible in animal studies; instead, we infer thirst from appetitive and drinking behaviors. I will present findings from larger mammals (including dogs and sheep) separately from smaller mammals (i.e., rats and mice) because these two categories present distinct advantages and disadvantages for the study of drinking and osmoregulation. One advantage of larger animals is that serial blood samples for analysis can be taken from the same animal without significant compromise of blood volume, whereas in small animals, unless reconstituted blood is replaced, only a single and sometimes terminal sample is advisable.

The first formal study of thirst after hypertonic NaCl administration was reported by Mayer (1901) in dogs. The definitive experiment that established intracellular dehydration as the primary cause of thirst was performed by Gilman (1937). He injected dogs with 2.5 mL/kg of either 20% NaCl or 40% urea solutions (both about 3 M), measured serum osmotic pressure after 30 minutes, and then allowed the dogs to drink. NaCl caused a rapid rise in osmotic pressure due to a shift of water from ICF to ECF compartments. When allowed to drink, dogs injected with

NaCl drank large amounts, mostly within the first few minutes of access, reversing their hypernatremia within one hour. After injection of urea, dogs drank only about half as much as after NaCl. This latter finding of a modest thirst after urea has not been found universally, including in the human work cited above (Zerbe & Robertson, 1983).

Holmes and Gregersen (1950) established dose dependency of osmotically evoked drinking in dogs and noted a threefold individual difference in the amount consumed due to a given stimulus. Kanter (1953) classified dogs as minimal internal regulators that drank copiously and excreted a near-isotonic urine or as maximal internal regulators that drank less and excreted a relatively low volume of hypertonic urine. It would be interesting to know how these individual intake differences might be related to sensitivity of the thirst mechanism described above for humans. Using slow intravenous infusions of NaCl, Wolf (1950) determined the mean osmotic threshold for drinking in dogs to be 2.9%, about double that reported for humans in the same paper, and with the explanation that "psychological factors" may underlie the difference.

A distinction between osmoreceptors and sodium receptors was first examined in goats. In those studies, infusions of small volumes of hypertonic solutions of Na^+ salts into the third ventricle were dipsogenic, whereas hypertonic glucose or sucrose was ineffective (Andersson et al., 1967; Eriksson et al., 1971). These findings suggested that hyperosmolarity of cerebrospinal fluid (CSF) and thereby of adjacent receptors was not a sufficient basis for drinking and, instead, that Na^+ concentration was important. McKinley et al. (1978) challenged this conclusion on the basis that intracerebroventricular ICV infusions of pure saccharides would dilute the natural ionic composition of CSF. Using sheep, they found that ICV infusion of 0.7 M sucrose in 0.15 M CSF produced a mean intake of 305 mL in eight out of eight sheep, whereas infusion of pure sucrose (1 M, the same total osmolality) produced less drinking (173 mL) and in only three out of seven sheep. They compared infusions into the carotid artery or CSF to preferentially stimulate receptors on a blood and brain side, respectively, of any blood–brain barrier. Intracarotid infusions of 1 M NaCl or 2 M sucrose were reliably and equally dipsogenic. In experiments without water available, NaCl infusion caused approximately 3% increases in both plasma and CSF Na^+ concentration, whereas sucrose infusion caused a 4% decrease in plasma and a 4% increase in CSF Na^+ concentration. Although elevated CSF Na^+ is thus the common element, it could be discounted as critical for drinking because intracarotid infusion of 2 M urea caused a comparable increase in CSF Na^+ but small amounts of unreliable drinking.

McKinley and colleagues concluded that osmoreceptors for drinking were in a brain region devoid of a blood–brain barrier, and thereby accessible to NaCl, sucrose, and urea. In contrast to the differences in drinking, all of the hypertonic solutes caused antidiuresis, but the onset of this effect was considerably slower and the magnitude less for urea than either NaCl or sucrose and could be a consequence of the increase in CSF Na^+ that would have occurred.

This result was extended by McKinley, Denton, et al. (1980), in which the time course of drinking during 90-minute ICV infusions was presented. Although 0.45 M NaCl in CSF caused drinking (1100 mL) throughout the infusion, an equiosmotic infusion of 0.3 M sucrose in high-sodium CSF (to prevent a fall in CSF Na^+ that occurs with 150 mM Na^+ CSF) caused similar initial drinking (300 mL in 15 minutes), but after that, very little was consumed. The authors interpreted the larger consumption with 0.45 M NaCl as a contribution from both osmoreceptors and Na^+ receptors. Collectively, these and other observations (McKinley, Olsson, Fyrhquist, & Liljekvist, 1980) show that ambient Na^+ is essential for osmoreceptor function, and, though a contribution from Na^+ sensors cannot be ruled out, the majority of the evidence points to osmoreceptors as initiators of intracellular dehydration-related drinking and antiduresis or AVP secretion.

Thrasher, Brown, Keil, and Ramsay (1980a) assessed in dogs whether drinking and AVP release were caused by an osmoreceptor or a Na^+ receptor mechanism. On separate occasions, they infused five dogs with 0.85 M NaCl or isosmotic (1.7 M) sucrose, glucose, or urea over a period of 45 minutes. Dogs had access to water, but if and when they initiated drinking it was removed until the 45-minute infusion was complete. Blood samples were taken before and during the infusion. At the end of the infusion, a CSF sample was taken. As expected, NaCl produced increases in plasma Na^+ (3%), osmolality (2–3%), and AVP (twofold), with a mean latency to drink of 14 minutes. CSF elevations of Na^+ and osmolality after 45 minutes were similar to those in plasma. Sucrose, which does not cross the blood–brain barrier, caused a slightly larger rise in plasma and CSF osmolality than NaCl, a decrease in Na^+, and a similar latency to drink (16 minutes). The rise of AVP was considerably larger, but the authors attribute this to stress or sickness since the dogs appeared agitated by sucrose infusion. Urea produced plasma and CSF changes similar to those with sucrose, but no drinking within the 45-minute period. Glucose increased osmolality but produced no drinking. Because drinking occurred with only two of the four solutes (i.e., NaCl, sucrose) that produced similar increases in plasma and CSF osmolality but opposite changes in plasma and CSF Na^+ (i.e., increase with NaCl, decrease with sucrose), the authors concluded that critical receptors for drinking and AVP secretion are osmoreceptors rather than Na^+ receptors and are located on the blood side of the blood–brain barrier.

Thrasher, Jones, et al. (1980) made a direct test of this hypothesis using ICV infusions of various hypertonic solutions via a surgically implanted third ventricular cannula. The solutions infused over 45 minutes were artificial CSF with added NaCl, sucrose, urea, or glucose (200 mOsm/L). Water was available for the duration of the infusion and the intake recorded. NaCl and sucrose had a similar dipsogenic effect (8–9 mL/kg body weight or 170 mL), whereas glucose and urea were ineffective. Plasma AVP at the end of the infusion was elevated two- to threefold above baseline by NaCl and sucrose, whereas neither glucose nor urea differed from the artificial CSF control. Thus, the adequate stimulus for drinking and AVP is an osmoreceptor. However, the latencies to drink after NaCl (12 minutes) and sucrose (22 minutes) were surprisingly long; drinking was estimated to have occurred with a CSF osmolality approaching 350 mOsm/kg, more than 15% above baseline and greater than fivefold the increase in comparable intravenous studies. It was suggested that the critical osmoreceptors are located some distance from the ventricular surface, a conclusion that seems at odds with the consensus that circumventricular organs (CVOs) are the critical sites. It is thus possible that dogs have an atypical permeability or other characteristic(s) of their CVOs and osmoreception.

Wood et al. (1982) studied osmotic drinking in rhesus monkeys. On separate test days, three monkeys were given via indwelling venous catheters 20-minute infusion of various concentrations of hypertonic NaCl (0.93–3.25 M), 1.7 M sucrose, or urea. Water was not available during this infusion, but after 20 minutes the infusion rate was cut to 10% to sustain the final osmolality for a further 15 minutes, during which time drinking was allowed and blood samples were taken. NaCl produced dose-dependent drinking of 10–30 mL/kg for the concentration range noted above. Sucrose also produced drinking, comparable to equiosmotic NaCl, but urea did not. In separate studies to determine thresholds, 1.7 M NaCl was infused with water present and a blood sample taken at the onset of drinking. The threshold so estimated was 2.3% (osmolality) or 2.9% (Na^+), similar to that in humans and many other mammals.

3.4   Intracellular Dehydration Drinking in Small Mammals

In this section, I review select studies of behavioral osmoregulation in rats or mice. These results are generally similar to or consistent with those in humans and large mammals, but they have enabled two major advances: electrophysiological/biophysical study of the receptors and tracing of their efferent pathways in the brain. These will be elaborated upon in Chapter 4.

As noted previously, the clearance of NaCl or other osmotic load by the mammalian kidney is rapid and efficient, via osmotic diuresis. In rats, more than 70% of an acute solute load is excreted in hypertonic (2–3x isotonic) urine within one hour, regardless of whether drinking has occurred (Cole, 1955; Corbit, 1965; Figure 3.4, panel A). The purely osmotic stimulus and associated cellular dehydration, with attendant expansion of plasma or ECF, are thus a description of the immediate consequence of an acute load. As that load is excreted by the kidney, the absolute solute load and thus osmotic pressure decline. Consequently, the potential stimulus to drinking changes with time. Of note, even without drinking, plasma Na^+ drops below the typical dipsogenic threshold (~2% above baseline) after 1–2 hours (Figure 3.4. panel B).

Adolph et al. (1954) found that within 30 minutes of i.p. injection, rats consumed enough water to substantially dilute a NaCl load. But if access to water was denied for periods up to eight hours, long after all of the NaCl load was fully excreted, the amount of water consumed was unchanged. Corbit (1965) and Novin (1962) found a slightly different result after intravenous infusions (more than 5–7 minutes) of hypertonic NaCl. Their results are shown in panel C of Figure 3.4. The amount consumed in one hour of access declined with time since injection, to a floor value after two hours of about 50% the amount consumed with immediate access. Novin (1962) additionally measured the electrical conductivity of the brain between two midline deep electrodes to continuously assess ionic concentration of tissue and/or CSF; an immediate ~7% elevation in conductivity decreased with a similar time course to drinking. Corbit suggested that the difference from Adolph et al. (and other studies) was the intravenous route, which produces a more rapid and less painful hypernatremia. Since all of the human and large animal studies used the intravenous route, it is appropriate to discuss the same route for rats.

Fitzsimons (1961a, 1963) circumvented this ambiguity by recording drinking behavior after rapid (two-minute) intravenous injection of hypertonic NaCl to acutely nephrectomized rats or sham-operated controls (Figure 3.4, panel D). He made five key observations:

- The osmotic threshold for drinking was comparable in sham-operated (1.6%) and nephrectomized (2%) rats, and in the range reported for larger mammals.

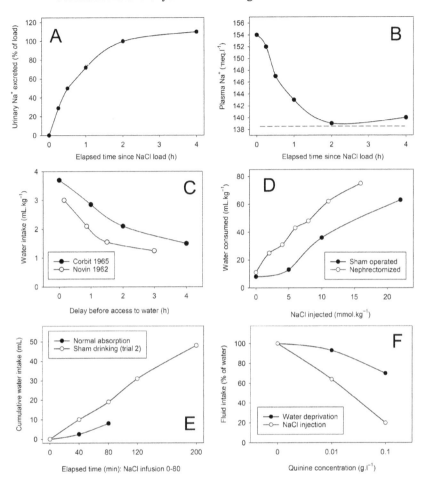

Figure 3.4 Effect of hypertonic NaCl loads in rats. Panels A and B are from Corbit (1965). Panel A shows time course of urinary excretion of an i.v. infusion over 2 min of approx. 10 mEq NaCl.kg^{-1}; 100% of the NaCl was excreted within 2 h. Panel B shows corresponding changes in plasma Na+ concentration. Panel C (from Corbit, 1965 and Novin, 1962) shows water intake when access to water after the infusion was delayed by various intervals. Panel D (from Fitzsimons, 1961a) shows water intake in 6 h following i.v. infusion of various doses of hypertonic NaCl in sham-operated and nephrectomized rats. Panel E (from Salisbury & Rowland, 1990) shows intake during and after 80-min i.v. infusion of NaCl in sham drinking rats with open fistulas, and on another occasion with the fistula closed (normal absorption). The sham drinking data are from the second of three trials reported. Panel F (from Burke et al., 1972) shows mean intakes in 2 h tests of different concentrations of quinine solution (0 = water) following either i.v. NaCl injection (1 mL of 3 M over 2 min) or 24 h water deprivation.

- Nephrectomized rats drank two to three times as much as sham-operated rats, in a dose-related manner, except at the highest doses. This indicates that excretion of Na^+ is an important factor in the water economy of intact rats.
- Nephrectomized rats drank, mostly in the first hour, an amount sufficient to dilute the load to isotonicity (in the total body water compartment), that is, perfect osmoregulation.
- If access to water was delayed by up to four hours after infusion, the amount of water consumed by nephrectomized rats was unchanged, showing that Na^+ or osmoreceptors do not adapt.
- Expansion of the extracellular space does not inhibit osmotic thirst. This was also shown by the fact that isotonic saline preloads did not inhibit thirst.

These findings suggest that, in a slow-drinking species such as rats, satiation of drinking at short times after infusion of NaCl is due to removal of hyperosmolality or hypernatremia. If drinking is delayed by several hours, the load is excreted and a smaller amount of water is consumed, but that drinking occurs in the absence of hypernatremia.

A different way of investigating postingestive factors is to eliminate them, using a sham drinking protocol in which water is consumed, but all of it drains out of a gastric or esophageal fistula without absorption. Salisbury and Rowland (1990) found that when NaCl was infused intravenously (1 mL of 3 M or about 10 mEq/kg over 80 minutes) during the early night, intake during the infusion at the first open fistula test was little more than with the fistula closed, but rose to about threefold this amount on subsequent tests (panel E of Figure 3.4). Sham drinking continued after the end of the infusion, presumably after much of the load was excreted. In the same study, s.c. injection of NaCl (4 mEq) elicited a one-hour sham intake about twice that with the fistula closed, but little increase across four consecutive open trials. Kraly (1978) also found a twofold amplification of water intake in a single one-hour sham drinking test starting one hour after i.p. injection of NaCl (10 mEq/kg). About 70% of that one-hour intake occurred in the first 15 minutes, suggesting a role for passage of water through the mouth in slowing sham drinking later in the session. The microstructure of drinking was not determined in either study, but the slowed average rate of drinking most likely reflects more frequent or longer pauses. Systemic hydration appears to be necessary to completely stop sham drinking.

One way to assess the motivating effects of hyperosmolality in rats is to make the available fluid less palatable. Burke et al. (1972) found that rats infused intravenously with NaCl then presented with mildly

(0.001–0.01%) quinine adulterated water drank substantially less than when drinking plain water (Figure 3.4, panel F). For comparison, intake after 24 hours of water deprivation was little affected by these levels of quinine adulteration. Additionally, when the NaCl load was given i.p., suppressions by quinine tended to be larger than with the intravenous route. The authors noted that rats drank quinine solutions for a few seconds and then backed away, groomed, and approached the spout from other angles or adopted abnormal postures. These and other findings show that acute hypertonicity produces an extreme taste reactivity to quinine that is not shared with natural dehydration. These findings were extended in studies by Nicolaïdis and Rowland (1975) and Rowland and Flamm (1977), who used rats that had been chronically adapted to quinine water (up to 0.08%) as their fluid source. Again, regardless of the route of administration, quinine drinkers took little or no fluid with acute hyperosmolality. In the latter studies, some quinine drinking occurred during the subsequent nocturnal period; the role of nychthemeral factors in drinking is discussed in more detail in Chapter 7. These adulteration studies show that the motivational stimulus provided by hypertonic NaCl is less than after periods of water deprivation that produce equivalent hypernatremia (see Chapter 8), or whether NaCl is administered in food (Rowland & Flamm, 1977). Thus, the context including route of administration is critical for full expression of osmoregulatory drinking.

House mice (*mus musculus*) have become popular subjects for drinking studies, in large part because of the availability of genetic engineering techniques to solve a number of previously intractable problems. Drinking studies in mice have been much more limited in scope than those in rats. Rowland and Fregly (1988a) injected albino (ICR:CD1) male mice with 10 mL/kg 1 M NaCl (10 mEq/kg i.p.) and recorded water intake for two hours. Mice drank 0.9 mL (3.1 mL/100 g body weight) compared with 0.1 mL after isotonic control injection. Johnson et al. (2003) used C57BL/6 male mice and two doses of NaCl (approximately 10 and 20 mEq/kg) and found dose-related drinks similar in magnitude to those reported by Rowland and Fregly (1988a). Additional analysis of drinking in C57BL/6 mice was performed in a gene knockout study that will also be described in Chapter 4 (Kinsman et al., 2014). For the present discussion, wild-type mice showed dose-related drinking after i. p. or s.c. hypertonic NaCl, with either immediate or 30-minute delayed access to water. Increases in plasma Na^+ achieved 30 minutes after injections of 5 and 10 mEq/kg were 3.4 and 7.6%, respectively. Mannitol (0.7 M) injection produced drinking similar to that evoked by 0.5 M NaCl, indicating that osmoreceptors rather than Na^+ receptors were involved. Thus, osmoregulatory drinking in mice appears to be similar to that in rats, with the caveat that relatively few protocols have been used and thresholds have not been determined.

Most of the animals and humans used in studies of osmoregulation have been young adults. Studies of osmoregulatory drinking during ontogeny and aging will be discussed fully in Chapters 6 and 10, respectively. To give a brief preview, osmoregulatory drinking develops early in life and remains substantially undiminished throughout most of the healthy life span. Those studies typically have not determined thresholds or solute specificity, but the available data strongly suggest that osmoreceptor function is likewise stable across the health span.

3.5   Peripheral Osmoreception

The focus of osmoregulatory drinking presented thus far has been on systemic osmolality changes and implicitly stimulation of systemic receptors, notably in the brain (see Chapter 4). However, there is a compelling case that functional osmoreceptors are found in the periphery, and notably along the orogastric axis and/or in the immediate postabsorptive field, including the splanchnohepatic venous complex. Collectively, these receptors have the capacity to sense relatively small water or osmotic loads either before they are absorbed or in the immediate post-absorptive region. Osmotically sensitive afferents from the hepatic portal regions have been known for many years, including their role in AVP secretion and drinking (Adachi et al., 1976; Chwalbinska-Moneta, 1984; Kahrilas & Rogers, 1984; reviewed by Bourque et al., 1994).

Some of the most compelling results have used intragastric administration of hypertonic solutions, mimicking the natural route by which solutes are ingested. In dogs, Kozlowski and Drzewicki (1973) found that infusion of 600 mOsm/kg NaCl into the portal vein reduced the threshold for drinking to intravenous NaCl. Chwalbinska-Moneta (1979) found that a five-minute infusion of 1.8% (0.3 M) NaCl into the hepatic portal vein of dogs increased plasma AVP by four- to fivefold without change in systemic osmolality. Higher concentrations had even greater effects. And in rats, Kahrilas and Rogers (1984) found that 75% of cells in the region of the nucleus of the solitary tract receiving hepatic afferents showed a sustained increase in firing rate to only a 1% increase in portal blood Na^+ concentration. Kraly et al. (1995) gave acute infusions (2 mL over 30 s) to rats through indwelling gastric catheters. The solutions were 0.6, 0.9, 1.2, or 1.8 M NaCl (approximately 3–9 mEq/kg) as well as equiosmotic mannitol or other Na^+ salts. These doses of NaCl elicited a dose-related increase in water intake but, except with 1.8 M, no

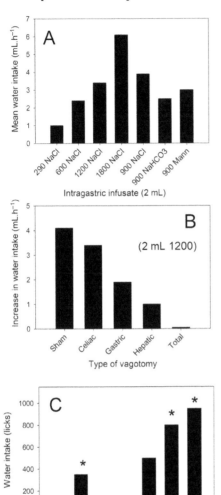

Figure 3.5 Effect of intragastric infusions of various solutions on drinking in rats. Panels A and B are from Kraly et al. (1995). Panel A shows mean water intake in 1 h following i.g. infusion (2 mL over 30 s) of the solutions and concentrations (mOsm.kg^{-1}) indicated. Mann = mannitol. All intakes were significantly elevated above isotonic (290 NaCl). Panel B shows effect of various vagotomies on 1 h intake following 2 mL i.g. infusion of 1200 mEq.kg^{-1} NaCl. Groups with gastric, hepatic, or total vagotomies drank less than sham-operated mean. Panel C (from Zimmerman et al. 2019) shows mean water intake (as licks) of mice following i.p. injection or i.g. infusion of NaCl in mice. Left bars are for euhydrated condition; right bars after 24 h water deprivation. *Significantly different from corresponding control (C) condition.

change in systemic osmolality (Figure 3.5, panel A). Thus, the stimulus is localized to the immediate perihepatic regions. Mannitol was about 80% as effective as NaCl. The authors found that total subdiaphragmatic vagotomy abolished drinking to intragastric hypertonic NaCl and that selective hepatic branch vagotomy strongly attenuated drinking, whereas celiac or gastric branch vagotomies were less effective (Figure 3.5, panel B). The results support the hypothesis of a gastrointestinal and/or hepatic portal osmosensitive mechanism for initiation of thirst. Using i.p. NaCl, Kraly (1978) had previously identified vagally mediated information as important for initiation of drinking. Latencies to drink were longer in vagotomized rats, and the amount consumed less, apparently due to their more rapid gastric emptying of water. The dose of NaCl (1% body weight 2 M) should have increased plasma osmolality in these rats and stimulated potential brain osmoreceptors. Thus, the markedly longer latencies (>20 minutes in vagotomized groups compared with ~10 minutes in sham-operated controls) suggest that central osmoreceptor mechanisms may operate over longer time frames than those in the periphery.

Zimmerman et al. (2019) reported that intragastric infusion of NaCl (0.15 mL of 1.5 M, approximately 10 mEq/kg) was not dipsogenic in euhydrated mice, whereas the same dose given i.p. was. However, when added to overnight water deprivation, both routes of administration produced more drinking than deprivation alone (Figure 3.5, panel C). In rats, Stricker et al. (2002) similarly showed a potentiation of drinking to intragastric NaCl after water deprivation. Zimmerman et al. (2019) suggest that a signal of gastric origin is effective to induce drinking only in states of dehydration. This conclusion diverges substantially from the foregoing view that peripheral osmoreception alone is effective. NaCl concentrations of 1 M and above are known to produce irritation of the gastric mucosa in rats (Takeuchi et al., 1986), so it would be interesting to revisit these studies using lower, physiologically relevant concentrations of NaCl. Additional aspects of the neural systems engaged by peripheral osmoreception will be discussed in Chapter 4.

3.6   Summary

Injection of solutes such as Na^+ or mannitol, which initially elevate ECF osmotic pressure and then draw water from cells to dilute the load to near isotonicity, cause reliable drinking in all species studied. This osmoregulatory drinking is accompanied by report of thirst in humans, and secretion of AVP. The threshold elevation of systemic osmolality to initiate these changes is in the range 1–3%. Regardless of whether drinking is allowed, the osmotic load is excreted by the kidney over the course of 2–4 hours. From sham drinking and other studies, osmoregulatory drinking is satiated when osmotic pressure is normalized and cellular water is restored. Many studies have shown that osmoreceptors for drinking and AVP secretion are located in or near the CVOs of the lamina terminalis. In addition, peripheral osmoreceptors in the gut or splanchnic regions monitor the osmolality of fluids absorbed from the gut and are sufficient to stimulate drinking in the absence of systemic hyperosmolality.

4   Intracellular Dehydration: Mechanism

4.1   Introduction

In the face of increased plasma osmolality, mammals have two principal mechanisms by which to dilute the stimulus: drinking behavior and excretion of the solute load by the kidney. Release of arginine vasopressin (AVP) from the posterior lobe of the pituitary gland and action at V2 receptors in the collecting tubules and duct of the kidney promote solute-free water reabsorption via increased expression of aquaporin channels. AVP is synthesized as a prohormone by magnocellular or neurosecretory neurons in the supraoptic (SON) and paraventricular (PVN) hypothalamic nuclei, transported axonally to nerve terminals in the posterior pituitary, and released in proportion to action potentials in those axons. A primary quest in this field has been to determine characteristics and location(s) of osmoreceptors that stimulate AVP synthesis and release. Regarding location or characteristics, these osmoreceptors might be the same as or different from those involved in drinking.

Pioneering work in relation to AVP release was performed by Jewell and Verney (1957), who restricted the spread of a hyperosmotic stimulus by ligating various branches of the internal carotid artery in dogs. This work revealed that critical osmoreceptors for the release of AVP were in the anterior hypothalamus or preoptic area, and were sensitive to about a 2% osmotic change. The osmoreceptors thus could be in the SON and PVN or in nearby location(s) that project to neurosecretory cells in the SON and/or PVN.

4.2   Osmoreceptors: Structure and Function

Osmoreceptors may be defined as cells that generate changes in their membrane potential as they shrink during intracellular dehydration. Many cells in the body have mechanisms to resist volume changes, but osmoreceptors do not and can sustain their volume changes for long periods. Cellular dehydration is transduced by stretch receptors in the osmoreceptor walls. Most such neurons are proportionally excited (i.e., increase firing rate) by extracellular hyperosmolality and are inhibited by hypo-osmolality. The basal firing rate of these neurons thus encodes a null or set point of the osmoregulatory system (see Bourque, 2008, for review).

Depolarization of the osmoreceptor membrane during hyperosmolality is caused by an increased probability of opening and hence conductance of nonselective cation channels. Conversely, hyperpolarization of the membrane during hypo-osmolality is via a decrease in the basal probability of opening of these channels. Nonselective cation channels often have a severalfold higher permeability to calcium than Na^+. The critical role of cell volume rather than solute exchanges in this process is shown by the finding that applying suction intracellularly in a patch clamp protocol can effectively mimic the effect of hyperosmolality on electrical excitability. Inflation of the cells produces opposite effects, including reversal of the effect of hyperosmotic stimulation (Figure 4.1).

Such analysis depends upon reliable localization of osmoreceptor cells for either in vivo or in vitro experimentation. Because magnocellular neurons in the SON and PVN were known for their role in AVP synthesis and secretion, many studies focused on the properties of these cells. These neurons in general increase their firing rates and/or adopt bursting patterns in response to increasing osmotic pressure. In vivo, these cells have many afferent connections; thus, establishing intrinsic osmosensitivity required the use of isolated cells in vitro (Oliet & Bourque, 1992). Increasing the osmolality of the perfusing solution by 5–40 mOsm/kg (approximately 2–13%) with mannitol or sucrose caused each of 36 cells isolated from rat SON to be depolarized, and accelerated the frequency of spike discharge, effects occurring within a few seconds and lasting for the duration of the stimulus.

To examine connectivity of the SON, Honda et al. (1990a) performed experiments in urethane-anesthetized rats in which electrical stimulation was applied to tissue surrounding the anteroventral third ventricle (including the vascular organ of the lamina terminalis [OVLT]; see next section), median preoptic area (MnPO), or SON and electrical recordings were made from single cells in these regions. Their results are consistent with a circuit of excitatory connections between the SON and OVLT, the OVLT and MnPO, and the MnPO and SON. Disruption of any part of this circuit by application of lidocaine prevented activation of SON cells by peripheral injection of hypertonic NaCl. The authors characterized the OVLT–MnPO–SON as an osmoreceptor complex that is involved in the release of AVP, with the whole complex being more sensitive than any of its components alone. These authors then

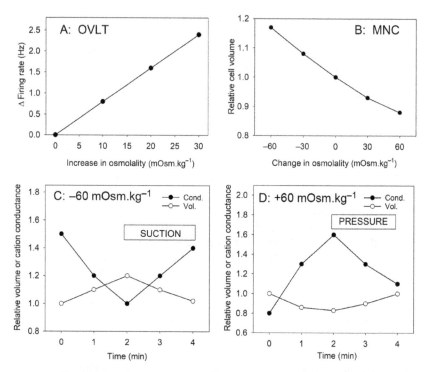

Figure 4.1 Properties of osmoreceptor neurons (from Bourque, 2008).
Panel A shows mean change in firing rate with increase in extracellular
osmolality in osmosensitive neurons in mouse OVLT. Panel B shows
change in relative volume of isolated magnocellular neurosecretory
neurons (MNCs) with change in extracellular osmolality. Panel
C shows decrease in extracellular osmolality of MNCs causes cell
expansion and decrease in cation conductance (0–2 min); shrinking the
cell by suction through a whole-cell patch clamp pipette causes a
reversal of these effects (2–4 min). Panel D shows reciprocal of effects in
C, with increase of extracellular osmolality and cell expansion by
application of pressure through the pipette.

showed that local osmotic stimulation of the MnPO produced excitatory
responses in most cells in the SON (Honda et al., 1990b) and
magnocellular PVN (Honda et al., 1992). Lesion of the OVLT impaired
the responsiveness of both vasopressin and oxytocin cells in the PVN to
plasma hyperosmolality. Thus, magnocellular neurons in both the SON
and PVN have intrinsic osmoreceptor properties and become more sensitive with concurrent excitatory input from osmoreceptors in the OVLT
and MnPO of the lamina terminalis.

The transduction process for cell shrinkage caused by hypernatremia or other extracellular solute is thought to occur via one or several types of transient receptor potential vanilloid (TRPV) channels. These channels have six transmembrane-spanning domains and a pore-loop domain that renders their class sensitive to a variety of thermal, mechanical, and chemical stimuli. Osmosensitive neurons in the OVLT have been shown to express TRPV1 and TRPV4, and magnocellular neurons in the supraoptic nucleus express TRPV1 and TRPV2. Though heterologous expression of TRPV1 does not impart osmosensitivity, it has been proposed that an N-terminal variant is an osmoreceptor. Functional experiments to delineate which receptor subtype(s) are critical to osmoreception have yielded inconsistent results. For example, it was reported that osmoreceptors of mice with knockout of the TRPV1 receptor gene shrank normally during hyperosmolality but did not change cation conductance. Relative to wild-type controls, TRPV1 mice had ~3% elevated basal plasma osmolality and about fourfold reduction in the slope of the AVP–osmolality relationship but showed only a 20% decrease in drinking following acute injection of 10 mEq/kg NaCl (Naeini et al., 2006). However, neither Kinsman et al. (2014) nor Taylor et al., (2008) were able to replicate these genotypic differences in either drinking or basal osmolality. Similarly, knockout of the TRPV4 receptor in mice either has (Liedke & Freidman, 2003) or has not (Ciura et al., 2011; Kinsman et al., 2014) been associated with functional osmoregulatory deficits. Moriya et al. (2015) have suggested that in vasopressin neurons of rat SON, the osmoreceptor may be a multimer of full-length TRPV1 with as yet unidentified macromolecules.

Grob et al. (2004) employed whole-cell patch clamp recordings in rat brain slices, including the MnPO. They showed that neurons in the MnPO have an intrinsic membrane permeability to Na^+ that transduces extracellular Na^+ concentration. Pharmacological and immunohisto-chemical probes revealed this was a previously identified concentration-dependent Na^+ channel known as Na_x, which is a family encoded by the SCN7A gene. In mice, the Na_x channel instead seems to be expressed only in glial cells (i.e., astrocytes and ependymal cells; Watanabe et al., 2000, 2006). This channel contributes to both water and NaCl intake under different conditions. I will discuss sodium intake further in Chapter 5, and for now focus on aspects related to water intake during hyperosmotic states.

To isolate the effects of Na^+ or osmotic change to the brain, Sakuta et al. (2016) administered hypertonic NaCl (4 μl of 1 M) or isosmotic sorbitol in artificial cerebrospinal fluid (CSF) to wild-type C57BL/6 mice and to mice with genomic knockout of either TRPV1, TRPV4,

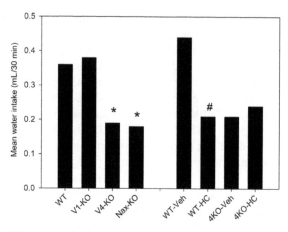

Figure 4.2 Group mean water intakes (mL/30 min) of mice following intracerebroventricular injection of hypertonic NaCl (4 μl of 1 M in artificial CSF; from Sakuta et al., 2016). The left set of data is from wild type (WT) mice and genomic knockouts (KO) of TRPV1, TRPV4, or Na_x receptors. The right set of data is from WT or V4-KO mice pretreated with either a vehicle (veh) or a TRP-V4 antagonist (HC) prior to injection of NaCl. *Different from WT. #HC differs from veh.

or Na_x. This NaCl infusion acutely increased CSF Na^+ concentration by about 10%. The water intakes in 30 minutes following injection are shown in Figure 4.2 (left side). Compared with injection of isotonic saline, which did not produce water intake, infusion of 1 M NaCl produced a similar and robust drink in both wild-type and TRPV1 knockout mice. In contrast, the intakes by either TRPV4 or Na_x knockouts were about half that of wild-type mice. Double knockout of Na_x and TRPV4 did not have an additional effect, suggesting that Na_x and TRPV4 engage the same mechanism. This was shown further using a TRPV4 antagonist (HC-067047), which reduced intake in wild-type mice but not in Na_x knockout mice (Figure 4.2, right side). Infusion of isosmotic sorbitol produced an intake only ~20% of that induced in wild-type mice by NaCl, and this was unaffected by gene knockout or antagonist procedures.

Other data suggested that the mechanism by which glial Na_x affects TRPV4, which has neuron-specific expression in the circumventricular organs, is via formation of epoxyeicosatrienoic acid from arachidonic acid. In support of this mechanism, drinking after intracerebroventricular (ICV) NaCl injection in wild-type mice was reduced to the level seen in Na_x knockout mice by miconazole, which inhibits synthesis of epoxyeicosatrienoic acids. Further, administration of epoxyeicosatrie-noic acid increased water intake of Na_x knockout mice to levels seen in the wild type. Water intake after sorbitol was unaffected by any of these manipulations. These results show that Na^+ sensing by glial Na_x in the subfornical organ (SFO) and/or OVLT produces, via modulation of TRPV4 in neurons, more than 50% of the water intake evoked in mice by acute hypernatremia in CSF. However, water intake after 24 or 48 hours of water deprivation (producing 5–10% increase in plasma Na^+ concentration; see Chapter 8) did not differ among the wild type or any of the knockout strains (Sakuta et al., 2016). This discrepancy does not seem to have been resolved satisfactorily. Further, given that different cell types express Na_x in mice compared to rats, it is not clear at this time whether these elegant results are specific to mice or would generalize to rats or other mammals.

4.3   Osmoreceptors and Drinking: The Lamina Terminalis

Andersson (1952) pioneered the use of intracerebral injections of hyper-tonic solutions, via indwelling cannulas, to assess brain regions involved in thirst and/or AVP secretion. He reported that injection of 0.1 mL of ~1.8% (2x isotonic) NaCl into the anterior hypothalamus caused rapid and vigorous drinking in 8 of 16 goats tested. Use of smaller injection volumes (Andersson & McCann, 1955) did not improve the localization or reliability of response. Andersson et al. (1967) showed that slow infusions (7.5 µl/min) of 0.85 M NaCl into the anterior third ventricle caused vigorous drinking and antidiuresis in goats, but identical infu-sions into the lateral ventricles were ineffective. Third ventricular infu-sions of fructose were also ineffective. These and other findings led to a proposal that there are Na^+ receptors rather than osmoreceptors on the brain side of the blood–brain barrier, specifically in the rostroventral third ventricle region (Olsson, 1973), a conclusion that has been chal-lenged (see later in this chapter).

In rats and rabbits, drinking was elicited by intracerebral (parenchymal) injections of hypertonic NaCl into several locations within the anterior hypothalamus and preoptic area, and only partially overlapping with effect-ive sites for AVP secretion (Peck & Blass, 1975). A fundamental question was whether the receptors are on the blood or brain side of the blood–brain barrier. McKinley et al. (1978) pointed out that circumventricular organs, by virtue of their reduced or absent blood–brain barrier, provide a logical substrate (see also Chapters 1 and 3).

Lesion studies in animals have played a key role in identifying osmor-eceptive regions critical to drinking. However, the interpretation of results can be difficult. For example, even if a lesion group were to drink reliably less than an intact or control group, this does not prove a defect at the osmoreceptor or downstream regions involved in the initiation of drinking. The abnormality could instead be at the level of maintenance or termination/satiation of drinking (Rolls et al., 1980). Direct observation and/or analysis of licking behavior may allow for discrimination among these alternatives but has rarely been performed. Determination of osmotic drinking thresholds by using low-intensity stimuli or constructing a dose–effect curve may be useful in identifying the nature of the deficit. This also has rarely been attempted in lesion studies.

In rats, the entire dorsoventral length of the lamina terminalis is only about 5 mm, and the width 0.5 mm. This small size, coupled with its vertical orientation, presents some difficulty in producing selective but complete stereotaxically guided damage restricted to only one subregion of the structure. As a result, lesion studies in rats often include many subjects only some of which will, upon histological analysis, have damage in or restricted to the organ or structure of interest. Mice have even smaller brains and in addition do not readily allow the richness of physiological study that has been performed in rats or other animals; investigators in this field must be cautious to avoid unwarranted interpretation. The anatomical and physiological situation is better in larger mammals, which is where I will start.

4.4   Lamina Terminalis and Osmoregulatory Drinking in Large Mammals

Thrasher and Keil (1987) tested dogs in which the OVLT had been ablated by prior electrolytic lesion. A particular advantage of dogs is that the OVLT can be approached ventrally and ablated without much involvement of the MnPO dorsal to the OVLT. These lesions had several temporary effects on fluid homeostasis, and drinking studies were not performed until the dogs had fully recovered. Several dipsogens were studied, but for now I focus on the osmotic stimulus, which was intravenous infusion of hypertonic NaCl at a rate of 0.32 mmol/kg body weight/min. Dogs with lesions destroying more than 90% of the OVLT showed a longer latency to drink compared with dogs with little or no damage to the OVLT (6 vs. 21 minutes). From blood samples, both OVLT-lesioned and control (damage sparing the OVLT) dogs had similar starting plasma osmolality (296 mOsm/kg), but the controls initiated drinking when osmolality had risen to 303 mOsm/kg (a 2.4% threshold) while the OVLT-lesioned dogs did not initiate drinking until osmolality reached 320 mOsm/kg (8.1%), more than a threefold higher threshold. Further, the amount drunk in the session was much reduced (15 vs. 28 mL/kg). Plasma AVP was measured in serial samples, and the slope of the AVP versus osmolality regression was some 60% lower in OVLT-lesioned dogs compared with control dogs. The authors concluded that the OVLT contains critical osmoreceptors for drinking and AVP secretion. The AVP result is consistent with the conclusion of Honda et al. (1990a) that an intact osmoreceptor complex (OVLT, MnPO, SON) is more sensitive than its component parts. This may be true for osmoregulatory drinking in dogs since OVLT lesion increased the threshold. The result implies that there are component(s) to the osmotic drinking system that are downstream from or in a circuit with osmoreceptors in the OVLT.

To determine the location of osmoreceptors for drinking in sheep, McKinley et al. (1982) administered intracarotid infusions of hypertonic NaCl (4 M, 1.3 mL/min for 20 minutes) before and after radiofrequency lesions through implanted electrodes targeting the OVLT. These lesions produced a few days of adipsia and/or hypernatremia, effects that had resolved by the time of the behavioral experiments. Before lesion, mean water intake to NaCl infusion was 1,105 mL, whereas after lesions destroyed the OVLT and a small amount of dorsally adjacent lamina terminalis, the intake was 109 mL. Sheep in which the lesion damaged tissue adjacent to but not including the OVLT consumed a near-normal amount (892 mL). The authors concluded that osmoregulatory drinking is dependent on tissue in or adjacent to the OVLT.

Subsequently, the same investigators (McKinley et al. 1999) performed an extensive study of the effects of lesions to various parts of the lamina terminalis on osmoregulatory drinking in sheep. Indwelling electrodes for lesions were radiographically targeted at the OVLT, MnPO, or SFO, or combinations thereof. Drinking was measured in the 30 minutes following intravenous infusion of 4 M NaCl (1.3 mL/min for 30 minutes) before and after full recovery from radiofrequency lesions through the electrodes. These results are shown in Figure 4.3. Lesions restricted to the OVLT or SFO had no effect on drinking and hypertonic NaCl. In contrast, combined lesions of the SFO and OVLT reduced drinking by ~50%, as did any lesion including the MnPO. Of particular note is the observation that OVLT lesion alone had no effect, but adding MnPO completely obliterated the drinking response. The plasma Na^+ concentration was similar in all groups before (145 mmol/L) and at the end of the 30-minutes infusion (155 mmol/L, about 7% increase). This study was not designed to examine drinking thresholds, and it remains possible that by not performing the drinking tests until after hyperosmolality had fully developed, any lesion effects on the initiation of drinking

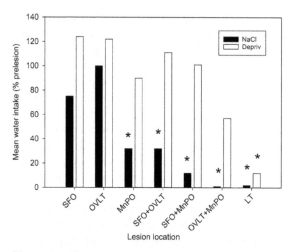

Figure 4.3 Group mean water intakes of sheep infused intravenously with hypertonic NaCl (156 mmol/30 min) or after 48 h water deprivation (from McKinley et al., 1999). Each animal was tested before and after brain lesion, and data are expressed as percent intake as after compared with before. Different groups of sheep had lesions histologically categorized as SFO, OVLT, MnPO, and combinations thereof, or of the entire lamina terminalis (LT). *Differs post- versus prelesion.

may have been obfuscated. The increase in plasma Na$^+$ or osmolality caused by this infusion was similar to the elevated drinking threshold reported by Thrasher and Keil (1987) in dogs with OVLT lesions.

All of these sheep were also tested for drinking after 48-hour water deprivation. Intake was not reduced from prelesion values in any group except complete ablation of the lamina terminalis. With the exception of the SFO- or OVLT-only groups, the increase in plasma Na$^+$ or osmolality was up to twofold higher after the lesion than before, and fourfold in the complete lamina terminalis group, suggesting a deficit in Na$^+$ excretion. Water deprivation studies will be examined further in Chapter 8.

As lesions are not available as an experimental tool in humans, the noninvasive imaging methods of positron emission tomography (PET) and functional magnetic resonance imaging (fMRI) have been used to assess regions activated by hyperosmolality (Egan et al., 2003). Subjects were given intravenous infusion of NaCl (0.51 M at 9.5 mL/kg over 50 minutes). Thirst began to emerge after approximately 25 minutes when plasma Na$^+$ concentration was increased by ~2%, and at this time a PET scan was performed in 10 subjects. There were significant increases or decreases in cerebral blood flow in many brain regions, including divisions of the hippocampus, cerebellum, cingulate gyrus, and caudate nucleus. The fMRI scans were conducted for the 10 minutes during which subjects reported a maximum increase of thirst rating and revealed activation in some regions not identified by PET. Among these were the OVLT in two subjects and anterior cingulate (ACC; Brodmann areas 24 and 32) in all four subjects. In OVLT and ACC, the fMRI signal (the difference from preinfusion baseline) continued to increase throughout the infusion. In the ACC, but not the OVLT, that signal abruptly reversed when drinking was allowed and well before ingested water was absorbed. It must be emphasized that fMRI data from only a few subjects are available using NaCl as the stimulus. In Chapters 8 and 9, studies using natural or hybrid thirst stimuli such as exercise-induced sweating yield will be reviewed; the results are generally consistent with the foregoing.

4.5   Lamina Terminalis and Osmoregulatory Drinking in Small Mammals: Evidence from Lesion Studies

Hosutt et al. (1981) examined drinking with intravenous infusions of two doses of NaCl in rats with complete lesions of the SFO. These results are shown in Figure 4.4, panel A. Compared with controls, the SFO-lesioned rats were severely impaired in drinking to the low dose, but most of the lesioned rats drank normally to the higher doses. No deficit to higher doses of NaCl was found by Eng and Miselis (1981) in rats with knife cuts to the ventral stalk of the SFO, and their data are presented in Figure 4.4, panel B. The data suggest an elevated osmotic thirst threshold in SFO-lesioned rats. In contrast, Lind et al. (1984) found that rats with similar knife cuts drank about 50% that of sham-operated controls following subcutaneous (s.c.) injection of relatively large doses of NaCl. The reason for this discrepancy is not clear, but the entirety of these data shows that although the SFO is not necessary for the initiation of osmoregulatory drinking, it is a critical site contributing to the Na^+ sensitivity (solutes other than NaCl were not tested) of the lamina terminalis complex and/or termination of such drinking.

Starbuck and Fitts (1998) examined the effect of SFO lesions on drinking in response to administration of low doses of NaCl via gastric gavage. The result in panel C of Figure 4.4 shows that for the first 30 minutes after a 2 mL gavage, intakes of lesioned and sham-operated rats were comparable with concentrations of 300 (isotonic) and 900 mOsm/kg NaCl, but intake was abolished at 1,200 mOsm/kg. In another study employing knife cuts of the anterior stalk of the SFO, Starbuck and Fitts (2002) reported that intake of the cut group (1.5 mL) was about half

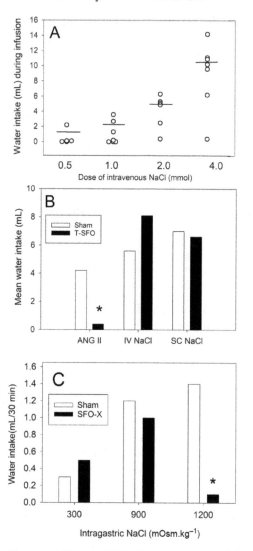

Figure 4.4 Effect of SFO damage on water intake of rats after hypertonic NaCl challenge. Panel A (from Hosutt et al., 1981) shows individual data of SFO lesioned rats (circles) and group means for intact control rats (lines) intake during intravenous infusion of 1 M or 2 M NaCl over 1 or 2 h for total doses shown. Panel B (from Eng & Miselis, 1981) shows group mean intakes during i.v. infusion of ANG II or NaCl (384 ng.kg^{-1}.min^{-1} for 20 min), NaCl (approx. 12 meq.kg^{-1} over 2 h), or in 2 h after s.c. NaCl (~6 meq.kg^{-1}). Shown are intakes of sham-operated rats and those with complete transections of the anterior stalk of the SFO (SFO-T). *SFO-T differs from sham. Panel C (from Starbuck & Fitts, 1998) shows group intakes by sham-operated rats and rats with complete lesions of the SFO (SFO-X) in the first 30 min following intragastric infusion of various doses of NaCl. *SFO-X differs from sham.

that of sham-operated rats (2.8 mL) after a 600 mOsm/kg load, but this effect was not significant due to one high drinker in the cut group. I have reanalyzed these data as fraction of rats consuming more than 2 mL. Eleven of 14 control and 1 of 7 lesioned rats met that criterion, a distribution that differs from chance ($p < 0.01$, χ^2 test). This result is consistent with those in the previous paragraph showing deficits at low doses of NaCl, but because the gastric loads do not cause appreciable change in systemic osmolality, the afferents from the peripheral osmo- or Na^+ receptors may be especially dependent on the SFO, whereas stronger stimuli may engage other osmosensory pathway(s).

Black (1976) was one of the first investigators to report on the effects of damage to the medial preoptic area and fluid homeostasis in rats. These were relatively large lesions, apparently extending well beyond the boundaries of the MnPO, and were associated with substantial postoperative death. However, for rats that were nurtured to recovery, daily water intakes were at or slightly above those of sham-operated controls, but the lesion group was persistently hypernatremic. Further, in response to intraperitoneal (i.p.) 1 M NaCl, the lesioned rats drank only 30% as much as sham-operated controls, despite equivalent natriuresis. Gardiner and Stricker (1985a, 1985b) significantly advanced this analysis by making smaller lesions aimed at the ventral MnPO. They also found postoperative adipsia as well as recovery, and some rats became hyperdipsic with mean daily water intakes two times that of sham-operated controls. This appeared to be a primary hyperdipsia because these rats were able to concentrate urine normally when fluid restricted. The rats were then subjected to several tests of fluid balance including osmoregulatory drinking to two doses of NaCl (2 and 4 mmol; about 4 and 8 mEq/kg, s.c., during the daytime). Because hyperdipsic rats might enter such tests overhydrated, I will focus only on the rats that were normodipsic after recovery from the lesion. Panel A of Figure 4.5 shows the percentage of these rats that drank either little or nothing (<2 and <3 mL for the low and high doses, respectively) following injection. Clearly, a greater fraction was impaired to the lower than the higher dose. The rats that failed to respond to either dose were then given two additional tests. In the first, the higher dose of NaCl was injected along with the stimulant caffeine, and in the second, the NaCl test was performed in the middle of the night phase. Panel B of Figure 4.5 shows that in both cases the formerly nonresponsive lesioned rats now had mean two-hour water intakes close to those of sham-operated controls. This result, reminiscent of other lesion studies (e.g., Rowland, 1976b, for lateral hypothalamus) shows that deficient drinking in this subset of MnPO-lesioned rats is not due to a primary impairment in osmoreception, but in the downstream processing of those signals. These effects on

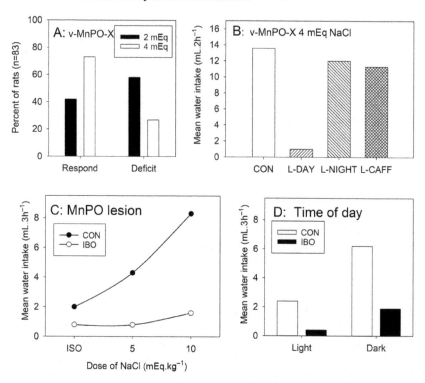

Figure 4.5 Effect of ventral MnPO damage (v-MnPO-X) on water intake of rats after hypertonic NaCl challenge. Panels A and B are from Gardiner and Stricker (1985b). Panel A shows distribution of 2 h drinking responses to 2 or 4 mEq NaCl injected s.c. These 83 rats had normal daily water intakes. Deficit was categorized as intake of 2 mL or less after NaCl. Panel B shows mean intake of sham-lesioned (CON) rats and of a subgroup of lesioned rats that did not respond to NaCl in daytime tests (L-day) but were later tested at night (L-night) or by day after pretreatment with caffeine (L-CAFF). Panels C and D are from Cunningham et al. (1992). Panel C shows effect of ibotenic acid (IBO) lesions of the MnPO on drinking in response to various s.c. doses of NaCl. IBO rats had ~80% cell loss in MnPO. Panel D shows water intake of control and IBO-lesioned rats when NaCl (10 mEq.kg^{-1}) was injected early in light or dark phases.

drinking were not correlated with any specific extent of lesion beyond the ventral MnPO, including lesions that also involved the OVLT or dorsal MnPO.

The interpretation of this study was challenged by Cunningham et al. (1992), who made excitotoxic lesions of the MnPO using microinjections of ibotenic acid. Postmortem histological examination revealed six rats with 75–80% loss of neurons in the MnPO with no involvement of the OVLT. The drinking response of these rats to low and high s.c. doses of NaCl (5 and 10 mEq/kg) are shown in Panel C of Figure 4.5, and the drinking in tests performed three hours after light onset (day) and three hours after light offset (night) are shown in panel D. The MnPO-damaged rats showed essentially no drinking after either dose of NaCl or at either phase of the nycthemeral cycle. Sham-operated control rats drank more in the night test, as also shown by Johnson and Johnson (1991), whereas the time-of-day difference in the intakes of sham-operated rats in the Gardiner and Stricker (1985b) study was modest – 10.7 and 12.3 mL – and consistent with many of my own laboratory observations. Since excitotoxic lesions should leave fibers of passage intact and functional, the differences in time-of-day effect in these studies could be reconciled if the coagulative lesion alters a net balance between excitatory and inhibitory signals coursing through the region, such as between the SFO and OVLT, that are modulated by timing or arousal effects (see Chapter 7). None of these lesion studies have used low-stress (intravenous) infusion protocols, and some of the behavioral results could thus have been influenced by nonspecific interfering aspects.

The effects of lesions to the OVLT or periventricular ventral third ventricle in relation to drinking in rats are challenging to evaluate because such lesions produce acute adipsia, from which many animals recover, but with persistent deficits in AVP secretion and control of natriuresis (Johnson & Buggy, 1978). However, microinjections of hypertonic NaCl or sucrose into the anteroventral third ventricle (Buggy et al., 1979) revealed this to be a more sensitive osmoreceptive site than other regions, including the lateral preoptic area previously identified by Peck and Blass (1975).

4.6   Neural Pathways of Systemic Osmoregulatory Drinking

The data reviewed above indicate that the osmoreceptor complex of the lamina terminalis is critical for optimal expression of drinking due to hyperosmolarity. One method to identify other regions or circuits that may be engaged was the induction of early genes or gene products as markers of neural activation. The most used protocol is immunohisto-chemical visualization of the perinuclear protein c-Fos (reviewed by Rowland, 1998). Oldfield et al. (1991) reported that intravenous hyper-tonic NaCl infused to rats at high doses that produced elevations of 4.4% or 9.2% in plasma osmolality in 10 minutes induced, relative to isotonic saline control, many strongly Fos-immunoreactive (Fos-ir) cells in the SON and PVN, as well as in the SFO, the dorsal and ventral MnPO, and the dorsal cap region of the OVLT. Similar but less intense activation was found with infusions of hypertonic sucrose, indicating that the cells activated were osmoreceptors rather than Na^+ receptors.

To determine whether the osmoreceptor complex was connected to AVP-secreting cells, Oldfield et al. (1994) made bilateral injections of the retrograde tracer, gold-conjugated cholera toxin, into the SON of rats. At least one week later, the rats were infused intravenously with hypertonic NaCl (2.25 mmol) and were then sacrificed for histochemical determination of the coincidence of retrograde label and Fos-ir. The mean percentages of retrogradely labeled cells inducing Fos-ir to hypertonic NaCl were 63, 24, and 35 in the OVLT, MnPO, and SFO, respectively. The respective percentages of Fos-expressing cells that did not contain retrograde tracer, and thus presumably projected to other brain regions, were 22, 32, and 14. These findings suggest that the SON is the efferent terminus of many osmotically activated cells in the OVLT, and to a lesser extent from cells in the MnPO and SFO. In an extension of this work, Bisley et al. (1996) found that leakage of intravenously injected horseradish peroxidase surrounded Fos-ir cells in the dorsal cap of the OVLT, indicating they are outside the blood–brain barrier.

Han and Rowland (1996) found that a relatively low dose (6 mmol/kg) of intravenous hypertonic NaCl induced strong Fos-ir in the SON and PVN of rats, but it did not produce visible Fos-ir in the SFO, MnPO, or OVLT. A higher dose (12 mmol/kg) induced Fos-ir in 25–50% more cells in the SON and PVN, but it also induced Fos-ir in the SFO, MnPO, and OVLT (Figure 4.6, panel A). The results shown are for 10-minute infusions with 90 minutes until tissue collection; slower infusions produced somewhat less activation but similar profiles.

A profile similar to that described above after the intravenous low dose by Han and Rowland (1996) was found in sham-operated rats given a low dose of NaCl (0.6 M, 3 mmol/kg) intragastrically (Starbuck & Fitts, 2002). They found that rats with knife cut transection of the ventral stalk of the SFO were generally similar, but with a roughly 50% reduction in the Fos-expressing cell numbers in the SON and PVN (Figure 4.6, panel B). Interestingly, Starbuck et al. (2002) found a similar reduction of Fos-ir in the SON and PVN of vagotomized rats treated with 6 mmol NaCl intragastrically, but no difference between sham-operated and vagotomized rats at the higher dose of 10 mmol/kg. Hochstenbach and Ciriello (1996) used a larger, relatively rapid, intravenous dose of NaCl (7.7 mmol/kg), raising plasma Na^+ by about 7%, and, consistent with the foregoing studies, found no activation of the SFO, some Fos-ir in the

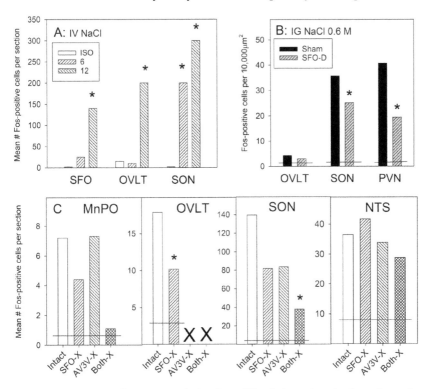

Figure 4.6 Group mean induction of Fos-ir in various brain regions of rats following treatment with hypertonic NaCl. Panel A (from Han & Rowland, 1996) shows cell counts in the SFO, OVLT, and SON 90 min after a 10 min i.v. infusion of 0.15 M NaCl (ISO control), or 6 or 12 mEq.kg^{-1} NaCl. *Increase above ISO. Panel B (from Starbuck & Fitts, 2002) shows Fos infuced in the OVLT, SON, or magnocellular PVN after intragastric gavage of 0.6 M NaCl (5 ml.kg^{-1}) in rats with cuts transecting the anterior stalk of the SFO (SFO-D) and sham operates. *SFO-D differs from sham. Horizontal lines indicate Fos after isotonic control procedure. Panel C (from Hochstenbach & Ciriello, 1996) shows mean Fos induced by i.v. infusion of NaCl (7.7 mEq.kg^{-1} over 10 min) in four brain regions of intact rats and those with complete lesions of the SFO (SFO-X), anteroventral third ventricle (AV3V-X), or both structures. *Differs from intact group. Horizontal lines indicate Fos after isotonic control procedure. (X indicates no data, structure lesioned.)

OVLT and MnPO, and strong activation of the SON and PVN. They included rats with lesions of the SFO, OVLT (anteroventral third ventricle), or both. These results are shown in Figure 4.6, panel C. Activation of the SON and PVN was reduced by about 50% after

SFO lesion, and this was also the case in the OVLT and MnPO but not in some other regions they reported, such as the nucleus of the solitary tract (NTS). Lesions of the OVLT likewise reduced activation of the SON and PVN. Lesions of both the SFO and OVLT substantially prevented activation of the MnPO, SON, and PVH, but again were without effect in the NTS.

These results consistently show minimal or no Fos-ir in the lamina terminalis, and especially the SFO, with low doses of NaCl in rats. This negative result, together with the reduced effect in the SON and PVN after lamina terminalis lesions, suggests that the Fos method may have an intrinsic insensitivity to low levels of neural activation. After higher doses, some Fos-ir is induced in these regions, especially in the peripheral rim of the SFO (Smith & Day, 1995) and dorsal cap of the OVLT (Bisley et al., 1996; see Rowland, 1998, for review). As a caution, it should also be noted that even these so-called low-dose systemic infusions produce elevations in plasma Na^+ that are often 200–300% in excess of the osmotic drinking threshold (~2%) and may never be attained under natural circumstances such as water deprivation. Further, whereas a high dose of NaCl produced Fos-ir only in the dorsal cap of the OVLT, neurons throughout the entire OVLT were found to be electrophysiologically responsive (Kinsman et al., 2020). Further, in mice, Fos-ir has been observed throughout the OVLT (Leib et al., 2017). This suggests that, at least in rats, some cells are activated by NaCl but do not express Fos (i.e., a false negative result). If this were confirmed more generally, it may require a reassessment of the utility of using Fos as a marker of neural excitation in the lamina terminalis.

Recent work in the field has focused on determining phenotypes of neurons in the osmoreceptor regions and manipulation of these identified cells using molecular/genetic approaches. Many of these studies have used mice and have investigated pathways engaged by water deprivation, to be discussed in Chapter 8. Drinking studies in the present narrative are restricted to studies of pure osmoregulation.

Using a retroviral method with local injections into the brain of rats, Kinsman et al. (2020) introduced an inhibitory photoresponsive channel into the OVLT (see Appendix). During 30-minute intravenous infusion of a high dose of NaCl (~15 mmol/kg), continuous laser stimulation of the OVLT completely inhibited the drinking response. In contrast, intermittent stimulation (20 Hz, 2 sec ON, 2 sec OFF) did not affect osmotically induced drinking, possibly because these stimulation parameters did not effectively silence OVLT neurons. The dose of NaCl used in this study was unusually high, and it would be of interest to determine whether parameters of laser-induced inhibition in this protocol differ as a function of dose of NaCl and/or rate of infusion. Broadly, this confirms that some neural excitation in the OVLT is needed for acute osmoregulatory drinking.

Zimmerman et al. (2016) investigated some functional properties of excitatory neurons (identified by the marker NOS-1) in the SFO of mice. Osmotic stimulation by i.p. injection of a high dose of hypertonic NaCl (>20 mmol/kg), increasing plasma Na^+ by more than 10%, led to a rapid increase in concentration of a free calcium indicator (GCaMP6s) in these cells as measured by optical recording. Hyperosmolality also caused robust drinking that was more than 80% prevented by chemogenetic inactivation of NOS-1-expressing cells in the MnPO (via hM4Di, Gi-coupled, or inhibitory designer receptor). This is consistent with osmotic activation of an excitatory glutamatergic projection from the SFO to the MnPO (Oka et al., 2015) onto glutamatergic cells in the MnPO. However, because lesion of rat SFO has little or no effect on osmoregulatory drinking to high doses of NaCl, this result does not prove that the SFO inputs to the MnPO are crucial for the observed chemogenetic inhibition of drinking.

Using rats, Marciante et al. (2019) investigated the role of glutamatergic cells in the MnPO via the technique of chemogenetic inhibition using clozapine-N-oxide (CNO). In vitro electrophysiological studies of single MnPO neurons in hypothalamic slices prepared from these animals found that bath application of hypertonic NaCl in artificial CSF (330 mOsm) caused an increase in spike discharge frequency. Both basal and stimulated discharge was abolished by focal application of CNO. In vivo release of AVP after hypertonic NaCl (~5 mEq/kg, i.p.) was fully inhibited in rats preinjected with CNO. In contrast, the drinking response to hypertonic NaCl was only partially attenuated (3.3 vs. 7.1 mL in CNO and vehicle-pretreated groups, respectively), suggesting that osmoreceptors in the MnPO may act in parallel or synergy with other regions or mechanisms to generate osmoregulatory drinking. Alternatively, the inhibitory effect of CNO in the MnPO was incomplete and may highlight a more general interpretational difficulty with pharmacological approaches.

The role of phenotypically identified OVLT neurons in osmoregulatory drinking of mice was studied by Leib et al. (2017). They found that 70% of OVLT neurons expressing Fos in response to a high dose of hypertonic NaCl (20 mmol/kg, i.p.) co-express the angiotensin 1A receptor gene *Agt1r*. In rats, coresponsiveness of neurons throughout the OVLT to both NaCl and Ang II has now been demonstrated electrophysiologically (Kinsman et al., 2020). Leib et al. (2017) showed that almost all of these neurons also expressed the glutamatergic marker

Vglut2 (Slc17a6). By then targeting channel rhodopsin (ChR2) to these OVLT[Agtr1a] neurons, they found that photostimulation of the OVLT elicited vigorous licking as well as operant responding to obtain water in water-replete animals. The operant aspect suggests this is a motivated behavior, with induction of a thirstlike state.

None of these results have proven that any one region or connection of the lamina terminalis is critical for the full expression or sensitivity of osmoregulatory drinking. The weight of the evidence suggests that the ventral division (i.e., OVLT and ventral MnPO) may be more involved than the dorsal division (i.e., SFO and dorsal MnPO). In the case of AVP secretion, the ventral part is more clearly dominant and consistent with the common embryological origins of the OVLT and neurohypophysis (see Chapter 1).

Zimmerman et al. (2016), using population recording of activation of NOS-1-expressing SFO neurons (presumptively, SFO[GLUT]) from free calcium dynamics and optical recording, found that the SFO of mice was activated in a dose-dependent manner by i.p. injection of NaCl (Figure 4.7, panel A). Shown are changes after 1 M and 3 M NaCl (estimated to be 7 and 21 mmol/kg, assuming typical body weights) and 2 M mannitol. The similarity of 1 M NaCl and 2 M mannitol curves shows this is an osmoreceptor and not a Na^+ receptor mediated effect. Interestingly, the act of drinking rapidly reversed the calcium signal (Figure 4.7, panel B). Water was made available 45 minutes after injection of 3 M NaCl, at which time plasma osmolality was 8% above baseline and the calcium signal remained well above baseline. Only 30 seconds after the first lick, the signal was reduced by about 40% toward baseline, and this occurred whether the fluid consumed was water or 0.3 M NaCl. Licking a cold surface produced a similar but smaller transient effect. By 300 seconds after the first lick of water, the calcium signal was fully suppressed to baseline, despite no change in systemic osmolality at this time. In contrast, in mice drinking 0.3 M NaCl, the signal had now reversed to the higher level that was observed before drinking. Thus, the act of drinking produced a nearly immediate effect to reverse the osmotic-related signal in the SFO, but this appears to be sustained only if the early postingestive effects predict rehydration.

Augustine et al. (2018) showed that mice with a CNO-activated inhibitory receptor inserted into the MnPO did not drink following i.p. injection of hypertonic NaCl after pretreatment with CNO. Additional recording of calcium signals from SFO[NOS-1] cells showed that SFO activity induced by i.p. NaCl was not changed by CNO pretreatment, suggesting that the SFO cells either are themselves osmoreceptors and/or

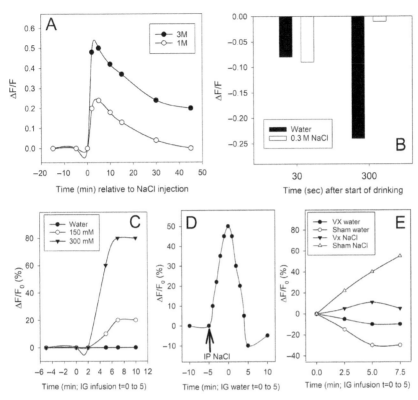

Figure 4.7 In vivo calcium imaging from NOS-expressing cells in the SFO of mice. Panels A and B are from Zimmerman et al. (2016). Panel A shows change in calcium signal across time after i.p. injection of 1 M or 3 M NaCl (150 μl). Panel B shows short (30 sec) and longer (300 sec) term effects of licking either water or 0.3 M NaCl on the still elevated calcium signal 45 min after 3 M NaCl i.p. injection. Panels C–E are from Zimmerman et al. (2019). Panel C shows effect of 5-min intragastric infusions of various solutions (1 mL/5 min) on the calcium signal from SFO neurons. Panel D shows rapid increase in calcium signal after i.p. injection of NaCl and reversal during intragastric infusion of 1 mL water. Panel E shows attenuated SFO calcium signal in vagotomized (Vx) mice during intragastric infusion of water or 300 mM NaCl.

receive input from osmoreceptors in other regions such as the OVLT. The authors also showed that MnPO neurons expressing glucagon-like peptide-1 receptor (MnPO$^{\text{GLP-1R}}$) are the principal source of inhibitory input to the SFO and are activated transiently by licking any fluid, regardless of taste; this may underlie the abovementioned acute inhibition of SFO cells by licking.

To further investigate the nature of the early postingestive signal, Zimmerman et al. (2019) fitted mice with indwelling intragastric catheters. They showed that intragastric infusion of 1 mL over 5 minutes of 0.5 M NaCl (about 25 mEq/kg) produced a near-linear rise in calcium signal from SFO^{NOS-1} neurons across the infusion duration and preceding any change in systemic osmolality (Figure 4.7, panel C). Additionally, 1 M mannitol produced a similar effect, indicating osmoreceptor involvement. In other mice, NaCl (about 12 mEq/kg) injected i.p. produced a similar rapid rise in SFO^{NOS-1} calcium signal, and this was reversed by intragastric infusion (0.2 mL/min) of water (Figure 4.7, panel D). These findings indicate a bidirectional drive on SFO^{NOS-1} neurons from nerve terminals in the gastrointestinal tract, effects that were greatly attenuated by subdiaphragmatic vagotomy (Figure 4.7, panel E). It is possible that, like oral inhibition (Augustine et al., 2018), these effects may be mediated via the MnPO.

In closing this section, I will iterate two cautions. First, the doses of NaCl used in the foregoing mouse studies are what I believe most physiologists would consider very large. While using strong treatments to demonstrate a principle is a logical first step, the results need to be demonstrated for the physiological range. This has been accomplished to some extent by applying these methods in water-deprived mice, protocols that will be discussed in Chapter 8. But, as a preview and an example, optical silencing of the SFO to OVLT pathway reduced drinking after water deprivation by about 50%, whereas SFO manipulations were without effect on water intake – although they did change intake of NaCl in choice studies (Matsuda et al., 2017). Second, mice are not small rats or indeed a good representative of mammals. In Chapter 5, especially, I will point out significant differences in drinking mechanisms in mice compared to rats: A perhaps extreme possibility is a different organization or distribution of function within the lamina terminalis of mice, including different cell type expression of and potentially contribution to drinking of Na_x. The relative lack of physiological studies of drinking in mice, compared to rats, leads to an uncomfortable gap in cross-species extrapolation.

4.7   Neural Pathways of Peripheral Osmoreceptive Drinking

Compelling evidence for peripheral osmoreceptors, most likely in the early postabsorptive gut, and which could be experimentally isolated using intragastric administration of small doses of NaCl, was reviewed in Chapter 3. The following is an analysis of the central mechanisms engaged by these receptors. Choi-Kwon and Baertschi (1991) infused, via indwelling catheter, 2 mL 0.6 M NaCl into the stomach of conscious rats. They found that the increase in AVP in sham-operated rats was attenuated by lesion of the splanchnic nerves innervating the upper small intestine and portal vein but was not diminished by subdiaphragmatic vagotomy. Other stimuli of osmoregulatory drinking, such as mannitol and sucrose, were also effective.

King and Baerschi (1991) showed that the central pathway mediating this effect on AVP secretion is an ascending catecholaminergic bundle ventral to the locus coeruleus and/or the ventrolateral medulla and then projecting to the SON and PVN. Lesions of the MnPO attenuated this response. Carlson et al. (1997) performed a similar study and found an increase in osmolality of hepatic portal blood from 294 to 302 mOsm/kg, peaking about five minutes after the end of the infusion, but with no change in osmolality of systemic blood. The infusion caused large increases in Fos-ir in the SON and PVN in brains harvested two hours later, substantial increases in the area postrema (AP), NTS, and lateral parabrachial nucleus (LPB), but no change in the SFO. The OVLT and MnPO were not mentioned, although the authors state that they surveyed many regions. It remains unclear whether the physiological (AVP) and behavioral (drinking) responses to stimulation of splanchno-hepatic receptors use either separate or redundant pathways in the brain, but it is clear these receptors have crucial roles in early detection of and responses to hyperosmolarity.

The pathway(s) eliciting drinking have not been fully identified, beyond AP and/or NTS termination of vagal afferents. It is possible that these hindbrain regions activate the forebrain osmoreceptor complex, but at levels below threshold for detection using Fos-ir as a marker. A study using jugular vein infusions of NaCl found Fos-positive cells induced in brain stem regions including the caudal NTS, rostroventro-lateral medulla, and LPB of rats (Hochstenbach et al., 1993). Most of the medullary neurons had a noradrenergic phenotype, suggesting they may be involved in cardiovascular responses to hypertonicity (Hochstenbach & Ciriello, 1995). Other experiments attempted to stimulate the natural route through which salt would enter the body, using intragastric or hepatic portal infusions of NaCl. Kobashi et al. (1993) found that intra-gastric administration of hypertonic NaCl induced strong Fos-ir in the AP, caudal NTS, and LPB, attributing this to activation of hepatic afferent sensory fibers to the caudal NTS. Morita et al. (1997) showed that intraportal infusion of 0.45 M NaCl, with simultaneous infusion of water into the vena cava to prevent increase in systemic osmolality, induced Fos-ir in the AP and NTS, as well as the SON and PVN. Infusions of hypertonic mannitol were ineffective, suggesting the transduction is via Na^+-specific receptors. These are probably on the terminals of afferent hepatic nerves because electrical stimulation of these nerves induced a similar pattern of Fos in the brain.

4.8   Summary

Cellular dehydration caused by stimuli such as hypertonic NaCl or mannitol causes a sustained shrinkage of osmosensitive cells, and in osmosensitive neurons this is transduced into a proportional change in firing rate. The basal firing rate of these neurons may encode an effective set point for osmoregulation. In the brain, these osmoreceptors seem to be predominantly in the SFO, MnPO, and OVLT. From selective lesions and other evidence, it appears that these regions act in a synergistic manner, such that optimal drinking and/or AVP secretion occurs when all three of these interconnected regions are functional. Some data suggest that there may be species differences in the details of this integrated functioning of the lamina terminalis.

5   Extracellular Dehydration Thirst and Drinking

5.1   Angiotensin II as a Dipsogen

Dire clinical conditions (including severe blood loss or diseases such as cholera) that are associated with frequent vomiting and diarrhea have been reported anecdotally to be accompanied by extreme thirst. These conditions are characterized by blood or extracellular fluid loss and are without significant change in osmotic pressure. It was not until Fitzsimons (1961b) systematically investigated conditions under which drinking occurs without rise in osmotic pressure that the concept of extracellular dehydration thirst came of age (see Fitzsimons, 1969, for extended discussion). As noted in the previous chapters, eliminating renal excretion of an osmotic load by nephrectomy was an important step in establishing osmoreceptor involvement in drinking (Fitzsimons, 1961a). But when Fitzsimons (1961b) performed nephrectomy prior to stimuli of extracellular thirst, he found an opposite effect – many of the drinking responses were attenuated or abolished. The logical sequel to this work was to determine the role of the kidney in extracellular thirst. This led to the discovery that exogenously administered angiotensin II (ANG II) is a potent dipsogen. It became apparent that endogenously generated ANG II contributes to, but is not the sole mediator of extracellular drinking. One of the themes of work over the past 40 years has been to determine the contribution and mechanism of action of endogenously generated ANG II to various extracellular thirst(s). To aid in following those arguments later in this chapter, it is useful to start by reviewing the dipsogenic effect and mechanisms for exogenously administered ANG II.

Endogenously produced ANG II is a potent vasoconstrictor and is one of several hormones generated during natural states of hypovolemia or hypotension. These states reduce arterial perfusion pressure to the kidney and increase sympathetic outflow, both of which stimulate the juxtaglomerular cells surrounding the afferent renal arterioles to secrete renin into the blood (see Chapter 2). Renin enzymatically cleaves a large precursor globulin, angiotensinogen, into a 10 amino acid fragment known as ANG I. ANG I then rapidly undergoes C-terminal cleavage to the octapeptide ANG II, or more accurately ANG (1-8), by action of a peptidase called angiotensin-converting enzyme (ACE1). More recently, it has become evident that a heptapeptide fragment, ANG (1-7), also has significant roles, and this may be formed by cleavage of ANG II in tissues expressing the enzyme ACE2. ANG II acts via two main classes of receptor (AT1R and AT2R) while ANG (1-7) acts via Mas-receptors. These receptors have diverse intracellular signaling cascades that often have opposing actions. Thus, the net action of ANG in a tissue will depend in part on the ratio of ANG II to ANG (1-7). This balance has been studied in cardiovascular research but less in the context of fluid homeostasis. Both forms of ANG have short half-lives in plasma (<30 seconds) before they are degraded by ubiquitous aminopeptidases into smaller and apparently inactive fragments. The concentration of ANG II in plasma thus is determined primarily by the rate of formation of ANG I from angiotensinogen, and this depends on the activity of renin in plasma (PRA). PRA, the measurement of which is relatively simple, has often been used as a surrogate for plasma ANG II concentration.

Initially, the juxtaglomerular cells of the kidney were thought to be the only source of renin, which, because of its size, will not penetrate the blood–brain barrier. It has since been shown that many tissues, including parts of the brain, have intrinsic renin–angiotensin systems. Unless noted specifically, my text refers to renin released from the kidney and the circulating renin–angiotensin system. One common way of experimentally manipulating the formation of ANG II is through the use of ACE1 inhibitors such as captopril (formerly SQ14225). Interpretation of findings using these agents must take into account the fact that they may have concentration-dependent penetration into the brain (Robinson & Evered, 1983). Common ways of obtunding or preventing action of ANG II are through genetic manipulation (e.g., knockdown or gene-silencing techniques) of thirst-critical type 1 receptors (AT1R) or through the use of direct receptor competitive antagonists such as losartan (formerly DuP753). The AT1R has at least two isoforms; only type 1a is expressed in rodents, and it can be assumed I am referring to this isoform.

5.1.1   Foundational Studies in Rats

The first clear indication that stimulating endogenous production of ANG II caused euhydrated rats to drink came from a study using intraperitoneal (i.p.) injection of partly purified hog renin (Fitzsimons,

1969). Fitzsimons and Simons (1969) then showed that intravenous infusions of ANG II produced a dose-related increase in water intake of rats, although the effective doses were quite large. Hsiao et al. (1977) lowered that dose or drinking threshold by almost a hundredfold through the use of the natural rat form (Ileu[5]) of ANG II, chronic indwelling venous catheters, prior experience of the rats with ANG II, and home cage testing. This emphasizes the importance of a low-stress behavioral test condition when the stimulus produces an adverse or sudden physio-logical effect such as, in this case, hypertension.

Circulating ANG II exerts its dipsogenic action in the brain. Booth (1968) reported that microinjection of ANG II into rat hypothalamus caused drinking. Systematic studies using injections into many brain regions suggested that access of the solutions to the anterior cerebral ventricles, either by direct injection or by leakage up the outside of cannulas that traversed the ventricles, yielded the lowest drinking thresh-olds (Johnson & Epstein, 1975). The latency to drink after central administration is remarkably short, often less than one minute, whereas the latency to drink during intravenous infusion is usually 10 minutes or longer. This may be in part because it takes some time for threshold levels of ANG II to be achieved at the relevant receptors. Combined with the principle that circulating peptides such as ANG II can only access the brain at circumventricular organs (CVOs) that have a minimal blood–brain barrier, these findings suggested one or more of these organs were the critical dipsogenic site for ANG II. Simpson and Routtenberg (1975) solidified this position by showing that microinjections of ANG II into the rat subfornical organ (SFO) yielded remarkably low drinking thresh-olds (<1 pmol) and that lesions of the SFO completely abolished drink-ing during intravenous infusion of ANG II.

One of the classic approaches to dissecting actions of an endogenous signal molecule such as ANG II is through the use of receptor antagon-ists. Early studies with ANG II antagonists were often difficult to inter-pret because these molecules were peptides with some agonist activity and lacked selectivity for receptor subtypes. The first selective AT1R competitive nonpeptide antagonist DuP753, now known as losartan, blocked drinking and pressor actions of peripherally administered ANG II (Wong et al., 1990). Fregly and Rowland (1991a) confirmed this result and extended it to show that peripheral injection of losartan blocked drinking evoked by intracerebroventricular (ICV) administration of ANG II to rats, indicating that losartan penetrates the CVOs. Importantly, the SFO was one of several brain regions with a high density of AT1R, determined autoradiographically (Mendelsohn et al., 1984; Rowe et al., 1991; Tsutsumi & Saavedra, 1991); other AT1R-rich regions known to be drinking-relevant included the organum vasculosum of the lamina terminalis (OVLT), median preoptic nucleus (MnPO), and paraventricular nucleus (PVN), as well as some hindbrain locations such as the area postrema (AP) and nucleus of the solitary tract (NTS).

Supporting evidence that the SFO is a primary site for transduction of circulating ANG II came from electrophysiological studies showing that peripheral administration of ANG II produced action potentials in SFO neurons in vivo (Gutman et al., 1988; Tanaka et al., 1985) and that the SFO has efferent connections to the MnPO, SON, and PVN (Gutman et al., 1986). Peripheral administration of ANG II increased cerebral glucose metabolism of rats in two brain regions, the SFO and pituitary gland (Gross et al., 1985). Mapping of Fos-ir proved to be a more useful method to identify regions activated by ANG II.

McKinley et al. (1992) reported that Fos-ir was induced in the SFO and OVLT of rats given intravenous infusions of ANG II, but not after the hypertensive catecholamine, phenylephrine. Fos-ir was induced by both ANG II and phenylephrine in the SON, PVN, and NTS, suggesting these regions are activated by hypertension. Rowland, Li, et al. (1994) confirmed this result and added the MnPO to the list of activated structures. They also found that either lesions of the SFO or ICV injection of losartan completely blocked ANG II–induced Fos-ir in all of these regions. Oldfield et al. (1994) injected rats with a retrograde tracer (fluoro gold) into the SON and subsequently examined Fos-ir in response to ANG II infusion. They found many doubly labeled cells in the OVLT, MnPO, and SFO, but the percentage of retrogradely labeled neurons expressing Fos-ir was almost double in the SFO (48%) than in the MnPO or OVLT. The number of Fos-positive cells that were not retrogradely labeled was higher in the SFO (72%) than in the other structures, suggesting that a large fraction of SFO cells project to brain regions other than the SON.

All of these findings point to the SFO as the critical site for dipsogenic action of circulating ANG II. Even if peripherally administered ANG II (and/or ANG II released as a transmitter from nerve terminals) did activate other brain regions containing AT1R, that activation alone is insufficient for drinking. At a minimum, a conditional or gating input originating with ANG II action in the SFO appears to be necessary. However, peripheral infusions of ANG II produce a sustained elevation in blood pressure, and signals from relevant baroreceptors could be inhibitory to neurons in the lamina terminalis and thereby to drinking. In regard to an inhibitory effect on drinking, Robinson and Evered (1987) found that co-infusion of a hypotensive agent potentiated the drinking to ANG II in rats. Procedures that block ANG II drinking, such as lesions of the SFO (Hosutt et al., 1981) or treatment with losartan (Wong et al., 1990), also block or attenuate the pressor action of peripheral ANG II by altering sympathetic outflow (Mangiapane & Simpson, 1980). Thus, if baroreceptor signals of the pressor response to ANG II were attenuated by these treatments, one might hypothesize that any pressure-sensitive drinking response to ANG II from sites other than the SFO might be potentiated. But they are not, indicating the unique role of the SFO in initiating the process in rats.

5.1.2 Angiotensin and Drinking in Other Species

Subcutaneous (s.c.; Wright et al., 1982) and intracerebral (Lotter et al., 1980; Sharpe & Swanson, 1974) injections of ANG II are dipsogenic in nonhuman primates, although no work appears to have been done concerning critical receptor sites. The dipsogenic action in humans is equivocal. Phillips et al. (1985) gave intravenous infusions of ANG II to healthy young men who, on another occasion, received isotonic saline control in a single-blind design. ANG II infusions started at 2 ng/kg/min and doubled every 15 minutes to 16 ng/kg/min for the last segment of a one-hour treatment. Subjects had no water available during the infusion but completed visual analog scales for thirst and mouth dryness every 15 minutes. Blood was taken every 15 minutes for measurement of ANG II and vasopressin (AVP) concentrations. By the end of infusion, plasma ANG II concentration rose from a baseline of about 20 pg/mL to 440 pg/ mL – considerably higher than would occur after fluid deprivation – and blood pressure rose by about 30 mm Hg. All 10 subjects showed similar changes in these measures, but only four of them reported increased thirst and dry mouth relative to the control condition and drank more water (426 mL vs. 150 mL control) in the one hour following infusion of ANG II. The remaining six subjects showed minimal differences in these measures between ANG II and isotonic saline control conditions. Notably, the four responders showed increases in plasma AVP after ANG II, whereas the six nonresponders did not. The authors were unable to account for these striking individual differences. Given a large natural individual variability in plasma AVP response to hyperosmolality (Chapter 3), it would be of interest to know whether the ANG II responders might have shown an atypical slope in their AVP-osmolality functions. Unfortunately, in part due to ethical concerns of infusing a hypertensive agent for basic research, it is now difficult to extend or follow up these types of studies in human subjects.

Intravenous infusions of ANG II induce drinking in several other species, including dogs (Fitzsimons et al., 1978) and sheep (Abraham et al., 1975). The threshold amounts infused in sheep were relatively high. Lesions of the SFO abolished drinking to peripheral infusion of ANG II in dogs (Thrasher et al., 1982) but not in sheep (McKinley et al., 1986). Thrasher and Keil (1987) subsequently reported that complete lesion of the OVLT abolished drinking, as well as AVP release, to intravenous infusion of ANG II in dogs. Thus, the importance of circulating ANG II and the role of the SFO within the sensory lamina terminalis may differ between mammalian species.

It might be expected that phylogenetically closer species such as mice and rats would be similar in regard to organization of the lamina terminalis. However, there are some differences between rats and mice that are not yet fully understood. Rowland and Fregly (1988a) reported that s.c. injections of ANG II did not have a statistically reliable effect on water intake in albino mice of the ICR strain, although the highest doses tested (600 and 1200 µg/kg, which are an order of magnitude larger than the effective doses by this route in rats) increased mean intake from a control mean of 0.2–0.4 mL/2 h. Consistent with this result, Johnson et al. (2003) reported a complete absence of drinking to s.c. ANG II in C57BL/6 mice but found robust drinking when doses as low as 10 ng ANG II were injected ICV. Rowland et al. (2003) found that s.c. injection of ANG I was marginally dipsogenic in mice in one of two studies, but it was not affected by cotreatment with an ACE1 inhibitor. Nonetheless, peripheral injection of ANG II induced Fos-ir in the same brain regions in mice as in rats, including the SFO, MnPO, and PVN (Rowland et al., 2003), and this was reduced but not eliminated by peripheral injection of losartan (Crews & Rowland, 2005). Crews and Rowland (2005) also found that ICV ANG II was dipsogenic in mice and was inhibited by peripheral treatment with losartan. ICV injection of ANG II induced Fos-ir in the same regions as the peripheral injection, and, like the drinking response, this was inhibited by peripheral losartan (Crews & Rowland, 2005). These studies show that peripherally administered ANG II does access the mouse brain at the CVOs but produces little or no drinking response, in contrast to the effect of central injections. This suggests that an inhibitory signal, possibly related to baroreceptors and hypertension (Robinson & Evered, 1987), has greater effect in mice than in rats. This may also be the case for some other species (see Chapter 11).

Oka et al. (2015) identified three nonoverlapping cell phenotypes in mouse SFO. One gives rise to excitatory efferent signals that co-express genes for CaMKII, NOS-1, ETV-1, and AT1R. A second class is inhibitory and GABA-ergic, and a third (glial) class expresses glial fibrillary acidic protein. By introducing the gene for a photosensitive channel

(ChR2) into the SFO, either by SFO injection of adeno-associated virus linked to a CaMKII promoter or using a transgenic line, mice could be induced to drink avidly during optogenetic stimulation of the SFO (see Appendix for further explanation). The drink was stimulation-bound, specific for water, and greatly inhibited by imparting a bitter (cyclohex-imide) or salty (0.3 M NaCl) taste to the fluid. This study does not prove that these neurons would be the same as those responding to either exogenous or endogenous ANG II, but the fact they express AT1R is suggestive that this would have been the case. These authors also showed that both the excitatory and inhibitory classes of SFO neurons project to the MnPO and OVLT, whereas the excitatory class additionally projects to the SON and PVN. These conclusions, notably with regard to expression of AT1R cells in the SFO and their projections, were confirmed and extended by Zimmerman et al. (2016), who showed that SFO^{glut} (excitatory) projection neurons express AT1a receptors. Matsuda et al. (2017) found consistent results, although they did not include ANG II as a stimulus; their findings are discussed in Section 5.6.

Nation et al. (2016) used a chemogenetic approach to activate CaMKII-expressing cells in the SFO. They injected an adeno-associated viral construct incorporating the gene for the excitatory DREADD hM3D into the SFO of mice to render transduced cells responsive to subsequent systemic administration of clozapine-N-oxide (CNO; see Appendix for further explanation). In mice with verified transfection of the hM3D receptor, s.c. injection of CNO produced a significant water intake (0.35 mL or 13 mL/kg in 1 h). When 0.3 M NaCl was simultaneously available, it was also consumed but in smaller amounts (0.15 mL). CNO injection was not dipsogenic in mice in which the receptor transfection failed. CNO injection induced Fos-ir in the SFO, MnPO, OVLT, SON, and PVN in successfully transfected mice. To address the question of whether these cells would have responded to ANG II, electrophysiological recordings from the SFO in vivo revealed two subsets of cells that responded to ICV injection of either ANG II or hypertonic NaCl. Subsequent infusion of CNO increased the firing rate of all of these neurons in transfected mice by a mean of four- to fivefold. With the caveat of a small sample size (Ns = 3), it appears that at least a subset of the excitatory class of SFO cells responds to ANG II.

In the next sections of this chapter, I will describe the dipsogenic effects of procedures designed to produce extracellular dehydration and/or hypotension, and the contribution of endogenously produced ANG II to that drinking. The role of ANG II in naturally occurring drinking will be addressed in Chapter 8.

5.2   Hemorrhage

The most direct way of producing hypovolemia is through hemorrhage. Blood volume cannot be transduced physiologically, so blood pressure is reported by stretch or mechanoreceptors in the walls of blood vessels. There are two classes of pressure or baroreceptors: arterial and cardiopulmonary. The arterial or high-pressure receptors are in the carotid sinus and aortic arch and, via afferents in the IX and X cranial nerves, synapse in the NTS to trigger a variety of baroreceptor reflexes. The majority of blood is contained in the low-pressure venous side of the circulation. The pressure in this system is monitored by cardiopulmonary baroreceptors, and these are thought to be involved in monitoring blood volume. Hemorrhage is a complex stimulus, and the receptor(s) engaged will depend on the extent and rate of onset of blood loss (Shadt & Ludbrook, 1991). Low levels or rates of hemorrhage engage sympathetic nervous system outflow, one result of which is vasoconstriction. Higher levels of hemorrhage cause arterial pressure to drop precipitously, engage arterial receptors, and cause release of adrenocorticotropic hormone (ACTH), AVP, and other factors (Darlington et al., 1986). Natural forms of hypovolemia, such as occur with extended water deprivation (Chapter 8), have a relatively slow onset and are not associated with hypotension; it could thus be anticipated that cardiopulmonary receptors are of particular relevance to drinking or thirst.

Constriction of the inferior vena cava is a model of central hypovolemia or hemorrhage. Thrasher et al. (2000) produced graded 10 Torr (mm Hg) drops in mean arterial pressure (MAP) of conscious dogs. This was done with no additional treatment and subsequently (on separate test occasions) during neural block of the cardiopulmonary receptors by infusing procaine pericardially, and after removing afferent arterial baroreceptor flow by sinoatrial denervation. In addition to recording cardiovascular parameters during each session, blood samples were taken for measurement of AVP and PRA. While cardiopulmonary receptor block increased basal heart rate and MAP, it had no significant effect on the relationship between MAP and either AVP or PRA. In contrast, sinoatrial denervation greatly obtunded the rise in both AVP and PRA as MAP dropped.

In humans, controlled blood loss occurs during blood donation; this is typically limited to less than10% of initial volume so that hypotension does not occur. Blood donors do not reliably report thirst (Holmes & Montgomery, 1953). Higher levels of hemorrhage are needed to induce thirst or drinking. Some early studies in rats showed that acute blood removal caused drinking (Fitzsimons, 1961b; Oatley, 1964), but a key study was that of Russell et al. (1975), who produced graded levels of blood loss through a venous catheter. Different groups of rats had 20, 30, 40, or 50% of estimated blood volume (assumed as 6% body weight; these would correspond to volumes of 5–12 mL) removed at approximately 1 mL/min. Although MAP was not measured, it is likely that these levels of hemorrhage caused substantial hypotension. The results (Figure 5.1, panel A) show that drinking was increased relative to control by all levels of hemorrhage, although 20% did not reach significance. The volumes of water consumed in the five-hour test were about half the respective volumes of blood removed. In other rats, 40% hemorrhage modestly (2×) increased plasma ANG II levels one hour later. Taken together with Fitzsimons' (1961b) finding that nephrectomy only slightly (~25%) attenuated drinking to hemorrhage, the data suggest only a minor contribution from ANG II.

In dogs, blood loss of about 22% over 13 minutes through a femoral catheter produced a drop in arterial blood pressure of 20 mm Hg and a 30% increase in heart rate, increased plasma levels of AVP and PRA, and led to a reliable drinking response of 9–14 mL/kg (Thrasher & Keil, 1987). Lesions of the OVLT had no effect on these drinking or neuroendocrine responses to hemorrhage (Figure 5.1, panel B). Also in dogs, blood loss has been reported to decrease the threshold for osmotic thirst (Kozlowski & Szczepanska-Sadowska, 1975). This effect was blocked by cutting the left vagosympathetic trunks, suggesting there is a tonic inhibitory signal to the brain from cardiopulmonary receptors.

The putative contributions of ANG II and baroreceptor inputs after hemorrhage have been examined using Fos-ir mapping in rats. Badoer et al. (1992) found that 4 mL (20–25%) rapid hemorrhage from an arterial catheter in rats transiently decreased MAP by some 50%. When sacrificed 1.5 hours later, increased expression of Fos-ir was observed in forebrain (SFO, OVLT, PVN [both magnocellular and parvicellular divisions], and SON) as well as in hindbrain (AP, NST, and ventrolateral medulla) regions. The latter are thought to mediate the cardiovascular responses to hemorrhage. In a subsequent study (Badoer, McKinley, Oldfield & McAllen, 1993), the thoracic spinal cord was injected with retrograde tracer, and a subsequent 4 mL hemorrhage induced Fos-ir in 22% of retrogradely labeled cells in the ventrolateral medulla and 14% in the PVN. Badoer, Oldfield, and McKinley (1993) stated that a high dose of captopril prevented hemorrhage-related Fos-ir expression in the SFO and OVLT but not in the PVN and SON. These data are consistent with ANG II action in the SFO and OVLT during hypotensive hemorrhage but do not rule out baroreceptor or other spinally mediated afferents.

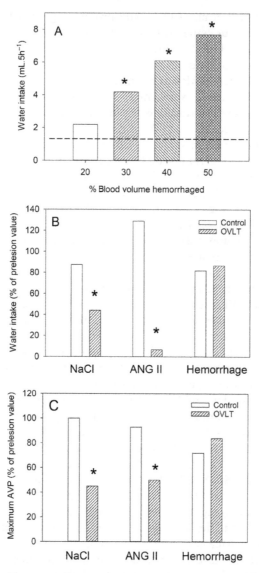

Figure 5.1 Hemorrhage as a dipsogenic stimulus. Panel A shows increase in water intake of rats after graded levels of hemorrhage (from Russell et al., 1975). The dashed line is the mean intake of untreated controls over 5 h. *Indicates significant increase from control. Panels B and C (from Thrasher & Keil, 1987) show drinking (B) and maximum posttreatment AVP (C) in dogs tested before lesion (=100%) and following lesion including >90% of the OVLT, or control lesions that were in adjacent tissue. *Different from prelesion value. The treatments were i.v. infusion of hypertonic NaCl or ANG II, or 22% hemorrhage.

5.3   Isovolemic Hypotension: Caval Ligation

Drinking was not measured in the caval constriction study cited above (Thrasher et al., 2000). In a previous study, these investigators reported that constriction of the inferior vena cava, which reduces cardiac return to the heart without loss of total blood volume, caused drinking with a mean latency of 22 minutes and a two-hour intake of 13.2 mL/kg (Thrasher, Keil, & Ramsay, 1982). Water intake was correlated with the reduction in arterial pressure but not with PRA. Intravenous infusion of a peptidergic ANG II receptor inhibitor, saralasin, caused a greater decline of blood pressure but had no effect on water intake or AVP levels. The role, if any, of ANG II in the drinking thus remains unclear.

Fitzsimons (1969) reported that complete ligation of the inferior vena cava, either above or below the renal veins, caused a strong drinking response in rats. The rate of drinking peaked in the first two hours after the procedure, and the six-hour intake was more than 40 mL/kg. This robust drinking response was almost completely prevented by bilateral nephrectomy but not by ligation of the ureters, suggesting the substantial dependence of caval ligation–induced drinking on renin release and its assumed action via generation of ANG II. Leenen and Stricker (1974) showed that PRA was increased five- to eightfold above levels in sham-operated rats throughout the 24 hours after caval ligation. Fitzsimons and Elfont (1982) reported that pharmacological inhibition of ACE1 with a high dose of captopril, and thus conversion of ANG I to ANG II in the brain, attenuated the drinking to caval ligation by about 50%. These authors concluded that drinking after caval ligation is multifactorial, involving ANG II–dependent and non-ANG mechanisms. Conversely, inhibition of ACE in the periphery, using lower doses of captopril or the less potent teprotide (SQ20881), produced a two- to threefold enhancement of water intake in the first few hours after caval ligation (Fitzsimons & Elfont, 1982; Lehr et al., 1975). An explanation for this is low doses of captopril that effectively block peripheral ACE1 do not reach sufficient concentrations in the brain to fully inhibit brain regions, such as CVOs, where the expression of ACE1 is particularly high. Thus, peripheral ACE1 inhibition causes plasma ANG I levels to rise to high levels, which are still converted to ANG II in the brain via the incompletely inhibited ACE1. These studies were performed before discovery of ACE2 and roles for tissue ANG (1-7), so some of these results may be understood better if the full spectrum of ANG peptides and actions in the brain were known.

Stricker (1971a) reported that cavally ligated rats drank water for two to three hours and then greatly slowed their rate of intake (six-hour and

24-hour intakes were about 30 and 60 mL/kg, respectively), whereas ligated rats given isotonic saline to drink showed robust drinking throughout the 24 hours for a total mean intake four- to fivefold higher than with water to drink. In water drinkers, plasma Na^+ concentration was reduced by about 10% relative to control, whereas plasma osmolality was increased by about 10%, attributed to increased plasma urea consequent to reduced urine output. The saline drinkers were not hyponatremic, and Stricker attributed the early cessation of water drinking to cellular overhydration. This may be relevant to understanding why the water intake after hemorrhage is relatively low (Section 5.2). The possible relationship between ANG II and sodium preference or appetite will be discussed in Section 5.6.

5.4   Isovolemic Hypotension: Vasodilator Drugs

A nonsurgical procedure to produce a simulated and rapid-onset hypovolemia is via injection of a hypotensive or vasodilator pharmacological agent. The mixed β_1, β_2 adrenergic agonist isoproterenol has been used most commonly, although other agents have been used (Fitzsimons, 1979). Isoproterenol has a dual mechanism: increasing heart rate and producing renin secretion from juxtaglomerular cells. The latter action occurs directly via β_1 receptor activation of those organs and indirectly via β_2 receptors that cause vasodilation and hypotension (Kirby et al., 1994). Isoproterenol causes a dose-dependent increase of water intake in rats (Leenen & McDonald, 1974; Lehr et al., 1967). A dose of 100 µg/kg, commonly used in drinking studies in rats, causes an almost instantaneous drop in MAP of about 50 Torr, with a return to baseline after 30–60 minutes due both to physiological counterresponses and to degradation or elimination of isoproterenol. PRA typically peaks after 15 minutes and remains substantially elevated after one hour. Drinking usually starts within 15 minutes, and it is substantially complete after one hour (Leenen & McDonald, 1974). A long-lasting antidiuresis also occurs, leading to net positive fluid balance. The drinking in rats was initially thought to be mediated entirely by ANG II generated by renin (Fitzsimons, 1979; Houpt & Epstein, 1971), although this is not the case in dogs (Fitzsimons & Szczepanska-Sadowska, 1974). In aging rats, isoproterenol no longer elicits renin release or drinking (Thunhorst et al., 2011; see Chapter 10).

Other studies have found that drinking following administration of low doses of isoproterenol is renin dependent, whereas higher doses additionally or instead engage baroreceptor mechanisms (Rettig et al., 1981). Studies that have investigated the role of ANG II using inhibitors of ANG II formation or action have produced mixed results (e.g., Fitzsimons, 1969; Fregly & Rowland, 1991a; Hosutt et al., 1978; Robinson & Evered, 1983), discrepancies that may in part be due to exacerbated hypotension that occurs when ANG II action is prevented or due to the use of different doses of isoproterenol. Fregly and Rowland (1991a) found drinking after a relatively low dose of isoproterenol (25 µg/kg) was not affected by peripheral injection of losartan; Figure 5.2, panel A). It must be emphasized that this dose of losartan completely blocks drinking to peripherally administered ANG II (Fregly & Rowland, 1991a). Peripheral injection of a peptide antagonist, sarile, also had no effect (Figure 5.2), replicating a result by Tang and Falk (1974), whereas the beta receptor antagonist propranolol and a high dose of captopril were effective. ICV injection of losartan also inhibited isoproterenol-induced drinking. One possible explanation is that peripherally administered losartan may not penetrate brain regions important for hypotension-related drinking, but it does penetrate regions engaged by circulating ANG II. In this regard, peripheral losartan attenuated by 60% Fos-ir induced in the SFO by ICV administration of ANG II (Rowland, Morien, & Fregly, 1996), suggesting only partial access of peripherally administered losartan to some regions of the SFO, at least at the dose tested. Alternatively, captopril is having actions other than blocking formation of ANG II. Subsequent work showed that the nonapeptide bradykinin, whose half-life is greatly extended by captopril, induced water intake when administered in combination with a low dose of ACE1 inhibitor. Apparently, this effect is not mediated by ANG II (Fregly & Rowland, 1991b; Rowland et al., 1995).

Fitzsimons (1979) reviewed evidence that not all hypotensive treatments are strongly dipsogenic. For example, the mildly hypotensive agent sodium nitrite produced only a modest drinking response in intact rats, but a robust drinking response after left cervical vagotomy (Moore-Gillon, 1980). This suggests that inhibitory as well as excitatory signals for drinking may be engaged.

Studies in which either blood pressure has been controlled or longer-acting hypotensive regimens are used have been informative. Evered (1990) found that bolus intravenous injection of the vasodilator diazoxide caused dose-related and stable drops of 10–65 Torr in MAP of rats lasting at least two hours. Drinking was stimulated and intake correlated with the degree of hypotension (Figure 5.2, panel B). A high dose of captopril exacerbated hypotension but abolished drinking, suggesting that ANG II alone mediates water intake. This result does not distinguish between peripherally generated ANG II and that which may be generated in the brain, since the dose of captopril used should have been sufficient to block ACE1 in critical brain regions.

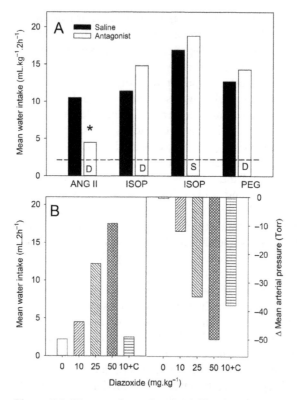

Figure 5.2 Hypotension-related drinking in rats. Panel A (from Fregly & Rowland 1991a, 1992) shows effect of pretreatment with either a saline vehicle or an ANG II receptor antagonist (D = DuP753 or losartan, 10 mg.kg^{-1}; S = sarile 0.5 mg.kg^{-1}) on 2 h water intake following s.c. administration of ANG II (150 μg.kg^{-1}), isoproterenol (25 μg.kg^{-1}), or polyethylene glycol (PEG; ~10 mL.kg^{-1} 30%; test started 4 h later). *Indicates significant attenuation of drinking by antagonist. Dotted line indicates no treatment baseline. Panel B (from Evered, 1990) shows i.v. bolus injection of minoxidil caused a dose-related increase in 2 h water intake and decrease in mean arterial pressure. A dose of 10 mg.kg^{-1} with captopril (10+C) abolished drinking but produced strong hypotension.

Kinsman et al. (2020) found that optogenetically mediated inhibition of OVLT greatly attenuated diazoxide-induced drinking in rats. Without laser stimulation, water intake in the first 30 minutes after treatment was about 8 mL, but it was at least 75% less with photoinhibition. When the laser was turned off after 30 minutes, water intake partially increased but did not reach levels achieved with no laser stimulus. Given that hypotension and ANG II production should have persisted at this time, the failure to observe complete catch-up of drinking is unexpected. A similar effect was seen when water intake was stimulated by hypernatremia, and electrophysiological studies in this paper show conclusively that individual neurons in the OVLT are both Na^+ and ANG II sensitive.

There are high concentrations of ANG II type 1 receptors (AT1R) in the lamina terminalis of most if not all mammals, including the SFO and OVLT, which lack a blood–brain barrier (Allen et al., 1988). The renin released after isoproterenol, and the ANG II subsequently generated, induces Fos expression in these regions of the brain (Rowland, Fregly, et al., 1994). The SON and PVN also are strongly activated. Low doses of an ACE1 inhibitor enhanced isoproterenol-related Fos-ir expression in the SFO, whereas high doses completely blocked this effect; activation of the SON or PVN was less affected by ACE1 inhibition (Rowland, Fregley, et al., 1994). Consistent with the view that the SFO is the principal site for dipsogenic action of ANG II generated by isoproterenol, Fitts (1994) found that lesions of the SFO abolished isoproterenol-induced drinking and Krause et al. (2008) found that partial knockdown of AT1R in the SFO by injection of antisense oligonucleotide produced a commensurate loss of isoproterenol-induced drinking. These studies found that neither lesions nor AT1R knockdown in the OVLT had any effect on drinking to isoproterenol.

Uschakov et al. (2009) examined functional efferents from the lamina terminalis to the periaqueductal gray (PAG). Rats were injected with a retrograde tracer into the PAG, with one week allowed for transport. At that time, some rats were injected with isoproterenol; they were sacrificed 90 minutes later and the brains processed for Fos-ir and tracer. Many cells in the lamina terminalis were retrogradely labeled, with relative abundance MnPO>OVLT>SFO. Only a small fraction of those cells were doubly labeled with Fos-ir after isoproterenol, but the relative fraction was higher in the SFO (16%) than the OVLT (9%) or MnPO (2%). Insofar as other stimuli tested produced a different profile of double labeling, the data suggest that the SFO has particularly prominent outputs to PAG that are engaged following isoproterenol. But many cells expressing Fos after isoproterenol were not doubly labeled, suggesting other functions and/or efferent pathways for those cells. Chan and Sawchenko (1994) characterized the induction by either hypotensive agent or hemorrhage of Fos-ir in hindbrain neurons, including in the NTS and the C1 catecholaminergic cell group of the ventrolateral medulla.

Much less work has been done with acute hypotension in mice. We know of no drinking studies using hemorrhage or caval ligation. Isoproterenol does cause a modest water intake of up to 10 mL/kg in mice, but there may be strain differences in effective dose (Johnson et al., 2003; Rowland & Fregly, 1988), as is the case in rats (Fregly et al., 1990). The dipsogenic effect is completely blocked in mice by lesion of the OVLT (Johnson et al., 2003). This differs from the findings in rats, and to my knowledge the mouse SFO has not been tested in this regard. In mice in which optical imaging of calcium signaling in the SFO was performed, Zimmerman et al. (2016) reported that i.p. injection of a high dose of isoproterenol caused a maximal and sustained rise in signal within 5–10 minutes. This rise was completely prevented by pretreatment with combined high doses of losartan and captopril. The result is consistent with the necessary generation and action of ANG II in the SFO to produce this effect. It is of interest that the magnitude of the change in calcium signaling was only about half that produced by polyethylene glycol (Section 5.5) or by various doses of hypertonic saline (Chapter 4). Thus, the physiological relevance of this finding awaits further clarification.

5.5   Nonhypotensive Hypovolemia

5.5.1   Colloid Treatment

The stimuli of real or simulated extracellular fluid (ECF) loss that I have discussed thus far, namely, hemorrhage, caval ligation, and isoproterenol, are all rapid-onset stimuli. As mentioned previously, subjecting animals to such a sudden and life-threatening situation without antecedent environmental events is most likely a highly stressful condition, and one under which appetitive behaviors and drinking may be easily disrupted. A distinctly different stimulus of hypovolemia is that caused by injection of a hyperoncotic colloid that relatively slowly sequesters isotonic fluid at the injection site and without drop in MAP. The mechanism for this sequestration is disruption of the Starling forces (Chapter 2) and net removal of fluid from capillaries. I know of no studies using large mammals in this regard: what follows is restricted to rats and mice.

The most commonly used hyperoncotic colloid is polyethylene glycol (PEG) of high molecular weight and delivered in concentrated (20–40% w/v) solution. The pioneering study (Fitzsimons, 1961b) used the natural resin gum Arabic, but results with PEG are similar. Fitzsimons (1961b) reported that i.p. injections of either gum Arabic or PEG to rats caused a dose-related accumulation of ascitic fluid that was maximal after four hours, and a dose-related water intake that typically occurred one to three hours after injection. The degree of hypovolemia produced increased linearly to a maximum after three hours, attesting to the relatively gradual onset of this extracellular fluid loss. PEG-induced drinking was normal in nephrectomized rats, indicating that it is not dependent on renin release. More studies have used the s.c. route of administration of PEG, and in this case, the fluid accumulation is as an edema at the injection site lasting several hours. Compared with rats given only water to drink, Stricker (1971a) found that (s.c.) PEG-treated rats given isotonic saline to drink after PEG consumed about fourfold more and in so doing repaired their plasma volume deficit. Since isotonic saline is spontaneously preferred over water by Sprague-Dawley rats, this result does not unequivocally indicate a specific sodium appetite. But such specific appetite was evident, especially more than six hours after PEG, when unpalatable hypertonic (0.45 M) NaCl was given in choice with water (Stricker, 1971b). In rats of the Fisher 344 strain that do not have a spontaneous preference for isotonic saline, PEG stimulated a threefold greater intake of 0.15 M NaCl than water, but the overall intakes corrected for body weight differences are less than 50% of those typical of Sprague-Dawley rats (Rowland & Fregly, 1988b).

Stricker (1971b) argued that due to hypovolemia-related antidiuresis, water intake after PEG produces cellular overhydration, which inhibits further intake. Such cellular overhydration does not occur when NaCl is available. This interpretation is partly supported by a sham drinking study (consumed water drains from an open gastric fistula without absorption) in which rats consumed about twice as much water in a two-hour drinking test starting two hours after PEG administration compared with when the fistula was closed (Salisbury & Rowland, 1990). It may be concluded that in the absence of food as a source of solutes, NaCl intake is required to restore plasma volume after PEG.

Hosutt et al. (1981) reported that SFO lesions that abolished the drinking response to ANG II in rats only partially attenuated water intake after PEG, and the attenuation was greater after a lower rather than a higher dose (20 vs. 30% PEG solutions; Figure 5.3, panel A). This suggests that the relative contribution of ANG II to the drinking response declines as the degree of hypovolemia increases. Consistent with this interpretation, Fregly and Rowland (1992) found that peripheral administration of the AT1R antagonist, losartan, had no effect on drinking after 30% PEG. This finding was replicated and extended by Rowland, Morien, and Fregly (1996) to a metabolite of losartan (EXP3174) that has better brain permeability than the parent compound. This study also

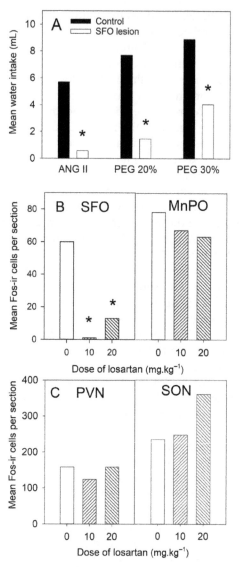

Figure 5.3 PEG-induced drinking: role of SFO in rats. Panel A (from Hosutt et al., 1981) shows effect of SFO lesions on 1 h water intake during i.v. infusion of ANG II, and in 7 h after s.c. injection of either 20% or 30% PEG. *Drinking was significantly lower in the lesion groups, but less so at the highest dose of PEG. Panels B and C (from Rowland, Morien, & Fregly, 1996) show effect of pretreatment with various doses of losartan on Fos-ir induced by 30% PEG in SFO and MnPO (B), and PVN and SON (C). *Indicates significant difference from no losartan condition.

found that PEG induced Fos-ir in structures of the lamina terminalis, as well as the SON and PVN; pretreatment with losartan abolished this Fos expression in the SFO, but it had no effect in the MnPO, SON, or PVN (OVLT was not reported; Figure 5.3, panel B). Since lesions of the SFO almost completely abolish Fos-ir induced in the MnPO, OVLT, SON, and PVN by intravenous infusions of ANG II (Rowland, Li, et al., 1994), the foregoing result with PEG implies that baroreceptor inputs to one or more of the MnPO, SON, and PVN are responsible for the induction of Fos-ir in these regions.

Rowland and Fregly (1988a) reported that a high dose of PEG (~30 mL/kg of 25% solution, s.c.) caused a robust water intake (~33 mL/kg/6 h) in ICR albino mice, with most of that occurring in the first two hours after injection. This is a substantial intake, comparable to that observed after 24 hours of water deprivation. In separate mice given both water and 0.15 M NaCl to drink, PEG evoked about twice this total fluid intake over six hours with a 2:1 ratio of saline to water. This is noteworthy because ICR mice do not spontaneously prefer isotonic saline to water. This result was confirmed by Johnson et al. (2003) in C57BL/6 mice and, in a choice between water and 2% NaCl, only water intake was stimulated in the six hours after PEG. Unlike in rats, there is no evidence that sodium appetite is stimulated in mice within this time range after PEG. A subsequent study reported that two hours after PEG, plasma protein was elevated by 18%, indicating substantial loss of extra-cellular fluid volume and that PRA was elevated more than thirtyfold (Rowland et al., 2003). Mice showed strong induction of Fos-ir in the SFO, MnPO, SON, and PVN six hours after PEG. Prior injection of the AT1R antagonist losartan completely eliminated the induction of Fos in the SFO, MnPO, and OVLT (the latter was not quantified), but it was without effect on that induced in the SON or PVN (Crews & Rowland, 2005). Importantly, losartan failed to attenuate drinking following PEG. This result shows that ANG II is generated and penetrates the circumventricular organs of the mouse brain during substantial hypovolemia but has no apparent role in the drinking response; whether such a role might be apparent at lower doses of PEG or lower levels of hypovolemia has not been tested. Additionally, activation of the SON and PVN is not dependent on signals originating with ANG II action in the lamina terminalis. Fos-ir induced in the MnPO and OVLT is blocked by losartan in mice, but not in rats. Consistent with this result, optical recording (calcium imaging) from the SFO of mice revealed that admin-istration of either PEG or isoproterenol increased the signal associated with nitric oxide synthase–expressing cells (Zimmerman et al., 2016). Those responses were reversed by pharmacological prevention of synthesis or action of Ang II. McKinley, Walker, et al. (2008) investigated drinking in mice with knockout of the angiotensinogen gene (Agt-/-). Wild-type mice consumed water and 0.3 M NaCl in the eight hours after PEG injection, whereas the Agt-/- mice did not increase intake of either fluid above that of a vehicle-treated group. These authors confirmed in wild-type mice the finding of Crews and Rowland (2005) that Fos-ir was induced in the SFO, MnPO, OVLT, SON, and PVN, but that in Agt-/- mice Fos-ir in the OVLT and SFO was about 80% less but was comparable in the other regions and was slightly increased in the MnPO (Figure 5.4).

These findings, that PEG activation of SFO can be prevented by losartan, losartan + captopril, or elimination of ANG II (Agt-/-), but that only the latter prevents drinking suggests that not all ANG action in brain evokes suprathreshold Fos-ir, and may indicate the possibility that ANG of central origin could be involved. It is notable that the drinking to PEG in mice, often approaching 100 ml/kg body weight, is extraordinarily robust and contrasts with the meager (10 ml/kg) intakes observed with isoproterenol. The reason for this disparity, not evident in rats, is unknown.

5.5.2   Diuretic Treatment

Diuretic agents like furosemide, also known as frusemide, are inhibitors of renal tubular sodium reabsorption and produce an acute (1–2-hour) loss of urine that is approximately isosmotic with plasma. Rabe (1975) performed a dose–response analysis of urinary losses and subsequent intakes of water and concurrently available 0.3 M NaCl solution in rats, measured four to six hours after the diuretic injection. Since approximately 75% of the urinary loss is in the first hour, this means the depleted state was present for at least three hours prior to the intake test. Panel A of Figure 5.5 shows that drinking of both water and 0.3 M NaCl occurred soon after presentation, such that rats consumed a mixture that is slightly hypotonic. The volume consumed was, however, substantially less than that lost in urine (panel B). Fitzsimons (1979) presented water immediately after furosemide injection to rats and found that almost nothing was consumed in the first hour, and even after six hours the intake was still only about 25% of the volume of urine lost (panel C). Longer delays between furosemide injection and the intake test induce robust intake of water and NaCl solution (Jalowiec, 1974). This has become a common procedure to induce sodium appetite (Section 5.6).

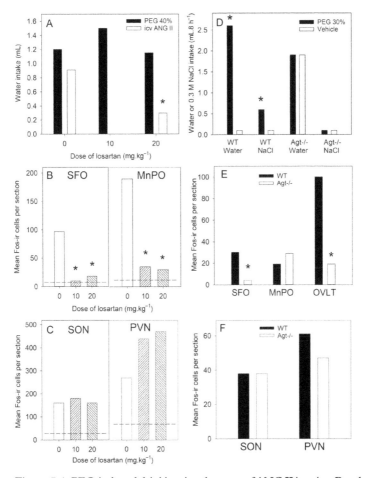

Figure 5.4 PEG-induced drinking: involvement of ANG II in mice. Panels A–C are from Crews and Rowland (2005). Panel A shows PEG-induced drinking is not affected by peripheral losartan, whereas drinking induced by cerebroventricular ANG II is attenuated. *Losartan inhibition relative to zero dose. Panels B and C show induction of Fos-ir in various brain regions measured 2 h after injection of 30 mL.kg^{-1} 40% PEG. Fos induced in SFO and MnPO is abolished by peripheral losartan while that in SON and PVN is not attenuated. *Significant effect of losartan. Panels D–F are from McKinley, McAllen, et al. (2008). Panel D shows PEG (20 mL.kg^{-1} of 30%) stimulated intake of water and 0.3 M NaCl in an 8 h test compared with vehicle treatment; in contrast, intake was not stimulated above baseline in mice lacking the angiotensinogen gene (Agt-/-). *PEG > vehicle. Panels E andF show Fos induced in SFO, OVLT, and SON of wild-type mice measured 6 h after PEG, whereas Agt-/- mice showed increase above baseline in SON only. *Agt-/- significantly lower than wild type.

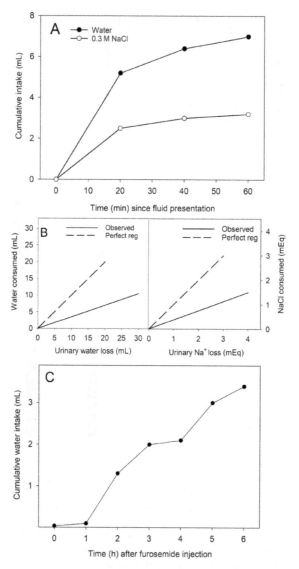

Figure 5.5 Drinking in rats following injection of furosemide. Panel
A (from Rabe, 1975) shows intakes of water and 0.3 M NaCl when they
were presented 4 h after injection of furosemide (20 mg.kg^{-1}). Panel
B (from Rabe, 1975) shows regression lines of water consumed as a
function of urine volume (left) or NaCl intake as a function of urinary Na^{+}
loss; the urinary data are for 6 h, and the intakes are for the last 2 h of that
time. Dashed lines indicate the theoretical replacement intakes. Panel
C (from Fitzsimons, 1979) shows drinking across time with immediate
access to water following injection of furosemide (15 mg.kg^{-1}).

5.6   Sodium Depletion and Sodium Appetite

To treat sodium appetite adequately is beyond the scope of this book. In this section, I will present studies that illuminate the neural circuitry of the lamina terminalis after body sodium depletion. As noted above, intake of both preferred and nonpreferred (i.e., hypertonic) NaCl solutions are stimulated to some degree in the few hours after some hypovolemic treatments, notably PEG or furosemide. Whereas feeding rats a Na^+-free diet for several days is insufficient to stimulate sodium appetite, treatment with furosemide and waiting about 24 hours produces a robust and selective intake of NaCl given in choice with water in rats (Jalowiec, 1974) and mice (Matsuda et al., 2017; Rowland et al., 2004; Rowland & Fregly, 1988a). The onset of sodium appetite is faster in the presence of a low dose of captopril (Johnson & Thunhorst, 1997).

Within three hours of injection of furosemide to rats (and access to sodium-free food), maximal levels of PRA, hypovolemia, and Fos-ir in the SFO and OVLT are achieved, yet the sodium appetite is minimal at this time and takes a further 21 hours to develop fully (Rowland & Morian, 1999). This may be due in part to slower secretion of aldosterone and its action in other brain regions. This study suggests that stimulation of the SFO and OVLT, probably by ANG II, is alone insufficient to produce salt intake. However, in mice that were sodium depleted for 24 hours with furosemide and a sodium-free diet, the specific appetite for 0.3 M NaCl solution seen in wild-type mice was completely absent in mice with knockout of the AT1a receptor (Matsuda et al., 2017). Using the same protocol, these authors showed that mice with knockdown of the AT1a receptor in the SFO (using a Cre-lox manipulation; see Appendix) had attenuated salt appetite, and that the degree of inhibition was linearly related to the loss of cells expressing AT1a receptors. In contrast, knockdown of the same receptors in the OVLT had no effect on salt appetite. They then showed that optogenetic silencing of the SFO to OVLT pathway had no effect on salt appetite, but silencing of a pathway from the SFO to the bed nucleus of the stria terminalis (BNST) again produced strong inhibition of salt appetite in proportion to the number of cells engaged by the manipulation. The authors thus suggest that a population of cells in the SFO expressing AT1a receptors and projecting to the BNST are essential for the expression of salt appetite, and, from other studies in the paper, this subset of SFO neurons is separate from a set that is involved in water intake. This finding still does not address the delayed appearance of salt appetite relative to stimulation of the SFO as assessed by Fos-ir, although this discrepancy might be addressed by identifying Fos-positive cells at different times, either by phenotype or efferent projection.

5.7   Summary

Acute depletion of ECF volume without change in osmolality is sufficient to induce drinking in many species. However, the threshold for drinking appears to be quite large, of the order of 10–20% loss of plasma volume. This change may occur without a significant drop in arterial pressure, due to effective physiological counter-regulation, including secretion of renin from the kidneys and subsequent generation of ANG II. Under many conditions of actual or simulated hypovolemia, ANG II appears to be involved in the drinking response and probably by action on AT1a receptors in the SFO. However, interference with ANG II production and/or action does not uniformly disrupt all forms of hypovolemia-related drinking, and it appears that afferents from cardiopulmonary pressure receptors may also be involved. There may be strain differences in the relative contribution of these two mechanisms, or others, to extracellular dehydration drinking. Restoration of ECF volume requires ingestion of NaCl as well as water, and mechanisms for this are discussed briefly.

6   Pregnancy and the Ontogeny of Thirst

6.1   Introduction

The principal topic of this chapter is the early development of thirst mechanisms. Because early postnatal development in mammals is dependent upon the prior intrauterine environment, the first part of this chapter will start with studies on fluid balance in the mother during pregnancy. The second part of the chapter will consider the developmental trajectory of fluid regulation. Newborn mammals all suckle, and milk is their unique source of both nutrition and fluid for some period. The age at which they are able to exhibit ingestion independent of milk and the mother will depend in part on the relative maturation of the sensory and motor functions of their nervous systems. The ability to respond to dehydration with ingestion will depend on an adequate transduction of the physiological signal(s) of dehydration, and the motoric ability to consume the fluid(s) available.

As will be developed in Chapter 8, fluid deprivation produces both intracellular and extracellular dehydration in adults, but their relative contribution varies with duration of deprivation and other factors. Adult rodents have most of their daily intake within a few minutes of ending a meal of dry food (Chapter 7), and, together with less common drinking immediately before meals, this has been called prandial drinking (Kissileff, 1969a). This raises important questions about whether prandial drinking is anticipatory of systemic dehydration and, if so, whether this behavior is learned during ontogeny. The present chapter will include the issue of early learning in relation to drinking behavior.

The magnitude and duration of impact of a given perturbation to fluid balance, and its action as a potential stimulus of drinking, will depend to a significant degree on the response of the kidney to that perturbation. For mammals, birth signifies the time at which the kidneys become the main organs of excretion, and it is not surprising that the neonatal kidney is not immediately able to assume adult levels of function. McCance (1948) was among the first to review the undeveloped function of human kidneys for the first few months of life, although he emphasized there were large individual differences. A species-typical timetable for postnatal maturation of renal function is present in all mammals, with mechanistic studies in rats showing that adultlike function is reached by weeks 4–5 postnatally.

6.2   Pregnancy

An adaptive feature of mammalian pregnancy is for the mother to provide a reasonably stable or buffered environment for the preterm offspring. One of the principal changes in the mother is lowered plasma osmolality and increased plasma volume, both of which ostensibly allow suitable fetal hydration.

6.2.1   Women

In the last trimester of pregnancy, basal plasma osmolality appears to be regulated at about 3% or 10 mOsm/kg lower than postpartum levels (Davison et al., 1984). To investigate the development and mechanism of this effect, Davison et al. (1988) infused volunteers with hypertonic NaCl (about 6 mEq/kg over 2 h) on six occasions. The first two tests were in a luteal phase of the menstrual cycle before they conceived, then during the first trimester at 5–8 and 10–12 weeks of gestation, in the third trimester at 28–33 weeks of gestation, and again 8–10 weeks postpartum while not breastfeeding. To investigate whether human chorionic gonadotropin (hCG) might be responsible for changes during pregnancy, the women were injected with hCG prior to one of the preconception tests. During the infusions, plasma osmolality and vasopressin (AVP) were measured every 15 minutes and thirst was rated on a 10 cm visual analog scale. Subjects also reported when they first experienced a strong, conscious desire to drink. Subjects were allowed to drink to satiety after the infusion period, but other details of this behavioral test were not given.

Figure 6.1, panel A, shows the mean osmolalities from each phase at the pre-infusion baseline and the corresponding first strong sensation of thirst. Basal levels of plasma osmolality were reduced by 10–11 mOsm/kg at all times during pregnancy compared with prepregnancy and post partum values. Not shown in the graph, hCG treatment before pregnancy resulted in a 5 Osm/kg lowering of mean basal osmolality. However, blood levels of hCG achieved by injection were generally less than those during pregnancy such that within-subject decrease in basal osmolality across treatments was highly correlated with plasma hCG

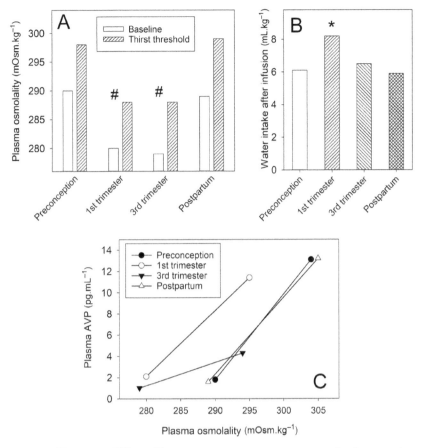

Figure 6.1 Effect of human pregnancy on responses to i.v. hypertonic NaCl 6 mEq.kg^{-1} over 2 h) infusion. Panels A–C are from Davison et al. (1988). Panel A shows basal osmolality at four different phases, and the osmolality at which thirst was first reported. #First and third trimester values are less than preconception or postpartum tests. Panel B shows amount of water consumed following the 2 h infusion. *Vs. all other times. Panel C shows initial and final (2 h) plasma osmolalities and AVP concentrations at the four different phases.

level. Thirst ratings were affected in a similar manner relative to osmolality, and in all phases the desire to drink occurred at 10–13 mOsm/kg above the initial value at that test. That is, the relative threshold and sensitivity of thirst were unchanged across the various phases. However, water intake after the infusion was about 30% greater in the first trimester compared with all other phases (Figure 6.1, panel B), but no discussion of this was offered.

Within a condition, AVP levels in plasma during NaCl infusion were linearly correlated with plasma osmolality. However, the abscissal intercept (extrapolation to zero AVP) was about 10 mOsm/kg lower during pregnancy than before or after (Figure 6.1, panel C), reflecting the differences in basal values shown in panel A. The slopes of the linear regressions between AVP level and osmolality were similar at all times except during the third trimester, when released AVP was cleared more rapidly because of an increase in degradative enzymatic activity. Because of this enzymatic degradation, it is likely that the actual release of AVP in the third trimester was similar to that during other times of testing.

Basal osmolality, as well as NaCl-related increases in AVP and thirst, also show a marked change during the normal menstrual cycle. Basal osmolality is 4–5 mOsm/kg lower in the luteal phase than in the follicular phase, with ovulatory phase intermediate, and absolute osmotic thirst thresholds are likewise 5 mOsm/kg lower in the luteal phase (Vokes et al., 1988). Thus, the use of the luteal phase in the foregoing pregnancy study (Davison et al., 1988) represents an effect of hCG beyond the lowest thresholds found during the menstrual cycle. Davison et al. (1990) noted that hCG infusions had no effect on osmoregulation in males. Additional aspects of the hormonal basis of these effects will be discussed in the subsequent section on rodents.

To investigate the role of plasma volume changes during pregnancy, Davison et al. (1990) gave hypertonic NaCl infusions identical to the foregoing to women during the first and third trimesters of pregnancy, and again 10–12 weeks postpartum. In each phase, two tests were administered in random order. One test was standard, in air, and the other was while they were subject to head-out immersion in water for three hours (1 h before then during the 2 h infusion) to increase thoracic blood volume. As before, basal plasma osmolality was 10 mOsm/kg lower during pregnancy compared with postpartum, and it was unaffected by water immersion. NaCl infusion produced similar increases in osmolality (9–14 mOsm/kg) in all tests and an increase in plasma volume of about 8%. Immersion for one hour before infusion caused an increase in plasma volume, ranging from 4.5% postpartum to 12.1% in the third trimester, and the infusion of NaCl produced comparable (7%) increases above this value at all tests. AVP and thirst ratings during the infusions were linearly correlated with osmolality. The slopes of these functions (i.e., change in AVP or thirst vs. change in plasma osmolality during the infusions) are shown in panel C of Figure 6.1. In the air condition, the slope of the AVP function was lower in the third trimester, as in the previous study (panel C). The slopes were decreased comparably by the water immersion procedure, which effectively increased plasma volume. In contrast, neither water immersion nor phase of the study had an effect on thirst slopes. Further, the absolute osmolalities at which thirst was first consciously noted were 10 mOsm/kg lower during pregnancy than postpartum, but they were minimally (2–3 mOsm/kg) increased by water immersion. Together, these data show that osmoreceptor function is reset downward throughout pregnancy, possibly due to the action of hCG, and that increased plasma volume attenuates osmotically induced AVP secretion but has no effect on thirst. It follows that with adequate water to slake normal maternal thirst, the human fetus is chronically exposed to a milieu that is hypo-osmolar relative to levels typically found outside of pregnancy.

6.2.2   Animals

In rats, the effects of pregnancy are generally similar to those in humans. Durr et al. (1981) reported that basal plasma osmolality was 281 mOsm/kg on the day before normal parturition, compared with 292 mOsm/kg in nonpregnant females. Blood volume was 15% higher before parturition. These differences were not observed by treating nonpregnant females with progesterone, estrone, or a combination for two weeks. Rats progressively increase spontaneous food and water intakes during pregnancy: In this study, water intake was about 50% elevated late in gestation; food intake was not recorded. Water deprivation for 48 hours (with dry chow freely available) produced an increase of 8–9 mOsm/kg in both pregnant and nonpregnant groups, thus showing that this extreme water deprivation during pregnancy did not elevate osmolality above normal or nonpregnant basal levels. Using graded levels of water deprivation (12, 24, and 48 h), it was found that the slopes of the lines relating osmolality to AVP secretion were identical in pregnant and virgin groups (Figure 6.2, panel A), but with basal levels about 11 mOsm/kg apart. An approximately linear relationship between AVP and plasma osmolality was found after injection of graded intraperitoneal (i.p.) doses of hypertonic NaCl, but the slope of these lines was about one-half those after water deprivation (Figure 6.2, panel A). Water was not presented in this study, but Kaufman (1981) found that three-hour water intake following intravenous (i.v.) injection of 10 mEq/kg NaCl was comparable in pregnant and nonpregnant rats.

In the previous study, I noted that the slope of the linear regressions between plasma AVP and osmolality was higher after water deprivation than after i.p. hypertonic NaCl. Water deprivation causes both

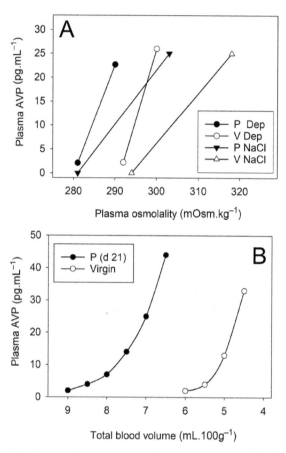

Figure 6.2 Effect of pregnancy on osmotic and volumetric control of AVP secretion in rats. Panel A (from Durr et al., 1981) shows linear regressions for plasma osmolality vs. AVP in pregnant (P, day 21) and virgin (V) rats sacrificed after various levels (0–48 h) of water deprivation (Dep) or 30 min after i.p. injection of various concentrations of hypertonic NaCl (200–1200 mOsm.kg^{-1}). Individual data points were distributed in a dose-related manner along the relevant regression line. Panel B (from Barron et al., 1984) shows curvilinear functions relating plasma AVP to blood volume (excluding conceptus) in day 21 pregnant and virgin rats following various doses of polyethylene glycol to induce hypovolemia. Blood volume was determined from plasma volume (Evans blue dilution) and erythrocyte mass (^{51}Cr labeling).

hyperosmolality and hypovolemia (Chapter 8), and the difference in slope may thus reflect a contribution from hypovolemia. To isolate the effect of volume depletion on AVP, Barron et al. (1984) treated virgin and 14–21-day pregnant rats with various i.p. doses of polyethylene glycol (PEG) (see Chapter 5) alone or in combination with NaCl. The graphs relating AVP to degree of hypovolemia are curvilinear (Figure 6.2, panel B) and of similar shape in both virgin and pregnant groups. However, basal volume was expanded by almost 50% in late pregnancy, with the result that the functions relating AVP to actual volume were significantly displaced in pregnancy (panel B). This would be consistent with no change in baroreceptor function during pregnancy but with the result that absolute volume is functionally regulated at a higher level. Drinking was not examined in this study.

Relaxin is a hormone, with some homology to insulin, secreted from the corpus luteum during pregnancy in the rat. Intracerebroventricular (ICV) injection of relaxin produced an acute drinking response (Summerlee & Robertson, 1995; Thornton & Fitzsimons, 1995). Intravenous infusion of relaxin likewise increased water intake, an effect that was abolished by lesion of the subfornical organ (SFO; Sunn et al., 2002) or by losartan (Sinnayah et al., 1999). Using isolated slices of the SFO, Sunn et al. (2002) showed that many neurons were excited by bath application of relaxin, and that most of these neurons were also excited by angiotensin (ANG) II. It is believed that relaxin, via specific receptors, causes local release of ANG II in the brain. Infusion of relaxin induced Fos-ir in the periphery of the SFO and dorsal cap of the organum vasculosum of the lamina terminalis (OVLT; Sunn et al., 2002), and the relaxin-stimulated neurons in the SFO and OVLT are connected to the supraoptic (SON) and paraventricular (PVN) nuclei (Sunn et al., 2001). Lesion of the OVLT abolished relaxin-induced Fos-ir in the SON and PVN, but it did not affect the drinking response; conversely, lesion of the SFO abolished the drinking response but had little or no effect on Fos-ir in the SON and PVN (Sunn et al., 2002).

To assess whether endogenous relaxin plays a role in increased water intake during pregnancy in rats, Zhao et al. (1995) infused a specific monoclonal antibody to relaxin from days 12–22 of pregnancy. Although the antibody reduced total water intake, this effect was restricted to the 14-hour light period and had no significant effect during the 10-hour dark period when most of the spontaneous drinking occurred. Assuming that the antibody achieved complete passive immunization, it appears that relaxin plays only a minor role in daily fluid intake during pregnancy.

More recent work has identified several forms of relaxin, all members of a relaxin–insulin superfamily. Of relevance to fluid balance, relaxin-3 is produced in the brain and acts with high affinity at a specific receptor (RXFP3) and with lower affinity at RXPF1. These receptors are found in circumventricular and neurosecretory regions, and ICV administration of relaxin-3 induced robust water intake in rats (de Avila et al., 2018).

Relaxin seems to be responsible for resetting the osmolality–AVP relationship in pregnancy. Weisinger et al. (1993) infused ovariectomized rats with relaxin for seven days, and at the end of that time they were either water deprived for 24 hours or received an acute injection of hypertonic NaCl (8 mmol/kg). Basal osmolality was reduced by 10 mOsm/kg by relaxin; the linear regression between osmolality and plasma AVP had the same slope but was shifted to lower osmolality in relaxin-treated rats compared with controls. These effects emulate those of natural pregnancy in rats (Durr et al., 1981) in much the same way that hCG treatment produced these effects in humans.

In closing this section on pregnancy, it should be noted that some effects are species-selective. Thus, whereas rats and humans have lower plasma osmolality during pregnancy, sheep do not (Bell et al., 1986), possibly because they do not produce relaxin.

6.3   Ontogeny of Drinking

6.3.1   Humans

Desor et al. (1975) tested the volumes of water and various tastants consumed from a test nipple by infants (1–4 days postnatal) fed from a bottle since birth. They consumed a mean of 9 mL water (0.3% body weight) in a three-minute test and, after a short rest, consumed a comparable volume of 0.07 M sucrose solution in three minutes. In another study, newborns rejected saline solution relative to water (Beauchamp et al., 1994); this relative rejection was smaller or absent by 4–8 months of age. None of these studies was able to manipulate level of deprivation. Mothers in modern Western cultures are advised not to give infants fluids other than milk to avoid possible interference with caloric intake.

Paque (1980) reported fluid consumption by nomadic Saharan Bedouin populations living (around 1960) in a relatively dehydrating environment. Of relevance to ontogeny, he noted that by 8–12 months of age postnatally, parents started to feed infants the unsalted foods and fluids that they themselves were eating. Water and tea brewed from brackish water also were consumed. Of particular note, during the hottest days (>40°C inside the tents), 1–2-year-old infants *incessantly* (Paque's emphasis) alternated between suckling at their mother's breast and drinking tea. They thus obtained a steady supply of nutrients, electrolytes, and water. Paque suggested that drinking of a mildly salted mixture by infants prevented hypovolemia. Although not specifically mentioning infants or children, Leshem et al. (2008) give a more recent account of high salt intake by Negev Bedouin women in tribal encampments.

In a physiologically less demanding environment (the United Kingdom), Petter et al. (1994) analyzed 48-hour drinking habits of preschool (2.1–4.3 yrs) and elementary school (5.5–7.0 yrs) children, using diary records maintained by the parents. In preschoolers, only 5% of all of the drinks taken were plain water, and over 70% of the children did not drink water at all. The preschoolers drank water slightly more frequently (15% of all drinks; 50% drank water at least once). The preponderance of drinks were flavored juices or milk. When parents were asked why water was consumed so little, the main response was children do not like the taste of water. Thus, even from a young age, independent fluid intake is usually associated with energy consumption and its associated flavor. It is thus difficult to distinguish hunger from thirst as the primary motivation of their drinking behavior.

6.3.2 Sheep

Catheterization and instrumentation of fetal sheep can be performed as early as 60% of the normal gestation period of 147 days (Back et al., 2012). The catheters pass through the skin of the dam, and studies may be performed a few days later without anesthesia. Drinking-related studies have been made at about 100 or 130 days of gestation (67% and 87% of term, respectively, sometimes distinguished as preterm and near-term). From a neurobiological perspective, the sheep brain at birth is about 50% of adult weight and at the preterm and near-term ages, respectively, is estimated (from McIntosh et al., 1979) to be about 65% and 90% of birth weight.

Near-term fetal sheep, like humans, exhibit spontaneous swallowing of amniotic fluid. In one study, near-term ewes were deprived of water for 54 hours, thereby increasing the plasma osmotic pressure in the fetus by some 4% from 300 to 311 mOsm/L, yet the frequency and amount of swallowing behavior was unchanged from baseline (Ross et al., 1991). The amniotic fluid was then infused with hypotonic saline (0.075 M; 1500 mL/90 min). This decreased osmolality and Na^+ concentration in amniotic fluid to levels somewhat lower than before deprivation, and osmolality of fetal blood returned to near baseline (303 mOsm/L). Swallowing decreased during the infusion period, suggesting that drinking of dilute amniotic fluid could not alone be responsible for normalization of fetal plasma osmolality.

In contrast to the lack of effect of maternal dehydration, fetal swallowing rate was increased sixfold in the near-term fetus by injection of hypertonic NaCl (4 M) to increase fetal plasma osmolality by about 5%. However, swallowing returned to baseline within five minutes, despite continued plasma hyperosmolality (Ross et al., 1989). The threshold increase in osmolality for stimulation of swallowing in the near-term fetus was about twofold higher than in adults, and, further, drinking could not be elicited earlier in gestation (see Ross & Nijland, 1998, for review). Like maternal water deprivation, slow infusion of ANG II (100 ng/kg/min) to the near-term fetus was ineffective in changing swallowing rate, despite robust cardiovascular effects (Ross et al., 1989). In contrast, acute ICV injection of high doses of ANG II caused a threefold increase in swallowing rate (Ross et al., 1985). Thus, in the near-term fetus, ANG II stimulates swallowing amniotic fluid only acutely and at high doses.

To determine at what fetal age brain osmoreceptive regions become functional, using the measure of increased Fos-ir expression, preterm or near-term fetal sheep were infused via i.p. catheter with hypertonic NaCl at doses designed to increase plasma osmolality by 10 mOsm/kg (~3%). Increased Fos-ir was observed in the OVLT, SFO, SON, PVN, and median preoptic nucleus (MnPO) at both ages, qualitatively comparable to the responses in adult sheep (Caston-Balderrama et al., 1999, 2001; Xu et al., 2001). The authors conclude that the absence of swallowing in the preterm infant was due to incomplete connectivity between the osmosensory regions and the relevant motor pathways, and not a result of undeveloped osmosensory apparatus.

6.3.3   Rats

Similar to humans, newborn rat pups have limited sensory and motor capacities, obtaining all of their food and fluid as milk from the dam. Rat dams nurse their pups intermittently, and primarily during the daytime in the first week postnatally (Ader &Grota, 1970; Redman & Sweney, 1976). Thus, the pups experience relatively short but repeated periods of maternal deprivation. Interestingly, lactating rat dams show decreased responsiveness to a variety of dipsogens administered during the daytime (Kaufman, 1981).

Friedman (1975) showed that imposed maternal deprivation for as little as two hours strongly stimulated milk intake from the dam in pups at postnatal day 10 (PND10), and this deprivation was associated with a

4.2% reduction in hematocrit ratio and (inferred) plasma volume. After eight hours of deprivation, the hematocrit ratio declined by 11.7% and milk consumption was greater, provided that the dam's milk supply was not a limiting factor. Hypovolemia after injection of the hyperoncotic colloid PEG modestly stimulated milk intake. Bruno et al. (1982) found that nipple attachment and milk intake of PND15 and PND20 pups deprived for four hours were unaffected by additional injection of low doses of PEG, possibly due to a ceiling effect. These findings suggest that mild hypovolemia is a natural stimulus of suckling during the nursing period. Neonatal rats have negligible ability to concentrate urine, and deprivation thus leads to decreased plasma sodium concentration and possibly osmolality (Heller, 1949). Thus, until pups start to sample and ingest dry food around PND15 in the laboratory, hypovolemia may occur regularly while hyperosmolality may occur rarely if ever. Hyperosmolality induced abruptly by injection of hypertonic NaCl potently inhibited nipple attachment and milk intake at PND15 (Bruno et al., 1982).

It is important to know whether these findings with milk intake in pups generalize to intake of water, which, of necessity, does not involve the dam. To investigate this question, three principal protocols have been used that require little more than reflexive swallowing. In a "drop protocol" similar to the human infant test reported previously, a fluid dropper is placed near the tongue or snout (Almli, 1973; Wirth & Epstein, 1976). In a "sucking protocol," the pup is placed on a fluid-impregnated surface such as filter paper and may suck and ingest the fluid, with minimal appetitive behavior (Hall & Bryan, 1980). Finally, in a "swallow/spit protocol," a flanged cannula is inserted under the anterior tongue and test fluids are infused or pulsed; the pup can actively swallow the fluid or allow it to drip passively out of the mouth (Hall, 1979). Because spontaneous micturition is rare at these ages, weight gain is usually the measure of intake over suitably short test durations.

In both swallow/spit and drop protocols, rat pups increased water or milk intake above baseline after ICV ANG II at PND2, to renin- and colloid-induced hypovolemia at PND4, and to β-adrenergic agonists at PND6 (Ellis et al., 1984; Leshem et al., 1988; Wirth & Epstein, 1976). Using the sucking protocol, Bruno (1981) confirmed many aspects of this timetable, but, in separate tests at PND6, the stimulated intake of water did not differ from intake of milk. In contrast, by PND12, water was consumed in greater amounts than milk. Bruno suggested that intake of milk was suppressed by development of dehydration anorexia; regardless of whether this is an accurate interpretation, it is clear that the taste of the fluids is having an effect by PND12. Of note, the above tests were the first exposure of pups to water, so no learning about different postingestive effects of milk and water could have occurred. Finally, in rat pups weaned as early as PND16, appetitive aspects of drinking were shown by locomotion to a spout (Bruno, 1981). Thus, pups as young as PND2 increase water intake in these protocols when dehydrated, but they do not start to differentiate water from milk until PND12.

After about PND16, appetitive components of water seeking become progressively more important. As will become apparent, the conditions for water need after weaning play a role, and it is thus relevant to include a description of spontaneous drinking during that period. Weaning in the laboratory often occurs at PND21, when rat pups are provided dry food and water, typically from a drinking spout in the cage. They normally start to sample dry food and drink about PND16, but also consume some mother's milk until weaning (Redman & Sweney, 1976). Kissileff (1971) weaned rat pups at PND17 to a liquid diet, available from a sipper spout, thereby limiting or eliminating prior exposure to dry food. At various ages thereafter, they were switched to dry food and water and their patterns of eating and drinking recorded for five days. Rats switched to dry food for the first time before PND28 all showed some drinking during meals (intrameal) for the five days of study. The median percentage of drinking that was classified as intrameal was 21, 33, 39, 56, and 46% on the five consecutive days, albeit with considerable individual variability. The persistence or transition of this intrameal pattern to the adult pre- and postmeal pattern was not studied. In contrast, rats switched to dry food for the first time after PND38 showed an adultlike pattern in which there was little intrameal drinking. Rats first given dry food at intermediate ages (PND28–34) had an intermediate level of intrameal drinking. These results indicate a maturational rather than an experiential factor. It follows that a good fraction of water consumed in the first two weeks after normal weaning occurs during meals, possibly due to dryness or discomfort of the oral cavity caused by the dry food.

Adult rats whose salivary production has been largely abolished, either by removal of salivary glands or by treatment with atropine, are known to show an extreme version of intrameal drinking in which drinking follows consumption of each mouthful of food (Chapman & Epstein, 1970; Kissileff, 1969b). This drinking provides necessary lubrication for swallowing. Before PND35, rats may normally have insufficient saliva to fully swallow a dry meal, although their intrameal pattern is less extreme than that of salivaless rats. This interpretation of partial development of meal-associated salivation before PND35 is consistent with observations that rat salivary glands grow and their maximal (pilocarpine-stimulated) secretion rates increase until about PND35 (Abe et al., 1987). An alternative interpretation is that, in the days immediately before weaning, rat pups start to show nipple-shifting (Cramer et al., 1980). This proclivity to switch nutrient source may be perpetuated by the discrete food pellets (45 mg) used in Kissileff's testing protocol. Nonetheless, weanling rats rarely drink when food is not being consumed, and it follows that in the studies of independent drinking to be described next there is minimal or no prior experience of consuming water in the absence of food.

Friedman and Campbell (1974) cite a report by Kreček and Krečkova (1957) that drinking in PND19–24 pups after hypertonic NaCl administration proceeded slowly compared with adults. Friedman and Campbell reexamined this issue using rats at PND16, 20, or 30, or adults. PND16 and PND20 cohorts were weaned to dry food and water one day earlier, while the PND30 cohort was weaned at PND21. Thus, all of the rats had an opportunity to establish independent drinking by licking from a sipper spout before the test session. On the test day, rats were injected with various doses of hypertonic NaCl (0.25–1 M, 20 mL/kg body weight, i. p.), PEG (10–30%, 20 mL/kg, s.c.), and isotonic saline or sham injection control. Other rats had their inferior vena cava (IVC) ligated, using ether anesthesia. In all cases, water intake (with food absent) was recorded for up to eight hours after the treatment.

Water intake at all ages was dose and time related, and representative results are shown in Figure 6.3. Panel A shows the water intake, normalized for body weight, of PND20 pups and adults following injection of the intermediate dose of NaCl (0.5 M, or 10 mEq/kg) or isotonic NaCl control. The intake by PND20 rats occurred throughout the six-hour test, whereas adults finished drinking after less than two hours. This result is consistent with the description of similarly aged pups by Kreček and Krečkova (1957). In PND16 pups (not shown), baseline water intake was a relatively high 2 mL/100 g body weight and was not increased by any dose of hypertonic NaCl. Because of the high baseline in this study, the conclusion by Friedman and Campbell (1974) that osmoregulatory thirst is absent at PND16 cannot be fully evaluated. At PND30, the water intake was 3% body weight, compared with 5% body weight in adults for loads of 20 mEq NaCl/kg. This 60% of adult response at PND30 agrees with an earlier report (Adolph et al., 1954) that the amount of water drunk in two hours starting four hours after injection of hypertonic NaCl (40 mEq/kg) increased from 7% body weight at PND30 (± 5) to an average of more than 12% between 35 and 69 days of age. That study also found that the high intake in young adulthood declined to about 7% of body weight by 200 days of age, comparable to that at PND30. Thus, age of the adults used for

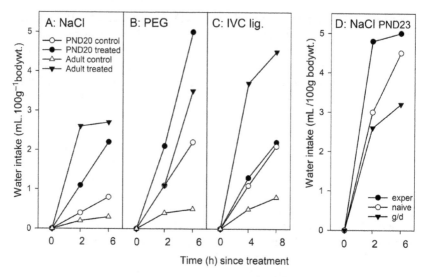

Figure 6.3 Ontogeny of drinking in rats. Panels A–C (from Friedman & Campbell, 1974) show mean cumulative water intakes, from drinking spouts, of postnatal day 20(PND20) pups or adults, given either a control procedure or injected with NaCl (20 mL.kg^{-1} i.p. of 0.5 M; Panel A) or polyethylene glycol (20% PEG, 20 mL.kg^{-1}, s.c.; Panel B) or after ligation of the inferior vena cava (Panel C). Panel D (from Myers & Hall, 2001) shows water intake induced by hypertonic NaCl on PND23 in pups that had a prior drinking experience after intracellular dehydration (exper), those that had not (naïve), and those that had been dehydrated but rehydrated by gavage (g/d).

comparison may be a relevant variable, although other differences (e.g., degree of physical restraint) between studies cannot be discounted.

Panel B of Figure 6.3 shows that drinking in response to PEG-induced hypovolemia was fully present by PND20 (Friedman & Campbell, 1974), as was also the case at PND15 (not shown). Drinking in adults was smaller relative to body weight, and the reason for this more prolific response in early life has not been explained. In our section on drinking in aging (Chapter 10), a decline in PEG response by rats seems to occur for a few months into young adulthood, and it may represent an extended decline of the high responsiveness very early in life shown here. In contrast to the result with PEG, drinking seen in adults following caval ligation (Figure 6.3, panel C) is completely absent at PND20, albeit compared to a relatively high intake in the sham-operated group. By PND30 and 42 (data not shown), caval ligation did cause drinking above sham-operated control levels (Friedman & Campbell, 1974), but that

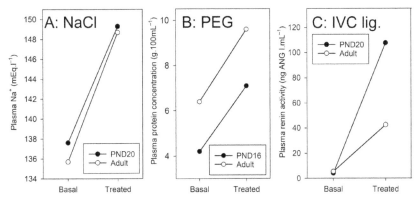

Figure 6.4 Physiological changes induced by hydration challenges in PND16 or PND20 pups and in adults (from Friedman & Campbell, 1974). Panel A shows plasma Na$^+$ at baseline and 90 min after i.p. NaCl (20 mEq.kg^{-1}). Panel B shows plasma protein concentration at baseline and 8 h after injection of 30% PEG. Panel C shows plasma renin activity at baseline and 1 h after ligation of the inferior vena cava.

effect can be attributed primarily to a decrease in the control group intake rather than an increase in the ligated group.

Given that water and electrolyte excretion is not fully developed early in life (Falk, 1955; Heller & Lederis, 1959; Trimble, 1970), it is important to consider the physiological changes caused by these putative dipsogenic stimuli. Figure 6.4 presents key physiological parameters collected at indicated times after treatment in rat pups and adults that did not have access to water (Friedman & Campbell, 1974). In all cases, the treatments caused greater plasma changes at younger compared with older or adult ages. Thus, the relatively low drinking response in the youngest groups after NaCl or caval ligation cannot be ascribed to a smaller stimulus.

In adults, PEG causes both hypovolemia and generation of plasma ANG II. Studies that have attempted to dissociate these responses (Chapter 5) have found that PEG drinking is substantially independent of ANG II. In contrast, drinking to caval ligation appears to be completely dependent on generation of ANG II. Thus, although infant (PND2) rats and prenatal sheep respond to ANG II by reflexive swallowing, the ontogeny of appetitive drinking to ANG II has not been examined. These data suggest that, as in adults, drinking to PEG in infants might be relatively independent of ANG II. No studies have investigated the neurobiological basis of the early-developing and purely hypovolemic drinking. Also in adults, PEG stimulates intake of both water and saline (Chapter 5); water intake alone coupled with anuria causes hyponatremia, and this may pose a ceiling on intake that is not evident when NaCl is available. No study has examined whether infant rats show salt appetite after PEG and/or whether even higher total intakes might be observed when NaCl is also offered compared to water alone.

Hall et al. (2000) examined the development of appetitive aspects of drinking in weanling rats. Rats were weaned at PND18 to dry food and water from a sipper spout. At PND21 or 35, rats received injection of hypertonic NaCl (2 M, 2 mL/kg, s.c.) or isotonic control and were presented water 45 minutes later for a one-hour test. Substantial intake above minimal control baselines occurred at PND35 but not PND21. To examine the potential role of drinking due to experience with dry food in this effect, other rats were weaned at PND18 and fed a complete liquid diet until testing at PND35. Drinking after NaCl injection was greatly reduced compared to the pups with the chow and water experience.

Myers and Hall (2001) further investigated, in rats weaned to the liquid diet at PND19, the effect of experience of drinking to intracellular dehydration with NaCl. In this study, to again avoid prior drinking with dry food, pups were weaned to a liquid diet and on PND21 received injection of either hypertonic (20 mEq/kg) or isotonic NaCl. One hour after the hypertonic injection, one group received water to drink for the remainder of the 24 hours, one group received intragastric gavage of the same amount of water in aliquots distributed across the 24 hours, and one group had no water to drink. The isotonic-injected control group also had no water during this 24-hour period. Liquid diet was then returned for 24 hours. At the main test two days later (PND23) all rats received hypertonic NaCl injection. The results are shown in panel D of Figure 6.3. The one- and two-hour intakes of the "experienced" group that on PND21 had been allowed to drink after NaCl was approximately twofold greater intake than that of any other group. Only the previous isotonic (control) group showed a significant increase in the remaining hours of the test, and by six hours their intake was similar to that of the experienced group. The authors note that no opportunity to drink – with or without repletion by gavage – was associated with the smaller drinking responses, a result they also found using intraoral infusion of water through a cannula at the first (PND21) test. The authors concluded that the full coordination of water-oriented appetitive behaviors requires associative learning in the form of prior experience with such drinking.

Hall et al. (2000) extended this analysis, showing that the one-hour water intake following hypertonic NaCl injection was much less at PND21 than PND35, but that the increased response at PND35 did not occur if the rats were raised on a liquid diet. Thus, the experience of meal-associated drinking with dehydration and drinking seems to be an important contributor to development of short-latency appetitive drinking responses by PND35. It should be noted that this analysis does not address the origin of the drinking stimulus during the experience period (viz., dry mouth, systemic, or both).

In closing this section, it should be noted that weanling rats in the natural environment would be exposed to a variety of foods of differing fluid content, and the influence of such variety on drinking has not been examined systematically. In one laboratory study (Overmann & Yang, 1973), weanling rats were given a free choice of two semipurified diets that differed in protein content and metabolic water requirement. One group of rats was given a restricted (60%) water ration throughout the study period, and it was observed that compared with a group with unrestricted water, the restricted group selected a lower proportion of the high-protein diet. This shows that young rats have some ability to adjust the type of food consumed on the basis of water availability and/or hydration status. The quantitative analog of this is dehydration anorexia, which may develop before weaning (Bruno, 1981; Friedman, 1975).

6.3.4 Other Rodents

Does the ontogenetic trajectory in rats apply to all rodents? Using a suckling test of attachment to the nipple of an anesthetized dam, Hall and Rosenblatt (1979) found that latency to attach after a seven-hour deprivation (which from the foregoing should represent a hypovolemia of at least 10%) decreased in rat pups during the first week and then remained low through the normal weaning age (PND21). Pups from Syrian hamsters (*Mesocrecitus auratus*) showed a similar decline in attachment latency through PND10, but by PND15 they showed a rapid rise in latency. Rowland (1991) examined drinking in young hamsters deprived for 4–6 hours and found vigorous water intake from an anterior oral cannula at both PND6 and PND18, with intakes at least as great as in rats of those ages. Drinking in hamsters seems to mature comparably to or faster than in rats.

In apparent contrast, mice (*Mus musculus*, C57BL6 strain) do not exhibit independent drinking at PND3, 6, or 9, but this starts to emerge at PND12 (Hall & Browde, 1986). Further, injection of hypertonic NaCl did not promote intake of water or milk at PND6, but it did so for both fluids at PND12. Since the neural development of the mouse brain is thought to be comparable to that of rats, the delayed appearance of independent drinking in mice relative to rats is unexpected and remains unexplained. Hall and Browde (1986) noted that PND6 mice did not show ratlike mouthing or other appetitive responses. A parallel may be found in the observation by Wilson et al. (1981) that PND6 mice pups, again unlike rats, did not show a milk ingestion reflex (torso stretching) when milk letdown occurred from the mother's nipple. Since this ontogenetic work was performed, mice have become a predominant species for study of the neurobiology of drinking, and potential differences from rats or other rodents in maturation of adultlike systems should be reexamined.

6.4   Ontogeny and Phenotypic Plasticity of Neural Structures

Consistent with the observations in preterm sheep, many neurons in the rat forebrain exhibit changes in firing rate during hyperosmolality by PND8 (Almli et al., 1976), although the osmotic threshold for drinking may be higher perinatally than in adults for both rats (Almli, 1973) and sheep (Xu et al., 2001). Rinaman et al. (1997) compared the expression of Fos-ir in PND2 rat pups and adults 15–30 minutes following s.c. injection of a high dose of hypertonic NaCl (20 mEq/kg), which increased plasma Na^+ by an average of 18% at PND2 and 12% in adults. Despite the immature brain at PND2, pups showed adultlike induction of Fos-ir in circumventricular organs (SFO, OVLT, and area postrema) and in the neurosecretory PVN and SON. However, unlike in adults, there was no induction of Fos-ir in the medial nucleus of the solitary tract (NST), lateral parabrachial nucleus (LPBN), locus coeruleus, and medial part of the central nucleus of amygdala. The authors suggested that the circumventricular osmosensitive regions may precipitate the osmotic drinking seen at this age, and that maturation of connections from these regions are responsible for behaviors such as dehydration anorexia (Leshem & Epstein, 1988). Work in decerebrate adult rats is consistent with this view (Flynn et al., 1995).

Several studies have examined the effect of fluid challenges to the pregnant rat dam on drinking in offspring, presumably via epigenetic programming mechanisms. Whereas many of these studies have focused on changes in the kidney, hypertension, or salt preference (see El-Haddad et al., 2004; Mecawi et al., 2015, for reviews), I will restrict this discussion to those that have examined changes in water intake of the offspring.

Zhang et al. (2011) subjected rats to 72 hours of water deprivation during the last three days of pregnancy. This procedure elevated the plasma osmolality of dams and fetal pups by 12–14% relative to dams and fetuses that were not deprived, and it reduced hematocrit ratio of pups by 10.6%. The expression of angiotensinogen mRNA in forebrain was approximately doubled in fetuses from water-deprived dams, and this effect remained undiminished when pups were five months of age. The expression of AT1 receptor mRNA was likewise elevated in both fetuses and five-month-old pups. The adult offspring were given a high dose of ANG II ICV and water intake was measured. Male but not female offspring of water-deprived dams showed a slightly higher water intake, although because of the high dose and intakes, the significance or interpretation of this finding is difficult.

Perillan et al. (2004, 2007) examined the effect of partial aortic ligation (PAL) of mother rats, performed prior to mating, on the ontogeny of thirst in pups using the dropper protocol described previously. PAL produced a twofold elevation in plasma renin activity (PRA), and inferred elevation of ANG II, in the dams. They found no change, relative to pups from sham-operated dams, in water intake in response to hypertonic NaCl at PND2 and to colloid-induced hypovolemia at PND4, but elevated drinking to β-adrenergic stimulation with isoproterenol at PND6. This effect was reversed by captopril, indicative of ANG II mediation. Using the same protocol, Arguelles et al. (2017) found that the induction of Fos-ir by isoproterenol at PND6 was elevated by some twofold in the OVLT, SFO, MnPO, and SON of pups from PAL mothers compared with pups from sham-operated mothers. This is consistent with increased ANG II signaling caused by isoproterenol in these regions of PAL offspring. Whether these neurobiological and behavioral effects would persist into adulthood was not reported, but the data indicate the occurrence of at least short-term phenotypic plasticity in these regions.

Repeated episodes of maternal hypovolemia using PEG in late gestation delayed the development of drinking, using the dropper method (Perillan et al., 2008). Consistent with the findings of Wirth and Epstein (1976), pups from sham-treated mothers increased water intake after hypertonic NaCl on PND2, after PEG on PND4, and after isoproterenol on PND6. The offspring from repeatedly hypovolemic dams showed no drinking to NaCl or PEG on PND2 and 4, respectively, although the response to isoproterenol on PND6 was normal. At what age responses to NaCl and PEG would have emerged was not studied, so the precise developmental delay cannot be specified from these results. Repeated hypovolemia during rat pregnancy is also known to increase salt appetite but not water intake of adult offspring (Galaverna et al., 1995; Nicolaidis et al., 1990).

Increased exposure to NaCl from food or fluid during late pregnancy and through weaning of the offspring has inconsistent effects. Curtis et al. (2004) reported that in adult rats, water intake in response to intravenous hypertonic NaCl was unaffected by the perinatal level of NaCl in food (in the range 0.1–3%). In contrast, Macchione et al. (2015) found that perinatal exposure to water and 0.45 M NaCl to drink caused the adult offspring to drink more in response to intravenous hypertonic NaCl than offspring not exposed to salt perinatally. However, examination of their data suggests that the difference is due to an unusually low drinking response by the no-salt group. Unless and until a coherent explanation for these diverse results can be advanced, this aspect of phenotypic plasticity remains poorly understood.

6.5   Summary

During pregnancy in humans and rats, plasma osmolality is regulated at a level about 3% lower than in nonpregnant females (or males). This may be, in part, caused by reproduction-related hormonal changes. Late in gestation, fetal sheep show acute swallowing responses to some dipsogens, and the relevant circumventricular organs (CVOs) in the brain appear to have full responsiveness to those dipsogens at this time. Postnatal development of independent drinking in rats shows that responses to hypovolemia are present and vigorous very soon after birth, whereas development of osmoregulatory drinking has a considerably slower ontogenetic trajectory. Further, this trajectory seems to be slower in mice than in rats and requires further study. Some aspects of osmoregulatory drinking in rats, as well as food-associated drinking, appear to have an experiential component. Hypovolemia or other circulatory challenges before birth in rats cause alterations in the ontogenetic trajectory of drinking, although the limits and mechanisms of this phenotypic plasticity have not been fully elucidated.

7 Food-Associated Drinking and Nycthemeral Rhythms

7.1 Introduction

Many studies of drinking, including protocols for intracellular and extracellular dehydration, are performed in the absence of food. This is, in part, because food intake is often associated with drinking. The first part of this chapter will consider drinking that is associated with food. The protocols to study intracellular (Chapter 3) and extracellular (Chapter 5) drinking involve highly controlled situations in which dehydration occurs rapidly and in the absence of contextual antecedent events. In animals, for example, an injection or another procedure is followed by an inferred, intense thirst in an environment in which drinking is the only behavior cued by the presence of a water source. In humans, an acute laboratory procedure is also involved, almost always with informed consent, including knowledge of likely effects. Fitzsimons (1979) called the thirst or drinking that arose under these conditions primary. Drinking that did not occur in this way, including meal-associated drinking, was considered secondary. The terms *homeostatic* and *nonhomeostatic* have also been used (Kissileff, 1973).

All living organisms exhibit nycthemeral (day–night) rhythms in almost all aspects, and most cells contain clock-related genes that confer a periodicity of about 24 hours. This periodicity is synchronized either directly (e.g., by light cycle) or indirectly; this occurs in mammals via connections with a master clock in the suprachiasmatic nucleus of the hypothalamus (for review, see Patke et al., 2020). Thus, behaviors such as eating and drinking occur primarily during an active phase (light = diurnal, dark = nocturnal) and are reciprocally intercalated with longer periods of inactivity, including sleep. Most of the examples of meal-associated drinking to be discussed in the first part of the chapter implicitly embrace nycthemeral rhythms. In the second part of the chapter, I will focus specifically on direct influences of nycthemeral factors in drinking.

7.2   Meal-Associated Drinking: Descriptive Analysis

7.2.1   Humans

In the absence of actual fluid deprivation (Chapter 8), extreme losses through sweating (Chapter 9), or some pathological conditions, fluid loss is relatively continuous. The principal short-term dehydrating event is eating food, which, from the time our ancestors developed central place foraging, occurs predominantly in predictable episodes that are designated as meals. Such meals usually contain a variety of food items of varying water, micronutrient (including sodium) and macronutrient content. Absorption and metabolism of that meal starts quite rapidly after the onset of eating, but it is not fully complete for several hours. Nonetheless, most of the elective intake of water or other beverage occurs during or immediately after the meal. That is, the drinking precedes physiological detection of the magnitude of systemic dehydration that will occur from the meal. Functional evaluation of this predictive aspect is difficult to achieve in humans, but it will be evident in some of the animal studies to be described.

Are there oral or early systemic effects of the meal that determine fluid intake? At the oral level, this might be represented by the dry mouth hypothesis (Chapter 1), with the possible embellishment that foods requiring more saliva to swallow are typically drier or saltier. At the early systemic level, the gut or hepatic osmoreceptors (Chapter 4) could provide a signal about the food or food mixture soon enough to modulate the amount of drinking. A corollary of both of these is that the quantity of fluid consumed will correlate with the amount of food or duration of eating.

Brandenberger et al. (1985) examined 24-hour oscillation in the plasma renin activity (PRA) of humans and found nycthemeral and ultradian oscillations that were modified by meal-related peaks with large variation in amplitude within and between individuals. The possible role of prandially released angiotensin II (ANG II) in meal-associated drinking of rats will be examined in Section 7.3.

De Castro (1988) had 36 adults keep self-report diaries of everything they ate or drank for seven days, along with the time of day. Derivative analyses from the raw data revealed that the amount of fluid ingested was primarily related to the amount of food ingested in a bout and correlated only weakly with self-reported thirst. In contrast, the amounts consumed in the relatively few drinks that occurred outside of eating bouts were strongly correlated with subjective thirst. Despite inherent inaccuracy of self-report, this result does suggest that prandial drinking is controlled differently than nonprandial drinking. De Castro (1992) subsequently found this relationship with food persisted throughout the adult life span.

7.2.2   Animals

Studies in the laboratory, and in particular in rats, have the advantage that single foods of known composition can be offered. Many of these studies have used a grain-based, natural ingredient chow of low water content (<10%), and some have used semipurified ingredients.

The quantitative relationship between amount of water consumed and daily food intake has been noted in several species under laboratory conditions (e.g., Cizek, 1959, 1961; Cizek & Nocenti, 1965). Most rats are nocturnally active, and most of their food and fluid intake occurs at night. A 12:12 artificial light–dark cycle is implied except as noted. Siegel and Stuckey (1947) reported ad libitum or spontaneous food and water intake of rats in six-hour time bins. Their results (Figure 7.1, panel A) showed that 70% of food and 84% of water intake was nocturnal. Further, the ratio of water to food (in mL/g) averaged 1.2 over the 24 hours but was higher in the second half of the night (1.8) than in the first half (1.2). Johnson and Johnson (1990a) likewise found that the water-to-food ratio was about twofold higher at night than by day, but without obvious change across the night phase.

Fitzsimons and Le Magnen (1969) made continuous recordings of food and water intake in rats (Figure 7.1, panel B) and found similar overall results, with a higher water-to-food ratio at night (1.6) than in the day (0.9). My inspection of three individual cumulative records they presented (their figure 2) shows that the water-to-food ratio was on average about 30% higher in the second compared with the first half of the night. They classified drinking as meal associated if it occurred within 10 minutes before the onset of a meal, during the meal, or within 30 minutes after the meal. Within this period, drinking could occur as several bursts, which they did not analyze further. About 10 meals were taken per day (typically, seven of these were during the night), with a mean size of about 2 g. Over 70% of total daily water intake was consumed with meals according to the above criterion, and in 9 of 10 rats the amount of water consumed in association with each meal was strongly correlated with meal size. Bealer and Johnson (1980) found a complete loss of this correlation between meal size and water intake in rats that had recovered near-normal daily food and water intake following lesions of the anteroventral third ventricle (including the organum vasculosum of the lamina terminalis [OVLT]); indeed, up to 50% of meals had no associated drinking using the Fitzsimons and

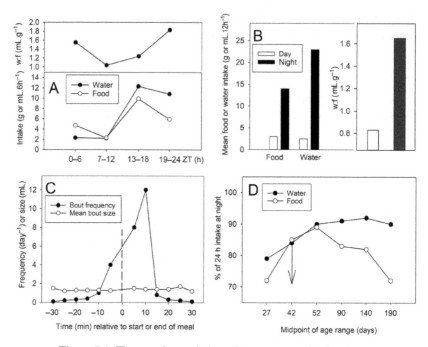

Figure 7.1 Temporal association of spontaneous food and water intake in rats. Panel A (from Siegel & Stuckey, 1947) shows the mean dry food (chow) and water intakes in 6 h bins. ZT = Zeitgeber time, where 0–12 = light and 13–24 = dark. The top panel shows the corresponding water-to-food ratios. Panel B (from Fitzsimons & Le Magnen, 1969) shows mean food and water intakes during the day and night, and the right panel shows the corresponding water-to-food ratios. Panel C (from Kissilefff, 1969a) shows the temporal association of drinking bouts in relation to the onset (negative x values) or after the end (positive x values) of spontaneous meals (vertical line). Mean bout size is also shown. Panel D (from Morris & Mogenson, 1980) shows the mean percentage of daily intake of food or water occurring in the dark period as a function of age. Each data point is the average of several days around that age range. The arrow shows the drop in nocturnal water fraction that occurred when food was rationed equally to day and night. This was also done around day 140, but there was no change in nocturnal water fraction.

Le Magnen criterion. These lesions also led to complete loss of day/night difference in either food or water intake, suggesting disruption of the master circadian oscillator (in the adjacent suprachiasmatic nucleus) and/or of its connections to circuitry involved in ingestive behavior.

Kissileff (1969a) examined the temporal relationship between food and water intake in rats using small grain-based food pellets (45 mg) delivered via a single lever press. (To avoid food hoarding or waste, a minimum five-second interpellet interval was in effect). Water intake was analyzed as drafts, where a draft or lick cluster was defined as a minimum of 10 licks terminated with either eating or a one-minute pause. Kissileff noted that feeding in normal rats occurred as discrete bouts lasting 3–6 minutes, usually uninterrupted, and that most such meals were associated with a single draft of water. Means of 17% and 45% of all drafts occurred in the five minutes preceding or following a meal, respectively, with a sharp drop-off in frequency at times more remote from meals (Figure 7.1, panel C). The mean size of these drafts was approximately 1.4 mL, regardless of timing with respect to meals. Applying the criterion of Fitzsimons and Le Magnen (1969) to Kissileff's data, 80% of all drinking was meal associated. These two studies have similar results, except for the absence of within-meal (intrameal) drinking in Kissileff's study, possibly because the "paw-sized" or quantal nature of the food items promoted more sustained feeding.

De Castro (1989) examined spontaneous food and water intakes in rats and again found that fluid intake was determined primarily by food intake. Zorilla et al. (2005) examined definitions for meals and provided an analysis in which drinking behavior was considered an integral or explicit part of feeding. Of relevance to the present discussion, rats took a mean of 4.7 pauses per night for drinking within nocturnal meals (i.e., about half of the meals), with 1.9 mL mean water intake in these pauses. Fitzsimons and Le Magnen (1969) considered several potential explanations for the prandial nature of ad libitum drinking, one of which was pure coincidence. That could mean that both eating and drinking are under the control of a common factor, such as an activity rhythm or oscillator, and the analysis of Zorilla et al. (2005) is consistent with this theoretical position. However, as I review below, there are limitations to the generality of this hypothesis.

Several investigators have approached the issue of synchrony of food and water intake by measuring drinking patterns when food was available only at restricted times. An extreme example is complete food deprivation. Rats typically drink 25–85% of their normal intake when food is absent (e.g., Fitzsimons & Le Magnen, 1969; Nicolaïdis & Rowland, 1975), which is considerably more than the nonprandial water intake under free-feeding conditions. Oatley (1971) found that the temporal pattern of drinking was unchanged during a 24-hour period without food, and, since this intake is well in excess of biological need, he proposed it is a manifestation of an underlying mechanism (e.g., oscillator) generating drinking in a programmed sequence independent of feeding. This does not refute a common timing mechanism for food and water intakes mentioned above, but it shows that feeding is not necessary for operation of the drinking mechanism. Oatley (1971) further examined patterns of drinking when food was spaced evenly through the 24-hour period either by delivery of 0.65 g every hour or 1.62 g every 2.4 hours. Food was consumed comparably rapidly at each meal delivery, but drinking remained 70–75% nocturnal; another way of stating this is that the water-to-food ratio at night was threefold higher than during the day. Further, while each meal was still accompanied by drinking, many drinking bouts occurred at times remote from meals. Johnson and Johnson (1991a) performed a similar study, with meals presented every two hours, and also found mainly nocturnal drinking; the probability of drinking with a meal was about 0.4 during the day and about 0.9 at night. Fitzsimons and Le Magnen (1969) came to a similar conclusion in rats fed for either two 1-hour periods or one 2-hour period during the daytime. Under these conditions in which large meal sizes developed over several days on the schedule, only 40% of water intake was associated with meals. Zucker (1971) reexamined this result using two daytime meals but with the second either right before lights out or in the middle of the day. In the latter protocol, only 15% of water intake occurred during the night (i.e., mostly near the food times), whereas in the former protocol 30% of water was consumed at night, presumably because it included some of the drinking associated with the second meal. Oatley's (1971) conclusion that the pattern of drinking is independent of eating thus has limited generality (see Kissileff, 1973, for additional concerns).

Morris and Mogenson (1980) examined the percentage of food and water consumed during the day and night phases under both ad libitum conditions and when a daily food ration was equally divided between day and night. Under ad libitum conditions, they found that both food and water intake rose to about 90% nocturnal during the age range 25–50 days, but after that age food became less nocturnal (about 70% by six months of age), whereas drinking remained 90% nocturnal (Figure 7.1, panel D). Thus, the higher water-to-food ratio at night mentioned previously has a developmental or maturational time course. Likewise, when food intake was equalized between day and night, young rats decreased their nocturnal intake (to about 70%) while older rats maintained 90%. Drinking behavior may become progressively less dependent upon eating during the first half of the rat's life span.

The above examples of temporal decoupling of food and water intake are all experimenter imposed. Would the same happen if restriction were imposed by the animal itself? Marwine and Collier (1979) examined this using a protocol in which rats were required to emit effort in the form of lever presses to gain access to water. This study was described in some detail in Chapter 2, so only the main result will be recapitulated here. When the effort or cost to access water was low, drinking occurred with almost every meal. However, as the effort or cost to access water increased, far fewer drinking bouts were initiated per day but the size of the bouts increased so that total water intake was relatively constant. The number of meals per day remained constant so that, at high water access effort, many meals occurred without drinking. Further, at low costs, 40% of the drinking bouts were categorized as postmeal, 25% premeal, and 20% within meal, a total (85%) that is consistent with the ad libitum patterns described previously. In contrast, at high cost of access, premeal bouts were predominant, suggesting that drinking was initiated by systemic dehydration and disinhibited feeding with relatively short latency, an apparently different mechanism than occurs under ad libitum or low-effort circumstances.

The amount of water consumed per day depends in part on the composition of the food consumed. Radford (1959) pointed out that different foods contain different amounts of preformed water as well as water to be recovered from oxidative metabolism. In rats fed chow, feces contain 70% water and account for about 25% of the water lost per day, whereas on purified (low-fiber) diets, that loss is much smaller. Thus, the overall water-to-food ratio will be diet dependent, but it will also vary with the electrolyte content. In general, adding water to food decreases the water consumed, but not to zero. For example, rats eating chow moistened with an equal weight of water for one hour at the start of the night after daytime food deprivation consumed 8.9 g food and 1.6 mL water (Rowland, 1995). When adjusted to dry food weight, the intake was 4.45 g chow and 6.05 mL water, or a water-to-food ratio of 1.36. In contrast, rats fed dry food in the same protocol ate 5.5 g and drank 3.5 mL, with a water-to-food ratio of 0.64. Rats consuming liquid diets likewise continue to drink water; for example, Kissileff (1973) found that rats drank a mean of 20 mL water per day while eating 42 mL of a diluted sweet condensed milk diet. However, water intake was only 4 mL perday in rats fed only fruit and vegetables for two days (Nicolaïdis & Rowland, 1975), possibly due to differences in fiber content and/or absorption rate compared to the liquid diet.

Fitzsimons and Le Magnen (1969) examined the prandial structure of drinking when rats were switched from a high-carbohydrate to a high-protein diet with low and high water requirements, respectively. The total water consumed and water-to-food ratio increased by roughly

50% on the first and subsequent days after the switch, but the fraction of water that was meal associated decreased from 82% before the switch to 48% on the first day after the switch, and several days were required for the additional water to become synchronized with meals. Lucas et al. (1989) manipulated the timing of access to water after spontaneous meals. Postprandial bouts increased in size as a result of the experience that water would later be withheld, but no preprandial drinking appeared in anticipation of restricted access.

Another way to increase water requirements of a diet is to add NaCl. Collier et al. (1991) added four levels of NaCl (0.5, 2, 3, or 4%) to a purified ingredient diet. Rats accessed the food by emitting a small procurement cost (10 lever presses), which served to stabilize the number of meals per day at about five with mean size 3–4 g throughout the study. The critical dependent variable was the effort or cost of water, which was available for 20 licks – the authors called this a sip – upon completion of a fixed ratio of lever presses (5–40 in five steps each for 10 days). Each sip yielded, on average, 0.13 mL and sips were usually clustered into bouts. The average water-to-food ratio for the respective diets was 0.9, 1.1, 1.5, and 2.8 mL/g and was independent of the cost per sip. The number of drinking bouts per day was 11–12 (i.e., two bouts per meal across 24 h) at the 0.5% and 2% salt levels, rising to 15 bouts per day (three per meal) with 4% NaCl added. Temporal patterns of water bouts were not analyzed in relation to meals, but the fact that the number of bouts increased with salt level while the meal number remained unchanged suggests that the added bouts were not prandial. Salt added to food also increases fluid intake and the water-to-food ratio by a physiologically adequate amount under conditions in which acute intracellular dehydration (i.e., injection or infusion of hypertonic NaCl) does not produce short-latency drinking. Three examples are shown in Figure 7.2. The first is when water is available via intragastric self-injection (Kissileff, 1973). The second is when the fluid available has been chronically adulterated with quinine (Nicolaïdis & Rowland, 1975). And the third is representative of neurological damage (zona incerta lesions; Rowland et al., 1979). None of these studies measured patterns of food and water intake, but it is reasonable to assume that most of the food intake was distributed through the night and that the nature of the osmotic load from the diet (e.g., onset, duration, and nycthemeral timing) thus differs substantially from acute primary thirst treatments.

It is likely that most species show meal-associated drinking under permissive conditions (Blair-West & Brook, 1969; Gregersen, 1932; Kutscher, 1969), although the details apparently differ between species and depend on the meal size and composition. Some of these differences

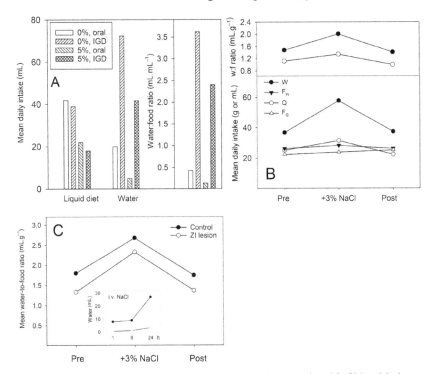

Figure 7.2 Increased water-to-food ratio in rats when NaCl is added to the food. Panel A (from Kissileff, 1973) shows rats fed a liquid diet with NaCl added (5%) or not (0%). Additionally, rats had water to drink either orally or via intragastric self-administration (IGD). The left bars show 24 h food intake, the middle bars the concurrent water intake, and the right bars the derived water-to-food ratio. Panel B (from Nicolaïdis & Rowland, 1975) shows the effect of chronic exposure to quinine-flavored water on response to added NaCl. The lower panel shows mean food (F) or fluid (W = water, Q = quinine), and the upper panel shows associated fluid-to-food ratio for regular chow in the pre- and postdays, and a 3-day average when 3% NaCl was added to the ground chow diet. Panel C (from Rowland et al., 1979) shows water intakes of control and zona incerta (ZI) lesion rats during a similar 2-day treatment with 3% NaCl added to chow. Inset shows ZI lesion rats did not drink to i.v. NaCl infusion.

will be considered in Chapter 11. Towbin (1955) allowed dogs to eat dry food ad libitum for six hours per day and found that daily water intake was highly correlated with food intake. The data suggest dogs may have taken about eight drinks per day with a mean size of about 75 mL, but the coincidence of such drinks with meals was not recorded.

7.3   Meal-Associated Drinking: Mechanism

In this section, I will discuss the potential mechanisms underlying food-associated drinking, mostly in rats. It is first important to review the passage of food and fluid through the gut in relation to eating. In a seminal study, Lepkovsky et al. (1957) showed that the gastric contents of rats eating dry food was about 50% water, with the fraction rising to 75% in the intestinal lumen. They state that the intestinal lumen "acts as though it were a part of the internal environment" (p. 327), and in particular a water reservoir of considerable capacity. Armstrong et al. (1978) found that the stomach content of rats fed ad libitum rose through the night and fell during the daytime, but at all times there was moist food in the stomach. The food content of the first 40 cm of intestine showed little nycthemeral variation. It follows that spontaneous meals always enter a partly filled upper gastrointestinal tract. When rats were deprived of food for two hours at the start of the night, while the stomach was relatively empty, the distal small intestine was still quite full (Wiepkema et al., 1972). At this time, the cecum contained about 1 g dry matter and 4 g water. Even after 24 hours of deprivation, the cecum contained 2 g water. By adding dye to food, these authors also showed that food from a meal was rapidly propelled far down the small intestine and mixed with still unabsorbed food from previous meals. To study entry of water into the gut, Oatley and Toates (1969) allowed food-deprived rats to eat for 30 minutes without water available and then sacrificed the rats at various times to measure food and fluid in the gut. They found that 70% of the food remained in the stomach for three hours and was associated with uptake into the stomach and upper intestine of about 1 mL water per gram of dry food. Rowland (1995) sacrificed rats after allowing them to eat (but not drink) for 15 minutes at the start of the night after daytime food deprivation. The rats ate a mean of 1.7 g chow, and the wet and dry weights of the stomach 15 minutes after the start of that meal were 3.2 and 1.2 g, respectively. Corresponding weights in unfed rats were 0.27 and 0.04 g. Thus, at about the time a spontaneous-sized meal ends, most of that food is still in the stomach and is associated with approximately its weight in water. Rowland (1995) also included rats that ate a 1:1 chow-to-water mixture for 15 minutes and found that while 6.4 g of the wet food was consumed, the wet stomach weight was 10.4 g. The fluid in the gut thus is not all drawn osmotically from plasma but presumably derives mainly from saliva or digestive secretions.

It is difficult to measure the salivary rate of rats while they are eating, but this has been accomplished in sheep with 2.7 mL saliva secreted per gram of dry chaff (Stacy & Warner, 1966). An estimate of the salivary contribution in rats can be made by examining the water intake of rats whose salivary glands have been removed. As noted previously, these rats exhibit a pattern of intrameal prandial drinking, and the overall water-to-food ratio is elevated two- to threefold above that of intact rats (Kissileff, 1969a). However, this may exceed the amount needed to swallow food because pellet-paired intraoral infusions of varying amounts of water produced complete cessation of oral drinking in salivaless rats when the injected volume was about 80% of their intake without oral infusions (Kissileff, 1969b). Based on these data, it is feasible that about 1 mL saliva is secreted for every gram of dry food consumed by rats and so accounts for the fluid in the stomach that occurs with meals, but we cannot discount an additional contribution from gastric secretions. That food then holds at least an equivalent amount of water during transit through the digestive system; it constitutes a substantial fluid reservoir that is not often considered in studies of systemic fluid regulation.

It has frequently been asserted that meal-associated drinking, at least in free-feeding rats, occurs too rapidly during or after a meal for physiological signals of dehydration to have occurred (Fitzsimons, 1979) – hence, its designation as secondary or anticipatory drinking. The evidence reviewed above shows that a substantial amount of fluid is translocated, initially from secretory glands, into the gut contemporaneously with feeding. The question then becomes not whether dehydration occurs rapidly but rather whether the resulting signals of dehydration have reached a critical or threshold value before the meal ends. In sheep, which have particularly copious prandial salivary secretion when eating dry chaff, Blair-West and Brook (1969) found that rapid eaters had a two- to fourfold elevation in plasma renin concentration within 30 minutes of the onset of eating. This was due to a large drop in plasma volume, and it was accompanied by a rise in blood pressure and renal conservation of Na^+ and water. These changes did not occur in intermittent or slow eaters or when fed lucerne, a more hydrated food. When the drop in plasma volume during a chaff meal was prevented by intravenous infusion at a rate and ionic composition similar to saliva, the rise in plasma renin did not occur. And in rats adapted to eat for one hour per day, eating a large meal for one hour without water present led to a 50% increase in plasma ANG II concentration, as well as a 5% increase in plasma Na^+ concentration (Mann et al., 1980). Kraly and Corneilson (1990) measured food and water intake over one hour after 24 hours of food deprivation and found that the water-to-food ratio was increased by a low dose of captopril and reduced by a high dose of captopril. This suggests that ANG II action in the brain mediates, at least in part, drinking associated with the large meal. However, these protocols do not fully address mechanisms that might be engaged by smaller, ad libitum meals.

Kraly (1984a) provided convincing evidence that physiological changes during spontaneous meals in rats are sufficient to explain meal-associated drinking. It was known that food in the stomach causes mucosal release of histamine, and that this activates local vagal afferent endings and may also engage histamine receptors in the kidney to release renin. In rats eating a spontaneous meal early in the night, Kraly showed that combined pharmacological blockade of H1 and H2 receptors abolished premeal drinking and reduced postmeal drinking by more than 60% (Kraly & Specht, 1984) This pharmacological block also abolished drinking caused by exogenous administration of histamine, but it had no effect on other types of drinking, including that induced by ANG II or after water deprivation. Using sham feeding in rats equipped with gastric fistulas so that no absorption occurred, Kraly (1984b) showed that pregastric or gastric stimulation was sufficient to engage this histaminergic mechanism. Food-deprived, sham-feeding rats consumed 62 mL liquid diet and 10 mL water in a one-hour test; pretreatment with the histamine H1 and H2 receptor antagonist combination blocked the water intake by more than 90% but had no effect on food consumption. Further, subdiaphragmatic vagotomy abolished this water intake without significant effect on liquid diet consumption, showing the critical participation of vagal afferents in this cascade. These data do not exclude the possible involvement of other locally acting factors, perhaps including bradykinin (Rowland & Fregly, 1997), although the latter has not been studied within the context of eating.

The aforementioned study by Kraly and Corneilson (1990), although in a large meal protocol, suggested that prandial histamine release – via vagal afferents to the brain stem and outputs to the kidney and/or by local action in the kidney – causes release of renin and formation of circulating ANG II (Radke et al., 1986). To show that this may occur in a small meal protocol, Rowland (1995) allowed rats to eat for 15 minutes early in the night after a daytime fast and found that a mean intake of 3.2 g dry chow produced a twofold rise in PRA at the end of these 15 min. Thus, ANG II is a likely contributor to drinking during or immediately after small meals. It should be noted that the small meal or spontaneous eating protocols used by Kraly and Rowland were conducted early in the night when feeding and drinking are normally high; the threshold for drinking to dipsogens may well be at their nycthemeral lowest at this time (Johnson & Johnson, 1990b). As noted previously, the finding by Johnson and Johnson (1991a) that equal-sized meals spaced every two hours had at least twice the probability of associated drinking at night compared with the day implies that the proposed histamine–ANG II cascade may be less engaged and/or effective during the day than at night. In a study examining dipsogenic effects of intravenously administered ANG II in rats, Hsiao et al. (1977) reported no significant difference in water intake (using a suprathreshold dose of 16 ng/min or ~40 pmol/kg/min) in tests early in the day or night, although the respective mean intakes were 1.0 and 1.6 mL; analysis of drinking thresholds might have revealed a higher sensitivity at night. Extrapolating from the findings of Mann et al. (1980), the 16 ng/min dose of ANG II would have produced plasma ANG II levels about fourfold above baseline. However, Hsiao et al. (1977) found that pretreatment with a low, nondipsogenic dose of NaCl lowered the drinking threshold for ANG II to 4 ng/min (10 pmol/kg/min), which would have produced about a twofold increase of plasma ANG II levels, similar to the fractional increase in PRA after a small meal (Rowland, 1995). Thus, this increase in PRA or inferred ANG II would be dipsogenic, especially if it occurred in the context of a subthreshold (i.e., <2%) hyperosmolality. Although the site of action of this ANG II is not known definitively, recall that OVLT lesions disrupt meal-associated drinking (Bealer & Johnson, 1980).

Collecting evidence for osmotic changes during small meals is difficult for at least two reasons. First, the effect may not involve changes in the general circulation, but instead local effects in the hepatic portal or other system. Such peripheral osmoreception is treated in Chapter 4. Second, systemic changes of 2% or less are often at the limits of experimental detection. In a study using serial blood samples in free-feeding pigs, no change in plasma osmolality was detected following spontaneous meals. There were 5% increases in plasma protein concentration and hematocrit ratio after meals (Houpt & Anderson, 1990). In rats eating the first of a cluster of 1.5 g dry chow meals offered on a 22-hour food deprivation schedule, Deaux et al. (1970) found that plasma osmolality was increased by 3.6% at the moment of initiation of drinking, which occurred 5.5 minutes after the start of that meal. It is thus plausible that increased plasma osmolality could contribute to drinking immediately after even small meals taken on an empty stomach.

Some studies attempted to approach the problem using meal-paired parenteral administration of fluids; the rationale is that such infusions should negate or prevent changes due to the meal itself. Kissileff (1969b) programmed intragastric infusions of water with each 45 mg pellet eaten by rats fed ad libitum. As the volume per injection was increased, oral water intake decreased and fell to zero when the total infused per day was only slightly above daily baseline water intake without infusion. Intraoral infusions produced a similar effect. Rowland and Nicolaïdis (1976) found a different result, and meal-paired intragastric or intravenous water infusions were only about 50% effective in suppressing oral intake. They attributed the difference to the fact that Kissileff had used a nasogastric catheter, which does not eliminate oral sensations (Altar & Carlisle, 1979; Holman, 1969), whereas they had used a catheter introduced through the abdomen. To verify that other differences in test procedure did not underlie the discrepancy, Rowland and Nicolaïdis (1976) replicated Kissileff's result using a nasogastric catheter. In hindsight, prandial water infusions by any route would not be expected to interfere substantially with the histamine–ANG II mechanism described above, so any suppression of drinking by meal-paired water administration would impact primarily an osmometric mechanism. Overhydration (hypo-osmolality) may eventually inhibit any prandial ANG-related drinking, but none of these studies measured plasma osmolality or PRA that would have allowed a direct assessment of this possibility.

In summary, meals cause rapid systemic hypovolemia and hyperosmolality. The magnitude of these changes are dependent on the water content of the food, its composition, and the size of the meal. It is feasible that even the small changes in osmolality of volume (and/or ANG II) can combine to exceed a threshold for drinking, although this has not been proven directly. The amount of water consumed during or after ad libitum meals occurs in small bouts, and the probability of their occurrence may be influenced by nycthemeral factors to be discussed below.

7.4   Nycthemeral Rhythms

Many authors use the term *circadian rhythms* when addressing time-of-day factors, but since most of their studies are performed in an environment with a 24-hour light–dark cycle, the involvement of a true endogenous circadian mechanism is inferred rather than demonstrated. To avoid overinterpretation, I will use the term *nycthemeral* when referring to time-of-day differences or rhythms. When relevant, for comparison between certain studies, I have converted times of day to Zeitgeber time (ZT) where ZT0 is lights on and ZT12 is lights off; thus, ZT0–12 is the light phase and ZT12–24 is the dark phase.

I previously distinguished the processes of drinking threshold, maintenance, and termination (Rolls et al., 1980). This distinction is particularly important in considering whether and how the time of day affects water intake. As exemplified in work on osmotic thirst in humans during pregnancy (Chapter 6), an altered threshold does not necessarily produce altered water intake or vasopressin (AVP) secretion. Further, both threshold and maintenance may be affected by actual or anticipated environmental dangers, such as during the light phase for a nocturnal species. Finally, mechanisms that terminate drinking, including feedback from oral or gastric sensors, might have different sensitivities at different times of day. As I will review below, numerous studies have found nycthemeral differences in the amount of water consumed either spontaneously or in association with dipsogenic stimuli, yet few have tried to address which of the aforementioned processes is or are involved. Thus, unless a particular result addresses or favors one process over another, I will not make specific attribution because it remains an open question.

In humans, although a relationship between nycthemeral and ultradian (typically, a few hours) sleep/activity rhythms and drinking has been made, including rhythms in PRA (Brandenberger et al., 1985), it should be noted that all of the human laboratory studies, including those that have assessed osmotic drinking (Chapter 3) thresholds, have been performed in the morning hours – presumably for logistical reasons. In a study designed to emulate normative eating and drinking patterns, Perrier et al. (2013) performed a residential laboratory study of humans (average age 24.8 years, mostly females) who, on the basis of preexperimental diaries of daily fluid intake, had been divided into low and high drinking groups. During the five-day study period, meals were provided at 0800, 1200, and 2000 hours and a snack at 1600 hours. For the low drinker group, 0.25 L water was provided at each of these times for a daily total of 1L. For the high drinker group, 0.5 L water was provided at each of these times with 0.25 L supplements at 1400 and 2200 hours, for a total of 2.5 L. There were no time-of-day differences in plasma or salivary osmolality, or between the low and high drinker groups, but urine production showed a nycthemeral rhythm (highest in the afternoon) and was substantially greater and with lower osmolality in the high drinkers. After two days, the water conditions were reversed for a final three days. Urinary adjustments matched to the new intake were complete within the first 24 hours. This study suggests there is no change in osmoregulatory set point with time of day. It is likely, however, that there are cultural or other effects: Athanasatou et al. (2019) reported that the fluid intake and urinary output of females in Greece were highest during the first six hours of the day.

In rats, as indicated earlier in this chapter, water intake is largely nocturnal and in part coupled with food intake. One possible explanation for this effect is that illumination has a suppressive effect on drinking and/ or other active behaviors. This hypothesis has been tested by comparing water intakes of rats housed in continuous illumination (LL) with those on a light–dark (LD) cycle (Gutman et al., 1969; Stephan & Zucker,

1972a, 1972b; Stoynev & Ikonomov, 1983). Each study found a modest (about 20%) suppression of 24-hour intakes in LL, and evidence of a free-running circadian rhythm with periodicity 25–26 hours. On the basis of changes in urinary parameters, Gutman et al. (1969) suggested that illumination may suppress the activity or sensitivity of osmoreceptors. The critical role of the suprachiasmatic nucleus in these rhythms was shown by the fact that its complete bilateral ablation abolished nycthemeral rhythms of food and water intake in an LD cycle, but an attenuated rhythm in urinary electrolyte excretion persisted (Stephan & Zucker, 1972a; Stoynev et al., 1982).

To determine whether drinking induced by specific dehydrating stimuli may differ with time of day, Oatley (1967a) imposed various durations of food deprivation in rats ending at specified times of day or night. The results (Figure 7.3, panel A) show that water intake was a function of food consumed during the water deprivation period and not the time of day of the test. Oatley concluded, "These results do not suggest or necessitate any hypothesis that the drinking controller has an intrinsic diurnal oscillation, or that it is influenced by a biological clock" (1967a, p. 185). Oatley (1967b) then showed that one-hour water intakes in response to various concentrations of hypertonic NaCl (2 mL/rat i.p. or ~7 mL/kg, yielding doses ranging from approximately 2.4 to 12.0 mEq/kg) were not systematically influenced by time of day of the injection (Figure 7.3, panel B). Both of these studies used hooded (non-albino) rats kept in a 12:12 LD cycle and a within-subjects design with randomized order of testing.

Johnson and Johnson (1990b) measured the spontaneous 24-hour drinking patterns of rats (Figure 7.3 panel C). Food intake was not measured but presumably had a good correlation with the drink pattern. Rats were then injected with various doses of hypertonic saline (10 mL/kg and 3.4–10.9 mEq/kg, s.c.) at either the nadir (ZT3) or peak (ZT12) of the spontaneous profile. At all doses, injections near the start of the active period (ZT12) produced 60% more drinking compared with the early light phase (ZT3; Figure 7.3, panel D). They also found that leaving the lights on for the ZT12 test did not affect the higher intake at this time, suggesting that light suppression does not account for the lower intake at ZT3. There were no differences in plasma Na^+ or osmolality at the time of injection that could explain this result. Johnson and Johnson (1991b) subsequently showed, in rats with free-running circadian rhythms in a constant light (LL) environment, increased osmotic thirst occurred specifically during the active phase compared with the inactive phase. Like Oatley (1967b), the Johnson and Johnson (1990b) study was within subjects but used albino rats, which may be more

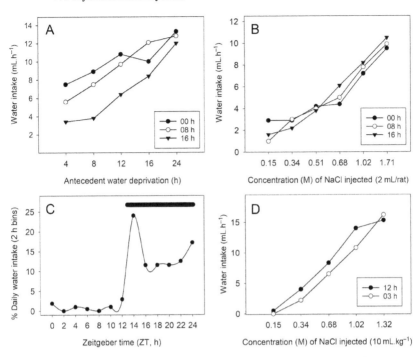

Figure 7.3 Time-of-day factors in drinking of rats. Panel A (from Oatley, 1967a) shows mean 1 h water intake following different durations of water deprivation ending at the circadian times shown. Panel B (from Oatley, 1967b) shows mean 1 h water intake following i. p. injection of different concentrations of NaCl solution (2 mL/rat). Panels C and D are from Johnson and Johnson (1990b). Panel C shows spontaneous drinking patterns of rats, averaged over several rats and day, expressed as percentage total daily intake in each 2 h bin; horizontal bar shows dark period. Panel D shows water intake in the first hour after s.c. injection of various concentrations of NaCl (10 mL.kg^{-1}) either in the early light phase (ZT03) or at the start of the night (ZT12).

light-sensitive than hooded rats. Comparison of panels B and D in Figure 7.3 reveals that the amount of water consumed was systematically higher in the Johnson and Johnson (1990b) study. This is consistent with the finding of Fregly et al. (1990) that albino rats (Sprague-Dawley) drank about twice as much in two hours after hypertonic NaCl injection than hooded rats (Long-Evans). In contrast, urinary excretion of the NaCl load was slightly (15%) greater in Long-Evans rats. Whether the time-of-day effect described by Johnson and Johnson (1990a) is restricted to albino rats that are particularly light-sensitive might be important to address. There are other strain differences that might indirectly contribute to the observed effects. For example, albino rat strains are generally more docile and easy to handle than hooded strains, which may produce additional stress during injection procedures in the latter, resulting in nonspecific suppression of drinking. This could, in part, be overcome using intravenous infusions.

Rats in the Oatley (1967b) and Johnson and Johnson (1990b) studies drank at the lowest dose of NaCl at all times of testing, suggesting that the threshold for drinking does not differ markedly with time of day. In another study, Johnson and Johnson (1991a) reported that meals of fixed size taken during the day had about 50% lower probability of being accompanied by drinking compared with the same meals at night. Unlike the osmotic drinking study, this result is consistent with an interpretation that the threshold for drinking may be lower at night than during the day. Again, intravenous infusions may be the best way to resolve this question.

Intravenous infusions of ANG II have been used to address the question of threshold. Hsiao et al. (1977) infused ANG II at 16 ng/min to rats either during the day or during the night using a within-subject design. They reported that the mean intakes at day and night were 1.6 and 1.0 mL, but this difference did not reach statistical significance. Corresponding latencies to drink were 12 and 10 minutes, respectively. However, in a dose-response study performed during the day, these authors found this dose of ANG II produced drinking in only 75% of rats (mean intake of 2.5 mL in drinkers), but in the time-of-day study, no mention was made of the percentage responding. Without that information, it is difficult to fully accept the authors' conclusion that time-of-day factors are definitively not involved.

The essential role of physiological rhythms in time-of-day behavioral differences was underscored in a study by Barney et al. (1995). Noting that core body temperature has a pronounced nycthemeral rhythm in rodents with night levels about 2°C higher than during the day (e.g., for rats, Satinoff et al., 1982; for mice, Castillo et al., 2005; Connolly & Lynch, 1981), they reasoned that thermoregulatory adjustments might likewise be dependent on time of day. Different groups of rats, housed in a 12–12 LD cycle, were exposed at six different times of day (starting at ZT0, 4, 8, 12, 16, 20) for three hours to either 25°C or 40°C, followed 15 minutes later by a two-hour drinking period at 25°C. Lights were on and food was absent throughout the exposure and drink periods. The results are shown in Figure 7.4. The majority of fluid lost during heat exposure was evaporative – due to saliva spreading and panting (see Chapter 9) – but was lowest (50 mL/kg) during exposures starting at

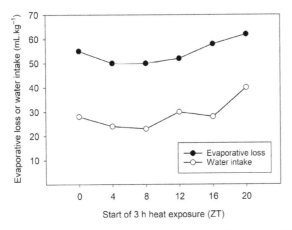

Figure 7.4 Effect of time of day on thermally induced drinking in rats (from Barney et al., 1995). Shown are the 3 h evaporative water losses during 3 h exposure to 40°C starting at the ZT indicated, and the 2 h water intakes following exposure.

ZT4 and 8 and was highest (62 mL/kg) at ZT20. This may be because core temperature was higher at the latter time and more evaporative cooling was necessary to prevent lethal hyperthermia. Water intake showed a similar rhythm, lowest at ZT8 and highest at ZT20 (23 and 40 mL/kg, respectively; note that the actual drinking periods started 3 h after these ZTs). Rats drank about 50% of their fluid losses in all tests. The almost twofold difference in the drinking response may best be viewed as secondary to an endogenous nycthemeral rhythm of body temperature.

There are conditions of brain damage or other factors that seem to enhance the importance of nycthemeral factors in drinking. When rats with lesions of the lateral hypothalamus recover adequate spontaneous drinking, it is all nocturnal and meal associated (Kissileff, 1969a; Rowland 1976a). Such animals did not drink following daytime injections of hypertonic NaCl or other dipsogens, or in the absence of food, so it was widely believed they had lost controls of primary drinking. However, Rowland (1976a) showed that after daytime injections these rats drank during the subsequent night, whereas when injected during the night they drank within a few hours. Median latencies to drink after injection at ZT0 or ZT12 were 11 hours and 0.5 hours, respectively. Lesion rats with enucleation showed free-running rhythms of drinking, with a similar dependence on whether the injection was at the start of their active or inactive periods, thus suggesting the response to NaCl was due to an endogenous clock-related process and not light suppression. Coburn and Stricker (1978) and Gardiner and Stricker (1985) then found a similar effect in rats with lesions of the lateral preoptic area or median preoptic nucleus (MnPO), respectively. The so-called drinking deficits in such rats are heavily modulated by the phase of an endogenous oscillator. The mechanism for such dependence was unknown at the time of those studies.

The direct influence of circadian oscillation by the suprachiasmatic nucleus on fluid regulatory neurons in the OVLT was investigated in an elegant study by Gizowski et al. (2016). They started with the finding that many studies in rodents (but not all; e.g., see Possidente & Birnbaum, 1979; Rowland et al., 2015; Tabarin et al., 2007) find a bimodal nycthemeral distribution of drinking and other behaviors (Johnson et al., 2003; Spiteri, 1982). Pigmented C57BL/6 mice show peaks in water intake early in the night (ZT12–14) and again at the end of the night (ZT23–24), with a preceding period (ZT20–22) of substantially less drinking (Figure 7.5, panel A). Compared with mice allowed to show this normal drinking peak at ZT23–24, mice prevented from drinking at that time had a 1% higher plasma osmolality and 2.5% lower volume at the end of the subsequent day period (ZT10). The authors suggest that the late-night drinking is anticipatory of and prevents dehydration during the subsequent day, although I caution that the degree of dehydration is subthreshold for drinking and the term *anticipatory* has perhaps unwarranted cognitive implications. In any event, the ingested water is most likely sequestered in the gastrointestinal tract as an internal reservoir (Gizowski et al., 2018). It was further shown that AVP neurons in the outer shell of the suprachiasmatic nucleus project to the OVLT and release AVP at times of peak drinking. Optogenetic activation of these neurons during the low drinking period (ZT20–22) caused drinking comparable to the normal peak at ZT23–24 while optogenetic inhibition of these cells during ZT23–24 prevented the normal drinking peak (Figure 7.5, panel B).

We must now ask the question whether the dichotomy between primary drinking and secondary drinking proposed some 50 years ago is or ever was a viable distinction. I have reviewed evidence that meal-associated drinking produces physiological signals soon enough to account for much if not all meal-associated drinking and, conversely, that output signals from the master clock (i.e., suprachiasmatic nucleus) impinge directly on osmoreceptive elements in the OVLT. This neuroanatomical arrangement again raises the question about whether it is the initiation/thresholds or maintenance/termination aspects of drinking that

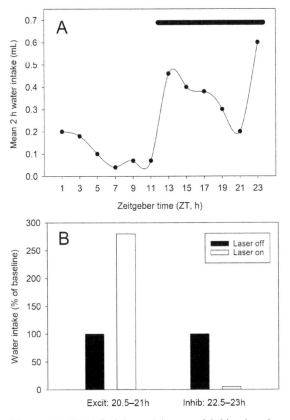

Figure 7.5 End-of-night anticipatory drinking in mice and dependence on vasopressin inputs to OVLT (from Gizowski et al., 2016). Panel A shows mean spontaneous water intakes of mice expressed as 2 h averages as a function of ZT; horizontal bar denotes dark phase. In panel B, left bars show that blue laser stimulation of vasopressin projections during the low drinking period greatly increases water intake. Right bars show that yellow laser inhibition of these projections during the peak drinking period abolishes water intake.

are so affected. Earlier, I noted that body temperature was higher at night than by day. It has been found that an increase of intracellular calcium in human embryonic kidney (HEK) cells transfected with the putative osmoreceptor cation channel TRPV1 is temperature sensitive, almost 30% higher at 36°C compared with 40°C (Nishihara et al., 2011). Further, in cells from rat supraoptic nuclei, application of the TRPV1 agonist, capsaicin, triggered cationic currents and increased intracellular calcium at 36°C but not at 24°C (Moriya et al., 2014). Thus, operation of osmoreceptive mechanisms may be temperature dependent.

Allen et al. (2017) engineered mice to permanently express the fluorescent marker *td*-tomato in neurons that expressed Fos-ir following water deprivation. These mice were subsequently exposed to 40°C for four hours and then sacrificed. In the MnPO, Fos was induced by the heat exposure in a population of cells that were intermingled but not overlapping with those expressing *td*-tomato. In this protocol, it is likely – but was not measured – that the core temperature of mice increased above 40°C and that they became dehydrated (see Chapter 8). While not identical to water deprivation, thermal exposure will cause primarily intracellular but some extracellular depletion, so why different sets of cells might be engaged by the two stimuli would not be predicted on the basis of fluid deficits alone. Instead, core temperature and/or thermal afferents from the periphery could be causing different subsets of cells to be activated by equivalent dehydrations. This is pure speculation, but collectively these observations imply that study of tissue temperature on lamina terminalis excitability and function may be warranted.

7.5   Summary

In free-feeding animals, including humans, most daily water consumption is prandial, occurring during or soon after meals. In contrast to earlier interpretations, it now appears that this drinking has a systemic basis and is not purely anticipatory. Those systemic changes include small increases in osmolality, especially in hepatic portal regions, or decreased plasma volume with increase in plasma ANG II, and together these may be suprathreshold for initiation of drinking. In addition, release of histamine during eating may promote prandial drinking. Because feeding and thus associated drinking normally has a species-typical nycthemeral rhythm, studies of drinking at different times of day are potentially informative. Despite many studies in this regard, it is not fully clear whether osmotic (and/or volumetric) mechanisms for initiation of drinking, and/or termination of drinking, have different thresholds at different times of day. Recent work has shown a direct pathway from the suprachiasmatic nucleus (master clock) to the OVLT, which suggests at least the potential for direct clock influences on osmoregulation. I speculate that nycthemeral changes in body temperature may also affect the sensitivity of osmoreceptive and/or other elements of the drinking circuitry in the brain.

8   Hybrid Dehydrations: Water Deprivation

8.1   Introduction

Water deprivation, meaning complete absence or withholding of water, is arguably the most natural antecedent of dehydration and thirst. Drinking after water deprivation may be studied formally in a laboratory or less formally in a natural environment. However, from physiological and neurobiological perspectives, it is a complex dehydration, as will be discussed below.

The physiological magnitude of dehydration is a function of the duration of deprivation, but it is not a linear function. As the duration of deprivation and attendant fluid loss increase, there are a spectrum of physiological countermeasures that are engaged to slow the rate of future water loss. Further, due to several nycthemeral factors (Chapter 7), the timing of the start and end of the deprivation period is of importance. Total deprivation of water may be a rare event in the natural environment because at least some of the foods available will contain significant amounts of water. Chronic restriction may thus be more common than total deprivation.

Food consumed during a period of water deprivation introduces two variables: the gain of water that is contained in the food and the loss of water due to excretion of solutes and other waste materials from that food. Characteristics of the food available during water deprivation thus greatly influence the rate of dehydration. Food is consumed according to either a schedule or a nycthemeral rhythm, and this will introduce a nonlinear temporal aspect to the dehydration process. Additionally, voluntary food intake diminishes as dehydration progresses, a phenomenon known as dehydration anorexia.

Water deprivation causes fluid to be lost from intracellular and extracellular fluid compartments. Each of these compartments has distinct sensory neural or hormonal signaling pathways (Chapters 3–5), and the resulting state is what I will term a *hybrid dehydration*. The term *double depletion* has also been used (Fitzsimons, 1979), but my use of the term *hybrid* invokes not only a mixture but also a result that may in some way (s) differ from the components. I will present some data in support of this position in subsequent parts of this chapter, but one simple difference is that dehydration thirst develops slowly with a passage of time, whereas the pure laboratory components of either intracellular or extracellular depletion are normally produced rapidly without natural antecedent circumstances.

As in previous chapters, I will also consider mammals ranging in size from humans to mice. Relative food intake or metabolic rate of different-size mammals introduces potential differences in the rate of dehydration. For example, a typical human weighs 70 kg and eats approximately 500 g or 7 g/kg dry food constituents (e.g., macronutrients and minerals) per day. In contrast, a typical laboratory mouse weighs 30 g and eats 3 g or 100 g/kg dry food constituents per day. Thus, relative to body weight and for similar dry food constituents, mice consume 14-fold more dehydrating components of food per day. Nonmammalian species have different mechanisms (see Chapter 11), but I will restrict this chapter to examples in a few well-studied mammals under laboratory conditions, including humans.

8.2   Solute Handling during Water Deprivation

The changes in body fluids during water deprivation, and hence in subsequent drinking, depend substantially on solute exchange during the deprivation period. It is important to start by reviewing these exchanges, which fall into two now-familiar categories, input and output.

8.2.1   Solute Avoidance: Dehydration Anorexia

Elective solute input originates in food and is determined by the composition, including water content of that food, and the amount consumed. Many animals in a natural arid habitat may rarely drink free water but instead derive all of their water from food and its metabolism. In the laboratory, the type of food may also vary between species and laboratories. When only low-moisture (<10%) or "dry" food is presented, most species show progressively reduced food intake – dehydration anorexia – but with varying magnitudes and time courses. Sheep fed a daily ration of 0.8 kg dry chaff showed no anorexia for the first 24 hours of water deprivation but a small (<10%) decrease during hours 24–48 (McKinley et al., 1983). Dogs (Metzler et al., 1986; Ramsay et al., 1977a) and macaque monkeys (Wood et al., 1982) were fed a ration of moistened food once daily and showed no anorexia. On the other hand, rabbits fed ad libitum decreased intake of a relatively low-sodium diet by 20% during 24 hours of water deprivation (McKinley et al., 1983). Rats decreased dry food intake by 30–40% on the first day of water deprivation (Bealer et al., 1983; McKinley et al., 1983) and by substantially more on the second day. Mice reduced dry chow intake by 10% and 25% after 24 and 48 hours of water deprivation, respectively (Bekkevold et al., 2013); food intake recovered substantially during chronic water restriction (McKenna & Haines, 1981).

Schoorlemmer and Evered (2002) examined the early stages of dehydration anorexia in rats. They measured food intake every 15 minutes for the first 7.5 hours of the night with water either present or absent. Panel A of Figure 8.1 shows that food intake was reduced during the first hour and, at the end of 7.5 hours, food intake was 40% lower in the group without water. This was due entirely to smaller meal size without change in meal frequency. In another study, lasting six hours at the start of the night, rats were deprived of water but were infused continuously with water (1.67 mL/h) into either the stomach, jejunum, cecum, vena cava, or portal vein. The total infused volume (10 mL) was about 70% of the water intake (14.3 mL) of a group with water available. The six-hour food intake in the various conditions is shown in panel B of Figure 8.1. A group not infused showed a 30–40% reduction in food intake compared to the group with water. Dehydration anorexia was almost completely reversed by infusion into any part of the gastrointestinal tract, but it was unaffected by either venous infusion. This study shows that, at least in the early stages, dehydration anorexia is mediated by sensors in the gastrointestinal tract or mesentery, and not at the level of blood circulation.

This conclusion is consistent with a reinterpretation of a study on brain mechanisms of dehydration anorexia. Rolls (1975) made large bilateral lesions of the lateral preoptic hypothalamus of rats, and, following recovery from acute effects, a subset of these rats failed to drink acutely when injected with hypertonic NaCl. In contrast, injection of hypertonic saline (10 mEq/kg) to 24-hour food-deprived rats inhibited 30-minute food intake by about 75% in both sham-operated and lesioned rats. It follows that dehydration anorexia is mediated by receptor(s) or pathway(s) distinct from those mediating osmoregulatory drinking. Likewise, rats with knife-cut lesions posterior to the organum vasculosum of the lamina terminalis (OVLT) have impaired osmoregulation, including natriuresis during food deprivation, but their dehydration anorexia after 24 and 48 hours was comparable to intact controls (Bealer et al., 1983).

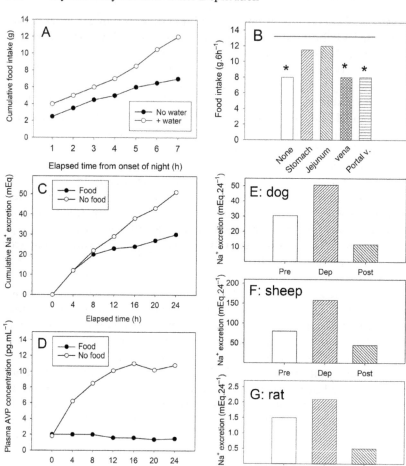

Figure 8.1 Effect of deprivation. Panel A (from Schoorlemmer & Evered, 2002) shows hourly cumulative dry food intake at the onset of the night in rats with and without water available. Intake of food-deprived rats was statistically lower at each time point. Panel B (from Schoorlemmer & Evered, 2002) shows food intake during the first 6 h of the night in rats without water available but infused into various body compartments. The horizontal line is intake with water available, and * denotes significantly less than this value. Panels C and D (from Metzler et al., 1986) show cumulative Na^+ excreted in urine and plasma AVP of dogs either fed a daily ration at t = 0 or fasted for 24 h. Panels E–G show mean urinary Na^+ excretion by dogs (Metzler et al., 1986), sheep, and rats (McKinley et al., 1983) over 24 h periods of baseline (pre), water deprivation (dep), and the following day (post).

There may be direct effects of dehydration on feeding circuits. Using a protocol in which rats were provided hypertonic saline (2.5%) only to drink for up to five days, progressive anorexia developed (Watts, 1999; Watts & Boyle, 2010). Across a wide range of durations of exposure, food intake was decreased by about 10% for each 1% increase in plasma osmolality. Peptide transmitters implicated in dehydration anorexia include corticotropin releasing factor, oxytocin, and nestafin (Rinaman et al., 2005; Watts, 2001; Yoshimura et al., 2014). Dehydration anorexia is reversed within a few minutes of drinking and is most likely mediated by preabsorptive mechanisms (Kakolewski & Deaux, 1970; Watts, 1999).

8.2.2   Solute Output: Natriuresis

For all species in which fluid balance studies have been performed, water deprivation is associated with a net increase in urinary Na^+ (natriuresis) and Cl^- (chloruresis) excretion (Luke, 1973; McKinley et al., 1983). K^+ excretion (kaliuresis) is less reliably increased. The net result of this natriuresis is to reduce the increase in plasma Na^+ concentration and osmolality that otherwise would occur, but at the expense of volume loss from plasma and various tissues. The magnitude of the natriuresis depends in part on the type and amount of food consumed during water deprivation.

Panel C of Figure 8.1 shows the time course of development of natriuresis in dogs that were fed at 0900 hours each day and quickly consumed their fixed ration of food containing 35 mEq Na^+, 110 mEq K^+, and 107 mL water (Metzler et al., 1986). In the water-deprived group, deprivation began at the time of meal presentation, and blood and urine samples (via catheters) were taken every 2–4 hours for 24 hours. In the nondeprived group, most of the natriuresis occurred in the eight hours after eating, whereas in the water-deprived group it continued throughout the 24 hours, for a net increase of 70%. Panel D of Figure 8.1 shows that the time (8–24 h) of increased natriuresis in the deprived group is associated with elevated levels of vasopressin (AVP). Panel E shows the 24-hour net Na^+ balance on the day before, the day of, and the day after deprivation. Notably, the day after is associated with reduced Na^+ excretion and recovery of Na^+ balance, and it was also associated with elevated plasma aldosterone. Panels F and G show the corresponding daily balances for sheep and rats similarly deprived of water for 24 hours (McKinley et al., 1983). In all of these species, plasma Na^+ levels or osmolality rose by approximately

5% during water deprivation, and it can be estimated that without natriuresis the increase would have been twice as great.

One putative mechanism for natriuresis is the action of AVP in the renal tubules (Luke, 1973). The time courses presented in Panels C and D of Figure 8.1 are consistent with this hypothesis. However, in rats with sagittal knife cuts caudal to the OVLT, cutting neural projections to the supraoptic nucleus (SON), water deprivation no longer produced natriuresis despite elevated AVP. As a result, after 48 hours of water deprivation, plasma Na^+ rose by 20 mEq/L compared with 4.5 mEq/L in sham-cut controls (Bealer et al., 1983). Because AVP secretion was intact, natriuresis was inferred to be due to other effect(s) of the knife cuts.

8.3   Systemic Effects of Water Deprivation and Drinking

Adolph (1950) compared initial drinking after water deprivation in several species. Relative to the water deficit incurred by dehydration, dogs were the fastest drinkers, humans the slowest, and rats intermediate. Passage of consumed water from the stomach into the intestine and its absorption start quite rapidly, but finding different rates of drinking across species suggests that the location and relative importance of pre-absorptive mechanisms of satiety may differ. Maximal rates of drinking under ideal or laboratory conditions depend in part on the motor actions associated with drinking. For example, fast drinkers such as dogs and sheep either use their tongues as scoops to transfer relatively large volumes per protrusion or may suck from the surface of the fluid. Further, these species must be able to breathe while swallowing. In contrast, humans use suction by the lips or gulping to place water in the mouth, with a separate swallowing action, and usually cannot breathe concurrently. In rats, the amount of water acquired per lick is two to four times greater licking from a bowl than from a sipper spout, but the total amounts consumed are comparable between the two modes of presentation (Gold et al., 1973). Species differences in mechanics of drinking probably dictate viable mechanisms for preabsorptive satiety. For this section, I will first consider humans and then various species of laboratory mammals together.

8.3.1   Humans

Thirst and water intake after deprivation in humans have been recorded informally for centuries. One of the first comprehensive scientific studies was by Rolls et al. (1980). Five young men (24–33 years old) gave predeprivation blood and urine samples and were asked to refrain from drinking any fluids or eating foods with high water content (e.g., salads, fruits, soups) for the next 24 hours. The next morning, they returned to the laboratory, gave postdeprivation blood and urine samples, and were allowed to drink room temperature water for one hour without food available. During and after this one-hour period, they completed visual-analog scale assessments of subjective sensations, including thirst and mouth discomfort. As summarized schematically in Figure 8.2, plasma Na^+ concentration, osmolality, and hematocrit ratio increased by 2–3% after deprivation, and plasma volume as indexed by protein concentration decreased by almost 6%. Ratings of thirst and mouth unpleasantness were increased substantially by deprivation. All subjects drank tap water promptly when offered, and thirst ratings returned to predeprivation levels within five minutes. Mean intakes after five and 60 minutes were approximately 10 and 14 mL/kg, respectively. In contrast, plasma Na^+, osmolality, and indices of volume did not change significantly until about 10 minutes after drinking onset and did not return to baseline until 30 minutes after onset. In similar studies in which young adults were given a fixed volume of water (10 mL/kg) and told to consume it within 5 minutes, thirst was again reversed immediately, as was plasma AVP (Geleen et al., 1984; Phillips et al., 1993). These findings indicate that thirst after water deprivation is associated with both hyperosmolality and hypovolemia (i.e., a hybrid thirst), and that sufficient water is absorbed within about 30 minutes after drinking to normalize these values. Ratings of thirst and mouth unpleasantness and AVP secretion reverse almost immediately upon drinking, indicating a preabsorptive contribution to satiation of thirst and cessation of water intake. Phillips et al. (1984, 1993) found similar results in young men but reduced postdeprivation drinking or fall in AVP in the elderly; the effect of aging on thirst and drinking will be discussed in Chapter 10.

The temperature of water in this study was ambient. In water-deprived rats (see Section 8.3.2), the intake of water rises modestly with its temperature from cold (12°C) through ambient to warm (37°C; Deaux, 1973; Gold et al., 1973). Likewise in dogs, intake of 38°C water after deprivation was 10% higher than 20°C water (Applegren et al., 1991), although this effect was not statistically significant. I know of no water deprivation study in humans that has compared intake at different water temperatures. Mildly thirsty people report that ice cubes are more quenching than water (van Belzen et al., 2017), and endurance athletes prefer and consume a greater volume of cool rather than warm beverages (Burdon et al., 2012; Sandick et al., 1984). Boulze et al. (1983) reported

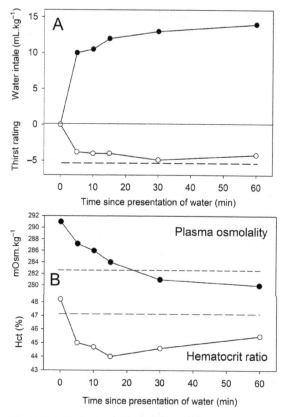

Figure 8.2 Drinking after 24 h water deprivation in young men (from Rolls et al., 1980). Panel A shows cumulative water intake at the end of the deprivation period and the corresponding thirst ratings; the rating before deprivation is shown by the dashed line. Panel B shows corresponding changes in plasma osmolality and hematocrit ratio (respective predeprivation values shown as dashed lines).

an inverted parabolic function of intake to temperature after heat exposure, with intakes of cool (16°C) water at least twofold higher than water at either ambient or cold (<10°C) temperature. Humans may thus differ from animals in their temperature dependence for water intake; this could in part be due to sociocultural factors. It follows that the amount of water consumed after deprivation (Rolls et al., 1980) and the resultant extent of restoration of the plasma indices of dehydration may be temperature sensitive.

8.3.2   Animals

Water deprivation, along with the type of food consumed during that period, is more readily controlled in animals than humans, allowing better-controlled mechanistic studies to be performed. In this section, I will review data from nonhuman primates, dogs, pigs, sheep, and rodents.

Rhesus monkeys (*Macaca mulatta*) deprived of water for 24 hours with a moist food ration showed a 4.4% increase in plasma osmolality and a 4.2% increase in plasma protein (Wood et al., 1980). This rise in osmolality is about 50% greater than in the human study described above, and the protein change a little smaller. In green African monkeys (*Cercopithecus sabaeus*), 48 hours of water deprivation produced a 5% increase in osmolality, a 10% rise in hematocrit ratio, and a three- to fourfold increase in plasma angiotensin II (ANG II; Wright et al., 1982). Different nonhuman primate species are involved in these two studies, but the data are consistent with rat studies to be reviewed below insofar as between 24 and 48 hours of deprivation there is almost no further increase in plasma osmolality, but marked additional decrease in plasma volume.

To investigate the relative contributions of intracellular and extracellular dehydrations, 24-hour water-deprived macaque monkeys were fitted with venous catheters and were infused with various amounts of water or isotonic saline (0.7 mL/min over 40 min) prior to a postdeprivation drinking test (Wood et al., 1982). The results are shown in panel A of Figure 8.3. Infusion of water produced a dose-related decrease in drinking, and the 100% infusion that restored osmolality decreased drinking by 85%. In contrast, an infusion of isotonic saline that restored plasma protein to normal suppressed drinking by only 5% (Rolls et al., 1980). It appears that almost all of the postdeprivation drinking in these nonhuman primates is of intracellular origin. On the other hand, removal of the postingestive effects of water, using a sham drinking preparation, produced almost continuous drinking for a one-hour test, whereas closed fistula controls were satiated after 5–10 minutes (Figure 8.3, panel B; Maddison et al., 1980). Preabsorptive factors alone thus are insufficient to produce termination of drinking. The initial rate of drinking in the primates in this study was 75 mL in 2.5 minutes, or 7–8 mL/kg/min.

Houpt and Yang (1995) examined blood changes during a 12-hour water deprivation in pigs, during which time they were free to eat dry food. Plasma osmolality fell by 2% until the first meal (after about 2 h) and thereafter rose by 10% during the remainder of the deprivation period. Pigs with neither water nor food showed a sustained drop in

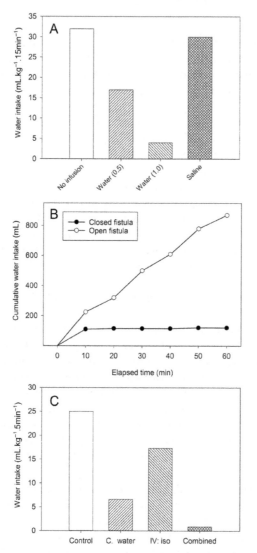

Figure 8.3 Effect of various manipulations on water intake after 24 h water deprivation. Panel A (from Wood et al., 1982) shows mean water intakes of rhesus monkeys under a no-infusion (control) condition, with intravenous water at 0.5 and 1.0x the estimated deficit prior to the drinking test, or the same volume of isotonic NaCl. Panel B (from Maddison et al., 1980) shows postdeprivation intake of rhesus monkeys with a gastric fistula closed (normal drinking) or open (sham drinking). Panel C (from Ramsay et al., 1977b) shows drinking by dogs after deprivation with either a control procedure, carotid infusion of water at $0.6 \text{ mL.kg}^{-1}.\text{min}^{-1}$, intravenous 0.15 M saline to restore blood volume, or the combined infusions.

osmolality, reaching about 6% after 12 hours. Controls with both food and water available showed no changes. The water-deprived group with food showed no change in blood volume over 12 hours. Pigs deprived of water with food present drank 47.8 mL/kg in five minutes to satiation, and the primary stimulus thus seems to be exclusively osmotic. Houpt et al. (1999) examined the effect of drinking on plasma osmolality after a five-hour deprivation of water with food present. In pigs drinking from an open bowl, the five-hour deprivation raised osmolality by about 2%, drinking (18 mL/kg) lasted 3.4 minutes, and at the end of this time, plasma osmolality had returned to baseline. When drinking time was increased by requiring an operant response, plasma osmolality at the end of drinking was in all cases reversed to predeprivation levels. Since only a fraction of the consumed water had been absorbed after 3–4 minutes, osmolality subsequently fell below baseline levels.

Sheep, like pigs, show a very rapid water intake to satiation following water deprivation and drink an amount close to the body weight lost during deprivation. Sheep deprived of water for 48 hours, with their normal dry chaff ration available, drank a mean of 2.7 L in two minutes (Bott et al., 1965) and only about 20% more over the next two hours. The two-minute intake was slightly more than their normal 24-hour intake of water. The deprivation caused a nearly 10% rise in plasma Na^+ concentration, but little change in plasma volume. These sheep were also fitted with an esophageal fistula that normally was closed with a bung. When tested with the fistula open after 48 hours of water deprivation, water sham-consumed after two minutes was comparable to that with the fistula closed. Thereafter, they drank large bouts intermittently such that the two-hour intake was 14.7 L, or four- to fivefold higher than the corresponding intake with the fistula closed. The authors concluded that the passage of water through the lower esophagus and rumen elicits powerful satiating signals. After 24 hours of deprivation, sheep showed a 3% increase in plasma Na^+ and osmolality but, as reviewed in Section 8.2.2, show natriuresis leading to a negative Na^+ balance of 100 mmol/kg. This obtunds the rise in osmolality during the first 24 hours of water deprivation (McKinley et al., 1983).

Dogs are another well-studied species that drinks extremely rapidly and, like sheep, they accurately drink an amount equal to their body weight loss (Adolph, 1950). Adolph (1939) reported that water-deprived dogs drank a mean of 1.4 L (~80 mL/kg) within 2–3 minutes. Ramsay et al. (1977b) prepared dogs with bilateral carotid artery loops so that water could be infused in small amounts to affect brain osmolality. Water deprivation for 24 hours produced a 3–4% rise in plasma osmolality and Na^+ concentration and an 11% increase in plasma protein concentration.

Carotid arterial infusions of water at 0.6 mL/kg/min reduced jugular vein osmolality to predeprivation level and reduced drinking by 72% (Figure 8.3, panel C). This infusion was insufficient to change peripheral (hindlimb venous) osmolality, indicating that brain osmoreceptors were controlling this effect on drinking. Carotid infusion of isotonic saline had no effect on drinking, but peripheral venous infusion of saline in an amount to normalize plasma volume reduced drinking by 27%. In non-infused dogs, drinking stopped rapidly (all drinking tests lasted 5 min) and well before any appreciable amount of the consumed water was absorbed. Thus, cerebral osmoreceptors are sufficient to modulate drinking in dogs, but intake is substantially terminated by preabsorptive factors, which might include gastric distention (Adolph, 1950). As in humans, the elevated plasma levels of AVP caused by deprivation return to basal levels within 3–5 minutes of drinking. The plasma half-life of AVP is a few minutes, so the time course of plasma levels after onset of drinking is consistent with cessation of AVP secretion as soon as water is sensed in the oral cavity (Nicolaidis, 1969).

In contrast to dogs or sheep, rats are slow drinkers and typically drink only about 50% of their weight loss in an initial drinking period (Adolph, 1950). The factors that terminate drinking in rats were analyzed in an elegant series of studies by and summarized in Blass and Hall (1976). Hall and Blass (1975) presented drinking patterns of individual rats following up to 48 hours of deprivation and showed an initial bout averaging five minutes, after which drinking became intermittent. The end of the first bout coincided with reversal of plasma osmolality to and eventually below normal (Figure 8.4, panel A). However, because gastric preloads of 100% fluid loss did not fully suppress drinking, the termin-ation of drinking appears to have been caused by cellular overhydration in close temporal proximity to the act of drinking (Hall & Blass, 1975). After 10 minutes, by which time drinking was completed, Hall and Blass (1975) estimated that 2.3 mL of the 10 mL consumed had been absorbed, with the remainder still in the stomach or intestine (Figure 8.4, panel B). This is the time at which plasma Na^+ and osmol-ality had returned to approximately baseline values, but plasma volume remained reduced. By closing a pyloric noose to prevent ingested water from entering the intestine, Hall and Blass (1975) found contributions to satiation both from postgastric and pregastric factors.

The relative contribution of intracellular and extracellular dehydration to postdeprivation drinking in rats was examined by Ramsay et al. (1977a) using the preinfusion strategy described earlier for monkeys and dogs. Rats that were deprived of water for 21 hours were given 10 mL preloads of water or isotonic saline either by gavage or

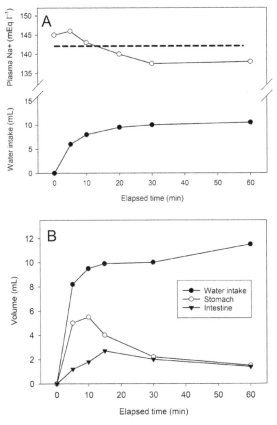

Figure 8.4 Drinking and fluid balance in rats after 24 h water deprivation (from Hall & Blass, 1975). The top part of panel A shows plasma Na+ concentration at various times after initiation of drinking at t = 0. The horizontal dashed line is the nondeprived or control value. Points at 20, 30, and 60 min are significantly lower than control. The lower part of panel A shows the time course of water intake. Panel B shows mean water intake and the amounts of water recovered from the stomach and intestines at different times after onset of drinking.

intravenous infusion and then were given an extended drinking test. In the first hour, the normal (no infusion) intake of 2.9 mL/kg was reduced by 65% and 17% by intravenous infusions of water and saline, respectively. Corresponding inhibitions by gastric preload were similar, 69% and 28%, respectively. Thus, approximately 67% of drinking after 21-hour deprivation by rats appears to be of intracellular origin. Other load sizes were given by gavage, but these will not be discussed because the conclusion is not altered.

A similar result using a different approach was reached by Barney et al. (1983). They deprived rats of water for 12, 24, 36, or 48 hours, with all of the deprivation periods ending in the early daytime (ZT3). Prior to a one-hour drinking test, rats were preinjected with either placebo or captopril (50 mg/kg) to block ANG II formation. In the placebo group, they found that the amount drunk increased monotonically with duration of deprivation (from 8 mL after 12 h to 18 mL after 48 h). The relative inhibition of those intakes by captopril rose from about 20% at 12 hours to 60% at 48 hours. Importantly, the residual and presumptively intra-cellularly related intakes in captopril-treated groups did not differ across the deprivation times. It is also evident that the relative contribu-tions of intracellular and captopril-dependent intakes change with time. These results are consistent with a study by Mann et al. (1980), who made direct measures of plasma osmolality and ANG II following 12, 24, or 48 hours of water deprivation in rats and found that osmolality reached a maximum within 12 hours, whereas plasma ANG II levels rose roughly fivefold between 12 or 24 and 48 hours of deprivation, indicative of a much larger volumetric and/or ANG contribution at longer deprivations.

Sham drinking or open fistula preparations have been used to examine drinking when no systemic rehydration occurs subsequent to the act of drinking. These results of studies in macaque monkeys are shown in panel B of Figure 8.3. Studies in dogs, sheep, or rats yield similar results. In all cases, compared with a closed fistula or natural absorption condi-tion, drinking continues for an extended period of time with the fistula open, often with only brief rests or pauses. In some studies, repeated testing with the fistula open produces a further increase in the amount consumed and less pausing, possibly due to learning about altered post-ingestive effects. For example, Waldbillig and Lynch (1979) found that the amount sham-ingested in two hours increased from about 50 mL to 100 mL across five open fistula tests, and that the latency to the first pause rose from 40 to 240 seconds across the same span. Blass et al. (1976) found that the amount of water sham-consumed increased with duration of deprivation and, conversely, that partial preloads of water one hour before the test session reduced the amount sham-consumed, whereas preloads of isotonic saline had no effect. Salisbury and Rowland (1990) found little or no increase in sham compared to real drinking when a combined stimulus of hypertonic NaCl and polyethylene glycol (PEG) was administered to emulate the physiological aspect of fluid deprivation. A speculative explanation for this unexpected absence of a sham drinking effect is that with the combined (injected) stimulus, food was not available during the development of dehydration.

Oatley (1967a) noted that the amount of water consumed by rats after a period of water deprivation correlated with the amount of food consumed in that time, a result corroborated by Ang et al. (2001). The effect of food intake during water deprivation in rats was revealed in a study by Bealer et al. (1983). Chow and water intakes and urinary parameters were measured daily for a baseline day and then for two consecutive 24-hour periods with one of three treatments, at the end of which time plasma was taken for analysis. The treatments were (a) food and water available ad libitum – the control condition, (b) deprivation of both food and water, and (c) deprivation of water but not food. Plasma osmolality and Na^+ were increased only slightly more in the with-food deprivation condition compared to food and water deprivation, yet plasma AVP was more than double in the former group, and their increase in plasma protein was likewise doubled. It thus appears that food ingested during dehydration (and with progressive dehydration anorexia) impacts plasma volume more than osmolality and that the higher levels of AVP are primarily due to this volumetric stimulus.

Mice have become an important species for transgenic manipulations, especially in relation to the brain. In general, physiological changes accompanying water deprivation in mice are similar to those in rats, although fewer studies have examined physiological indices. One major difference in drinking between rats and mice is the failure of mice to drink to peripheral administration of ANG II (Johnson et al., 2003; Rowland & Fregly, 1988a; Rowland et al., 2003), although PEG treatment does induce ANG-dependent drinking in mice (Chapter 5).

Bekkevold et al. (2013) examined the effects of total water restriction in mice for 12, 24, or 48 hours. Dry food intake averaged 89% and 64% of controls during the first and second days of deprivation. Changes in plasma parameters and body weight are shown in panels A–D of Figure 8.5. Urine osmolality refers to bladder samples taken at the time of sacrifice and, at all deprivation durations, approached a physiological ceiling near 3,000 mOsm/kg. Similar changes with water deprivation in mice have been reported by others, but, to my knowledge, no report has been made assessing the relative contributions of intracellular and extracellular dehydrations to drinking.

8.4   Physiological and Neural Mechanisms of Deprivation-Induced Drinking

As described in previous chapters, the brain regions most implicated in mammalian drinking of both intracellular and extracellular origin are the

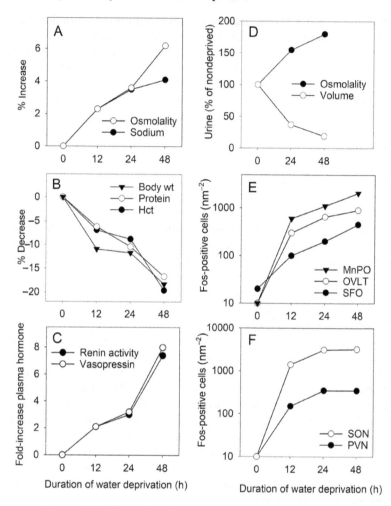

Figure 8.5 Effects of various durations of water deprivation in mice. Panels A and B (from Bekkevold et al., 2013) show percentage increase in plasma osmolality and Na+ concentration (A) and decrease in body weight and plasma volume (protein and hematocrit; B) after water deprivations ending in the morning. Panel C shows corresponding fold increase in plasma renin activity (PRA; from Bekkevold et al., 2013) and AVP (wild-type mice from Nagakura et al., 2010). Panel D (from Nagakura et al., 2010) shows 24 h urine measures without deprivation (0) or the first and second 24 h of water deprivation. Panels E and F (wild-type mice from Watanabe et al., 2000) show Fos-immunoreactivity induced in various brain regions by different durations of water deprivation. Note logarithmic ordinate scales.

nuclei of the lamina terminalis, namely, the subfornical organ (SFO), median preoptic nucleus (MnPO), and OVLT. In the present section, I consider how these are integrated within the brain using the hybrid stimulus of water deprivation as the dehydrating operation.

Using the induction of Fos as a marker of neuronal activation, it was shown that water-deprived rats expressed Fos-ir in many cells of the dorsal boundary of the OVLT, in the MnPO both dorsal and ventral to the anterior commissure, in the magnocellular SON and paraventricular nucleus (PVN), and more weakly in the SFO (McKinley et al., 1994; Morien et al., 1999; Rowland, 1998). Morien et al. (1999) compared the effects of water deprivation for 5, 16, 24, and 48 hours, and with deprivations starting at lights out (ZT12) or lights on (ZT0). Select results for the ZT12 groups are shown in Figure 8.6. Within five hours of water deprivation at the start of the night, plasma osmolality and hematocrit ratio were significantly elevated compared to nondeprived controls, and this was associated with increased Fos-ir in the MnPO and OVLT, but not the SFO. By 24 hours of deprivation, all of these measures were increased relative to baseline, and, despite only small additional changes in plasma measures between 24 and 48 hours, Fos-ir increased substantially in the SFO. The Fos-ir values after 48 hours are consistent with those reported by McKinley et al. (1994). This result suggests that, relative to the OVLT, the SFO is engaged (by the Fos-ir metric) only at high levels of plasma renin activity (PRA; ANG II) and/or more prolonged exposure to dehydration. In this regard, Barth and Gerstberger (1999) found a significant region-specific upregulation of AT1 receptor and angiotensinogen mRNAs in the SFO after 48 hours of water deprivation, suggesting that the SFO may become more responsive to ANG signaling. Using a retrogradely transported tracer injected into the SON, McKinley et al. (1994) reported that about 30% of labeled cells in the OVLT and MnPO coexpressed Fos after water deprivation compared with only 6% of cells in the SFO. Consistent with this result, Xu and Herbert (1996) showed that lesion of the OVLT abolished 24-hour water deprivation–induced Fos-ir in the SON but was without effect in the SFO. Following 24-hour water deprivation in virgin female rats, Fenelon et al. (1993) found that 72% of vasopressin-expressing cells in the SON also expressed Fos-ir, whereas double labeling was only half as frequent (37%) in oxytocin-expressing cells. These results suggest that the Fos-ir in the SON and inferred release of AVP after water deprivation in rats is completely dependent on input from the OVLT and/or MnPO.

Results in sheep are consistent with this view. Water intake and AVP secretion were attenuated by lesions that ablated both the OVLT and MnPO, although ablation of either structure alone produced only partial

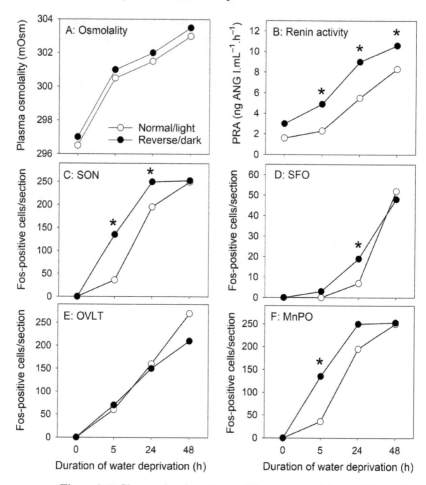

Figure 8.6 Changes in plasma osmolality, renin activity, and Fos-ir in various brain regions following different durations of water deprivation, with dry food available, in 3-month-old rats (from Morien et al., 1999). Separate groups were housed in either a normal light cycle with sampling in the middle of the light phase or in a reversed light–dark cycle with sampling in the middle of the dark phase. *p < 0.05, difference between groups sacrificed in light and dark at the same duration of water deprivation.

effects (McKinley et al., 1984). In dogs, using a refined surgical approach through the roof of the mouth, Marson et al. (1985) found that lesions restricted to the OVLT produced hyperdipsia, which allowed correction of lesion-produced hypernatremia, but that lesions which additionally encroached on the MnPO produced adipsia. These authors did not examine water deprivation per se, but their conclusion that pathways through the MnPO are critical for drinking is consistent with the foregoing. In rats, cell destruction in the MnPO by injection of an excitotoxin did not affect drinking to water deprivation (McGowan et al., 1988). Further, electrolytic lesions confined to the anteroventral third ventricle, not involving the MnPO, did not affect deprivation drinking. Rats with coronal knife cuts between the OVLT and SON showed increased drinking after water deprivation (Bealer et al., 1984), possibly due to impaired AVP secretion. This result indicates that connections running caudally from the OVLT (the cuts extended 1.5 mm on either side of midline and 2.5 mm up from the base of the brain) are not critical for drinking.

In addition to water intake and the hormonal changes described above, dehydration produces alterations in sympathetic nervous system activity. Brooks et al. (2004) examined the contribution of excitatory transmitter input to the rostral ventrolateral medulla (RVLM) in supporting blood pressure. Basal arterial pressure was not changed by water deprivation, but bilateral injection of the excitatory amino acid antagonist kyneurenic acid into the RVLM reduced blood pressure in water-deprived but not water-replete rats. Restoration of plasma osmolality by water (plus 5% glucose) infusion attenuated the kyneurate effect by more than 50%, although isotonic replacement of plasma volume had no effect (Figure 8.7, panel A). Thus, hyperosmolality and not hypovolemia initiates increased sympathetic outflow under these conditions. Stocker et al. (2005) addressed the role of the PVN in sympathetic nerve activity by injecting the GABA$_A$ antagonist muscimol bilaterally into the PVN and recording renal and lumbar sympathetic nerve activity in rats deprived of water for 0, 24, or 48 hours. The results (Figure 8.7, panel B) show the hypotensive effect of muscimol was amplified by water deprivation, and that both renal and lumbar activity were reduced but significantly more after 48 hours than 24 hours of deprivation. These authors did not address relative contributions of hyperosmolality or hypovolemia to this effect because a group that was dehydrated for 48 hours and then allowed two hours to drink and rehydrate did not differ in either osmolality or protein, or sympathetic activity, from nondeprived rats. The foregoing discussion that a major change between 24 and 48 hours of deprivation often is a volumetric component might suggest this is the critical difference in the sympathetic sensitivities to inhibition of the PVN. However, in this study (Stocker et al., 2005), plasma osmolality rose by 4.5% and 7.2% after 24 and 48 hours, and this alone could account for the result, although the reason for the atypically large rise of osmolality in the

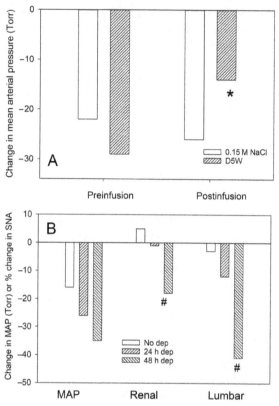

Figure 8.7 Changes in sympathetic nerve activity with water deprivation in rats. Panel A (from Brooks et al., 2004) shows the drop in blood pressure of water-deprived rats in response to bilateral injection of kynurenate into the rostral ventrolateral medulla before and after i.v. infusion of either isotonic saline or distilled water containing 5% glucose (D5W). *Denotes decreased effect after infusion. Panel B (from Stocker et al., 2005) shows change in mean arterial pressure (left bars) and renal (center) or lumbar (right) sympathetic nerve activity in nondeprived rats, or in groups deprived of water for 24 or 48 h. #Indicates 48 h deprived group differs from 24 h and no-deprivation groups.

second 24 hours of this study is not clear. The OVLT is the most likely origin for the osmotic signal because osmosensitive neurons in the OVLT project monosynaptically to the PVN (Shi et al., 2008), and microinjection of hypertonic NaCl into the OVLT increased lumbar and decreased renal sympathetic activity, effects that were attenuated by inhibition of the OVLT by microinjection of muscimol (Kinsman et al., 2017).

In mice, water deprivation for 24 hours induces Fos-ir in the OVLT, MnPO, SON, and PVN (Figure 8.6). The results are similar to those in rats including the lowest density of Fos in the SFO, whereas the SFO response after 48 hours was almost threefold higher than after 24 hours. Oka et al. (2015) reported that 30% of SFO neurons in mice expressed Fos-ir after 48 hours of water deprivation. As described in Chapter 1, they identified three nonoverlapping cell phenotypes in the SFO: an excitatory glutamatergic population (SFO^{GLUT}, which coexpresses calcium/calmodulin-dependent protein kinase type II [CaMKII] and neuronal nitric oxide synthase [nNOS]), an inhibitory GABA-ergic population (SFO^{GABA}, which expresses the vesicular GABA transporter Vgat), and a glial population that expresses glial acidic fibrillary protein (GFAP). Mice deprived of water were found to lick 35–40 times in five-second trials, indicative of sustained licking at 7–8 Hz. Optogenetic stimulation of the SFO^{GABA} cells reduced licking by 80%, primarily by inhibiting drinking once it had started. This suggests that the SFO generates an inhibitory signal acting within the SFO or projecting to the MnPO and OVLT once a drinking bout is initiated, independent of continued dehydration because the amount consumed in these five-second trials was small relative to an expected intake of up to 1 mL/mouse in 1–2 minutes after this level of deprivation.

As Zimmerman et al. (2016) later noted, the discovery of inhibitory drinking–related efferents from the SFO, in addition to sensory drinking–excitatory signals, prompts a reexamination of the earlier studies showing that ablation or disconnection of the SFO had little effect on postdeprivation drinking. Using 24-hour water-deprived mice and a transgenic method that allowed inhibition of SFO^{GLUT} cells during photostimulation, they showed that whereas controls (no light) took about 300 licks in 2–3 minutes and then were substantially satiated for the rest of a 30-minute session, photostimulation for the first 15 minutes reduced licking by about 90%; these latter mice drank as soon as the light was turned off. This finding suggests that the excitatory output from the SFO is essential for deprivation-induced drinking in mice. If the SFO^{GLUT} output can be regarded as sensory (i.e., ANG II, osmolality/Na$^+$, or both), this result suggests the SFO is essential for initiating drinking after deprivation, a conclusion that is different from the majority of results from ablation studies in rats and other species. It should be noted that lesion studies potentially allow some time-dependent recovery or reorganization within spared tissue, whereas optogenetic studies are acute and circumvent that possibility. The effect of SFO ablation has not been reported in mice, and it remains possible that mice would return a result diverging from many other species. A clue that this is a plausible situation is that, of all the mammals reviewed in Chapter 5, mice alone do not drink to peripheral administration of ANG II – a dipsogenic action that in most species is dependent on the SFO. If mouse SFO does not encode and initiate such a drinking response, it could imply a different functional organization. It is important for investigators using mice to acknowledge and address this knowledge gap. Nonetheless, the fact that the SFO and possibly other areas can influence downstream regions to inhibit drinking both by removal of an excitatory signal (viz., rehydration) and by a short-term inhibitory signal (i.e., peripheral water sensing) is an important integrative advance. For further discussion in relation to osmometric drinking, see Chapter 4.

Matsuda et al. (2017) found that 48-hour water-deprived mice, with a roughly 9% increase in plasma osmolality and fourfold increase in plasma ANG II, drank 50 mL/kg water in a two-hour test. Most of that intake occurred in the first 30 minutes. Wild-type mice additionally consumed 20 mL/kg 0.3 M NaCl, also mostly in the first 30 minutes. This could be to avoid plasma dilution (cf. Blass & Hall, 1976), although that has not been studied directly in mice. About 50% of the SFO neurons expressing Fos-ir after this level of dehydration also expressed the ANG II AT1A receptor, and all were glutamatergic (i.e., the excitatory pathway above). Knockout of this receptor had no effect on water intake after water deprivation, but it abolished concurrent intake of 0.3 M NaCl. On the basis of this and other studies involving Na^+ depletion, Matsuda et al. (2017) suggested that the SFO is involved in both water and NaCl intake, whereas the OVLT seems to be exclusively involved in water intake. Further, optogenetic silencing of the SFO to OVLT pathway throughout a two-hour test inhibited water intake after 48 hours of deprivation by about 40%, although in both controls and silenced groups almost all of the drinking was completed within the first 15 minutes. This suggests that the OVLT either alone or with involvement of the MnPO produces a physiologically significant water intake after deprivation, but not as large as when the SFO is engaged. It is possible that the early satiation in the absence of excitatory input from the SFO reflects a relatively unopposed inhibitory (SFO^{VGAT}) signal. Until the temporal or other aspects of potential osmodilution during drinking after deprivation are clarified in mice, these interpretations remain speculative. While systemic repletion has been addressed in relation to osmoregulatory drinking (Zimmerman et al., 2019), water deprivation with associated dehydration anorexia is a distinctly different physiological situation to which extrapolation cannot be made with confidence.

Augustine et al. (2018) found that chemogenetic inhibition of nNOS-expressing neurons in the MnPO completely blocked water intake of water-restricted mice, but this was without effect on food intake of food-restricted mice. A similar inhibition occurred when drinking was induced by optogenetic stimulation of the SFO nNOS cells, suggesting that SFO^{GLUT} projections to the MnPO may be critical for drinking after water deprivation. Further, by inducing loss of function in nNOS cells of either the OVLT or MnPO using caspase 3, only the MnPO site inhibited licking induced by photostimulation of the SFO.

Zimmerman et al. (2016) found that SFO^{GLUT} neurons in mice can be driven by either hyperosmolality or hypovolemia, including both angiotensin-dependent and -independent mechanisms. As expected, these neurons were activated (via photometric measurement of calcium in nNOS-expressing cells of the SFO) after 24 hours of water deprivation. However, such recording, which integrates across many cells, cannot distinguish between a decline occurring in all cells versus a complete inhibition of progressively more cells; the latter would imply different sensitivities of subgroups of cells to rehydration. Mice drank water for 4–5 minutes after deprivation, by which time the calcium signal had returned to predeprivation levels and before any change in systemic osmolality had occurred. The authors suggest that the act of drinking causes a resetting of SFO activity in functional anticipation of systemic repletion. Rapid inhibition of calcium signaling immediately after the onset of drinking in 24-hour water-deprived mice was also found in SON cells that project to the posterior pituitary (Mandelblat-Cerf et al., 2017). This is consistent with the known rapid inhibition of plasma AVP secretion. This effect could be mediated directly by an excitatory SFO^{GLUT} pathway to the SON (Oka et al., 2015) or indirectly via the MnPO (Zimmerman et al., 2019); the transport of retrograde tracer from the SON to the SFO is extremely weak in rats (McKinley et al., 1994). Anteroventral third ventricular lesions in rats abolished drinking and Fos-ir expression in the SON but not the SFO after 24 hours of water deprivation (Xu & Herbert, 1996), suggesting that critical efferents from the SFO go via the MnPO and/or OVLT. As noted before, an alternative but speculative interpretation is that mice may differ from rats in functional neuroanatomy of the lamina terminalis.

8.5   Hybrid Thirst: Perspective

I started this chapter by mentioning that the double depletion model of thirst and drinking had become something of a dogma in the field by the time of Fitzsimons's (1979) book. Implicit within those early formulations was that osmoregulatory drinking would be transduced by osmoreceptors in one or more locations and give rise to a total signal of intracellular dehydration. Separately, cardiopulmonary and/or ANG II receptors would give rise to a total signal of extracellular dehydration. Those signals would then become integrated at downstream brain regions. From a functional perspective, such integration is necessary because hybrid dehydrations, and in particular those caused by deprivation, can be composed of a theoretically infinite number of combinations of these two basic components.

What has emerged rather gradually at first, but quite rapidly with recent optogenetic and molecular genetic tools, is that the two types of transduction or integration can occur within the same cell. This is exemplified by findings that ANG II receptors are on osmosensitive cells in the lamina terminalis, and those cells can be shown to respond to both types of stimulus. This is a major advance, but if we view the lamina terminalis as a sensory surface, it leaves open the important question of sensory coding. For example, we have seen that using Fos-ir as a measure of activation (or activation above a threshold for detection using this method) produces a time-dependent recruitment of SFO cells. Is this because individual cells in the SFO have different intrinsic thresholds for their hybrid signal, because they have different ratios of responsiveness to the component signals, or something else? Sensory organs in general are not known for their redundancy, but instead their component cells are "tuned" to certain characteristics of the signal. Do the sensory circumventricular organs follow this model or instead have a unique organization? Is this organization subject to developmental programming or plasticity? I believe the field now has suitable tools to address these difficult problems but will need to apply the classic procedure of dose–response analysis, rather than a sledgehammer approach, to tease apart issues related to neurophysiological thresholds and ultimately individual differences in behavior.

8.6   Summary

Water deprivation or restriction is arguably the most natural of all dehydrations. The magnitude and rate of dehydration depends on the water and electrolyte content of available food, and the extent to which dehydration anorexia mitigates the net dehydrating effect of food. The early stages of water deprivation produce primarily intracellular dehydration, whereas longer durations of deprivation cause progressively greater extracellular fluid losses. Thus, the resulting stimulus to drink is a combination or hybrid of intracellular and extracellular drinking. There are considerable species differences in the rates of postdeprivation drinking and in the mechanisms that terminate such drinking, although in all cases some contribution or preabsorptive controls are evident. The principal structures of the lamina terminalis (i.e., OVLT, MnPO, SFO) collectively contribute to postdeprivation drinking, although the relative contribution of these structures may depend on the duration or degree of net dehydration and/or have species differences. Many neurons of the lamina terminalis are excited by both hyperosmolality and ANG II, and so act as integrators, but it has not been established whether the nature of that integration (or threshold) differs between cells within a region, or between regions.

9   Hybrid Dehydrations: Thermal Stress and Exercise

9.1   Thermoregulation

In the absence of drinking or eating moist food, terrestrial animals are continuously losing water through respiration, evaporation, and excretion. As the environmental temperature rises above the thermoneutral range for a given species, various thermolytic or heat loss mechanisms are engaged. Physical activity increases endogenous heat production (i.e., thermogenesis) and elicits the same thermolytic mechanisms. Conductive heat loss occurs by cutaneous vasodilation if core temperature exceeds that of the environment; this gradient may be modified if core temperature rises above a normal near 37°C in many mammals. As will be shown later in this chapter, controlled elevations of up to about 4°C may occur for limited durations. As the ambient temperature approaches or exceeds body temperature, conductive heat loss becomes insufficient. Progressively more heat loss is then accomplished by evaporative cooling, either via tachypnea (i.e., panting) and/or cutaneous moistening (i.e., sweating or saliva spreading). These latter physiological adaptations cause fluid loss and associated dehydration. They cannot be sustained for long periods without compensatory drinking. There are at least two reasons why thermal dehydration is a topic of contemporary interest. The first is the reality that climate change is bringing more frequent heat waves to more regions of the planet. The second relates to a burgeoning elderly population and their potential hydration problems (Chapter 10).

   Thermoregulatory mechanisms are combined anatomically with fluid sensors at early stages of neural processing. Electrophysiological data are compelling in this regard. Figure 9.1 shows the coincidence of thermal and osmotic or volume sensitivity in single neurons in the median preoptic nucleus (MnPO) of rats (Hori et al., 1988; Koga et al., 1987). Neurons were classified in vitro (slices, top row) or in vivo (urethane anesthesia, bottom row) as either warm sensitive, which increased firing rates above 37°C; cold sensitive, which decreased firing rates below 37°C; or temperature insensitive. About 75% of temperature-sensitive cells also changed their firing rate in response to small changes (~5%) of local osmolality, with more showing inhibitory compared with excitatory responses. In vivo, a similar fraction of temperature-sensitive cells changed firing rate in response to a modest roughly 15 mm Hg change in arterial pressure (bottom row). A high fraction of temperature-insensitive cells were unresponsive to changes in either osmolality or arterial pressure. No thermally sensitive cell was pressure sensitive after transections of the glossopharyngeal, vagus, and sympathetic nerves, indicating that pressure inputs to these neurons are from peripheral baroreceptors. Most temperature-sensitive cells also responded to changes in hepatoportal osmotic pressure (Hori et al., 1988), indicating functional afferents from peripheral osmoreceptors to the MnPO in addition to the intrinsic osmosensitivity demonstrated in the slice preparations.

The above electrophysiological studies used temperature changes of the brain tissue, via thermistor or bath temperature, but it is likely that afferents to these regions from skin temperature sensors may have similar interactive effects with hydration-related signals. Early studies that directly warmed the hypothalamus were unable to demonstrate reliable drinking behavior (see Fitzsimons, 1979, for review). As I will discuss below, drinking is reliably elicited by exposure to hot environments. Some older literature named this *thermogenic drinking*, but, to avoid confusion with physiological thermogenesis, I will use operational terminology such as *thermally induced drinking*.

9.2   Thermal Dehydration in Humans

The earliest systematic studies in this field had the objective of examining or improving physical performance during sustained occupational heat exposure, including in natural (e.g., desert, mines) or industrial (e.g., furnace) settings (Adolph et al., 1947; Pitts et al., 1944). More recent growth of competitive and individual sports has ushered in the study of fluid intake during or after exercise; exercise-related dehydration may today be one of the more common occurrences of thirst and fluid need. Thermal exposure, with or without exercise, has eclipsed water deprivation as a stimulus of choice for experimental study of dehydration in humans. Specific hemodynamic changes are influenced by the parameters of the exposure, such as environmental temperature and duration, the antecedent conditions, and whether the exercise is upright or recumbent (Harrison, 1958). Many of the studies of drinking to be described below have used only male subjects, but, when it has been examined,

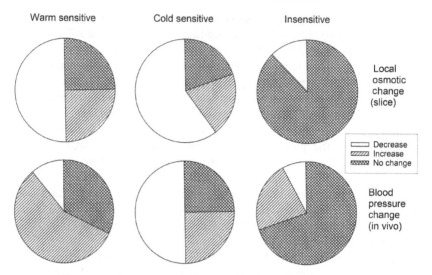

Figure 9.1 Pie charts showing the fraction of single cells in rat MnPO identified electrophysiologically as warm sensitive, cold sensitive, or temperature insensitive that respond to local changes in osmolality (in vitro, top row) or blood pressure (in vivo, bottom row; from Hori et al., 1988; Koga et al., 1987).

females often show different physiological responses than men (e.g., Ormerod et al., 2003; Röcker et al., 1977).

Many authors find that fluid intake during or shortly after thermal exposure is typically only about one-half of the total water lost, which is most usually assessed by body weight loss. This has been called both voluntary (e.g., Adolph et al., 1947) and involuntary (Greenleaf, 1992) dehydration. To prevent confusion, the term *hypohydration* is preferable. Full physiological rehydration takes several hours and includes eating food that contains adequate fluids and electrolytes (Adolph et al., 1947).

The phenomenon of hypohydration, as described in men in a desert environment by Adolph et al. (1947), is shown in panel A of Figure 9.2. Groups of 10–28 men were studied at low (<400 g/h), moderate (400–600), or high (>600) sweat or weight loss levels, and their hypohydration at the end of the exertion period derived from the difference relative to concurrent fluid intake. The graph has an apparent threshold and a slope of approximately 0.5, indicating that hypohydration increases (i.e., their remaining fluid deficit increases) in proportion to water loss. Panel B shows typical rate of water loss at different sustained running speeds in either cool and dry or warm and humid conditions

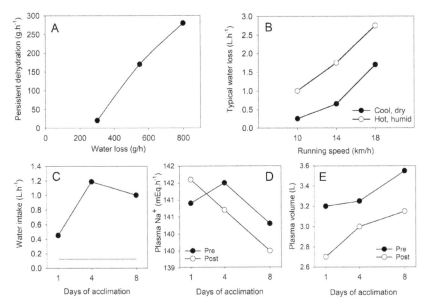

Figure 9.2 Effects of thermal dehydration in humans. Panel A (from Adolph et al., 1947, p. 259) shows hypohydration (water lost minus water consumed) at three different levels of exertion. Panel B (from Sawka et al., 2001) shows typical water loss as a function of running speed in two climates. Panels C–E (from Greenleaf et al., 1983) show water intake, plasma Na^+, and plasma volume before or after drinking on 8 successive days of 2 h ergometer exercise at 40°C. The horizontal line in panel C is intake of a control group performing identical exercise at 24°C.

(Sawka et al., 2001). Fluid loss during vigorous exercise in the heat is typically 1–2 L/h, and occupational activities in similar climates may produce loss of 1 L/h, although there is a wide individual range.

Another important dimension is acclimation. While laboratory studies are usually acute, it is evident that natural exposure to a hot environment is often a chronic or seasonal condition and occupational or recreational exertion is repeated or habitual. To assess the effects of acclimation, groups of young men were given eight daily two-hour ergometer exercise sessions at 75 W (~45% peak VO_2; Greenleaf et al., 1983). One group exercised in a warm (dry bulb 39.8°C) environment, and a control group exercised at ambient room (23.8°C) temperature. Subjects could request cool water (16°C) at any time during the sessions, but they were not informed that drinking was a dependent variable. The water intakes of the warm group on days 1, 4, and 8 are shown in panel C of Figure 9.2. Water intake on day 4 was almost three times that on day 1. By contrast, the water intake of the control group was low (about 150 mL/h) and did not change across sessions. Over the two hours, controls took 3–4 drinks, averaging 100 mL each day. In contrast, the warm group took larger (180 mL) drinks on day 1, but in the same number (3–4) and latency (25–30 min) as the controls. Across days, the mean size of each drink remained the same (180 mL), but the number increased almost threefold to 10–12 per session, and with shorter latency (10–15 min). Sweat rate in the warm group also increased, from 1.2 L/h on day 1 to a maximum of 1.6 L/h on day 4; the increase in water intake was at least double the rise in sweat rate. As a result, the degree of hypohydration was reduced but not eliminated by acclimation.

The increased fluid intake across days of heat acclimation has some effects on body fluid parameters. Panels D and E of Figure 9.2 (adapted from figure 3 of Greenleaf et al., 1983) show mean plasma Na^+ concentration and plasma volume before and immediately after the two-hour exercise session on days 1, 4, and 8 of acclimation. On day 1, plasma Na^+ rose during exercise, whereas on days 4 and 8 it fell, although these effects were relatively small (<1%). In contrast, plasma volume decreased by 10–15% during exercise, and this was not greatly affected by days of acclimation despite a trend for pre-exercise plasma volume to increase. These data suggest that one of the effects of hypohydration is avoidance of further osmotic dilution of plasma despite ongoing and substantial plasma volume deficits.

An extreme example of acclimation was described in people indigenous to the Sahara Desert (Paque, 1980). The Berbers there frequently tolerate thirst for long periods; perhaps as a result, they sweat much less than unacclimated visitors and drink frugally (600–700 mL/day, all with planned meals). The fluid they consume often contains modest amounts of salt, supporting extracellular volume, but at the same time they avoid excessive salt consumption, which would require additional water for excretion.

Figaro and Mack (1997) investigated factors that contribute to water satiation despite hypohydration. In their study, young adults performed a two-hour cycling exercise without water in dry heat (38°C, <30% RH, target heart rate 130), thereby achieving a mean body weight loss of 3%. After a 50-minute rest at room temperature without water, subjects had a nasogastric tube inserted. Each subject took part in three such dehydration sessions. On the first session, the tube was inserted as a control procedure and subjects had 75 minutes of rest, during which time they could freely drink cool (15°C) water. In another condition, water at 37°C was infused through the tube in an amount and temporal pattern equal to the intake of that individual at the first session; this was mostly in the first 10 minutes. After 20 minutes, cool water was again presented. The other condition was free drinking as in the first session, except water was aspirated from the tube at the rate it was consumed. Thus, although water was swallowed, none accumulated in the stomach or was absorbed – this was effectively a sham drinking procedure.

The results are shown in Figure 9.3 and indicate that free drinking occurred rapidly, leaving a residual dehydration of about 33% initial deficit. The thirst and dry mouth ratings in this group dropped from a high level before drinking to baseline or low levels within 10 minutes, although the 3% initial increase in plasma osmolality did not start to decline until after 10 minutes. This suggests, as in other studies (see, e.g., Chapters 3 and 8), that there is a potent preabsorptive effect of oral water on thirst and drinking behavior. This conclusion is supported by the results from the other two conditions. The gastric load produced a more rapid decline of osmolality than the oral load, and when drinking water was provided after 20 minutes, plasma osmolality had returned to baseline. Nonetheless, the thirst ratings had declined only partly from the peak, drinking occurred, and by the end of the session amounted to almost one-half that consumed in the free drink trial. As a result, plasma osmolality dropped 1–2% below normal, and it is likely that osmotic dilution was an inhibitory factor. Finally, in the sham drinking condition, no water was absorbed and plasma osmolality remained at its high level throughout, yet thirst ratings declined as rapidly as in the free drink condition. Drinking was sporadic through the rest of the session, such that intake was only about 50% higher than in the free drink condition. The authors concluded that oral factors are particularly potent in producing satiation in humans and that thirst may be dissociated from systemic osmolality. It should be noted that in all of these conditions, the plasma volume deficit of about 5% incurred by the dehydration was largely unchanged at the end of the drinking period.

Nicolaïdis (1969) studied the onset of sweating in water-deprived humans exposed to mild heat (33°C for 30 min). He found that forehead sweating increased within a few seconds of taking a small drink (120 mL), well before any non-oral factor could have triggered an effector response. Further, because cool (12°C) and warm (37°C) water had similar effects, a mouth-cooling effect does not seem to be involved.

Sweat is hypotonic relative to plasma, with Na^+ concentration ranging from about 10–50% that of plasma. It varies in composition across body regions (Takamata et al., 2001) and degree of adaptation to the environment (Kirby & Convertino, 1985). Moderate or high levels of sweating

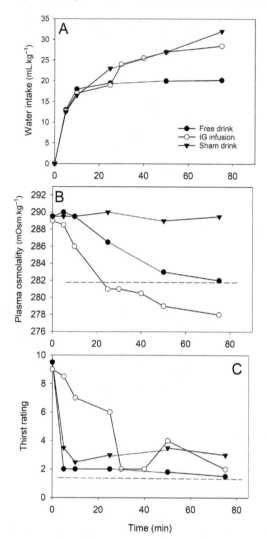

Figure 9.3 Drinking in humans following 2 h cycling in dry heat (from Figaro & Mack, 1997). Panel A shows cumulative water intake, panel B shows plasma osmolality, and panel C shows thirst rating at times indicated. Controls were presented water at t = 0 and consumed freely. Subjects in the sham drinking condition also drank from t = 0, but water was aspirated from their stomach as they drank. In the infusion condition, water (mean 20 mL.kg⁻¹) was infused i.g. for the first 25 min and then water was presented for 25–75 min. The dotted horizontal lines in panels B and C represent the average pre-exercise baselines for those variables.

lead to significant electrolyte loss and, without repletion of these solutes, plasma volume is not fully restored. This is, in part, why food is a viable restorative strategy. Alternatively, electrolyte-containing fluids can be beneficial both during and after fluid loss.

Meischer and Fortney (1989) examined dehydration due to sweating in young and old cohorts (see also Chapter 10). Subjects sat in a hot environment (45°C) for four hours. In the first three hours, both groups lost comparable body weight (1.5%), but the elderly had a much greater decline in plasma volume (11.3% vs. 4.9%) and increase in osmotic pressure (5.0% vs. 1.1%) compared with the young, possibly indicating impaired movement of fluid from tissues to support plasma volume. During the fourth hour, cool water (11°C) was presented and intake was measured. Both groups drank about 50% of their fluid loss (500 mL or 7 mL/kg), although intake of the elderly was palpably insufficient to restore osmolality or volume to baseline values. Thirst ratings increased less in the elderly compared with the young during dehydration. Both groups showed a rapid decline of thirst when allowed water, although the absolute decline was greater in the young.

Mack et al. (1994) produced a greater weight loss (2.5%) in young and old groups by exercising in the heat (36°C, 105 min). Subjective thirst ratings increased about twofold more in the young compared with the elderly group despite comparable weight loss. Subjects were then restored to a thermoneutral environment, and after 30 minutes cool (15°C) water was presented. The young consumed twice as much water as the elderly, consistent with their thirst ratings. This result is consistent with other reports of reduced thirst and drinking in the elderly (see Chapter 10), but it differs from the result of Miescher and Fortney (1989) described above. There are some procedural differences, including whether exercise was involved, or whether the drinking occurred during heat exposure or after return to a cooler environment. This latter aspect may be important and will be revisited at the end of this chapter in relation to exercise.

Brain regions involved in dehydration and rehydration have been investigated using either positron emission tomography (PET) or functional magnetic resonance imaging (fMRI) methods. Farrell et al. (2011) asked healthy but not physically trained participants (19–41 years old) to cycle on a stationary bicycle for 30 minutes at 60% heart rate reserve. This was followed by 4.5 hours without drinking, although various dry, salty snacks were available. Subjects then underwent pulsed arterial spin labeling fMRI in three successive conditions. The conditions were dehydrated (before drinking), during or immediately after ad libitum drinking of water while in the scanner, and 2.5 hours later as a rehydrated or reference condition. Blood flow changes in the cingulate and prefrontal cortices were correlated with those in the organum vasculosum of the lamina terminalis (OVLT) osmosensitive region, suggesting functional connectivity. Drinking caused a reduction in blood flow in the rostral cingulate cortex that was correlated with the quantity consumed, whereas such change was not evident in the posterior cingulate cortex. This difference is consistent with PET results in mildly fluid-deprived subjects before and after drinking to satiety (De Araujo et al., 2003). Farrell et al. (2011), noting similarities in the fMRI with that after hypertonic NaCl infusions (Chapter 4), suggested that these regions do not show additional responses to concurrent blood volume loss after exercise. It should be noted that the supine posture in the scanner tunnel may alter baroreceptor or other fluid-related signals relative to those in the species-typical erect posture.

Saker et al. (2014) performed another bicycle exercise study, using 60 minutes of cycling at 65% heart rate reserve, followed by one hour of rest before two sets of fMRI scans. The first set was while the subjects were still dehydrated, and it involved delivery of small (5 mL) volumes of water into the mouth every 30 seconds. These deliveries were judged to be in the pleasant range on a 10-point scale. The second set was a similar procedure, but it was performed after a period out of the scanner during which subjects consumed water beyond normal satiation, to the "comfortable limits of their tolerance" and reaching the unpleasant range of the 10-point scale. Pleasantness of drinking was associated with activation of the anterior cingulate and orbital frontal cortices. Overdrinking was associated with activation in the midcingulate cortex and insula.

Saker et al. (2016) conducted a follow-up imaging study of dehydration and rehydration, focusing on the role of oral factors. The basic procedure was similar: cycling dehydration, fMRI scans while thirsty, drinking to beyond normal satiation, and a second set of fMRI scans. In a scanner trial, subjects viewed a fixation cue that indicated 5 mL of fluid was about to be delivered into their mouth. They were instructed to hold that liquid in the mouth for 7 seconds, and then a cue would prompt them to swallow. They then completed brief ratings of pleasantness/ unpleasantness (10-point scale) of the liquid and also assessed the effort required to swallow it (10-point scale). A new fixation and trial then occurred. Both water and sugar (8% sucrose) solutions were rated moderately pleasant in the thirst condition and moderately unpleasant in the overhydrated condition. Swallowing effort was very low for both fluids in the thirst condition and increased to moderate effort in the overhydrated condition. Examination of the scans performed during the pre-swallow period in the dehydrated and overhydrated conditions showed activation of several cortical and subcortical regions, but in a few regions the activation was larger in the overhydrated condition. Bilaterally, these included the prefrontal cortex and amygdala, and several other structures showed a unilateral effect; the magnitude of that effect was inversely correlated with swallowing effort. These data show that swallowing, or swallowing effort, is represented in the cortex and may be the origin of inhibitory signals for drinking. Further analysis of these data (Saker et al., 2018) suggests that activation of the anterior midcingulate cortex facilitates swallowing when thirsty.

9.3   Thermal Dehydration in Animals

I will first consider select laboratory results obtained in dogs and sheep, both species that use tachypnea as a primary mode of thermolysis. Gregersen and Cannon (1932) made the observation that dogs exposed to 40°C for two hours showed almost continuous panting and drank water during this time. O'Connor (1977) examined the relationship between thermal exposure via an overhead radiant heat lamp and drinking in female mongrel dogs. Mean water lost by evaporation was almost 4 mL/kg in a one-hour exposure (range 2.0–4.8). Water was presented for two minutes every 10 minutes and intake recorded. Intake was minimal at the first presentation, but small drinks were taken at most of the succeeding opportunities. The total water intake was equal to or greater than the evaporative water loss in six of eight dogs tested, but with a high individual variability evident from the range of intakes (0.2–9.3 mL/kg). This stimulus heated the dorsal skin but did not greatly affect overall core temperature, suggesting that the panting, which started early and produced the evaporative loss, and drinking originated with cutaneous temperature receptors.

Four of the dogs were examined for evaporative loss and drinking while running at 7–10 km/h for one hour (O'Connor, 1977). Running at ambient temperature (18–24°C) caused a less than 1°C increase in core temperature relative to a sedentary control condition, was associated with panting, and produced a mean evaporative fluid loss of about 5 g/kg. The mean water intake was 70% of that loss, again with a wide individual range (1.2–5.4 g/kg). When running was instead under the radiant heat lamp, fluid loss increased to 8.6 g/kg and water intake also increased; in two dogs, it was more than the loss (mean 13.0 g/kg) and in the other two less (mean 5.7 g/kg). Thus, both exogenous (heat lamp) and endogenous (running) heat production caused comparable fluid losses and drinking.

A conspicuous and unexplained aspect of these data is the high individual variability in water intake despite little variance in fluid loss.

Several studies have shown that water-deprived animals have impaired tolerance to the heat because the mechanisms for fluid conservation in dehydration conflict with signals for evaporative fluid loss to ensure adequate thermolysis. Baker and Turlejska (1989) examined the effect of rehydration on thermally induced panting in dogs. Each of five male dogs was studied in five conditions of one-hour exposure to 40–41°C. The conditions were normally hydrated, water deprived for 48 hours, water deprived and infused intravenously with saline-dextran to restore plasma volume to hydrated levels before the exposure, water deprived but allowed to drink water for four minutes after 30 minutes of heat exposure, and the same but with 0.15 M NaCl to drink. This 48-hour water deprivation caused an increase of 8% in plasma osmolality and a decrease of 17% in plasma volume. The results from the last 30 minutes of heat exposure are shown in panel A of Figure 9.4. Hydrated dogs sustained a high rate of respiration or panting (280 breaths/min) throughout the session. Dehydrated dogs had lower panting rates (200 breaths/min) that were unaffected by plasma volume restoration by the saline-dextran infusion. In contrast, when dogs were allowed to drink water in the amount of 1,300 mL (42.2 mL/kg) in the four-minute access period, their panting rate rose to levels in the hydrated condition, and this most likely occurred before significant absorption had occurred. Finally, consumption of 1,245 mL (40.5 mL/kg) of isotonic saline produced a rapid partial restoration of panting to euhydrated levels, but with a decline later in the 30-minute period. These findings show a preabsorptive effect of drinking on panting and a postabsorptive effect of water (inferred relief of hyperosmolality) but not saline (inferred relief of hypovolemia). Thus, at the dehydration levels achieved by this deprivation, hyperosmolality has a greater inhibitory effect on panting than hypovolemia.

In sheep deprived of water for 48 hours but maintained at normal ambient temperatue (20°C), McKinley et al. (2009) reported a marked elevation in respiration rate when they were allowed to drink water at 39°C, an effect that was sustained for at least 100 minutes (recall that drinking in sheep is typically for <5 min). Drinking 1% NaCl produced a similar tachypnea, but this was not sustained for the entire session. Drinking water at 30°C produced a smaller tachypnea, whereas water at 20°C produced a transient drop in respiration rate. Gavage of the same volume of 39°C water produced a slow emergence of a much smaller degree of tachypnea as oral water. Thus, oral factors produce an immediate effect, and when water is absorbed that effect becomes longer lasting. McKinley et al. (2008) showed that panting by euhydrated sheep

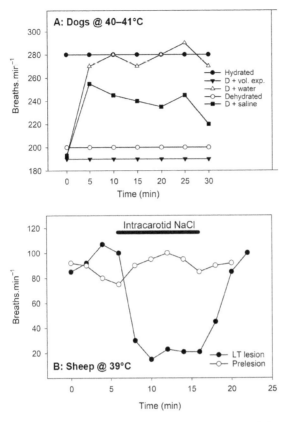

Figure 9.4 Thermoregulatory panting in dogs and sheep. Panel A (from Baker & Turlejska, 1989) shows the effect of prior dehydration on thermoregulatory panting in dogs exposed to 40–41°C for 30 min (t = 0 prior to placing in heat). D = 48 h prior water deprivation; vol. exp.= dehydrated and then volume expanded with saline-dextran; D + water or saline = allowed to drink water or saline for the first 4 min of the test period. Panel B (from McKinley et al., 2008) shows that panting in a hot environment (39°C) is inhibited during intracarotid infusion of hypertonic NaCl, but the effect is abolished after lesion of the lamina terminalis (LT).

at 39°C is acutely inhibited by intracarotid injection of hyperosmotic solutions and that this effect is abolished by lesion of the ventral lamina terminalis. Osmoreceptors in the lamina terminalis thus mediate panting-induced thermolysis, and most likely their activity is strongly influenced by signals from the oral cavity or esophagus.

Rats and many other small mammals do not sweat, but instead lose heat by vasodilation, especially from the hairless tail (Hainsworth, 1968; Harrison, 1958) and by grooming or spreading saliva on the fur and skin of the chest. At less severe environmental temperatures (up to 32°C in male and 36°C in female rats), conductive heat loss is important and salivation is not greatly increased. Rand et al. (1965) estimated that 17% of total heat produced can be lost from the rat tail in a warm environment. The role of heat loss from the tail has been examined using rats with amputated tails. At moderate (<36°C) temperatures, tailless rats show greater reliance on alternate thermolytic mechanisms – hyperthermia and evaporative loss – than rats with tails (Spiers et al., 1981; Stricker & Hainsworth, 1971). At a supraphysiological environmental temperature (44°C), normal rats spread copious saliva and thereby maintain an elevated core temperature for several hours, but tailless rats can only sustain this for a short duration before developing lethal hyperthermia (Stricker & Hainsworth, 1971).

Heat loss via vasodilation of the tail can be studied in a thermoneutral environment using the β-adrenergic agonist isoproterenol to increase metabolic rate. Administration of isoproterenol causes a modest increase in core temperature and a larger increase in tail skin temperature, indicating vasodilation, which rapidly reverses the initial change in core temperature. Tailless rats do not have this heat loss mechanism available, and they show much greater and prolonged core hyperthermia after isoproterenol (Spiers et al., 1981). It is of interest to point out that about 50% of the tail skin temperature response to isoproterenol is due to endogenously produced angiotensin II (ANG II; Fregly & Rowland, 1993) and that exogenous administration of ANG II (a vasoconstrictor in most vascular beds except the tail) increases tail skin temperature like isoproterenol (Wilson & Fregly, 1985). Systemic hypovolemia caused by fluid loss of evaporative cooling (see later in this section) will generate endogenous ANG II, and the above anomalous effect of ANG II in the tail ensures that it does not prevent lifesaving vasodilation.

Given the key role of salivary glands in thermolysis in hot environments, it is appropriate to review some basics about salivation. There are three bilateral pairs of major salivary glands: submandibular (also known as submaxillary), sublingual, and parotid (Proctor, 2016). The submandibular and sublingual glands are adjacent in the floor of the oral cavity, whereas the parotids are in the cheeks. Reciprocal sympathetic and parasympathetic innervation from the salivatory nuclei in the medulla causes these glands to secrete saliva at a low basal rate, increase that rate during eating, and, in saliva-spreading species, produce very high rates during thermal stress.

Saliva has many important constituents, but I focus only on the hydromineral aspects. The acinar cells of the salivary glands filter plasma; Na^+ is substantially recovered in the ducts of the glands but to different degrees across glands and flow conditions. Saliva secreted by the submandibular gland during heat stress has a low Na^+ concentration (<20 meq/L), whereas that from the parotid glands is much higher (>100 meq/L; Hainsworth & Stricker, 1971). Using retrograde trans-synaptic transport of pseudorabies virus injected into the submandibu-lar/sublingual glands of rats, it has been shown that many brain regions, including the lamina terminalis, have a polysynaptic efferent pathway to those glands (Hübschle et al., 1998, 2001; Jansen et al., 1992). Thus, it is possible that neurons in the lamina terminalis that sense or integrate systemic dehydration to produce drinking simultaneously decrease salivary secretion. This would have two important consequences. First, in regard to thermal stress, the submandibular and submaxillary glands would sustain high secretion rates only until a threshold of systemic dehydration is reached, at which point their output should decline. Second, of broad application to the relationship between thirst drinking and dry mouth, systemic dehydration causes drinking *and* a reduction in salivary flow mediated at least in part via mechanisms in the lamina terminalis.

Stricker and Hainsworth (1970b) reported that rats exposed to 40°C showed an initial and regulated rise in core temperature of about 3°C and were able to sustain that for up to 10 hours, provided they had water to drink. Intake was slow in the first two hours, but after that it proceeded steadily at about 25 mL/kg/h. However, rats that were not allowed to drink during the exposure, or who drank well below the group mean, were unable to last more than about five hours before developing lethal hyper-thermia (Hainsworth et al., 1968). Rats subjected to acute intracellular (hypertonic NaCl) or extracellular (polyethylene glycol [PEG]) dehydra-tion prior to heat exposure or were water deprived for 72 hours beforehand were even more impaired with regard to heat tolerance (Figure 9.5). In hydrated groups, most of the critical heat loss came from spreading of saliva from the submandibular glands because rats with selective removal of this gland (plus the sublingual, which is believed to have only a minor contribution in the heat) reached heat exhaustion in less than one hour at 40°C, whereas rats with selective parotid gland duct ligation were more resilient (Hainsworth & Stricker, 1971). Submandibular saliva is substan-tially hypotonic (see above), and it follows that the principal manifestation of dehydration from this saliva spreading should be hyperosmolality.

Hainsworth et al. (1968) reported plasma changes in rats after various durations at 40°C without water. Within one hour, plasma volume had

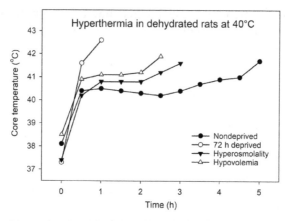

Figure 9.5 Hyperthermia in dehydrated rats in a 40°C environment without water to drink (from Hainsworth & Stricker, 1971). Different groups of rats were either nondeprived, deprived of water for 72 h, or were made hyperosmotic (NaCl injection) or hypovolemic (PEG injection) prior to the exposure. The graphs terminate when most of the group reached heat exhaustion.

decreased by 13%, with little further drop through hours 4–6. In contrast, plasma Na^+ concentration increased by 2.7% after one hour and continued to rise to 6.6% after 4–6 hours.

Removal of salivary glands is well-known to impair heat tolerance (e.g., Stricker & Hainsworth, 1970a) and to reduce drinking during 5 h at 36°C by >75% (Lund, et al., 1969). Bilateral damage to the chorda tympani, which includes the parasympathetic innervation of the submandibular gland, has the same effect as salivarectomy. Clark et al. (1939) were the first to show that lesion damage to the preoptic-anterior hypothalamic area greatly impaired heat tolerance, and Toth (1973) analyzed this syndrome more carefully in rats. After lesions that bilaterally damaged medial and lateral preoptic areas, the increase in body temperature during exposure to 38°C was similar to that of surgically desalivate rats, and the lesion animals spread little or no saliva. A similar effect of anterior hypothalamic lesions, sparing the MnPO, was reported by Stricker and Hainsworth (1970a). Preoptic lesion animals were, however, able to produce normal amounts of saliva in response to pharmacological stimulation (pilocarpine) and to thermoregulate behaviorally by operant responding for a water shower. These rats thus were able to detect thermal stress, but they were unable to respond with saliva production. This suggests that the preoptic and/or anterior hypothalamic area contains critical efferents from brain thermoregulatory centers to the salivatory nuclei in the brainstem. Hübschle et al. (2001) discuss this in the context of involvement of the lamina terminalis and, although the preoptic lesions probably spared the lamina terminalis, they are consistent with a more lateral efferent pathway from forebrain to hindbrain. This conclusion is consistent with the results of a study in which submandibular salivary secretion was stimulated by local thermal stimulation of preoptic area or anterior hypothalamus of rats (Kanosue et al., 1990).

Barney and West (1990) described changes in body fluid parameters of rats, without concurrent access to water, as a function of ambient temperature and duration of exposure. The left-hand panels of Figure 9.6 show the effects of exposure for four hours to various ambient temperatures. Evaporative water loss increased linearly as a function of temperature. At 32.5°C, this loss was purely from the extracellular fluid compartment, whereas at higher temperatures, fluid loss progressively occurred from the intracellular compartment as well; the relative change from these compartments thus depends on the thermal load. At the end of four hours, water was presented and intake was recorded. Temperatures above 32.5°C resulted in progressively larger intakes, which were correlated with and reversed the change in plasma osmolality. However, that intake replaced only about 50% of the fluid lost, as estimated from body weight loss. That is, hypohydration was observed comparable to that found in the human studies mentioned earlier in this chapter.

Hypohydration following thermal exposure in rats was analyzed further by Nose and colleagues. In these experiments, to avoid influence of solutes from food, rats were deprived of food for 12 hours prior to and throughout the experimental period. They first exposed rats to 36°C for 6–8 hours to achieve 10% weight loss (equivalent to 17% total water loss) and then measured changes in body fluid distribution. Some 41% of the total loss was from intracellular and 59% from extracellular compartments, the latter being distributed between interstitial fluid and plasma. As a result, plasma osmolality was increased and plasma volume was decreased (Nose et al., 1983). In a later study using heavier rats, the same exposure caused 7% body weight loss, a 4.1% increase in plasma osmolality, and a 12.8% reduction in plasma volume (Nose et al., 1985). After a 30-minute post-exposure period to bring body temperature to normal, rats were allowed to drink either water or saline solutions. As expected, those drinking water sustained hypohydration, whereas those drinking saline consumed twice as much and completely restored plasma parameters to those of controls (Nose et al., 1985; Yawata et al., 1987). The

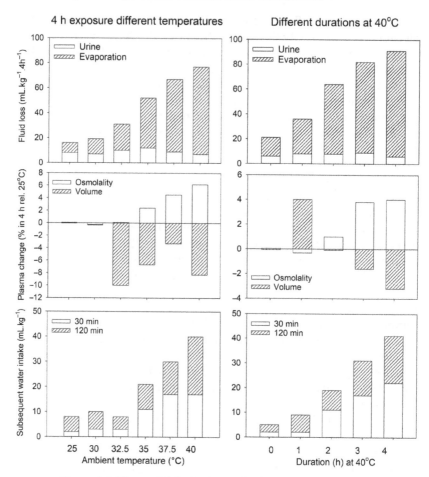

Figure 9.6 Thermal dehydration and subsequent drinking in rats (from Barney & West, 1990). The left panels show effects of 4 h exposure to different ambient temperatures and (bottom panel) mean water intake. The right panels show the hour-by-hour changes in dehydration and subsequent drinking at the highest temperature (40°C) reported in the left-hand panels.

authors concluded that hypohydration is a result of inhibition of water drinking by osmotic dilution, and full rehydration requires replacement of electrolytes lost in saliva during heat exposure. Further, restoration of plasma osmolality occurs faster and/or more completely than that for plasma volume (Nose et al., 1987).

To determine the contributions of osmotic and volumetric components to drinking, Barney (1997) exposed rats to 40°C for four hours, returned them to 25°C, and administered intravenous infusions of water or 0.15 M saline (40 mL/kg, about one-half of the total fluid lost). Then, after a 15-minute delay, water was presented and intake measured for two hours. Other rats were treated similarly but had blood samples taken at the time the drinking groups were given access to water. The water infusions completely normalized plasma osmolality, exacerbated the decrease in plasma volume, and reduced water intake (above that of controls maintained at 25°C throughout) by 85%. In contrast, saline infusions reduced the elevated plasma osmolality by only 40%, restored the plasma volume deficit by 80%, and reduced water intake by less than 30%. In another study, Barney et al. (1991) showed that water intake after thermal dehydration was unaffected by nephrectomy or a high dose of angiotensin converting-enzyme (ACE) inhibitor, whereas drinking after water deprivation was reduced, suggesting that ANG II has little or no contribution to post-thermal drinking.

Together, these data suggest that the principal stimulus for drinking after thermal dehydration in rats is osmotic. A volume-related signal, but probably not circulating ANG II, may contribute to saline consumption when it is available. It cannot be ruled out that the volumetric signal may functionally reduce the osmotic threshold, although the foregoing studies were not designed to investigate this possibility.

Some aspects of adaptation to heat exposure in humans were discussed earlier in this chapter. Barney and Kuhrt (2016) examined this phenomenon in rats. For seven consecutive days, male rats were placed in metabolism cages in an environmental chamber at either 37.5°C or 25°C (control) for four hours. Some rats had access to water during the exposure, while others had no water; none had food available. At the end of this time, all rats were placed at 25°C for a further three hours with water available. In all cases, water provided was at ambient temperature. Evaporative water loss during the four-hour exposure was determined from body weight loss, fecal and urine output, and water intake. Evaporative water loss was about 10% greater in rats with water in the heat compared to those without water, and that loss (in mL/kg body weight) declined slightly across the seven-day period; this change could have been due to body weight gain over the seven-day period. In contrast, the water intake during exposure increased about threefold over the seven-day period (Figure 9.7). Water intake in the three-hour period after heat exposure decreased across days, even in the group that had no water during the thermal exposure. As a result, the hypohydration at the end of the three-hour post-heat period was markedly divergent

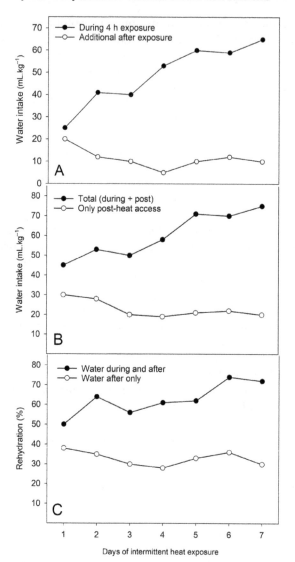

Figure 9.7 Effect of water access during and after seven consecutive daily 4 h exposures of rats to 40°C (from Barney & Kuhrt, 2016). Panel A shows the water intake of rats during the 4 h exposure and for an additional 3 h after return to 25°C. Panel B shows the total (during and after) intakes of the rats in panel A, and of a separate group of rats that were heat exposed without water available and were allowed to drink only during the 3 h after return to 25°C. Panel C shows the percentage of rehydration achieved by the water intakes shown in panel B relative to the evaporative plus urinary losses in the heat.

(Figure 9.7). Specifically, although the group with water during exposure was able to reduce their degree of hypohydration to about 25% at the end of the three hours, the group without water during exposure first drank far less postexposure than the group during their exposure, and because their intake did not increase across days, hypohydration was almost 70% at the end of the seven days. This result emphasizes the important point that drinking during thermal dehydration is much greater than if it is deferred until after the thermal exposure. Note the possible relevance of this result to the discrepancy between the Miescher and Fortney (1989) and Mack et al. (1995) studies in young and older humans discussed earlier in this chapter.

Whyte, Thunhorst, and Johnson (2004) examined the effect of thermal exposure in young (7–8 months old) and old (23 months old) cohorts of rats (aging and fluid intake is treated more fully in Chapter 10). They placed a radiant heat lamp overhead to raise colonic temperature by about 0.05°C/min for up to one hour. Young and old groups showed comparable body weight loss (3–4%), but when allowed to drink after the exposure, the young group consumed almost twice as much as the old group, such that the hypohydration was about 50% in the young and 70–80% in the old. A similar deficit was reported in two hours of water intake of 30-month-old brown Norway rats compared with a four-month-old cohort, despite similar weight loss in the heat (Begg et al., 2012). To my knowledge, these are the only animal studies to have examined the clinically relevant issue of aging and fluid restoration during or after heat exposure. While there are similarities in the design of these studies to the human study by Miescher and Fortney (1989) described earlier in this chapter, including access to water after rather than during the exposure, there are many translationally relevant aspects that remain unstudied. For example, since intake in post-heat tests is lower than when intake occurs in the heat, would aging subjects still drink less than young subjects if water were available during heat exposure? Would repeated intermittent exposure produce increased intakes and reduce hypohydration? Would intake of saline or electrolytes be greater than that of water and likewise alleviate the hypohydration?

Relatively little work has been done on brain mechanisms of post-thermal drinking, possibly due to the confounding effect of the stress of heat exposure alone. Patronas et al. (1998) examined regional expression of Fos-ir in the brain of rats exposed to one of four conditions: (a) standard temperature (22°C) and ad libitum food and water, (b) 22°C and 24 hours water deprived, (c) 48 hours at 34°C (60% RH) and ad libitum food and water, (d) four hours at 34°C and deprived of water for the last 24 hours. This is a relatively mild heat exposure, and it caused only about 20% more drinking than at 22°C. Two regional clusters had many Fos-positive cells: a body hydration cluster and a thermoregulatory cluster. In the hydration cluster, Fos was induced by deprivation in the OVLT, subfornical organ (SFO), MnPO, supraoptic nucleus (SON), and paraventricular nucleus (PVN), and, compared with deprivation at 22°C (group b), to a larger degree in the 34°C deprived rats (group d) in the PVN (+15%), SON (+40%), and MnPO (+80%). Of these structures, only the MnPO was activated by heat exposure without deprivation (group c), and effects of heat plus deprivation were approximately additive in this structure. Maruyama et al. (2003) and Uschakov et al. (2009) also noted that acute heat exposure (2–3 h at 39–40°C) induces Fos in the MnPO of rats.

A recent study by Allen et al. (2017) using Fos-TRAP transgenic mice yielded complementary findings. They found that 48 hours of water deprivation induced Fos in a spatially intermingled but nonoverlapping population of MnPO cells compared to those activated by acute heat exposure (4 h at 37°C). Abbott and Saper (2017) found that optogenetic stimulation of glutamatergic (Vglut-expressing) cells in the MnPO caused strong cutaneous vasodilation in 62% of mice, with an associated drop of core temperature. Most of these mice also consumed water (almost 1 mL or 40 mL/kg) during a 20-minute stimulation, and the sites supporting drinking overlapped substantially with those causing hypothermia. While this study does not show that the same cells can produce both responses, the electrophysiological data with which this chapter opened strongly suggest that at least some cells might have this dual property. This role of vasodilation in mouse thermoregulation was the subject of some early studies (e.g., Harrison, 1958), but I know of no systematic work on evaporative loss and thermal dehydration in mice.

9.4   Implications for Endurance Performance

From the foregoing, it is evident that both exercise and thermal exposure cause dehydration, and their combination is particularly potent. Further, when only water is available, rehydration is usually incomplete, especially as it relates to the extracellular fluid compartment (Sawka et al., 2001). Physiological dehydration impairs thermolysis, with the result that core temperature rises and inhibits physical and sometimes cognitive performance. The degree of physical training or adaptation is also important. Under some conditions, flavoring the beverage and inclusion of glucose and electrolytes can stimulate consumption relative to water and thereby attenuate hypohydration (Kemefick & Cheuvront, 2012; Wilk & Bar-Or,

1996). I will review a handful of studies, among many, that illustrate some points in regard to water intake.

In addition to the pioneering studies of Adolph and associates (1947), mentioned earlier in this chapter, many studies have affirmed that prolonged exercise in the heat impairs performance. For example, Gisolfi and Copping (1993) studied trained men running for 1.5–2.5 hours on a treadmill at 33.5°C. On separate test occasions, the runners had different water regimens including pre-exercise or drinking cold or warm water every 20 minutes. One finding was that the rise in rectal temperature was related to the percentage of weight loss, which in turn was related to water consumed. In a similar study, trained endurance cyclists performed for two hours at 33°C and received graded amounts of fluid to drink aimed to replace between 20 and 80% of the fluid loss in sweat (Montain & Coyle, 1992). They found that the increase in esophageal temperature was greater at smaller intakes, which in turn were associated with greater increases in plasma osmolality. Adams et al. (2018) reported that performance of elite cyclists in a 5 km simulated time trial following two hours of exercise at 35°C was better when covert hydration (a total of 2 L water at 37°C infused through a nasogastric tube every 5 min) was added to oral hydration (25 mL every 5 min for a total of 0.7 L) than without any covert hydration, even though thirst ratings were similar in both conditions.

Cheuvront and Haymes (2001) examined fluid intake and thermoregulation in eight elite female marathon runners. Each subject completed three laboratory sessions at approximately monthly intervals that coincided with the follicular phase of the menstrual cycle. Each session consisted of a 30 km treadmill run at each subject's competitive marathon pace and 71% VO_{2max}. Test sessions differed in ambient temperature, approximately 30°C, 20°C, and 12°C in random order. Cool water was offered for 30 seconds every 5 km, a timing that is familiar to distance runners. Both sweat loss and water consumed after 30 km increased at the highest temperature, but the ratio of intake to loss was approximately 65% under each condition. Subjects consumed water at each opportunity, but the amounts drunk each time were generally greater (~300 mL) than at the lower temperatures (~200 mL). After the first 30 minutes of running, subjects maintained a rectal temperature of about 38.5°C throughout each session. Thus, the amount drunk sustained adequate thermoregulation despite hypohydration. For a recent and comprehensive review of fluid balance and hydration in women, see Giersch et al. (2020).

Kenefick and Cheuvront (2012) suggested that a weight loss of 2% from acute exercise is a threshold above which performance decreases. In the above study of female marathon runners (Cheuvront & Haymes, 2001), weight loss at 30 km was 2.4–2.8% under all three temperature conditions, suggesting that the amount of water consumed was adequate to stay near this threshold. However, the intake was periodic as prompted by offering water. Expression of thirst and unprompted or self-determined consumption seems less reliable or consistent. Cotter et al. (2014) have carefully considered self-determined versus institutionally advocated fluid intake in a variety of conditions and recommended self-determined intake as the most useful or reliable. These and other (e.g., Perrier, 2017) authors have also reconsidered the definition of hypohydration and euhydration as part of a healthy lifestyle. These concepts and implications go beyond the scope of the present text.

9.5   Summary

Thermolytic responses are required in either high ambient temperatures when conductive heat loss is low, or during states of increased heat production such as during exercise. Most of the thermolytic responses involve fluid loss, including panting (i.e., tachypnea) and evaporative cooling from skin moistened by sweating or saliva spreading. The relative contribution of these mechanisms is species dependent. In all cases, the principal systemic change produced by the fluid loss is hyperosmolarity, although hypovolemia can also be considerable. Humans and animals usually do not drink sufficient water to replace the lost fluid, resulting in a state of hypohydration. This can be partially mitigated by repeated exposure (e.g., adapation) or by providing electrolytes to drink. Sustained hypohydration and/or elevated core temperature produces loss of physical performance and, in the extreme, can be lethal. Available evidence suggests that the OVLT and/or MnPO play important roles in detection of heat stress and execution of the thermolytic responses.

10 Thirst in Aging and Clinical Populations

The other chapters in this volume have considered thirst or drinking in physiologically normal subjects. (A possible exception is pregnancy, in Chapter 6, although the extent to which this is abnormal is debatable.) The present chapter considers several conditions, ranging from common to rare, in which the physiological and/or behavioral aspects of thirst and drinking are abnormal and present potential problems to health and well-being.

10.1 Aging

10.1.1 Human Studies

Aging is a natural condition, but one that has assumed major health significance only within the last 100 years. Until about 1920, worldwide life expectancy was about 30 years. Since that time and due largely to spectacular advances in medicine, nutrition, and sanitation, the current expectancy is over 70 years, with women living longer than men. In a comprehensive review of age-associated abnormalities of water homeostasis (Cowen et al., 2013), the most common problem identified was hyponatremia, which, depending on the criteria used, occurs in up to 30% of individuals. Hyponatremia is associated with many secondary effects ranging from neurocognitive disorders to bone fractures and is a strong independent predictor of premature mortality. Hyponatremia is most usually due to a syndrome of inappropriate antidiuretic hormone secretion (SIADH), which leads to excessive water retention.

Conversely, and of relevance to thirst, consider the incidence of hypernatremia and increased plasma osmolality in elderly populations (Cowen et al., 2013; Lešnik et al., 2017). This is a consequence of what Beck (2000) termed *homeostatic inelasticity*, especially in regard to kidney structure and function. Vasopressin (AVP) release in response to increased osmolality is either the same or even increased in elderly relative to young populations (Helderman et al., 1978), indicating that brain osmoreceptors are functional. Nonetheless, the intensity of thirst is often reduced. In all the studies to be described, subjective sensations such as degree of thirst or dry mouth have been measured periodically and typically using visual analog scales. The change in sensation is derived as distance between marks on the scale at different times. It is known that the elderly use these and similar measurements of subjective state differently than young people (Schwartz, 2003), possibly as a result of less effective working memory. Thus, absent any assessment of working memory in these aging cohorts, it is a logical possibility that their ratings relating to dehydration do not reflect state or changes of state with the same accuracy as in young cohorts.

In a classic study, Phillips et al. (1984) examined thirst and drinking following 24 hours of fluid deprivation in young (20–31 years old) and healthy old (67–75 years old) men. The physiological effects of the deprivation were similar to or greater in the elderly than those in the young, but the elderly had lower ratings of thirst and consumed less water than the young. Phillips et al. (1993) subsequently reported a study in which subjects were given a fixed oral load of water (10 mL/kg) at the end of the deprivation period and the time course of changes in thirst and AVP were followed. Thirst after deprivation was again higher in the young compared with the old group, and oral water loads rapidly reduced thirst to basal levels in both age groups (Figure 10.1, panel A). Interestingly, plasma AVP declined rapidly (i.e., preabsorptively, via orally mediated inhibition as discussed in previous chapters) in only the young group. This suggests that a particular physiological level of dehydration produces a smaller emotional or motivational signal in the elderly compared with young adults, and that the inhibitory effects of oral water on thirst and AVP may also differ in the elderly.

To analyze the relative contribution of osmometric and/or volumetric mechanisms to reduced thirst in aging, several studies have investigated these aspects separately. Phillips et al. (1991) gave intravenous infusions of hypertonic NaCl (~6 mEq/kg over 2 h) to recumbent, healthy young or old men and recorded various plasma parameters as well as visual analog reports of thirst and dry mouth. Despite comparably increased Na^+ and AVP concentrations in plasma, the elderly showed a smaller increase in thirst and dry mouth ratings as the infusion progressed (Figure 10.1, panel B). In a 30-minute drinking test when the infusion was complete, the elderly consumed only about 30% as much room temperature water as the young group. Both young and old groups showed strong correlations between thirst rating and plasma Na^+, but the slope was shallower in the elderly. Further, whereas all of the young subjects reported increased thirst relative to preinfusion baseline before Na^+ levels rose

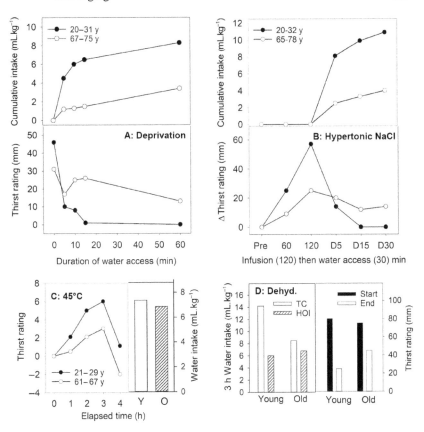

Figure 10.1 Drinking and thirst in young and old cohorts of humans. The upper part of panel A shows water intake across time following 24 h water deprivation, and the lower part shows the corresponding thirst ratings on a visual analog scale (from Phillips et al., 1993). The upper part of panel B shows water intake after a 2 h i.v. infusion of hypertonic NaCl, and the lower part shows the growth of thirst during infusion and effect of drinking (D) for 30 min after the infusion (from Phillips et al., 1991). The left part of panel C shows growth of thirst during 4 h exposure to 45°C with water presented for the last hour, with intakes shown in the right part (from Miescher & Fortney, 1989). Panel D shows the effects of head-out immersion (HOI) or time control (TC) on 3 h water intake (left part) and on thirst ratings (right part). Subjects were dehydrated by 2 h exercise and overnight deprivation before this procedure.

above 135 mEq/L, many of the elderly did not report thirst until 140–145 mEq/L. There was no significant difference in thirst threshold between groups as indexed by the x-axis intercepts of linear regressions of thirst and Na^+, but individual responses suggest a trend toward higher osmotic thirst threshold in the elderly. Constructs of threshold and sensitivity are not always clearly separable within these experimental designs.

A similar study with intravenous infusion of about 6 mEq/kg NaCl over two hours followed by a 30-minute rest and then a 30-minute drinking period yielded a different conclusion (Stachenfeld et al., 1996). In young and old populations, the infusion increased plasma osmolality (18–20 mOsm/kg) and volume (16–18%) by the same amounts and produced almost identical increases in thirst rating. Further, the amount and time course of cool (15°C) water intake was identical in young and old (18 and 30 mL/kg after 1 and 3 h, respectively). AVP levels were increased comparably during the infusion and dropped to baseline within a few minutes of drinking onset. However, the decline of thirst ratings during drinking was slower and less complete in the elderly. This result provides another distinction between inhibitory mechanisms on thirst and AVP, but obviously different from those reported by Phillips et al. (1991), discussed above.

Davies et al. (1995) found results comparable to those of Stachenfeld et al. (1996). In this study, a two-hour infusion of hypertonic NaCl produced similar increases in plasma osmolality and thirst in young and old groups, and the amount of room temperature water consumed in the two hours after the infusion was the same in both groups. The authors suggest that the lack of thirst or drinking deficits in the old group may be due to their careful screening for healthy subjects. Both Davies et al. (1995) and Stachenfeld et al. (1996) included females and males in the studies, but they made no mention of sex differences in the results. I can find no other systematic differences in procedure that might have caused these diverse results in regard to pure osmometric thirst: The conclusion must be that under at least some conditions, healthy elderly people experience comparable thirst and drink comparable amounts of water to young cohorts.

In regard to AVP secretion, these studies differ from an earlier report (Helderman et al., 1978) in which a similar two-hour hypertonic NaCl infusion produced a twofold greater increase in AVP in the elderly. Further, the slope of the linear regression between AVP and plasma osmolality was twofold higher in old men than in young men. The authors suggest that the higher AVP is functionally important to compensate for age-related loss of renal concentrating ability and resultant ability to excrete Na^+ and water. From animal studies, this may be related to lower expression of aquaporin (AQP2) channels in the renal tubules (Cowen et al., 2013).

Mack et al. (1994) examined the osmotic control of thirst and water clearance during a three-hour drinking period following a dehydration equal to 2.4% body weight. This dehydration was achieved by having the overnight-fasted subjects cycle for 105 min at 60% maximum heart rate on a semi-recumbent bicycle in a hot and dry environment (36°C; <30% RH). Subjects were allowed water 30 minutes after the end of the exercise period, and the amount consumed was recorded along with various plasma parameters. The elderly group drank about half as much as the young group, but with a similar time course: Most of the drinking occurred within the first hour. Thirst ratings indicated that the osmotic threshold for thirst was shifted to a higher plasma osmolality in the elderly. Analysis of the amount of water consumed as a function of thirst rating was a single function, with the elderly data clustering around a functionally higher set point. The authors concluded that the elderly do not have a deficit in thirst per se, but rather a shifted set point (hence, threshold) for body fluid homeostasis. However, the possible contribution of volumetric factors in this thermal dehydration (Chapter 9) cannot be discounted.

In another study of aging and thermal dehydration, Miescher and Fortney (1989) exposed young (21–29 years old) and old (61–65 years old) men to three hours of thermal dehydration at 45°C without access to water. This study was also described in Chapter 9; to summarize, both groups showed comparable weight loss (1.5%), but the elderly had smaller increases in thirst ratings and greater plasma changes in volume and osmolality. Nonetheless, both groups drank 50% of their fluid loss in the hour following exposure. Insofar as the major signal of dehydration may be osmotic, this result is consistent with the foregoing conclusion that osmometric thirst is essentially intact in a healthy aging population.

The contribution of volume receptors in thirst was assessed by examining the inhibitory effect of head-out water immersion (HOI) in dehydrated subjects. Stachenfeld et al. (1997) dehydrated young and old subjects via a two-hour evening session of exercise in the heat followed by overnight abstinence from fluids. The following day, subjects underwent a 195-minute HOI in water or a control (water suit) procedure. Fluid loss from exercise and the overnight abstinence was less in the elderly (1.2 kg) than the young (2.0 kg). Water (15°C) was available for the last three hours of the procedure. Intake in the control condition was some 50% lower in the elderly compared with the young, and, in comparison, HOI produced a large attenuation of water intake in the young (6.5 vs. 14.3 mL/kg) but not in the elderly (6.7 vs. 8.5 mL/kg). This result is consistent with the interpretation that the elderly have functionally loaded cardiopulmonary baroreceptors such that additional central volume expansion by water immersion has no effect on thirst and drinking. Some evidence suggested that the elderly, compared with the young, recruit arterial baroreceptors to deal physiologically with HOI. This important study points to a substantial decrement in cardiopulmonary control over drinking in the elderly, and this stands in striking contrast to their generally adequate or normal osmometric function.

In a study to identify changes in neuronal activity in the brain during dehydration and rehydration, Farrell et al. (2008) examined regional blood flow using positron emission tomography (PET) imaging of intravenously administered $H_2{}^{15}O$ in young and old men of mean ages 24 and 68 years, respectively. Ten scans were completed before the infusion, during a 68-minute intravenous infusion of hypertonic NaCl, and after a drinking period of eight minutes. The increases in plasma osmolality and thirst ratings were comparable in young and old cohorts during the infusion, but AVP was initially higher in the elderly and increased very little during the infusion. After access to water, during which time the young drank twice as much as the elderly (3.9 and 1.9 mL/kg, respectively), thirst ratings and AVP decreased more slowly or less completely in the elderly than in the young. Both age groups showed activation of the anterior midcingulate cortex (aMCC) and pregenual anterior cingulate cortex (pACC) at the time of maximum thirst or at the end of the infusion. After drinking, both groups showed a decline of activation in the aMCC, but the reduction was larger in the elderly in relation to the amount drunk. It was suggested that the reduced drinking in the elderly was due to greater satiation. Notably, the time allowed for drinking and the amounts consumed in this study were considerably less than in those previously discussed. Because thirst ratings did not differ with age, the amount consumed relative to peak thirst was lower in the elderly. The reasons for these discrepancies from some other studies is not clear, but they might include the unusual conditions (e.g., noise, restraint) associated with PET scanning.

Discrepancies notwithstanding, all of these studies demonstrate some difference between the young and old in fluid regulation and/or drinking. Cowen et al. (2013) suggest that different inclusion criteria for "healthy" subjects may underlie some of the discrepancies, although the test environments, including specifics of the visual analog scales, cognitive load, and water presentation, may be important. In addition to environmental factors noted for the PET study, almost all of these studies have used supine subjects – an abnormal posture for drinking – and various degrees of tethering.

The apparent insensitivity of volumetric thirst systems in the elderly, exacerbated by other problems including polypharmacy, dementia, and reduced mobility, places a particular burden on caregivers to ensure that their charges are adequately hydrated (Cook et al., 2018). Since females may be at higher risk for these problems than males, perhaps in part because they live longer, additional studies with female subjects especially more than 70 years old are warranted. Finally, it is relevant to recall that de Castro (1992) did not find age-related differences in fluid consumption in free-living humans. Participants maintained seven-day diaries of ad libitum food and fluid intake, and the vast majority of fluid consumed was with meals and ensured adequate hydration. It follows that if this habitual and therefore highly learned or anticpated access to food and fluid at the same time is decoupled, as in the foregoing laboratory studies or under adverse environmental conditions such as a heat wave in a temperate zone, deficient fluid intake may be more likely to occur.

10.1.2 Animal Studies

Animal studies, mostly using rats, have examined components of drinking (i.e., intracellular, extracellular) separately, as well as in hybrid dehydration conditions. Several different strains of rats have been used in these studies. Fischer 344 and Fischer-brown Norway cross have long life spans and are favored models of healthy aging because they are relatively free of organic diseases into later life. However, the main results are similar across strains, so this aspect will not be a focus of this discussion.

In regard to osmoregulatory thirst, several studies have been published that used rats of two or more ages, along with different doses of NaCl (1–10 mEq/kg), concentrations (0.4–2 M), and routes of administration. In an attempt to standardize these data for economical presentation in Figure 10.2, reported intakes were transformed to mL/kg/2 h, adjusted upward by the volume of the injection (in mL/kg), and the sum was divided by the dose of NaCl (mEq/kg) administered. Other transforms or derivations might have been applied (see Thunhorst et al., 2009), but all yield comparable conclusions. Most studies used only males, one used females (Martin et al., 1985), and two used both males and females (Begg et al., 2012; Rowland et al., 1997). Sex differences in these latter studies were generally small, and data from these are presented as the mean for males and females. Munich Wistar (McKinley et al., 2006), brown Norway (Thunhorst & Johnson, 2003; Thunhorst et al., 2009), Fischer 344 × brown Norway (Thunhorst et al., 2014), Sprague Dawley

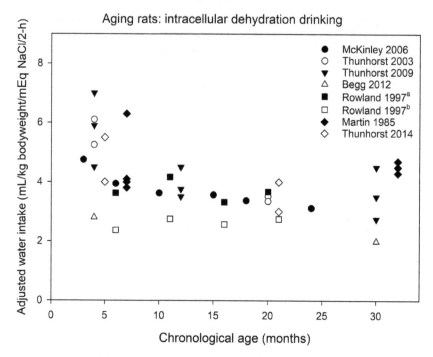

Figure 10.2 Water intake in rats at various chronological ages in response to intracellular dehydration with hypertonic NaCl. Intakes in 2 h have been adjusted for mean body weight and dose of NaCl administered. Each study tested several ages, all identified with the same symbol. For Rowland et al. (1997); [a]indicates Sprague Dawley and [b]Fischer strains.

(Rowland et al., 1997), and Wistar (Martin et al., 1985) strains show relatively similar adjusted intakes to NaCl as a function of age, with the most notable trend for intakes to decline before about six months of age (about 20% of life span), after which time they remain fairly constant. For unknown reasons, and at all ages, Fischer 344 (Rowland et al., 1997) and La Trobe brown Norway (Begg et al., 2012) rats had the lowest adjusted intakes.

Each of the studies that used the youngest rats (McKinley et al., 2006; Thunhorst et al., 2009, 2014; Thunhorst & Johnson, 2003) found that the steepest decline in intake is at the young rather than the old end of the range (Figure 10.2). While the excretion of the NaCl load may require slightly more water in old compared with young rats (Thunhorst et al., 2009), reflecting loss of renal concentrating power, water intakes were in all cases adequate to respond to the administered challenge. This perspective reframes the question from one of age-related decline in drinking to one of why drinking is exuberant in young adult rats. There is no informed answer to that question, but it is remarkable that the majority of studies in the physiology and neurobiology of fluid homeostasis in rodents have used young (2–4 months) subjects and therefore provide results that may be unrepresentative of the major part of the life span. Whether, and at what age, a similar early decline in osmoregulatory thirst may occur in humans is unknown.

Several studies have included peripheral administration of angiotensin II (ANG II) as part of a battery of dipsogens in rats of various ages and strains. The results of these studies for the youngest (3–4 months) and oldest (22–30 months) cohorts are shown in Figure 10.3. There is no systematic change in ANG II–evoked drinking with age. Many of these studies include intermediate ages (not shown), and these also show no difference from either young or old cohorts (Begg et al., 2012; McKinley et al., 2006; Rowland, DelBianco, & Fregly, 1996; Rowland et al., 1997; Silver et al., 1993; Simpkins et al., 1983). Because the adjusted water intakes after osmotic stimulation were comparable across studies (Figure 10.2), the fourfold difference in water intake evoked by similar doses of ANG II in the different studies is striking and one for which I have no explanation.

Only one study has used the preferred intravenous route of administration of ANG II (50 ng/kg/min × 3 h; Thunhorst et al., 2010) and found that intake was lower (11 mL/kg) in four-month-old rats than in 12- or 29-month-old cohorts (18 and 16 mL/kg, respectively). These data are consistent with an absence of age-related decline, but they were not included in Figure 10.3 because of the smaller dose administered. When the normal rise in blood pressure caused by ANG II was prevented by prior injection of minoxidil, intake was elevated in the young cohort (to 19 mL/kg/3 h), but it was unchanged in the middle-aged and old cohorts. This suggests that drinking in the youngest group is inhibited by hypertension, presumably mediated via baroreceptors, but this effect is lost by middle age. The threshold dose for onset of drinking to ANG II has not been examined as a function of age.

As described in Chapter 5, peripherally administered ANG II must reach receptors in the sensory lamina terminalis to exert a dipsogenic effect. The number of ANG II type 1 (AT1) receptors, assessed either autoradiographically by the binding of radiolabeled ANG II in the paraventricular nucleus (PVN) and organum vasculosum of the lamina terminalis (OVLT; Rowland et al., 1997) or by AT1A mRNA expression in a hypothalamic block (Begg et al., 2012), were about 50% lower in old

Aging rats: ANG I or II induced drinking

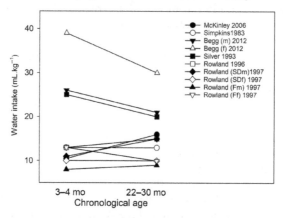

Figure 10.3 Mean 1 or 2 h water intakes, adjusted for body weight, of young (3–4 month) and old (22–30 month) cohorts of rats following subcutaneous injection of ANG I or ANG II (100–200 µg.kg⁻¹). Each study is indicated with a different symbol. Intakes in young and old cohorts are joined to facilitate comparison.

compared with young cohorts. In contrast to the PVN and OVLT, Rowland et al. (1997) did not find a reliable decline of AT1R binding in the subfornical organ (SFO) or median preoptic nucleus (MnPO). It appears that the dipsogenic potency of ANG II is maintained in aging rats despite some apparent and possibly heterogeneous loss of relevant receptor expression in AT1-rich regions of the brain that have been associated with drinking and/or AVP secretion.

In contrast to the results with exogenous ANG II, dipsogenic treatments that are thought to depend on endogenously generated ANG II show an unequivocal age-related decline. The results for acute hypotension are compiled in Figure 10.4. In this figure, water intakes are unadjusted for isoproterenol dose (15–40 µg/kg). Data are shown for males (McKinley et al., 2006; Simpkins et al., 1983; Thunhorst et al., 2011), females (Hardy et al., 2018; Martin et al., 1985), or both (Rowland et al., 1997) and represent rats of several different strains. The age-related decline in drinking is particularly marked after six months of age. Similar results were obtained using the alternative hypotensive agents salbutamol (Thunhorst et al., 2011), minoxidil (Thunhorst, et al., 2009), or bradykinin plus captopril (Rowland, Del Bianco, & Fregly, 1996). Not all of these studies reported water intakes after a placebo or control treatment, but these tend to be 5–10 mg/kg at

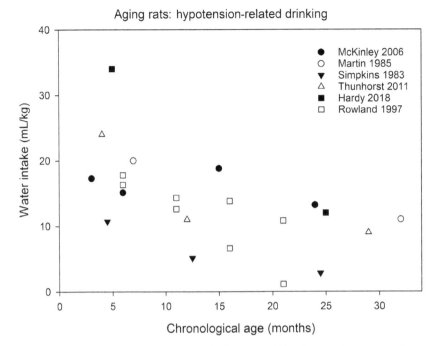

Figure 10.4 Mean water intake in 90- or 120-min tests by groups of rats at various chronological ages following injection of agents causing acute hypotension; most studies used isoproterenol in the range 15–40 μg.kg^{-1}. Each study tested several ages, all identified with the same symbol.

all ages, so the data in Figure 10.4 indicate a loss of almost all the dipsogenic response after middle age.

Measurement of plasma renin activity (PRA) 30 minutes after isoproterenol or salbutamol revealed the expected high level in four-month-old rats, but it was reduced to about 60% of this level at 12 months and was completely absent at 29 months (Thunhorst et al., 2011). Further, isoproterenol caused a large increase (relative to 0.15 M saline) in Fos-ir in the SFO and OVLT of young (five months) but not old (25 months) female brown Norway rats (Hardy et al., 2018). A similar loss of increase was found in the AP and NTS, but this may have been due to an increase in the number of labeled cells after the control injection rather than a change in number after isoproterenol. Using a hypotensive combination, bradykinin plus captopril, Rowland, Del Bianco, and Fregly (1996) likewise found greatly reduced Fos-ir in the SFO, MnPO, and supraoptic nucleus (SON) of old (22 months) compared with young (four months) female Sprague Dawley rats. These findings are consistent with a gradual age-related loss of renin secretion and resultant lack of elevation in circulating ANG II to produce brain activation and drinking. Hardy et al. (2018) suggested that increased expression of glial marker protein (GFAP) in aging could produce interference with neuronal activation by ANG II in the SFO and other regions. However, ANG II is not generated by isoproterenol in aging, and, as discussed above, the dipsogenic response to exogenous ANG II is maintained into late life (Figure 10.3), suggesting that neuronal activation is maintained. Use of near-threshold doses of ANG II might reveal deficits in transduction.

Whether the loss of PRA response is due to direct loss of β-adrenergic responsiveness in the kidney, including mild glomerulopathy, or to a factor related to blood pressure cannot readily be determined. Baylis et al. (1997) reported that the PRA response of rats to ACE1 inhibition was greatly reduced, and the hypotensive reaction amplified. This almost complete loss of PRA response was also found using other stressors (Baylis et al., 1998). Simpkins et al. (1983) reported that the maximum chronotropic response to isoproterenol fell from about 110 beats/minute at four months to 70% and 30% of that at 12 and 24 months of age, respectively. This was confirmed and extended by Thunhorst et al. (2009) using the longer-acting hypotensive agent minoxidil, with maximum chronotropic response at 12 and 30 months of age about 80% and 50% of that at four months. Further, the associated drop in mean arterial pressure, stable over a three-hour measurement period, was comparable (−25 Torr) in four- and 12-month-old cohorts but was greatly increased (−60 Torr) in the 30-month-old group. This latter effect is probably due to a combination of decreased chronotropic response and a complete failure to generate ANG II. This raises a potential confound in the drinking data in Figure 10.4 because the aging cohorts would have been more hypotensive. To control for this, Thunhorst et al. (2009) examined water intake as a function of degree of hypotension by adjusting minoxidil dose ranges from 1 to 20 mg/kg in the young cohort to 0.5–3 mg/kg in the oldest cohort; in this way, there were overlapping pressure changes in all of the groups. The overall slope of the water intake (mL/100 g body weight) versus blood pressure change (Torr) curve was linear at each age, but the slope was reduced by about 40% and 80% at 12 and 30 months, relative to four months (Figure 10.5). Further, when cumulative intake was plotted for specific levels of hypotension and as a function of duration, it may be seen that there is a clear and progressive decline of intake with age, and, with the exception of the lowest degree of hypotension, drinking occurred throughout the session. These changes in dipsogenic response to minoxidil closely reflect the abovementioned age-related

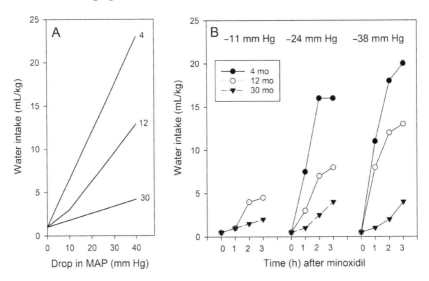

Figure 10.5 Effect of monoxidil on water intake and arterial pressure in 4-, 12-, and 30-month-old cohorts of rats (from Thunhorst et al., 2009). Doses of minoxidil were adjusted downward with age. Panel A shows mean water intake at various levels of hypotension as a function of age. Panel B shows the time course of drinking after minoxidil at doses titrated to produce similar ranges of hypotension at all three ages.

changes in PRA secretion to isoproterenol (Thunhorst et al., 2009). These data suggest that it is the loss of PRA response and presumably in plasma ANG II so generated, rather than differences in arterial pressure, that underlie the age-related loss of dipsogenic potency of hypotensive drugs.

Another way in which the contribution of ANG II to drinking has been tested is with the use of ACE1 inhibitors administered chronically at a low dose. Rowland, Del Bianco, and Fregly (1996) mixed enalapril into the food of young (five months) and old (22 months) Fisher 344 rats and found a tenfold stimulation of daily intake of isotonic NaCl above pre-treatment baseline in the young cohort, but only a twofold increase in the old group. Concurrent water intake was not different across ages or condition. (Unlike many strains of rats, Fisher 344 rats drink very little isotonic NaCl under baseline conditions.) At the end of the regimen, PRA was threefold higher in young compared with old cohorts; the old rats had typical baseline values, although those were not measured in this study, again implying a near-total loss of PRA response. A consistent result was found using the ACE 1 inhibitor ramipril mixed into food and

0.45 M NaCl as the salt available, but in this case PRA was elevated in both five- and 20-month-old cohorts (Rowland et al., 1997). Thunhorst and Johnson (2003) found that captopril, administered in drinking water, increased daily intake of 0.3 M NaCl in young but not old cohorts of brown Norway rats, without a change in concurrent water intake. These studies are consistent with the interpretation that chronically elevated PRA and ANG II increase preference for or intake of NaCl solutions, and this does not occur in old rats. The study by Rowland et al. (1997) gives some insight into the chronology of this effect, with a partial loss by 10 months and an almost complete loss by 15 months of age. This is consistent with the time course for decline of minoxidil-induced drinking revealed by Thunhorst et al. (2009).

Sodium depletion has been used to produce extracellular fluid loss and, with overnight maintenance of the depleted state, induces a relatively selective sodium appetite that is believed to be at least in part ANG II dependent. Begg et al. (2012) injected young (four months) and old (30 months) rats with the diuretic furosemide, and after 24 hours without food they were given a two-bottle choice between water and 0.5 M NaCl. After two hours, NaCl intake was 10 mL/kg and 2 mL/kg in young and old rats, respectively, averaged for males and females. Water intake was also stimulated, but, notably, the resultant mixture was near isotonic (0.14 M) for young rats but was markedly hypotonic (0.07 M) for old rats. Thunhorst et al. (2014) performed a similar study using 0.3 M NaCl and found two-hour intakes of 5 mL/kg in young rats and, with their concurrent water intake, made an approximately isotonic mix. In contrast, old rats consumed undetectable amounts of NaCl and only 1 mL/kg of water. These authors repeated the same test three times at 8–12-day intervals and found that intakes of NaCl approximately doubled over that series in the young rats, with the mixture rising to 0.21 M, whereas the older rats still consumed very little salt or water. Both young and old rats excreted about 4 mmol of Na^+ per kilogram of body weight at each test, but the old rats restored less than 15% of that loss by drinking NaCl even at the third test. Rowland et al. (1997) used dilute NaCl (0.05 M) to slow repletion after furosemide; they found a partial decline (~40%) in NaCl consumed at 20 months compared with younger ages, and a larger residual Na^+ deficit at the end of the drinking test. Thus, all studies performed have found an age-related deficit in repletion of extracellular fluid loss via NaCl intake.

The final method to produce purely extracellular thirst, using polyethelene glycol (PEG) as the dipsogen, has been performed in only one study in aging, using Munich Wistar male rats (McKinley et al., 2006). The youngest rats (three months) showed the highest six-hour water intake (22 mL/kg); those of intermediate ages (6–15 months) averaged 14 mL/kg, and the oldest (18–24 months) were markedly impaired (5 mL/kg). NaCl solution (0.3 M) was also present but was not consumed in significant amounts by any group. The plasma volume deficits, measured in separate six- and 18-month cohorts, were comparable, but no measures of PRA or blood pressure were taken. Since PEG-induced drinking in young rats is thought to be independent of PRA and hence ANG II (Chapter 5), then either there is an age-related dependence on renin and/or while the hypotensive action of PEG is negligible in the young, it could be more substantial in older rats and produce resultant behavioral impairments.

In response to stimuli that produce mixed intracellular and extracellular dehydration, rats tested with water but no food show inconsistent age-related effects. Martin et al. (1985) reported that drinking in the 30 minutes following 24-hour water (but not food) deprivation also remained unchanged with age. An essentially similar result was found by Rowland et al. (1997): Male Sprague Dawley rats showed the largest decline (again, largely a function of the high intake by the youngest group) – amounting to only about 30%. In contrast, McKinley et al. (2006) found that two-hour water intake after 24 hours of water deprivation was reduced from about 45 mL/kg at three months of age to 30 and 20 mL/kg at six and 24 months, respectively. A similar 60% reduction in 30-versus four-month-old rats was reported by Begg et al. (2012). Notably, the intakes of the young groups differed substantially between these studies, presumably reflecting the Na^+ content of the stock food available during the deprivation period and/or the degree of dehydration anorexia. However, both the relatively high (45 mL/kg; McKinley et al., 2006) and low (12 mL/kg; Begg et al., 2012) intakes by the three- to four-month-old groups were linked with greater than 50% declines in the oldest groups. Begg et al. (2012) also reported about 50% less drinking in 30-month-old compared with four-month-old rats after a thermal stress (40°C for 1 h) despite comparable weight loss, a result consistent with Whyte et al. (2004), which was mentioned in Chapter 9.

Martin et al. (1985) reported that 24-hour food and water intakes were comparable in seven- and 32-month-old cohorts of females. Two studies in male rats (McKinley et al., 2006; Silver et al., 1993) found age-related declines of around 33% in spontaneous water intake, whereas another study found no age difference (Thunhorst & Johnson, 2003). Silver et al. (1993) found no age-related change in the day–night distribution of water intake. McKinley et al. (2006) measured concurrent food intake and found that it decreased in proportion to water intake (i.e., the water-to-food ratio was constant). In a one-hour test with both food and water following overnight food deprivation, Silver et al. (1993) reported an age-related decline in intakes of both commodities, but the water-to-food ratio was similar in all age cohorts. Thus, when both food and water are concurrently available, the intakes are strictly proportional across all ages.

One study has examined drinking in aging C57BL/6 mice (Silver et al., 1991). These authors measured the number of licks rather than actual intake. Assuming there is no age-related change in volume per lick, they found some deficits in 25-month-old compared with three-month-old mice in the first few minutes of testing sessions following water deprivation or hypertonic NaCl injection, but over a longer period (up to 4 h) the older mice caught up with the young groups. The authors argue that drinking induced by deprivation is impaired, but a more reasonable interpretation is that it is slower to be expressed. In rat studies discussed above that included time courses for drinking, there is little evidence for a delayed onset.

10.2   Polydipsia

Fitzsimons (1979) classified syndromes of excessive drinking – polydipsia- as either symptomatic or pathological. Symptomatic polydipsia occurs most commonly when there is a primary fault in fluid retention by the kidney and the increased drinking is a natural and appropriate response to the physiological condition of increased urinary losses. Diabetes insipidus is an example of this, and has several categories. One category is loss of AVP secretion from the anterior pituitary gland, and this can be either genetic or subsequent to a tumor or other brain damage. A second category is insensitivity of the kidney to AVP or other renal pathology. Other conditions producing polydipsia due to fluid loss include fever (excessive sweating), diabetes mellitus, and kidney dialysis. I will not discuss these syndromes of symptomatic poly-dipsia further because they do not involve a dysfunction of thirst.

Barlow and de Wardener (1959) defined *compulsive drinking* as excessive consumption of fluid due to psychological disturbance. The population that they described was 80% female and was characterized by plasma hypo-osmolality (269 vs. 280 mOsm/kg in normal controls), with most common incidence in the age range 35–59 years. These patients often presented a history of psychiatric problems, including various psychoses including schizophrenia or irrational belief in a therapeutic effect of water (Goldman et al., 1988; Goldman et al., 1997). To study osmoregulatory thirst and drinking, patients with a diagnosis of compulsive drinking and age-matched normal controls (average age 30 years) were given a two-hour intravenous infusion of hypertonic NaCl (855 mmol/kg total solute load), during which blood samples and thirst ratings were obtained every 30 minutes (Thompson et al., 1991). Subjects were allowed to drink water for two hours starting 15 minutes after the end of the infusion. The results are shown in the left-hand panels of Figure 10.6. Basal osmolality of the compulsive drinkers was 1–2% below that of controls, but the changes produced by the infusion were strictly parallel. The absolute levels and changes of AVP were also similar in both groups. In contrast, the thirst ratings were consistently higher in the compulsive drinkers before, during, and after infusion. The compulsive drinkers consumed more than twice as much water as controls. The authors argued that the osmotic threshold for thirst was reduced by 4.4% in compulsive drinkers compared to controls, although that analysis depends on assumptions concerning linear extrapolation of these functions to zero thirst. Nonetheless, compulsive drinkers clearly experience greater thirst than controls, even after drinking to temporary satiation after the infusion. There was no deficit in water excretion in polydipsic patients.

Another identified clinical syndrome is inappropriate ADH (or AVP) secretion (SIADH). An identical infusion of hypertonic saline was given to SIADH patients and normal controls (average age 52 years; Smith et al., 2004). The results from this study are shown in the right-hand panels of Figure 10.6. The SIADH patients had almost 10% basal reductions in plasma osmolality, due in part to high baseline AVP secretion, but thirst ratings and amount of water consumed after the infusion did not differ between groups. A lowered set point of osmoregulation is suggested. Note also that drinking to satiation did not suppress ADH levels below the normally elevated baseline in the SIADH patients.

In a discussion of polydipsia and psychosis (McKinley et al., 2004), it was suggested there is no animal model to advance the analysis. A model of inappropriately excessive drinking in rats has been described by Falk (1961) and is known as either schedule-induced polydipsia or adjunctive drinking. The critical features of this protocol are reduction of body weight by food restriction and delivery of small food morsels according to a fixed interval or time schedule in daily sessions lasting up to several hours. Under these conditions, rats become highly agitated and often drink compulsively after delivery of each food morsel. In such sessions, animals can drink approaching their own body weight in water, and this has now been shown in several species. Of particular interest to clinical polydipsia, mice show a strong gene-linked propensity for adjunctive drinking. Symons and Sprott (1976) showed that DBA/2 mice developed, over the course of about six sessions with food delivered every

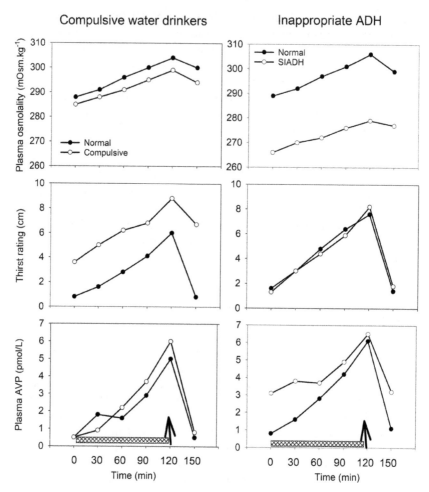

Figure 10.6 Changes in plasma osmolality, thirst rating, and plasma AVP concentration before, during, and after intravenous infusion of hypertonic NaCl (855 mmol.kg^{-1}) in humans. The left panels show data for compulsive water drinkers and normal controls (from Thompson et al., 1991). The right panels show data from patients with a syndrome of inappropriate ADH secretion (SIADH) or normal controls (from Smith et al., 2004). Hatched bar indicates the infusion time and arrows show the time at which water was presented. (There was in fact a 15-min hiatus between the end of infusion and water presentation.)

150 seconds (an FI 150 schedule), intakes averaging 7 mL per three hours. The food intake during this time was about 1.4 g, which normally would be accompanied by 1–2 mL of water intake. In contrast, C57BL/6 mice on the same FI 150 schedule did not develop intakes in excess of 1–2 mL. This suggests a single gene locus for polydipsia, and backcross experiments yielded results consistent with this interpretation (Symons & Sprott, 1976). A more recent study (Ford et al., 2013) did not find such a large difference between DBA/2 and C57BL/6 mice, possibly in part because the level of food restriction or weight loss was only about one-half that of the Symons and Sprott study. The parametric study by Ford et al. (2013) revealed that drinking by the C57BL/6 mice was strictly a function of food consumed because as the schedule interval was increased, the amount of food received and water intake decreased. In contrast, water intake of DBA/2 mice increased with intervals up to a maximum at FI 180 seconds, indicating true polydipsia.

Adjunctive drinking is a complex protocol, and, aside from a clear genetic link, its physiological basis remains unclear. Pharmacological studies have been conducted in rats, and, in general, drugs that may be useful in the treatment of obsessive-compulsive disorder attenuate polydipsia (Rodriguez et al., 2017).

10.3   Hypodipsia

When intake is chronically insufficient to replace fluid losses, a new steady state will be reached in which body fluid content is reduced (as measured by increased plasma osmolality and/or decreased plasma volume), yet thirst or drinking is not apparent. One clinical presentation of this is essential hypernatremia, in which plasma osmolality and Na^+ are chronically elevated. DeRubertis et al. (1971, 1974) described several such patients and found one feature to be diuresis with hypernatremia, indicating a loss of osmotic control of AVP secretion. Fluid loading was therefore an ineffective treatment. However, AVP synthesis and secretion during hypovolemia was normal, and the authors thus suggested there was a selective defect in the neural apparatus coupling osmoreceptors to AVP secretion. Hiyama et al. (2017) reported three new patients as well as one from a previous study in whom thirst and AVP secretion were absent or deficient despite hypernatremia. Magnetic resonance imaging of their brains did not indicate any structural lesions in the hypothalamus. However, the blood serum from all these patients contained antibodies reactive to mouse SFO and, in one case, OVLT. Injection of the immunoglobulin fraction of serum from one patient caused wild-type mice to develop hypernatremia and caused cell death in the SFO. The authors suggested that autoimmune destruction of the SFO may underlie the clinical syndrome.

In animals, mostly rats, many different locations of brain lesions were shown to produce hypodipsia. Aside from acute adipsia with certain locations of damage (for review, see Epstein & Teitelbaum, 1972; Grossman, 1990), other lesions produced chronically reduced daily water intake without change in food intake, hence reducing water-to-food ratios. One such lesion is in the zona incerta, dorsal to the lateral hypothalamus (Evered & Mogenson, 1977; Rowland et al., 1979) which also produces a deficit to acute osmoregulatory thirst. The total fluid balance of such preparations was not routinely investigated. The observation by Buggy and Johnson (1977) that lesions of the preoptic-periventricular or anteroventral third ventricle (AV3V, now known to include the OVLT) caused rats to be hypernatremic ushered in the focus on the lamina terminalis which has been discussed in many previous chapters. Relevant to the clinical syndrome, rats with AV3V damage had defective osmoregulatory drinking, but drank normally to PEG-induced hypovolemia. Immediate postlesion natriuresis without appropriate drinking led to hypernatremia which was never corrected (Bealer, 1983). Further, hypothalamo-hypophyseal explants from AV3V lesion rats showed no release of AVP to increased osmolality of the perfusion medium (Sladek & Johnson, 1983). Lesion of the SFO did not cause hypernatremia in dogs (Marson et al., 1985) and did not abolish drinking to hypertonic saline. Lesions that include the ventral MnPO cause either hyperdipsia or hypodipsia, often with hypernatremia and deficits in osmotic thirst and AVP secretion (Gardiner & Stricker, 1985; McKinley et al., 2004; Marson et al., 1985). We cannot ignore the possibility of species differences in regard to the role of these structures of the lamina terminalis, but the studies in rats, dogs, and sheep suggest that the clinical presentation of hypernatremia described by Hiyama et al. (2017) may also have included primary or secondary degeneration within parts of the MnPO.

10.4   Summary

Experimental analysis of drinking in humans has yielded inconsistent results, ranging from no deficits relative to young groups, to substantial deficits. It is possible that cognitive or other factors can account for some of these differences between studies. Age-related dehydration in at-risk human populations may be minimized by ensuring adequate food intake and meal-associated drinking and/or provision of foods with high fluid content. With the exception of hypotension-related stimuli, age-related declines in drinking by rats after about 25% of the life span are small. Increased drinking at youngest ages (3–4 months) seems to be the unexplained anomaly; a generic explanation would be maturation in late adolescence of an as-yet unrecognized inhibitory mechanism.

Symptomatic polydipsia occurs when fluid losses from the body are increased, whereas pathological polydipsia occurs when increased drinking occurs without any defect in fluid retention. These clinical conditions are considered, as are cases of hypernatremia, when the effective set point for plasma Na^+ appears to be elevated. There is evidence that these conditions may in some cases be linked to pathology of the lamina terminalis.

11   Comparative Aspects of Body
         Fluid Regulation

Over 1 million species of animals have been described with some degree
of scientific scrutiny. All of them are faced with a common problem of
regulating body fluids. They achieve this through regulation of various
combinations of intake (e.g., drinking) and output (e.g., urine). The
purpose of this chapter is to briefly review some of the diverse mechanisms used by species other than the select few mammals that are featured
in the previous chapters of this book, and to apply this perspective to
understand some aspects of drinking in those mammals from developmental or evolutionary perspectives.

11.1   Aquatic Species

Aquatic vertebrate species include bony fish and mammals. I will briefly
consider marine mammals at the end of this section, but first I discuss
teleost fish, which evolved at least 150 million years ago and comprise
almost half of all known vertebrate species. Life evolved in oceans,
probably of lower salinity than today, but nonetheless a saltwater milieu.
Today, fish can be characterized as permanently living in seawater (e.g.,
haddock), which has NaCl content of 30–40 g/kg, permanently living in
fresh water (e.g., goldfish), or migrating into or though brackish water
(Figure 11.1, panel A). Brackish water has a range of NaCl contents
between fresh (zero) and seawater, and may change over a short distance;
tidal river estuaries are a good example of such a transitional environment of salinity. Only salmon and eels truly migrate between the
extremes. Another classification for fish is stenohaline versus euryhaline.
Stenohaline fish are those unable to adapt to major changes in salinity –
they are intrinsic freshwater or seawater species. Euryhaline fish are able
to adapt to changes in ambient salinity and do so by salinity-related
changes in expression of endogenous elements such as genes and gene
products that confer alterations in fluid regulation (Takei et al., 2014).

   Unlike more primitive aquatic animals that change their internal
milieu to some extent as the salinity of the environment changes, both

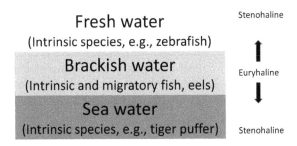

Figure 11.1 Schematic representation of the range of environments to which aquatic species have adapted. Intrinsic species do not migrate between zones (stenohaline), whereas euryhaline species can migrate between zones with attendant physiological changes.

of these classes of teleosts maintain the osmolality of their extracellular fluids at about 300 mOsm/kg (approximately 9 g/kg NaCl). Ambient salinity drives a spectrum of physiological responses to maintain the internal osmotic milieu in the face of a different external NaCl level. Table 11.1 describes some of the phenotypic differences in osmoregulatory function as a function of hypotonic (0.15 M NaCl) or hypertonic (>0.15 M NaCl) environments, with those adaptations becoming more vigorous as the disparity from isotonic increases. The gill is one of the key organs for regulation of water and salt balance, and it contains specialized epithelial cells called ionocytes that express a variety of ion transporters (Kültz, 2015; Takei et al., 2014), including those from two major clades, NKCC (Na^+-K^+-$2Cl^-$ cotransporter) and NCC (Na^+-Cl^- cotransporter).

Fish may drink in some situations, especially in a high-salinity environment. Fish always have water in their mouths, and drinking is accomplished via a swallowing reflex (i.e., relaxation of the esophageal sphincter) that appears to be organized in the brainstem. Swallowing high-NaCl water drives absorption of water through the wall of the gastrointestinal tract. This, coupled with excretion of NaCl by the kidney and gill and/or the overlying operculum, leads to an effective defense against the hypertonic milieu. Swallowing is an integral component of that defense. In contrast, fish living in hypotonic environments rarely if ever drink because their problem is to prevent water from diluting their internal fluids. In this very brief overview, I have neglected many other linked functions, including divalent ion transport and acid–base balance; for a full consideration, especially of the gill contribution, see Evans et al. (2005).

Table 11.1 *Major phenotypic differences in osmoregulatory function of teleost*

	FW: <9 g.kg^{-1} salinity	SW: >9 g.kg^{-1} salinity
Salt diffusion	Passive salt loss	Passive salt gain
Water movement	Passive hydration	Passive dehydration
GI tract		
Drinking	Low (with food)	High
NaCl-coupled water absorption	Absent	High
Water permeability	Low	High
Gill		
Ionocyte number	Low	High
NKCC activity	Low	High
Epithelial tight junctions	Relatively tight	Relatively leaky
NaCl permeability	Low	High
Water permeability	High	Low
Active NaCl transport	Absorption	Secretion
Kidney		
Urine volume	Large	Small
Urine osmolality	Very low	Isosmotic
Distal tubule water reabsorption	Very low	High
Distal tubule Na$^+$ reabsorption	High	Very low

Note. Adapted from Kültz (2015). FW = fresh or low brackish water; SW = sea or high brackish water; GI = gastrointestinal.

Evans et al. (2005) note that relevant osmoreceptors may be present in the branchial epithelium (i.e., gill), vasculature, or central nervous system. Such osmoreceptors presumably serve as the initiating part of a sequence orchestrating secretion of a large number of hormones shown to modulate changes in proliferation, differentiation, transcription, and transcriptome regulation that underlie the system changes shown in Table 11.1. Major advances have been made using molecular biological techniques in zebrafish (*Danio rerio*) and medaka (rice fish, *Oryzias latipes*; Guh & Hwang, 2017; Yan & Hwang, 2019). Key hormones include vasotocin and isotocin, homologs of mammalian vasopressin and oxytocin, cortisol, atrial natriuretic peptide (ANP), and angiotensin II (ANG II; Takei, 2000; Takei et al., 2014).

Osmotic changes in fish often are accompanied by changes in plasma volume (Anderson et al., 2007). For example, in dogfish adapted to normal seawater, within about four hours of transfer to 20% lower or higher salinity, blood volume was, respectively, increased or decreased by at least 10%. Reductions in volume have been shown to be an effective stimulant of drinking or swallowing in dogfish (Anderson et al., 2007), probably mediated by production of ANG II and its action at the area postrema in the brainstem (Katayama et al., 2018; Nobata et al., 2013).

Kobayashi et al. (1983) made a systematic analysis of drinking induced by application of ANG II in many species of teleosts. Of 20 species of stenohaline freshwater fish, only seven exhibited swallowing to ANG II. In contrast, 11 out of 17 stenohaline seawater fish exhibited swallowing, as did euryhaline species. The authors proposed that ANG II–induced drinking may represent an emergency reaction to encountering a more hypertonic environment in which they are at risk of dehydration.

Katayama et al. (2018) and others have argued that this reflexive swallowing in fish is not true thirst, and this is not exhibited until animals locomote or propel themselves from dry to wet situations. Such behaviors are first found in amphibians such as mudskippers or toads. For example, mudskippers (gobies) spend most of their time on dry land, but when dehydrated or injected cerebroventricularly with ANG II, they migrate to water and drink and/or absorb water through their skin. Interestingly, drying of the perioral region is also a sufficient stimulus for drinking, suggesting that thirst may be mainly a local rather than a general sensation (Katayama et al., 2018). Although mudskippers have a forebrain circumventricular organ (CVO; the organum vasculosum of the lamina terminalis [OVLT]), there is no evidence that this is activated by dipsogenic doses of ANG II; instead, as in fish and eels, the main site of action of ANG II is in the hindbrain area postrema, although sensations from a dry mouth may activate forebrain regions.

Marine mammals do not have gills; instead, the principal organ for fluid and electrolyte regulation is the kidney. In general, the kidneys of marine mammals have an anatomy consistent with the ability to produce concentrated urine, although there are marked differences between Cetacea (dolphins and whales), Pinnipedia (seals, sea lions, and walruses), and Sirenia (manatees; Ortiz, 2001). Concentrating ability may be indexed by urine-to-plasma ratios of osmolality, and these range from about 4 to 7 in various marine or aquatic mammals. This ratio is comparable to that in humans but substantially less than values at least twofold higher found in many small desert-adapted mammals. Some drinking of seawater (i.e., mariposia) has been reported in marine mammals, but it is not thought to be a major or essential contributor to fluid homeostasis and may instead reflect incidental ingestion while eating. An exception may be drinking during thermal stress, such as in tropical or other hot environments (Ortiz, 2001).

11.2 Amphibians and Reptiles

Water conservation mechanisms of amphibians are relatively poor: They are unable to excrete a concentrated urine, and their skin is permeable to water loss (discussed by Fitzsimons, 1979). Amphibians acquire water through their skin via a water absorption response in which the seat and hindlimbs are pressed against a moist substrate. This has been studied in some detail in tree frogs (Maejima et al., 2010) and toads (Goldstein et al., 2003; Propper et al., 1995). Taylor et al. (1999) identified both intracellular and extracellular components to water absorption behavior in spadefoot toads indigenous to an arid environment. ANG II stimulates the water absorption response and is effective after injection of small amounts into the third cerebral ventricle (Maejima et al., 2010; Taylor et al., 1999). The diencephalon of tree frogs expresses ANG II AT1 receptors, but the specific neural circuitry involved is not known.

Reptiles were among the first terrestrial vertebrates and were more successful than amphibians in regard to colonizing many diverse habitats, including arid regions. In distinction from amphibians, the skin of reptiles is much less water permeable. This means that cutaneous water losses are small, but it also precludes water absorption by that route. Most reptiles are carnivorous and often do not have to drink. But when they are dehydrated, they do drink and restore fluid balance rapidly relative to the slow cutaneous absorption of amphibians. For example, rat snakes dehydrated for up to 19 days were found to replace their fluid loss in a single drinking episode (Myer & Kowell, 1971). Consistent with this, sea snakes (*Hydrophilus platurus*) dehydrate during seasonal drought, and they will drink if captured at that time, but they do not do so during the rainy season, when they imbibe fresh water from lenses on the surface (Lillywhite et al., 2019). Murphy and DeNardo (2019) examined the widely held premise that xeric-adapted reptiles do not need to drink because they obtain sufficient metabolic water from their food. They found that meal consumption by dehydrated gila monsters (*Heloderma suspectum*) and rattlesnakes (*Corotalus atrox*) did not improve their hydrational status, but rather exacerbated it. They conclude that such carnivorous species must in fact drink free water, although their tolerance of wide levels of systemic osmolality does not make drinking a short-term necessity.

Common iguanas, whose natural environment lies between xeric and aquatic, were studied under laboratory conditions by Fitzsimons and Kaufman (1977). Intracellular dehydration, produced by acute injections of hypertonic NaCl or sucrose, produced drinking in an amount to accurately dilute the load to isotonicity (Figure 11.2); this resembles drinking in a nephrectomized rat because solute excretion by lizards is extremely slow. The latency to drink (0.5–4 hours) was longer than typically seen in mammals, but when drinking occurred it was as large, discrete bouts. Injection of ANG II also stimulated water intake in

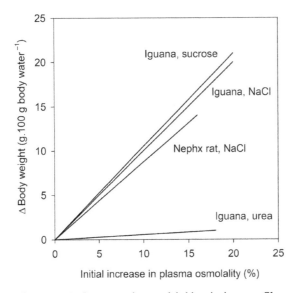

Figure 11.2 Osmoregulatory drinking in iguana. Shown are regression lines from various doses (Fitzsimons & Kaufman, 1977) of hypertonic NaCl, sucrose, or urea. Water intake is equated to weight gain because animals are anuric during the 6 h test period. For comparison, drinking by nephrectomized rats is included.

iguanas, with latency of only a few minutes, and this drinking was additive with that caused by concurrent hypertonic NaCl injection (Fitzsimons & Kaufman, 1977). The location of receptor(s) for these functions have not been reported. The dipsogenic responsiveness of several other species of reptiles in response to peripheral ANG II is described by Kobayashi et al. (1979).

Wilson (1984) noted that juxtaglomerular-like cells and components of the renin-angiotensin system are present in most species of vertebrates, and these are involved in various aspects of osmoregulation, ionic regulation, and vascular control. While water acquisition is often observed, one of the more universal effects of ANG II is to stimulate the sympathetic nervous system.

11.3   Birds

Birds and mammals have both evolved from reptiles and, with the exception of aquatic mammals mentioned previously, might be expected to have similar characteristics of thirst and drinking behavior. One of the first confirmations of this idea was the observation by Akerman et al. (1960) that electrical stimulation of the pigeon forebrain near the ventricular wall of the preoptic area elicited drinking. Peripherally administered hyperosmotic stimuli, principally NaCl, cause reliable dose-related drinking in pigeons (Thornton, 1984), quail (Takei et al., 1988, and chickens (Yeomans & Savory, 1988). Hawkins and Corbit (1973) found the water consumed in the first hour after intraperitoneal (i.p.) injection of graded doses of hypertonic NaCl was almost exactly the amount required to dilute that load to isotonicity, which in pigeons is about 0.17 M NaCl (Figure 11.3, panel A). When access to fluid was prevented for up to four hours after injection, the amount consumed declined by about 10% for every hour, a much less steep decline than in rats. The interpretation of these data is that pigeons, and birds in general, have relatively slow or inefficient renal excretion of an acute osmotic load, and they are much more dependent on drinking to dilute that load compared with typical mammals. Yeomans and Savory (1988) made a similar observation. Pigeons with permanent access to a dilute quinine-flavored water were challenged with NaCl injection (Yeomans & Savory, 1989). Similar to rats (Nicolaïdis & Rowland, 1975), pigeons drank only about 50% of the amount required to dilute the load and, as a result, sustained systemic hyperosmolality for many hours.

Thornton (1984, 1986) further analyzed the contribution of central Na^+ or osmoreceptors to drinking in pigeons. He first showed that pigeons deprived of water for 24 hours lost between 2% and 7% of body weight but, unlike mammals (Chapter 8), completely restored that loss within one hour when water was presented. Infusion of either 0.15 M or 0.3 M NaCl through a cannula ending in the third cerebral ventricle had no effect on drinking after deprivation. In contrast, infusion of water produced a substantial decrease in intake. Infusion of 0.3 M sucrose almost abolished drinking. Thornton interpreted these results to mean that drinking is controlled by an osmoreceptor mechanism and that a normal concentration of Na^+ in the cerebrospinal fluid is necessary for it to operate effectively. Using ^{14}C-2-deoxyglucose uptake to assess metabolic activity, Heuston and Zeigler (1994) examined the subfornical organ (SFO) of pigeons following 0, 24, or 72 hours of water deprivation. They found that mean uptake (optical density of autoradiograms) was increased by about 50% and 150% after 24 and 72 hours of deprivation, respectively, and this change occurred in each of four parts of the SFO examined. There were no changes in the paraventricular nucleus, archistriatum, or neostriatum.

Pigeons and many other avian species drink reliably in response to either central or peripheral administration of ANG II (Kobayashi et al., 1979;

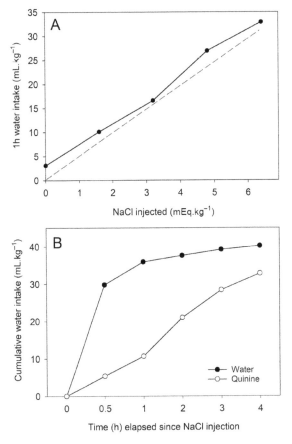

Figure 11.3 Osmoregulatory drinking in pigeons. Panel A (from Hawkins & Corbit, 1973) shows mean water intake in 1 h tests after four different i.p. doses of NaCl. The dashed line is the amount needed to dilute the loads to isotonicity. Panel B (from Yeomans & Savory, 1989) shows time course of intake of water or quinine solution (in birds adapted to quinine) after i.v. injection of 6 mEq NaCl.kg^{-1}.

Massi et al., 1986; Takei, 1977). The SFO is particularly sensitive to local injection of ANG II, and the drinking response to peripheral ANG II is completely eliminated by lesion of the SFO. These lesions do not affect drinking to osmotic stimuli or after water deprivation. Thus, as in mammals, the SFO seems to be a critical region for transduction of circulating ANG II, but it does not seem to play an important role in osmoregulatory drinking, including drinking after water deprivation.

The brain regions responsible for osmoregulatory drinking do not seem to have been characterized.

11.4   Mammals

There is an extensive literature on the adaptations of various species of mammals to harsh climates, and in particular those that are hot and dry and pose a challenge to body fluid homeostasis (e.g., Cooper, 2017; Schmidt-Nielsen & Schmidt-Nielsen, 1952). There are a wide variety of physiological adaptations. For example, desert goats deprived of water for four days had a 25% loss of total body water but only a 5% drop in blood volume, presumably to maintain blood fluidity (Khan et al., 1979). The water was instead translocated from gut and cells, which sustained a net 41% loss during this time. Depending on body mass, ungulates may either drop their core body temperature at night or sustain high daytime core temperatures that would be lethal for humans or rats (Taylor, 1970), both strategies minimizing the need for evaporative cooling and water loss (Chapter 9). My present purpose is not to review what is known about thirst or drinking in these species, but rather to place in context the differences between mammals studied in the laboratory that I have mentioned previously in the text. Kobayashi et al. (1979) made an extensive survey of ANG II–induced drinking in many species of mammals. Notable nonresponders were mice (*Mus musculus*) and gerbils (*Meriones unguiculatus*). The authors noted that these two species originate in arid regions of central Asia and may normally have access to relatively little free water. They speculated that this ecological heritage may have minimized the need for development of robust ANG II–related drinking.

The failure of mice to drink to peripheral administration of ANG II has since been demonstrated by many investigators (e.g., Johnson et al., 2003; Morley & Flood, 1989; Rowland & Fregly, 1988a). In contrast, they do drink to cerebroventricular administration of ANG II (Johnson et al., 2003; Katafuchi et al., 1991). This profile is shared by gerbils, which drink to central but not peripheral administration of ANG II (Block et al., 1974; Wright et al., 1984). Hamsters (*Mesocrecitus auratus*) and spiny mice (*Acomys cahirinus*) are relatively insensitive to peripheral ANG II, requiring high doses to elicit small drinking responses (Czech & Vander Zanden, 1991; Rowland, 1988). Whenever it has been tested, all of these species drink robustly following hypovolemia induced by polyethylene glycol (PEG). They also drink robustly to peripheral administration of hyperosmotic NaCl, although Almli and Weiss (1975) suggested that the threshold for drinking may be two to three times higher in gerbils than rats. It thus seems important that these species as well as strain differences (Kutscher, 1969) are applied to the question of possible variation in structures, connectivity and function of the lamina terminalis, and its role in water intake and/or sodium appetite.

11.5 Summary

Mechanisms of water acquisition, including drinking, are quite varied across species, reflecting their evolutionary and ecological histories. Increased osmolality seems to be a near-universal stimulus to water acquisition, but responsiveness to ANG II is considerably more restricted.

Appendix Methods in Physiology and Neuroscience

A.1 Physiological Measurements

In this section, I give brief descriptions of select methods and relevant assumptions used for measurement of various body fluid compartments, as referred to throughout the text.

A.1.1 Blood and Urine Sampling

Assays performed on blood samples are the primary way in which fluid compartments are measured. The amount of blood needed for a test, or for a battery of tests, will depend on the specific volume(s) required for a particular assay. In humans, a one-time sample is usually via venipuncture, whereas for multiple samples a catheter is inserted, for example, into the forearm. There is brief pain associated with the puncture and, in animals, it may introduce adverse reactions to stress. The ideal is to implant a venous sampling catheter under general anesthesia some hours or days beforehand, and then withdraw single or serial blood samples from the catheter. Acute samples may be obtained in rodents by heart puncture, orbital sinus puncture, or amputation of the tip of the tail, but animal welfare considerations have now either banned or discouraged these methods unless they are part of a terminal procedure that includes anesthesia. Laboratory mice have a total of only about 1 mL blood; consequently, blood sampling in mice is often a terminal procedure.

In a few studies, it is necessary to have an arterial blood sample for which a catheter is introduced beforehand into an appropriate artery. This is often a femoral artery, but in large species it is possible to use a carotid artery surgically routed into a skin flap for convenient access (known as a carotid loop).

Urine is produced continuously but is voided intermittently, so, depending on the type of urine analysis one may use urine from a catheter (continuous) or voided either spontaneously or by pubic pressure. Rodent pups must be induced to void by light pressure, which occurs naturally by the mother licking their genitals. Over longer collection periods, animals are often housed in metabolic cages in which spontaneously voided urine is collected via a funnel beneath a mesh floor. In addition to the ionic composition of urine (see below), the volume voided in unit time or across times may be of relevance.

A.1.1.1   Ionic Concentration and Osmolality The ions most usually assayed for body fluid determinations in urine or blood are sodium (Na^+) and potassium (K^+). Ion-specific electrodes are used most often; these transduce the concentration of a given ion into an electrical potential, read by a voltmeter. Predating the miniaturization and improved selectivity of these electrodes, a more common method was flame photometry. In this method, the component ion(s) in a small fixed volume of sample are thermally excited by a flame. Decay from this state emits light at an ion-specific wavelength, and the total energy at that wavelength (intensity) measured by photometer is proportional to the number of ions.

The total number of dissolved particles in solution gives rise to its osmotic pressure. This is often determined by measuring the freezing point of the solution (i.e., blood plasma or urine) relative to pure water: The depression of the freezing point is proportional to the number of dissolved particles.

A.1.1.2   Plasma Volume Unlike concentrations of ions described above, the total volume of blood plasma cannot be measured directly from a discrete sample. The most accurate method is by injecting intravenously a small volume of solution containing a known concentration of a tracer substance to which cells are impermeable; after a suitable time to achieve homogeneity in the blood, a blood sample is taken and the concentration of the tracer determined. Several tracers are available, including radioisotopes such as [51]Cr (usually as the EDTA salt) or dyes of known maximum wavelength of absorption, such as Evans blue or indocyanine green. These methods provide a single determination and cannot be repeated, at least not until the original tracer has been completely eliminated.

Many experimental designs call for measurement of volume at multiple, frequent times, and the indirect measurements of hematocrit ratio or plasma protein concentration are more useful. Hematocrit ratio is the fractional volume of a blood sample that is, after centrifugation, occupied by packed red blood cells. Because the packed cells still contain small amounts of plasma between them, an adjustment is needed to calculate the true fraction. More usually, however, an experimenter is interested in the change of hematocrit ratio after a procedure or compared between two conditions, and in this case the fractional difference in hematocrit ratio is often used and expressed as percentage change. A key assumption is that the red blood cell number and size do not change or differ significantly across samples during the experiment. Note that a 10% increase in hematocrit ratio (e.g., from 40 to 44) would be interpreted as a reciprocal 10% fall in plasma volume.

Plasma protein concentration may be measured directly by protein binding assays, but more conveniently this is inferred from the refractive index of plasma. The refractive index depends on total dissolved large solids, mainly proteins. Thus, as for the hematocrit ratio, changes in plasma protein concentration across time or between treatment groups can be used to assess percentage differences in plasma volume. A key assumption is that over the time course of the study, the total amount of protein in plasma does not change, such that changes in plasma protein concentration are reciprocal to changes in plasma volume.

In many cases, the hematocrit ratio and plasma protein change in similar but not identical amounts (see Fitzsimons, 1979, for further discussion). In the text, I have usually indicated the specific metric used.

A.1.1.3   Plasma Hormones Relevant to body fluids, the principal blood-borne hormones of interest include the steroids aldosterone and cortisol (corticosterone in rodents), the enzyme renin, and the peptide hormones angiotensin II (ANG II) and arginine vasopressin (AVP), also known as antidiuretic hormone. Because blood contains enzymes that degrade these peptides, plasma preparation must involve immediate inactivation of these enzymes in drawn blood to stabilize the peptide of interest. All of these hormones are measured using either radioimmunoassay (RIA) or enzyme-linked immunosorbent assay (ELISA). These use antibodies specific to the substance of interest (the antigen) and are usually highly sensitive and selective. Before these methods became available in commercial kits 40+ years ago, less sensitive bioassays were used. It should be noted that the kits used for measurements in animal samples are marketed for clinical use; there is a possibility that the antibody appropriate to humans may not be as sensitive or selective for the animal antigen. In these methods, a standard curve is constructed using known concentrations of the antigen, and the concentration in each sample is calculated from the standard curve.

A.2   Measurement and Manipulation of Neural Activity

A.2.1   Lesions and Pharmacology

The aspirational goal for understanding how the brain organizes behavior in general, or a rather specific and episodic behavior such as drinking, is to identify all of the neurons involved, their phenotypes, and the timing of their activity in relation to the end product behavior. The use of lesions – permanent damage, either accidental or experimental, to a known brain region – was one of the first widely used methods. The logic is that a behavior will not occur after lesion of a region critical to that behavior. The method has been used for drinking behavior, and some lesion results are included in the text. Many of these involve putative sensory regions. Damage to more integrative regions "downstream" of sensors is subject to a multitude of interpretational problems, including the following:

- Lesions damage all classes of neurons in the region rather than a homogeneous'subset.
- Lesions also damage axons of passage and blood vessels, thus impacting other'regions.
- The behavioral effect is probably not clear-cut: It may be nonselective, partial, or'complex.
- Functional reorganization of the brain may occur with time after focal'damage.

The converse experiment, to stimulate a brain region of interest, has some of the same interpretation problems, but chemical stimulation in or near putative sensory regions has proven important, and the text contains several examples. Typically done in rodents, a brain cannula (i.e., injection guide) is inserted toward a brain region of interest using stereotaxic surgery. After full recovery, chemical agent(s) may be introduced to the region using a micro-injector. For example, injection of very small doses of ANG II into the subfornical organ (SFO) produce an immediate and compelling drinking response, a result that was pivotal in unraveling functions of the lamina terminalis. Such spectacular or significant results are the exception rather than the rule.

In a broader sense, pharmacological manipulation, using either agonists or antagonists, does start to address the question of phenotypes of neurons involved. Even using local brain injection, the spread of agent(s) from the injection site is of concern in relation to specificity. This concern is greater when the more common routes of peripheral administration are used.

During the past decade or so, new approaches to these questions have become available using methodology from molecular genetics. I will describe some of these methods later in this section, but for the foreseeable future, these will be applicable only to animal models.

A.2.2   Brain Activity Imaging Methods

A.2.2.1   Noninvasive For ethical reasons, noninvasive methods are the only ones available in humans, with the rare exception of measures during a neurosurgical intervention. Because the neuronal activity of a brain region is closely linked to blood flow through that region (and extraction of key raw materials such as oxygen and glucose by brain tissue), blood flow integrated over a suitable time frame has been used as a surrogate measure. The methods are limited in spatial and temporal resolution.

Positron emission tomography (PET) and functional magnetic resonance imaging (fMRI) are techniques to measure the amount of local neural activity using cerebral blood flow as an indirect indicator. They differ in principle. PET uses decay of a positron-emitting radionuclide attached to a blood-restricted carrier molecule, detecting derivative gamma rays that leave the brain and engage a surrounding detector array that interpolates the location and time of decay; a region with greater blood flow will emit more. However, fMRI has almost completely replaced PET and instead measures induction and relaxation of spin alignment of electrons in a high magnetic field. The relationship to blood flow is that the blood-borne hemoglobin has a different magnetic state when oxygenated compared to being deoxygenated. The amount of oxygen stripped from hemoglobin as it passes through a capillary bed thus produces some degree of deoxygenation. These forms of hemoglobin modify the applied magnetic field locally, giving rise to a signal that is blood oxygenation level dependent (BOLD).

In both methods, there are limitations of spatial resolution and time to complete a scan. Thus, each yields an averaged signal over a given tissue cube (i.e., voxel), which may contain tens of thousands of neurons and is carried out over typically 10 or more seconds. For studies of dehydration or thirst, this time constraint is not a critical issue, but the resolution (i.e., voxel size) may be because regions of interest such as the organum vasculosum of the lamina terminalis (OVLT) and SFO can often not be subdivided. These scans also require the subject to be supine and with head immobilized, neither of which are normal drinking positions. Drinking, if allowed, is through a straw that will minimize gross head movements. The supine position may lead to some movement of blood from the legs into the thoracic region, which in turn could affect functional baroreceptor activity.

A.2.2.2 Invasive: Fos Immunoreactivity and Pathway Tracing
These methods are used in animal studies. They provide a level of analysis that cannot be achieved in humans using the above noninvasive methods. Detection of the protein c-Fos by immunohistochemical methods (referred to in the text as Fos-ir) was one of the first attempts to describe activation of multiple brain regions following treatment with a

dipsogen or other drinking-related treatment. The gene *c-fos* is a widely expressed early transcript in response to strong excitation of a cell (Morgan & Curran, 1986; see Rowland, 1998, for a review relevant to fluid homeostasis). While some studies have measured *c-fos*, its time course may be relatively short and since these are terminal studies (usually in rodents), it is often not feasible to study multiple times; instead, the translated protein c-Fos has a suitably long half-life and is readily stained in the cytoplasm of expressing cells. The original procedure thus is to administer the acute treatment to rodents, usually in a multiple-group design using appropriate controls or dose ranges, and to sacrifice them after an elapsed time (1–2 h is common) using a brain perfusion method. The brains subsequently are sectioned appropriately, are exposed to a primary Fos antibody, and then undergo visualization procedure(s). Under a microscope, Fos-containing cells have stained cytoplasms. Using appropriate region outline and object-counting procedures, a quantitative estimate of cell activation can be achieved. Some shortcomings of this method limit it as rigorously quantitative. First, it is essential to include a placebo-treated control to ensure that the region(s) of interest have little or no basal Fos-ir. Second, the counting method involves a thresholding procedure; that is, some cells may express Fos-ir but at an intensity too low to be "seen" or to be deemed important. All cells above this threshold normally are weighted the same, but they may in fact have quite different suprathreshold levels of Fos. Third, although comparing results between groups of animals within a study may be valid, comparison of results between labs may be difficult because of differences in procedure, including tissue thickness and primary antibody used. Last, some cells may not express Fos after activation: The risk of a false negative result is present, although probably small. In the text, data are either described qualitatively (e.g., strong Fos was observed) or graphically as cell counts with the underlying assumption that more suprathreshold Fos-ir cells means more activation. Use of additional primary antibodies (e.g., double staining) has allowed extra phenotypic properties to be revealed.

The Fos-ir method frequently identifies several regions as activated by a given stimulus. It does not, however, give information about how those regions are interconnected. Pathway tracing makes use of either anterograde or retrograde axonal transport systems of neurons using appropriate marker molecule(s) that subsequently can be detected histologically. In these methods, the marker is injected using a stereotaxic method and microinjection into a specific brain region, either cell bodies (anterograde transport) or putative terminal regions (retrograde transport). The animal then recovers for several days, during which the axonal transport occurs; then it is sacrificed and the brain sectioned for visualization of the marker using microscopy. This method is usually only semi-quantitative (e.g., strong or weak projection) but in combination with other phenotypic markers can be made more specific. Most tracers do not cross synapses, but some do (e.g., pseudorabies) and are used to trace polysynaptic pathways.

One limitation of this method, and some of the following, is that the precise localization of the injected substance often varies a little from rodent subject to subject, and spread of the marker by diffusion from the injection site will limit the specificity of the result.

Both Fos and pathway tracing methods have subsequently been improved and harnessed to cell-specific applications using molecular genetic strategies (Luo et al., 2018).

A.2.2.3 Calcium Imaging Depolarization of a neuron (i.e., firing) is tightly coupled to opening of voltage-gated calcium (Ca^{2+}) channels and a relatively large and brief increase in cytoplasmic free Ca^{2+} concentration. The changes in Ca^{2+} concentration can be followed optically using fluorescent calcium-sensitive probes. The most common of these, mentioned in the text, is the green fluorescent protein-based sensor GCaMP6, which is a fusion of fluorescent protein with calmodulin, an endogenous Ca^{2+} binding protein – an example of a so-called genetically encoded Ca^{2+} indicator (GECI). To achieve further specificity, GECIs can be restricted to specific cell types using gene-targeting (transgenic) techniques. For this reason, most mammalian studies have to date been in mice. For in vivo imaging, the GECI is first expressed in the region of interest (e.g., the SFO), and an optical fiber is implanted ending in or above the SFO. The optic fiber eliminates the problem of light scattering of the emitted fluorescence, and it defines the field of view for an external camera; see Jennings et al. (2015) and Luo et al. (2018) for further details and extensions of the method. The recorded Ca^{2+} signal is an average across all of the GECI-expressing neurons in that field of view.

A.2.3 *Direct Stimulation or Inhibition of Neural Activity*

To demonstrate that activity in a region of interest is sufficient to change (e.g., initiate or terminate) a target behavior, it is ultimately essential to be able to control those neurons. Pharmacological or electrical stimulation has been used traditionally, but I now describe the more powerful and selective molecular approaches. These are invasive methods, involving genetic modification of the host, and among mammals they have to date been almost exclusively in rats or mice. There are two main approaches: chemogenetic and optogenetic, both of which are used in studies cited in the text.

A.2.3.1   Chemogenetic Manipulation The principle behind this method is that a non-native G-protein-coupled muscarinic-like receptor, constructed to recognize a non-native ligand, is introduced into and expressed by neurons in the region of interest. Subsequently, administration of that non-native ligand will engage this receptor, which may have either an excitatory (depolarizing) or inhibitory (hyperpolarizing) net effect. These are known as designer receptors exclusively activated by designer drugs (DREADD; see Roth, 2016, for a review). These receptors are introduced using a viral vector (usually adeno-associated virus [AAV]) via local injection into the region of interest. The non-native receptor is thus incorporated into the DNA of infected cells. The most commonly used excitatory (Gαq-linked) moiety is the hM3Dq-DREADD, and the most commonly used inhibitory (Gαi-linked) moiety is the hM4Di-DREADD. Once expressed in the region of interest, these are "silent" receptors with (ideally) no discernible effect on normal neural function. The non-native ligand of choice has been clozapine-N-oxide (CNO), which crosses the blood–brain barrier and so can be administered peripherally. CNO-based methods are particularly useful for longer-term behavioral studies (i.e., hours or days) that correspond to the duration of DREADD engagement. Ideally, CNO will have no effects on other cells or behaviors (this may be assessed by injecting CNO into animals that have not received the non-native receptors); however, there is evidence that CNO metabolism may release clozapine, which is an antipsychotic and itself may affect activity of certain receptors (this and other limitations of chemogenetics are discussed by Luo et al., 2018). In the chemogenetic studies cited in the text, suitable control procedures were performed to have confidence in the result.

A.2.3.2   Optogenetic Manipulation In brief, optogenetics allows stimulation (or inhibition) of neurons in a region of interest in a phenotypically specific manner. A prerequisite for this is to identify the phenotype of the cells in that region to be targeted: for example, glutamatergic neurons and then a suitable marker such as glutamate transporter, which is expressed constitutively. The (known) regulatory sequence in the DNA of that marker is then used to drive the expression of a transgene that has been introduced into that cell type, and with the subsequent production of an effector protein. There are two ways in which the transgene can be introduced: either by viral infection (e.g., AAV) or using a genetic recombination method (e.g., *cre-lox*; see Luo et al., 2018, for further details and modifications).

Relevant to optogenetics, that effector protein would be a light-sensitive ion channel. The most commonly used transgenes for in vivo stimulation are those encoding channel rhodopsin (ChR) and in particular ChR2, which is excited by blue light (470 nm peak absorbance). This opens a nonspecific cation channel leading to depolarization (Kim et al., 2017). Blue light has limited spread in vivo, so local stimulation from a laser source via an optical fiber to the region of interest has a reasonably circumscribed field of activation. Light is usually pulsed several times per second, the transduction is very efficient, and it produces waves of depolarization. Neurons may also be hyperpolarized or inhibited using halorhodopsin and yellow light, which opens a Cl$^-$ channel, a so-called opsin pump. However, opsin pumps are considerably less sensitive than ChRs and to date have been employed with less success.

In some studies mentioned in the text, ChRs have been linked to axonal transporters such that projection regions of a region of interest become photosensitive (Luo et al., 2018). In a broader sense, these methods of genetic access to cells are being expanded and improved at a very fast pace, and new types of results should continue to deluge the drinking field for years to come.

References

Abbott, S. B. G., & Saper, C. B. (2017). Median preoptic glutamatergic neurons promote thermoregulatory heat loss and water consumption in mice. *Journal of Physiology*, 595, 6569–6583. https://doi.org/10.1113/JP274667

Abe, K., Hikada, S., Ishibashi, K., et al. (1987). Developmental changes in the volumes, protein, and some electrolyte concentrations of male and female rat submandibular saliva secreted in response to methoxamine and pilocarpine. *Journal of Dental Research*, 66, 745–750. https://doi.org/10.1177/00220345870660030801

Abraham, S. F., Baker, R. M., Blaine, E. H., Denton, D. A., & McKinley, M. J. (1975). Water drinking induced in sheep by angiotensin: a physiological or pharmacological effect? *Journal of Comparative and Physiological Psychology*, 88, 503–518. https://doi.org/10.1037/h0076405

Adachi, A., Niijima, A., & Jacobs, H. L. (1976). An hepatic osmoreceptor mechanism in the rat: electrophysiological and behavioral studies. *American Journal of Physiology*, 232, 1043–1049. https://doi.org/10.1152/ajplegacy.1976.231.4.1043

Adams, J. D., Sekiguchi, Y., Suh, H.-G., et al. (2018). Dehydration impairs cycling performance, independently of thirst: a blinded study. *Medical Science and Sports Exercise*, 50, 1697–1703. https://doi.org/10.1249/MSS.0000000000001597

Ader, R., & Grota, L. J. (1970). Rhythmicity in the maternal behaviour of *Rattus norvegicus*. *Animal Behaviour*, 18, 144–150. https://doi.org/10.1016/0003-3472(70)90083-7

Adolph, E. F. (1939). Measurements of water drinking in dogs. *American Journal of Physiology*, 125, 75–86.

Adolph, E. F. (1943). *Physiological regulations*. Lancaster, PA: Jacques Cattell Press. et al. (1947). *The physiology of man in the desert*. New York: Interscience. (1950). Thirst and its inhibition in the stomach. *American Journal of Physiology*, 161, 374–386. https://doi.org/10.1152/ajplegacy.1950.161.3.374

Adolph, E. F., Barker, J. P., & Hoy, P. A. (1954). Multiple factors in thirst. *American Journal of Physiology*, 178, 538–562. https://doi.org/10.1152/ajplegacy.1954.178.3.538

Akerman, B., Andersson, B., Farbicius, E., & Svensson, L. (1960). Observations on central regulation of body temperature and of food and water intake in the pigeon (*Columba livia*). *Acta Physiologica Scandinavica*, 50, 328–336. http://doi.org/10.1111/j.1748-1716.1960.tb00187.x

Allen, A. M., McKinley, M. J., & Mendelsohn, F. A. (1988). Comparative neuroanatomy of angiotensin II receptor localization in the mammalian hypothalamus. *Clinical and Experimental Pharmacology and Physiology*, 15, 137–145. https://doi.org/10.1111/j.1440-1681.1988.tb01055.x

Allen, W. E., DeNardo, L. A., Chen, M. Z., et al. (2017). Thirst-associated preoptic neurons encode an aversive motivational drive. *Science*, 357, 1149–1155. https://doi.org/10.1126/science.aan6747

Almli, C. R. (1973). The ontogeny of the onset of drinking and plasma osmotic pressure regulation. *Developmental Psychobiology*, 6, 147–158. https://doi.org/10.1002/dev.420060209

Almli, C. R., McMullen, N. T., & Golden, G. T. (1976). Infant rats: hypothalamic unit activity. *Brain Research Bulletin*, 1, 543–552. https://doi.org/10.1016/0361-9230

Almli, C. R., & Weiss, C. S. (1975). Behavioral and physiological responses to dipsogens: a comparative analysis. *Physiology and Behavior*, 14, 633–641. https://doi.org/10.1016/0031-9384(75)90192-4

Altar, A., & Carlisle, H. J. (1979). Intragastric drinking in the rat: evidence for a role of oropharyngeal stimulation. *Physiology and Behavior*, 22, 1221–1225. https://doi.org/10.1016/0031-9384

Anderson, C. R., & Houpt, T. R. (1990). Hypertonic and hypovolemic stimulation of thirst in pigs. *American Journal of Physiology: Regulatory, Integrative and Comparative Physiology*, 258, R149–R154.

Anderson, W. G., Taylor, J. R., Good, J. P., et al. (2007). Body fluid volume regulation in elasmobranch fish. *Comparative Biochemistry and Physiology, Part A*, 148, 3–13. https://doi.org/10.1016/j.cpba.2006.07.018

Andersson, B. (1952). Polydipsia caused by intrahypothalamic injections of hypertonic NaCl solutions. *Experientia*, 8, 157–158.

Andersson B., Jobin, M., & Olsson, K. (1967). A study of thirst and other effects of an increased sodium concentration in the 3rd brain ventricle. *Acta Physiologica Scandinavica*, 69, 29–36. https://doi.org/10.1111/j.1748-1716.1967.tb03488.x

Andersson, B., Leksell, R. G., & Lishajko, F. (1975). Perturbations in fluid balance induced by medially placed forebrain lesions. *Brain Research*, 99, 261–275. https://doi.org/10.1016/0006-8993(75)90028-1

Andersson, B., & McCann, S. M. (1955). A further study of polydipsia evoked by hypothalamic stimulation in the goat. *Acta Physiologica Scandinavica*, 33, 333–346. https://doi.org/10.1111/j.1748-1716.1955.tb01213.x

Andersson, B., Olsson, K., & Warner, R. G. (1967). Dissimilarities between the central control of thirst and the release of antidiuretic hormone (ADH). *Acta Physiologica Scandinavica*, 71, 57–64. https://doi.org/10.1111/j.1748-1716.1967.tb03709.x

Ang, K. K., McKitrick, D. J., Phillips, P. A., & Arnolda, L. F. (2001). Time of day and access to food alter water intake in rats after water deprivation. *Clinical and Experimental Pharmacology and Physiology*, 28, 764–767. https://doi.org/10.1046/j.1440-1681.2001.03519.x

Applegren, B. H., Thrasher, T. N., Keil, L. C., & Ramsay, D. J. (1991). Mechanism of drinking-induced inhibition of vasopressin secretion in dehydrated dogs. *American Journal of Physiology: Regulatory, Integrative and*

Comparative Physiology, 261, R1226–R1233. https://doi.org/10.1152/ajpregu .1991.261.5.R1226

Arguelles, J., Perillan, C., Beltz, T. G., et al. (2017). The effects of experimental gestational hypertension on maternal blood pressure and fluid intake and pre-weaning hypothalamic neuronal activity. *Appetite*, 116, 65–74. https:// doi.org/10.1016/j.appet.2017.04.008

Armstrong, S., Clarke, J., & Coleman, G. (1978). Light-dark variation in laboratory rat stomach and small intestine content. *Physiology and Behavior*, 21, 785–788. https://doi.org/10.1016/0031-9384

Athanasatou, A., Kandyliari, A., Malisova, O., & Kapsokefalou, M. (2019). Fluctuation of water intake and of hydration indices during the day in a sample of healthy Greek adults. *Nutrients*, 6, 793. https://doi.org/10.3390/nu11040793

Augustine, V., Gocke, S. K., Lee, S., et al. (2018). Heirarchical neural architecture underlying thirst regulation. *Nature*, 555, 204–209. https://doi.org/10 .1038/nature25488

Back, S. A., Riddle, A., Dean, J., & Hohimer, A. R. (2012). The instrumented sheep as a model of white matter injury in the preterm infant. *Neurotherapeutics*, 9, 359–370. https://doi.org/10.1007/s13311

Badoer, E., McKinley, M. J., Oldfield, B. J., & McAllen, R. M. (1992). Distribution of hypothalamic, medullary, and lamina terminalis neurons expressing Fos after hemorrhage in conscious rats. *Brain Research*, 582, 323–328. https://doi.org/10.1016/0006-8993

(1993). A comparison of hypotensive and non-hypotensive hemorrhage on Fos expression in spinally projecting neurons of the paraventricular nucleus and rostral ventrolateral medulla. *Brain Research*, 610, 216–223. https://doi.org/ 10.1016/0006-8993

Badoer, E., Oldfield, B. J., & McKinley, M. J. (1993). Haemorrhage-induced production of Fos in neurons of the lamina terminalis: role of endogenous angiotensin II. *Neuroscience Letters*, 159, 151–154. https://doi.org/10.1016/ 0304-3940

Baker, M. A., & Turlejska, E. (1989). Thermal panting in dehydrated dogs: effects of plasma volume expansion and drinking. *Pflügers Archiv: European Journal of Physiology*, 413, 511–515. https://doi.org/10.1007/BF00594182

Barlow, E. D., & de Wardener, H. E. (1959). Compulsive water drinking. *Quarterly Journal of Medicine*, 28, 235–258. (PMID 13658352)

Barney, C. C. (1997). Effects of preloads of water and saline on thermal dehydration-induced thirst. *Physiology and Behavior*, 61, 763–769. doi.org/ 10.1016/s0031

Barney, C. C., & Kuhrt, D. M. (2016). Intermittent heat exposure and thirst in rats. *Physiological Reports*, 4, e12767. doi.org/10.14814/phy2.12767

Barney, C. C., Threatte, R. M., & Fregly, M. J. (1983). Water deprivation-induced drinking in rats: role of angiotensin II. *American Journal of Physiology: Regulatory, Integrative, and Comparative Physiology*, 244, R244–R248. doi.org/10.1152/ajpregu.1983.244.2.R244

Barney, C. C., Vergoth, C., Renkema, L.-A., & Meeuwsen, K. W. (1995). Nycthemeral variation in thermal dehydration-induced thirst. *Physiology and Behavior*, 58, 329–335. doi.org/10.1016/0031-9384

Barney, C. C., & West, D. R. (1990). Control of water intake in thermally dehydrated rats. *Physiology and Behavior*, 48, 387–395. doi.org/10.1016/0031-9384

Barney, C. C., Williams, J. S., & Kuiper, D. H. (1991). Thermal dehydration-induced thirst in rats: role of angiotensin II. *American Journal of Physiology: Regulatory, Integrative and Comparative Physiology*, 261, R1171–R1175. doi.org/10.1152/ajpregu.1991.261.5.R1171

Barron, W. M., Stamoutsos, B. A., & Lindheimer, M. D. (1984). Role of volume in the regulation of vasopressin secretion during pregnancy in the rat. *Journal of Clinical Investigation*, 73, 923–932. doi.org/10.1172/JCI111316doi.org/10.1172/JCI111316

Barth, S. W., & Gerstberger, R. (1999). Differential regulation of angiotensinogen and AT1A receptor mRNA within the rat subfornical organ during dehydration. *Molecular Brain Research*, 64, 151–164. doi.org/10.1016/S0169

Baylis, C., Engels, K., & Beierwaltes, W. H. (1998). Beta-adrenoceptor-stimulated renin release is blunted in old rats. *Journal of the American Society of Nephrology*, 9, 1318–1320. (PMID 9644645)

Baylis, C., Engels, K., Hymel, A., & Navar, L. G. (1997). Plasma renin activity and metabolic clearance rate of angiotensin II in the unstressed aging rat. *Mechanisms of Ageing and Development*, 97, 163–171. https://doi.org/10.1016/S0047

Bealer, S. L. (1983). Sodium excretion following lesions of preoptic recess periventricular tissue in the rat. *American Journal of Physiology: Regulatory, Integrative and Comparative Physiology*, 244, R815–R822. https://doi.org/10.1152/ajpregu.1983.244.6.R815

Bealer, S. L., Carithers, J., & Johnson, A. K. (1984). Fluid regulation, body weight and drinking responses following hypothalamic knife cuts. *Brain Research*, 305, 239–245. https://doi.org/10.1016/0006-8993

Bealer, S. L., Crofton, J. T., & Share, L. (1983). Hypothalamic knife cuts alter fluid regulation, vasopressin secretion, and natriuresis during water deprivation. *Neuroendocrinology*, 36, 364–370. https://doi.org/10.1159/000123482

Bealer, S. L., & Johnson, A. K. (1980). Preoptic-hypothalamic periventricular lesions alter food-associated drinking and circadian rhythms. *Journal of Comparative and Physiological Psychology*, 94, 547–555. https://doi.org/10.1037/h0077685

Beauchamp, G. K., Cowart, B. J., Mennella, J. A., & Marsh, R. R. (1994). Infant salt taste: developmental, methodological, and contextual factors. *Developmental Psychobiology*, 27, 353–65. https://doi.org/10.1002/dev.420270604

Beck, L. H. (2000). The aging kidney: defending a delicate balance of fluid and electrolytes. *Geriatrics*, 55, 26–28. (PMID 10771700)

Begg, D. P., Sinclair, A. J., & Weisinger, R. S. (2012). Reductions in water and sodium intake by aged male and female rats. *Nutrition Research*, 32, 865–872. https://doi.org/10.1016/j.nutres.2012.09.014

Bekkevold, C. M., Robertson, K. L., Reinhard, M. K., Battles, A. H., & Rowland, N. E. (2013). Dehydration parameters and standards for laboratory mice. *Journal of the Association for Laboratory Animal Sciences*, 52, 233–239. (PMID 23849404)

Bell, R. J., Laurence, B. M., Meehan, P. J., Congiu, M., Scoggins, B. A., & Winotour, E. M. (1986). Regulation and function of arginine vasopressin in pregnant sheep. *American Journal of Physiology: Renal*

Bellows, R. T. (1939). Time factors in water drinking in dogs. *American Journal of Physiology*, 125, 87–97. https://doi.org/10.1152/ajplegacy.1938.125.1.87

Bernard, C. (1856). *Leçons de physiologie expérimentale appliquée à la médicine faites au Collège de France*. Vol 2. Paris: Baillière.

Bisley, J. W., Rees, S. M., McKinley, M. J., Hards, D. K., & Oldfield, B. J. (1996). Identification of osmoresponsive neurons in the forebrain of the rat: a Fos study at the ultrastructural level. *Brain Research*, 720, 25–34. https://doi.org/10.1016/0006-8993(96)00079-0

Black, S. L. (1976). Preoptic hypernatremic syndrome and the regulation of water balance in the rat. *Physiology and Behavior*, 17, 473–482. https://doi.org/10.1016/0031-9384

Blair-West, J. R., & Brook, A. H. (1969). Circulatory changes and renin secretion in sheep in response to feeding. *Journal of Physiology*, 204, 15–30. https://doi.org/10.1113/jphysiol.1969.sp008895

Blass, E. M., & Hall, W. G. (1976). Drinking termination: interactions among hydrational, orogastric, and behavioral controls in rats. *Psychological Review*, 83, 356–374. (PMID 1005582)

Blass, E. M., Jobaris, R., & Hall, W. G. (1976). Oropharyngeal control of drinking in rats. *Journal of Comparative and Physiological Psychology*, 90, 909–916. https://doi.org/10.1037/h0077268

Block, M. L., Vallier, G. H., & Glickman, S. E. (1974). Elicitation of water ingestion in the Mongolian gerbil (*Meriones unguiculatus*) by intracranial injections of angiotensin II and l-norepinephrine. *Pharmacology, Biochemistry and Behavior*, 2, 235–242. https://doi.org/10.1016/0091-3057

Booth, D. A. (1968). Mechanism of action of norepinephrine in eliciting an eating response on injection into the rat hypothalamus. *Journal of Pharmacology and Experimental Therapeutics*, 160, 336–348. (PMID 4296696)

Bott, E., Denton, D. A., & Weller, S. (1965). Water drinking in sheep with oesophageal fistulae. *Journal of Physiology*, 176, 323–336. https://doi.org/10.1113/jphysiol.1965.sp007553

Boulze, D., Montastruc, P., & Cabanac, M. (1983). Water intake, pleasure and water temperature in humans. *Physiology and Behavior*, 30, 97–102. https://doi.org/10.1016/0031-9384

Bourque, C. W. (2008). Central mechanisms of osmosensation and systemic osmoregulation. *Nature Reviews Neuroscience*, 9, 519–531. https://doi.org/10.1038/nrn2400

Bourque, C. W., Oliet, S. H., & Richard, D. (1994). Osmoreceptors, osmoreception, and osmoregulation. *Frontiers in Neuroendocrinology*, 15, 231–274. https://doi.org/10.1006/frne.1994.1010

Brandenberger, G., Follenius, M., Muzet, A., Ehrhart, J., & Schieber, J. P. (1985). Ultradian oscillations in plasma renin activity: their relationships to meals and sleep stages. *Journal of Clinical Endocrinology and Metabolism*, 61, 280–284. https://doi.org/10.1210/jcem-61-2-280

Brooks, V. L., Freeman, K. L., & O'Donaughy, T. L. (2004). Acute and chronic increases in osmolality increase excitatory amino acid drive of the rostro ventrolateral medulla in rats. *American Journal of Physiology: Regulatory, Integrative and Comparative Physiology*, 287, R1359–R1368. https://doi.org/10.1152/ajpregu.00104.2004

Bruno, J. P. (1981). Development of drinking behavior in preweaning rats. *Journal of Comparative and Physiological Psychology*, 95, 1016–1027. https://doi.org/10.1037/h0077844

Bruno, J. P., Craigmyle, L. S., & Blass, E. M. (1982). Dehydration inhibits suckling behavior in weanling rats. *Journal of Comparative and Physiological Psychology*, 96, 405–415. https://doi.org/10.1037/h0077888

Buggy, J., Fisher, A. E., Hoffman, W. E., Johnson, A. K., & Phillips, M. I. (1975). Ventricular obstruction: effect on drinking induced by intracranial injection of angiotensin. *Science*, 190, 72–74. https://doi.org/10.1126/science.1166302

Buggy, J., Hoffman, W. E., Phillips, M. I., Fisher, A. E., & Johnson, A. K. (1979). Osmosensitivity of rat third ventricle and interactions with angiotensin. *American Journal of Physiology: Regulatory, Integrative and Comparative Physiology*, 236, R75–R82. https://doi.org/10.1152/ajpregu.1979.236.1.R75

Buggy, J., & Johnson, A. K. (1977). Preoptic-hypothalamic periventricular lesions: thirst deficits and hypernatremia. *American Journal of Physiology: Regulatory, Integrative and Comparative Physiology*, 233, R44–R52. https://doi.org/10.1152/ajpregu.1977.233.1.R44

Burdon, C. A., Johnson, N. A., Chapman, P. G., & O'Connor, H. T. (2012). Influence of beverage temperature on palatability and fluid ingestion during endurance exercise: a systematic review. *International Journal of Sport Nutrition and Exercise Metabolism*, 22, 199–211. https://doi.org/10.1123/ijsnem22.3.199

Burke, G., Mook, D. G., & Blass, E. M. (1972). Hyperreactivity to quinine associated with osmotic thirst. *Journal of Comparative and Physiological Psychology*, 78, 32–39. https://doi.org/10.1037/h0032184

Cannon, W. B. (1919). *The physiological basis of thirst. Proceedings of the Royal Society*, 90, 283–301.

(1939). *The wisdom of the body.* 2nd ed. New York: Norton.

Carlson, S. H., Beitz, A., & Osborn, J. W. (1997). Intragastric hypertonic saline increases vasopressin and central Fos immunoreactivity in conscious rats. *American Journal of Physiology: Regulatory, Integrative and Comparative Physiology*, 272, R750–R758. https://doi.org/10.1152/ajpregu.1997.272.3.r750

Castillo, M. R., Hochstetler, K. J., Greene, D. M., et al. (2005). Circadian rhythm of core body temperature in two laboratory mouse strains. *Physiology and Behavior*, 86, 538–545. https://doi.org/10.1016/j.physbeh.2005.08.018

Caston-Balderrama, A., Nijland, M. J., McDonald, T. J., & Ross, M. G. (1999). Central Fos expression in fetal and adult sheep after intraperitoneal hypertonic saline. *American Journal of Physiology: Heart and Circulatory Physiology*, 276, H725–H735. https://doi.org/10.1152/ajpheart.1999.276.2.H725

(2001). Intact osmoregulatory centers in the preterm ovine fetus: Fos induction after an osmotic challenge. *American Journal of Physiology: Heart and Circulatory Physiology*, 281, H2626–H2635. https://doi.org/10.1152/ajpheart .2001.281.6.H2626

Chan, R. K., & Sawchenko, P. E. (1994). Spatially and temporally differentiated patterns of c-Fos expression in brainstem catecholaminergic cell groups induced by cardiovascular challenges in the rat. *Journal of Comparative Neurology*, 348, 433–460. https://doi.org/10.1002/cne.903480309

Chapman, H. W., & Epstein, A. N. (1970). Prandial drinking induced by atropine. *Physiology and Behavior*, 5, 549–555. https://doi.org/10.1016/ 0031-9384

Cheuvront, S. N., & Haymes, E. M. (2001). Ad libitum fluid intakes and thermoregulatory responses of female distance runners in three environments. *Journal of Sports Sciences*, 19, 845–854. https://doi.org/10.1080/ 026404101753113796

Chew, R. M. (1961). Water metabolism of desert-inhabiting vertebrates. *Biological Reviews of the Cambridge Philosophical Society*, 36, 1–31. doi.org/ 10.1111/j.1469-185x.1961.tb01430.x

Choi-Kwon, S., & Baertschi, A. J. (1991). Splanchnic osmoreception and vasopressin: mechanisms and neural pathways. *American Journal of Physiology: Endocrinology and Metabolism*, 261, E18–E25. https://doi.org/10.1152/ ajpendo.1991.261.1.E18

Chwalbinska-Moneta, J. (1979). Role of hepatic portal osmoreception in the control of ADH release. *American Journal of Physiology: Endocrinology and Metabolism*, 236, E603–E609. https://doi.org/10.1152/ajpendo.1979.236.6 .E603

Ciura, S., & Bourque, C. W. (2006). Transient receptor potential vanilloid 1 is required for intrinsic osmoreception in organum vasculosum lamina terminalis neurons and for normal thirst responses to systemic hyperosmolality. *Journal of Neuroscience*, 26, 9069–9075. https://doi.org/10.1523/JNEUROSCI .0877-06.2006

Ciura, S., Liedtke, W., & Bourque, C. W. (2011). Hypertonicity sensing in organum vasculosum lamina terminalis neurons: a mechanical process involving *TRPV1* but not *TRPV4*. *Journal of Neuroscience*, 31, 14669–14676. https://doi.org/10.1523/JNEUROSCI.1420-11.2011

Cizek, L. (1959). Long-term observations on relationship between food and water ingestion in the dog. *American Journal of Physiology*, 197, 342–346. https://doi.org/10.1152/ajplegacy.1959.197.2.342

(1961). Relationship between food and water ingestion in the rabbit. *American Journal of Physiology*, 201, 557–566. https://doi.org/10.1152/ajplegacy.1961 .201.3.557

Cizek, L. J., & Nocenti, M. R. (1965). Relationship between water and food ingestion in the rat. *American Journal of Physiology*, 208, 615–620. https://doi .org/10.1152/ajplegacy.1965.208.4.615

Clark, G., Magoun, H. W., & Ranson, S. W. (1939). Hypothalamic regulation of body temperature. *Journal of Neurophysiology*, 2, 61–80. https://doi.org/ 10.1152/jn.1939.2.1.61

Coble, J. P., Grobe, J. L., Johnson, A. K., & Sigmund, C. D. (2015). Mechanisms of brain renin angiotensin system-induced drinking and blood pressure: importance of the subfornical organ. *American Journal of Physiology: Regulatory, Integrative and Comparative Physiology*, 308, R238–R249. https://doi.org/10.1152/ajpregu.00486.2014

Coburn, P. C., & Stricker, E. M. (1978). Osmoregulatory thirst in rats after lateral preoptic lesions. *Journal of Comparative and Physiological Psychology*, 92, 350–361. https://doi.org/10.1037/h0077464

Cole, D. L. (1955). The excretion of intravenously administered saline by the rat. *Acta Endocrinologica*, 19, 397–405.

Collier, G., Johnson, D. F., & Stanziola, C. (1991). The economics of water and salt balance. *Physiology and Behavior*, 50, 1221–1226. https://doi.org/10.1016/0031-9384

Connolly, M. S., & Lynch, C. B. (1981). Circadian variation of strain differences in body temperature and activity in mice. *Physiology and Behavior*, 27, 1045–1049. https://doi.org/10.1016/0031-9384

Cook, G., Hodgson, P., Hope, C., Thompson, J., & Shaw, L. (2018). Hydration practices in residential and nursing care homes for older people. *Journal of Clinical Nursing*, 28, 1205–1215.

Cooper, C. E. (2017). Endocrinology of osmoregulation and thermoregulation of Australian desert tetrapods: a historical perspective. *General and Comparative Endocrinology*, 244, 186–200. https://doi.org/10.1016/j.ygcen.2015.10.003

Corbit, J. D. (1965). Effect of intravenous sodium chloride on drinking in the rat. *Journal of Comparative and Physiological Psychology*, 60, 397–406. https://doi.org/10.1037/h0022558

Cotter, J. D., Thornton, S. N., Lee, J. K. W., & Laursen, P. B. (2014). Are we being drowned in hydration advice? Thirsty for more? *Extreme Physiology and Medicine*, 3, 18. https://doi.org/10.1186/2046-7648-3-18

Cowen, L. E., Hodak, S. P., & Verbalis, J. G. (2013). Age-associated abnormalities of water homeostasis. *Endocrinology and Metabolism Clinics of North America*, 42, 349–370. https://doi.org/10.1016/j.ecl.2013.02.005

Cramer, C. P., Blass, E. M., & Hall, W. G. (1980). The ontogeny of nipple-shifting behavior in albino rats: mechanisms of control and possible significance. *Developmental Psychobiology*, 13, 165–180. https://doi.org/10.1002/dev.420130208

Crews, E. C., & Rowland, N. E. (2005). Role of angiotensin in body fluid homeostasis of mice: effect of losartan on water and NaCl intakes. *American Journal of Physiology: Regulatory, Integrative and Comparative Physiology*, 288, R638–R644. https://doi.org/10.1152/ajpregu.00525.2004

Cunningham, J. T., Beltz, T., Johnson, R. F., & Johnson, A. K. (1992). The effects of ibotenate lesions of the median preoptic nucleus on experimentally-induced and circadian drinking behavior in rats. *Brain Research*, 580, 325–330. https://doi.org/10.1016/0006-8993

Curtis, K. S., Krause, E. G., Wong, D. L., & Contreras, R. J. (2004). Gestational and early postnatal dietary NaCl levels affect NaCl intake, but not stimulated water intake, by adult rats. *American Journal of Physiology: Regulatory, Integrative and Comparative Physiology*, 286, R1043–R1050. https://doi.org/10.1152/ajpregu.00582.2003

Czech, D. A., & Vander Zanden, J. M. (1991). Drinking behavior in the spiny mouse (*Acomys cahirinus*) following putative dipsogenic challenges. *Pharmacology Biochemistry and Behavior*, 38, 913–916. https://doi.org/10.1016/0091-3057(91)90263-2

Darlington, D. N., Shinsako, J., & Dallman, M. F. (1986). Responses of ACTH, epinephrine, norepinephrine, and cardiovascular system to hemorrhage. *American Journal of Physiology: Heart and Circulatory Physiology*, 251, H612–H618. https://doi.org/10.1152/ajpheart.1986.251.3.H612

Davies, I., O'Neill, P. A., McLean, K. A., Catania, J., & Bennett, D. (1995). Age-associated alterations in thirst and arginine vasopressin in response to a water or sodium load. *Age and Ageing*, 24, 151–159. https://doi.org/10.1093/ageing/24.2.151

Davison, J. M., Gilmore, E. A., Durr, J., Robertson, G. L., & Lindheimer, M. D. (1984). Altered osmotic thresholds for vasopressin secretion and thirst in human pregnancy. *American Journal of Physiology: Renal Physiology*, 246, F105–F109. https://doi.org/10.1152/ajprenal.1984.246.1.F105

Davison, J. M., Shiells, E. A., Philips, P. R., & Lindheimer, M. D. (1988). Serial evaluation of vasopressin release and thirst in human pregnancy: role of human chorionic gonadotrophin in the osmoregulatory changes of gestation. *Journal of Clinical Investigation*, 81, 798–806. https://doi.org/10.1172/JCI113386

(1990). Influence of humoral and volume factors on altered osmoregulation of normal human pregnancy. *American Journal of Physiology: Renal Physiology*, 258, F900–F907. https://doi.org/10.1152/ajprenal.1990.258.4.F900

De Araujo, I. E. T., Kringelbach, M. L., Rolls, E. T., & McGlone, F. (2003). Human cortical responses to water in the mouth, and the effects of thirst. *Journal of Neurophysiology*, 90, 1865–1876. https://doi.org/10.1152/jn.00297.2003

Deaux, E. (1973). Thirst satiation and the temperature of ingested water. *Science*, 181, 1166–1167. https://doi.org/10.1126/science.181.4105.1166

Deaux, E., Sato, E., & Kakolewski, J. W. (1970). Emergence of systemic cues evoking food-associated drinking. *Physiology and Behavior*, 5, 1177–1179. https://doi.org/10.1016/0031-9384

De Avila, C., Chometton, S., Lenglos, C., Calvez, J., Gunlach, A. L., & Timofeeva, E. (2018). Differential effects of relaxin-3 and a selective relaxin-3 receptor agonist on food and water intake and hypothalamic neuronal activity in rats. *Behavioural Brain Research*, 336, 135–144. https://doi.org/10/1016/j.bbr.2017.08.044

de Castro, J. M. (1988). A microregulatory analysis of spontaneous fluid intake by humans: evidence that the amount of liquid ingested and its timing is mainly governed by feeding. *Physiology and Behavior*, 43, 705–714. https://doi.org/10.1016/0031-9384

(1989). The interactions of fluid and food intake in the spontaneous feeding and drinking patterns of rats. *Physiology and Behavior*, 45, 861–870. https://doi.org/10.1016/0031-9384

(1992). Age-related changes in natural spontaneous fluid ingestion and thirst in humans. *Journal of Gerontology*, 47, P321–P330. https://doi.org/10.1093/geronj/47.5.p321

De Luca, L. A., Menani, J. V., & Johnson, A. K. (2019). *Neurobiology of body fluid homeostasis: transduction and integration.* Boca Raton, FL: CRC Press.

DeRubertis, F. R., Michelis, M. F., Beck, N., Field, J. B., & Davis, B. B. (1971). "Essential" hypernatremia due to ineffective osmotic and intact volume regulation of vasopressin secretion. *Journal of Clinical Investigation*, 50, 97–111. https://doi.org/10.1172/JCI106489

DeRubertis, F. R., Michelis, M. F., & Davis, B. B. (1974). "Essential" hypernatremia: report of three cases and review of the literature. *Archives of Internal Medicine*, 134, 889–895. https://doi.org/10.1001/archinte.1974.00320230099021

Desor, J. A., Maller, O., & Andrews, K. (1975). Ingestive responses of human newborns to salty, sour, and bitter stimuli. *Journal of Comparative and Physiological Psychology*, 89, 966–970.

Durr, J. A., Stamoutsos, B., & Lindheimer, M. D. (1981). Osmoregulation during pregnancy in the rat: evidence for resetting of the threshold for vasopressin secretion during gestation. *Journal of Clinical Investigation*, 68, 337–346. https://doi.org/10.1172/jci110261

Duvernoy, H. M., & Risold, P.-Y. (2007). The circumventricular organs: an atlas of comparative anatomy and vascularization. *Brain Research Reviews*, 56, 119–147. https://doi.org/10.1016/j.brainresrev.2007.06.002

Egan, G., Silk, T., Zamarripa, J., et al. (2003). Neural correlates of the emergence of consciousness of thirst. *Proceedings of the National Academy of Sciences USA*, 100, 15241–15246. https://doi.org/10.1073/pnas.2136650100

El-Haddad, M. A., Desai, M., Gayle, D., & Ross, M. G. (2004). In utero development of fetal thirst and appetite: potential for programming. *Journal of the Society for Gynecological Investigation*, 11, 123–130. https://doi.org/10.1016/j.jsgi.2003.12.001

Ellis, S., Axt, K., & Epstein, A. N. (1984). The arousal of ingestive behaviors by chemical injection into the brain of the suckling rat. *Journal of Neuroscience*, 4, 945–955. https://doi.org/10.1523/JNEUROSCI.04-04-00945.1984

Eng, R., & Miselis, R. R. (1981). Polydipsia and abolition of angiotensin-induced drinking after transections of subfornical organ efferent projections in the rat. *Brain Research*, 225, 200–206. https://doi.org/10.1016/0006-8993

Epstein, A. N., & Teitelbaum, P. (1962). The lateral hypothalamic syndrome: recovery of feeding and drinking after lateral hypothalamic lesions. *Psychological Review*, 69, 74–90. https://doi.org/10.1037/h0039285

Eriksson, L., Fernandez, L., & Olsson, K. (1971). Differences in the antidiuretic response to intracarotid infusions of various hypertonic solutions in the conscious goat. *Acta Physiologica Scandinavica*, 83, 554–562. https://doi.org/10.1111/j.1748-1716.1971.tb05113.x

Evans, D. H. (2010). A brief history of the study of fish osmoregulation: the central role of the Mt. Desert Island Biological Laboratory. *Frontiers in Physiology*, 1, 13. https://doi.org.10.3389/fphys.2010.00013

Evans, D. H., Piermarini, P. M., & Choe, K. P. (2005). The multifunctional fish gill: dominant site of gas exchange, osmoregulation, acid-base regulation, and excretion of nitrogenous waste. *Physiological Review*, 85, 97–177. https://doi.org/10.1152/physrev.00050.2003

Evered, M. D. (1990). Relationship between thirst and diazoxide-induced hypotension in rats. *American Journal of Physiology: Regulatory, Integrative and*

Comparative Physiology, 259, R362–R370. https://doi.org/10.1152/ajpregu .1990.259.2.R362

Evered, M. D., & Mogenson, G. J. (1977). Impairment in fluid ingestion in rats with lesions of the zona incerta. *American Journal of Physiology: Regulatory, Integrative and Comparative Physiology*, 233, R53–R58. https://doi.org/10 .1152/ajpregu.1977.233.1.R53

Falk, G. (1955). Maturation of renal function in infant rats. *American Journal of Physiology*, 181: 157–170. https://doi.org/10.1152/ajplegacy.1955.181.1.157

Falk, J. L. (1961). Production of polydipsia in normal rats by an intermittent food schedule. *Science*, 133, 195–196. https://doi.org/10.1126/science.133.3447 .195

Farrell, M. J., Bowala, T. K., Gavrilescu, M., et al. (2011). Cortical activation and lamina terminalis functional connectivity during thirst and drinking in humans. *American Journal of Physiology: Regulatory, Integrative and Comparative Physiology*, 301, R623–R631. https://doi.org/10.1152/ajpregu .00817.2010

Farrell, M. J., Zamarripa, F., Shade, R., et al. (2008). Effect of aging on regional cerebral blood flow responses associated with osmotic thirst and its satiation by water drinking: a PET study. Proceedings of the National Academy of Sciences USA, 105, 382–387. https://doi.org/10.1073/pnas.0710572105

Fenelon, V. S., Poulain, D. A., & Theodosis, D. T. (1993). Oxytocin neuron activation and Fos expression: a quantitative immunocytochemical analysis of the effect of lactation, parturition, osmotic and cardiovascular stimulation. *Neuroscience*, 53, 77–89. https://doi.org/10.1016/0306-4522

Figaro, M. K., & Mack, G. W. (1997). Regulation of fluid intake in dehydrated humans: role of oropharyngeal stimulation. *American Journal of Physiology: Regulatory, Integrative and Comparative Physiology*, 272, R1740–R1746. https://doi.org/10.1152/ajpregu.1997.272.6.R1740

Fitts, D. A. (1994). Angiotensin II receptors in SFO but not in OVLT mediate isoproterenol-induced thirst. *American Journal of Physiology: Regulatory, Integrative and Comparative Physiology*, 267, R7–R15. https://doi.org/10 .1152/ajpregu.1994.267.1.R7

Fitzsimons, J. T. (1961a). Drinking by nephrectomized rats injected with various substances. *Journal of Physiology*, 155, 563–579. https://doi.org/10.1113/ jphysiol.1961.sp006647

(1961b). Drinking by rats depleted of body fluid without increase in osmotic pressure. *Journal of Physiology*, 159, 297–309. https://doi.org/10.1113/ jphysiol.1961.sp006809

(1963). The effects of slow infusions of hypertonic solutions on drinking and drinking thresholds in rats. *Journal of Physiology*, 167, 344–354. https://doi .org/10.1113/jphysiol.1963.sp007154

(1969). The role of a renal thirst factor in drinking induced by extracellular stimuli. *Journal of Physiology*, 201, 349–368. https://doi.org/10.1113/jphysiol .1969.sp008760

(1979). *The physiology of thirst and sodium appetite*. Cambridge: Cambridge University Press.

Fitzsimons, J. T., & Elfont, R. M. (1982). Angiotensin does contribute to drinking induced by caval ligation in rats. *American Journal of Physiology:*

Regulatory, Integrative and Comparative Physiology, 243, R558–R562. https://doi.org/10.1152/ajpregu.1982.243.5.R558

Fitzsimons, J. T., & Kaufman, S. (1977). Cellular and extracellular dehydration, and angiotensin as stimuli to drinking in the common iguana. *Journal of Physiology*, 265, 443–463. https://doi.org/10.1113/jphysiol.1977.sp011724

Fitzsimons, J. T., Kucharczyk, J., & Richards, G. (1978). Systemic angiotensin-induced drinking in the dog: a physiological phenomenon. *Journal of Physiology*, 276, 435–448. https://doi.org/10.1113/jphysiol.1978.sp012245

Fitzsimons, J. T., & Le Magnen, J. (1969). Eating as a regulatory control of drinking in the rat. *Journal of Comparative and Physiological Psychology*, 67, 273–283. https://doi.org/10.1037/h0026772

Fitzsimons, J. T., & Simons, B. J. (1969). The effect on drinking in the rat of intravenous infusion of angiotensin, given alone or in combination with other stimuli of thirst. *Journal of Physiology*, 203, 45–57. https://doi.org/10.1113/jphysiol.1969.sp008848

Fitzsimons, J. T., & Szczepanska-Sadowska, E. (1974). Drinking and antidiuresis elicited by isoprenaline in the dog. *Journal of Physiology*, 239, 251–267. https://doi.org/10.1113/jphysiol.1974.sp010567

Flynn, F. W., Curtis, K. S., Verbalis, J. G., & Stricker, E. M. (1995). Dehydration anorexia in decerebrate rats. *Behavioral Neuroscience*, 109, 1009–1012. https://doi.org/10.1037/0735-7044.109.5.1009

Ford, M. M., Steele, A. M., McCracken, A. D., Finn, D. A., & Grant, K. A. (2013). The relationship between adjunctive drinking, blood ethanol concentration and plasma corticosterone across fixed-time intervals of food delivery in two inbred mouse strains. *Psychoneuroendocrinology*, 38, 2598–2610. https://doi.org/10.1016/j.psyneuen.2013.06.011

Fregly, M. J., Paulding, W., & Rowland, N. E. (1990). Comparison of the dipsogenic responsiveness of Long-Evans and Sprague-Dawley rats. *Physiology and Behavior*, 47, 1187–1192. https://doi.org/10.1016/0031-9384.

Fregly, M. J., & Rowland, N. E. (1985). Role of renin-angiotensin-aldosterone system in NaCl appetite of rats. *American Journal of Physiology: Regulatory, Integrative and Comparative Physiology* 248, R1–R11. https://doi.org/10.1152/ajpregu.1985.248.1.R1

(1991a). Effect of a nonpeptide angiotensin II receptor antagonist, DuP753, on angiotensin-related water intake in rats. *Brain Research Bulletin*, 27, 97–100. https://doi.org/10.1016/0361-9230

(1991b). Bradykinin-induced dipsogenesis in captopril-treated rats. *Brain Research Bulletin*, 26, 169–172. https://doi.org/10.1016/0361-9230

(1992). Effect of DuP753, a nonpeptide angiotensin II receptor antagonist, on the drinking responses to acutely administered dipsogenic agents in rats. *Proceedings of the Society for Experimental Biology and Medicine*, 199, 158–164. https://doi.org/10.3181/00379727-199-43341

(1993). Role of angiotensin II receptors in tail skin temperature response to isoproterenol. *Proceedings of the Society for Experimental Biology and Medicine*, 203, 157–162. https://doi.org/10.3181/00379727-199-43341

Friedman, M. I. (1975). Some determinants of milk ingestion in suckling rats. *Journal of Comparative and Physiological Psychology*, 89, 636–647. https://doi.org/10.1037/h0077432

Friedman, M. I., & Campbell, B. A. (1974). Ontogeny of thirst in the rat: effects of hypertonic saline, polyethylene glycol, and vena cava ligation. *Journal of Comparative and Physiological Psychology*, 87, 37–46. https://doi.org/10.1037/h0036567

Galaverna, O., Nicolaïdis, S., Yao, S. Z., Sakai, R. R., & Epstein, A. N. (1995). Endocrine consequences of prenatal sodium depletion prepare rats for high need-free NaCl intake in adulthood. *American Journal of Physiology: Regulatory, Integrative and Comparative Physiology*, 269, R578–R83. https://doi.org/10.1152/ajpregu.1995.269.3.R578

Gardiner, T. W., & Stricker, E. M. (1985a). Hyperdispia in rats after electrolytic lesions of nucleus medianus. *American Journal of Physiology: Regulatory, Integrative and Comparative Physiology*, 248, R214–R223. https://doi.org/10.1152/ajpregu.1985.248.2.R214

(1985b). Impaired drinking responses of rats with lesions of nucleus medianus: circadian dependence. *American Journal of Physiology: Regulatory, Integrative and Comparative Physiology*, 248, R224–R230. https://doi.org/10.1152/ajpregu.1985.248.2.R224

Geleen, G., Keil, L. C., Kravik, S. E., et al. (1984). Inhibition of plasma vasopressin after drinking in dehydrated humans. *American Journal of Physiology: Regulatory, Integrative and Comparative Physiology*, 247, R968–R971. https://doi.org/10.1152/ajpregu.1984.247.6.R968

Giersch, G. E. W., Charkoudian, N., Stearns, R. L., & Casa, D. J. (2020). Fluid balance and hydration considerations for women: review and future directions. *Sports Medicine*, 50, 253–261. https://doi.org/10.1007/s40279

Gilman, A. (1937). The relation between blood osmotic pressure, fluid distribution and voluntary water intake. *American Journal of Physiology*, 120, 323–328. https://doi.org/10.1152/ajplegacy.1937.120.2.323

Gisolfi, C., & Copping, J. (1993). Thermal effects of prolonged treadmill exercise in the heat. *Medicine & Science in Sports & Exercise*, 25, 310–315. (PMID 8455443)

Gizowski, C., Zaesler, C., & Bourque, C. W. (2016). Clock-driven vasopressin neurotransmission mediates anticipatory thirst prior to sleep. *Nature*, 537, 685–688. https://doi.org/10.1038/nature19756

(2018). Activation of organum vasculosum neurons and water intake in mice by vasopressin neurons in the suprachiasmatic nucleus. *Journal of Neuroendocrinology*, 30, e12577. https://doi.org/10.1111/jne.12577

Gold, R. M., Kapatos, G., Proswe, J., Quackenbush, P. M., & Oxford, T. W. (1973). Role of water temperature in the regulation of water intake. *Journal of Comparative and Physiological Psychology*, 85, 52–63. https://doi.org/10.1037/h0034881

Goldman, M. B., Luchins, D. J., & Robertson, G. L. (1988). Mechanisms of altered water metabolism in psychotic patients with polydipsia and hyponatremia. *New England Journal of Medicine*, 318, 397–403. https://doi.org/10.1056/NEJM198802183180702

Goldman, M. B., Robertson, G. L., Luchins, D. J., Hedeker, D., & Pandey, G. N. (1997). Psychotic exacerbations and enhanced vasopressin secretion in schizophrenic patients with hyponatremia and polydipsia. *Archives of*

General Psychiatry, 54, 443–449. https://doi.org/10.1001/archpsyc.1997 .01830170069010

Goldstein, J., Hoff, K., & Hillyard, S. D. (2003). Comparison of dehydration and angiotensin II-stimulated cutaneous drinking in toads, *Bufo punctatus*. *Comparative Biochemistry and Physiology Part A: Molecular & Integrative Physiology*, 136, 557–563. https://doi.org/10.1016/S1095

Greenleaf, J. E. (1992). Problem: thirst, drinking behavior, and involuntary dehydration. *Medicine & Science in Sports & Exercise*, 24, 645–656. (PMID 1602937)

Greenleaf, J. E., Brock, P. J., Keil, L. C., & Morse, J. T. (1983). Drinking and water balance during exercise and heat acclimation. *Journal of Applied Physiology: Respiratory, Environmental and Exercise Physiology*, 54, 414–419. https://doi.org/10.1152/jappl.1983.54.2.414

Gregersen, M. I. (1932). Studies on the regulation of water intake. II. Conditions affecting the daily water intake of dogs as registered continuously by a potometer. *American Journal of Physiology*, 102, 344–349.

Gregersen, M. I., & Cannon, W. B. (1932). Studies on the regulation of water intake I: The effect of extirpation of the salivary glands on the water intake of dogs while panting. *American Journal of Physiology*, 102, 336–343.

Grob, M., Drolet, G., & Mouginot, D. (2004). Specific Na+ sensors are functionally expressed in a neuronal population of the median preoptic nucleus of the rat. *Journal of Neurophysiology*, 24, 3974–3984. https://doi.org/ 10.1523/JNEUROSCI.3720-03.2004

Grob, M., Trottier, J.-F., Drolet, G., & Mouginot, D. (2003). Characterization of the neurochemical content of neuronal populations of the lamina terminalis activated by acute hydromineral challenge. *Neuroscience*, 122, 247–257. https://doi.org/10.1016/j.neuroscience.2003.07.005

Gross, P. M., Kadekaro, M., Andrews, D. W., Sokoloff, L., & Saavedra, J. M. (1985). Selective metabolic stimulation of the subfornical organ and pituitary neural lobe by peripheral angiotensin II. *Peptides*, 6, 145–152. https://doi .org/10.1016/0196-9781

Grossman, S. P. (1990). *Thirst and sodium appetite: physiological basis*. San Diego, CA: Academic Press.

Guh, Y.-J., & Hwang, P.-P. (2017). Insights into molecular and cellular mechanisms of hormonal actions on fish ion regulation derived from the zebrafish model. *General and Comparative Endocrinology*, 251, 12–20. https://doi.org/ 10.1016/j.ygcen.2016.08.009

Gutman, Y., Benzakein, F., & Chaimovitz, M. (1969). Effect of illumination on water intake, thirst, and urine output in the rat. *American Journal of Physiology*, 217, 471–474. https://doi.org/10.1152/ajplegacy.1969.217.2.471

Gutman, M. B., Ciriello, J., & Mogenson, G. J. (1986). Electrophysiological identification of forebrain connections of the subfornical organ. *Brain Research*, 382, 119–128. https://doi.org/10.1016/0006-8993

(1988). Effects of plasma angiotensin II and hypernatremia on subfornical organ neurons. *American Journal of Physiology: Regulatory, Integrative and Comparative Physiology*, 254, R746–R754. https://doi.org/10.1152/ajpregu .1988.254.5.R746

Hainsworth, F. R. (1968). Evaporative water loss from rats in the heat. *American Journal of Physiology*, 214, 979–982. https://doi.org/10.1152/ajplegacy.1968.214.5.979

Hainsworth, F. R., & Stricker, E. M. (1971). Evaporative cooling in the rat: differences between salivary glands as thermoregulatory effectors. *Canadian Journal of Physiology and Pharmacology*, 49, 573–580. https://doi.org/10.1139/y71

Hainsworth, F. R., Stricker, E. M., & Epstein, A. N. (1968). Water metabolism of rats in the heat: dehydration and drinking. *American Journal of Physiology*, 214, 983–989. https://doi.org/10.1152/ajplegacy.1968.214.5.983

Hall, W. G. (1979). The ontogeny of feeding in rats: I. Ingestive and behavioral responses to oral infusions. *Journal of Comparative and Physiological Psychology*, 93, 977–1000. https://doi.org/10.1037/h0077628

Hall, W. G., Arnold, H. M., & Myers, K. P. (2000). The acquisition of an appetite. *Psychological Science*, 11, 101–105. https://doi.org/10.1111/1467-9280.00223

Hall, W. G., & Blass, E. M. (1975). Orogastic, hydrational, and behavioral controls of drinking following water deprivation in rats. *Journal of Comparative and Physiological Psychology*, 89, 939–954. https://doi.org/10.1037/h0077162

Hall, W. G., & Browde, J. A. (1986). The ontogeny of independent ingestion in mice: or, why won't infant mice feed? *Developmental Psychobiology*, 19, 211–222. https://doi.org/10.1002/dev.420190307

Hall, W. G., & Bryan, T. E. (1980). The ontogeny of feeding in rats: II. Independent ingestive behavior. *Journal of Comparative and Physiological Psychology*, 94, 746–756. https://doi.org/10.1037/h0077695

Hall, W. G., & Rosenblatt, J. S. (1979). Developmental changes in the suckling behavior of hamster pups: a comparison with rat pups. *Developmental Psychobiology*, 12, 553–560. https://doi.org/10.1002/dev.420120605

Han, L., & Rowland, N. E. (1995). Sodium depletion and Fos-immunoreactivity in lamina terminalis. *Neuroscience Letters*, 193, 173–176.

(1996). Dissociation of Fos-like immunoreactivity in lamina terminalis and magnocellular hypothalamic nuclei induced by hypernatremia. *Brain Research*, 708, 45–49. https://doi.org/10.1016/0006-8993

Hardy, R. N., Simsek, Z. D., Curry, B., et al. (2018). Aging affects isoproterenol-induced water drinking, astrocyte density, and central neuronal activation in female brown Norway rats. *Physiology and Behavior*, 192, 90–97. https://doi.org/10.1016/j.physbeh.2018.03.005

Harrison, G. A. (1958). The adaptability of mice to high environmental temperatures. *Journal of Experimental Biology*, 35, 892–901.

Hawkins, R. C., & Corbit, J. D. (1973). Drinking in response to cellular dehydration in the pigeon. *Journal of Comparative and Physiological Psychology*, 84, 265–267. https://doi.org/10.1037/h0035276

Helderman, J. H., Vestal, R. E., Rowe, J. W., Tobin, J. D., Andres, R., & Robertson, G. L. (1978). The response of arginine vasopressin to intravenous ethanol and hypertonic saline in man: the impact of aging. *Journal of Gerontology*, 33, 39–47. https://doi.org/10.1093/geronj/33.1.39

Heller, H. (1949). Effects of dehydration on adult and newborn rats. *Journal of Physiology*, 108, 303–314. (PMID 18149766)

Heller, H., & Lederis, K. (1959). Maturation of the hypothalamo-hypophysial system. *Journal of Physiology*, 147, 299–314. https://doi.org/10.1113/jphysiol.1959.sp006244

Heuston, K., & Zeigler, H. P. (1994). Water deprivation and subfornical organ activity in the pigeon: a [^{14}C]2-deoxyglucose study. *Brain Research*, 654, 331–335. https://doi.org/10.1016/0006-8993

Hiyama, T. Y., & Noda, M. (2016). Sodium sensing in the subfornical organ and body-fluid homeostasis. *Neuroscience Research*, 113, 1–11. https://doi.org/10.1016/j.neures.2016.07.007

Hiyama, T. Y., Utsunomiya, A. N., Matsumoto, M., et al. (2017). Adipsic hypernatremia without hypothalamic lesions accompanied by autoantibodies to subfornical organ. *Brain Pathology*, 27, 323–331. https://doi.org/10.1111/bpa.12409

Hochstenbach, S. L., & Ciriello, J. (1995). Plasma hypernatremia induces c-Fos activity in medullary catecholaminergic neurons. *Brain Research*, 674, 46–54. https://doi.org/10.1016/0006-8993(94)01434-J

(1996). Effect of lesions of forebrain circumventricular organs on c-Fos expression in the central nervous system to plasma hypernatremia. *Brain Research*, 713, 17–28. https://doi.org/10.1016/0006-8993

Hochstenbach, S. L., Solano-Flores, L. P., & Ciriello, J. (1993). Fos induction in brainstem neurons by intravenous hypertonic saline in the conscious rat. *Neuroscience Letters*, 158, 225–228. https://doi.org/10.1016/0304-3940

Holman, G. L. (1969). Intragastric reinforcement effect. *Journal of Comparative and Physiological Psychology*, 69, 432–441. https://doi.org/10.1037/h0028233

Holmes, J. H., & Gregersen, M. I. (1947). Relation of the salivary flow to the thirst produced in man by intravenous injection of hypertonic salt solution. *American Journal of Physiology*, 151, 252–257. https://doi.org/10.1152/ajplegacy.1947.151.2.252

(1950). Observations on drinking induced by hypertonic solutions. *American Journal of Physiology*, 162, 326–337. https://doi.org/10.1152/ajplegacy.1950.162.2.326

Holmes, J. H., & Montgomery, A. V. (1953). Thirst as a symptom. *American Journal of Medical Science*, 225, 281–286. (PMID 13030465)

Honda, K., Aradachi, H., Higuchi, T., Takano, S., & Negoro, H. (1992). Activation of paraventricular neurosecretory cells by local osmotic stimulation of the median preoptic nucleus. *Brain Research*, 594, 335–338. https://doi.org/10.1016/0006-8993(92)91147-7

Honda, K., Negoro, H., Dyball, R. E., Higuchi, T., & Takano, S. (1990a). The osmoreceptor complex in the rat: evidence for interactions between the supraoptic and other diencephalic nuclei. *Journal of Physiology*, 431, 225–241. https://doi.org/10.1113/jphysiol.1990.sp018238

Honda, K., Negoro, H., Higuchi, T., & Takano, S. (1990b). Activation of supraoptic neurosecretory cells by osmotic stimulation in the median preoptic nucleus. *Neuroscience Letters*, 119, 167–170. https://doi.org/10.1016/0304-3940(90)90825-t

Hori, T., Nakashima, T., Koga, H., Kiyohara, T., & Inoue, T. (1988).

Convergence of thermal, osmotic and cardiovascular signals on preoptic and anterior hypothalamic neurons in the rat. *Brain Research Bulletin*, 20, 879–885. https://doi.org/10.1016/0361-9230

Hosutt, J. A., Rowland, N., & Stricker, E. M. (1978). Hypotension and thirst in rats after isoproterenol treatment. *Physiology and Behavior*, 21, 593–598. https://doi.org/10.1016/0031-9384(78)90136-1

(1981). Impaired drinking responses of rats with lesions of the subfornical organ. *Journal of Comparative and Physiological Psychology*, 95, 104–113. https://doi.org/10.1037/h0077759

Houpt, K. A., & Epstein, A. N. (1971). The complete dependence of beta-adrenergic drinking on the renal dipsogen. *Physiology and Behavior*, 7, 897–902. https://doi.org/10.1016/0031-9384

Houpt, T. R., & Anderson, C. R. (1990). Spontaneous drinking: is it stimulated by hypertonicity or hypovolemia? *American Journal of Physiology: Regulatory, Integrative and Comparative Physiology*, 258, R143–R148. https://doi.org/10.1152/ajpregu.1990.253.1.R143

Houpt, T. R., & Yang, H. (1995). Water deprivation, plasma osmolality, blood volume, and thirst in young pigs. *Physiology and Behavior*, 57, 49–54. https://doi.org/10.1016/0031-9384

Houpt, T. R., Yang-Preyer, H., Geyer, J., & Norris, M. L. (1999). A rapid feedback signal is not always necessary for termination of a drinking bout. *American Journal of Physiology: Regulatory, Integrative and Comparative Physiology*, 276, R1156–R1163. https://doi.org/10.1152/ajpregu.1999.276.4.r1156

Hsiao, S., Epstein, A. N., & Camardo, J. S. (1977). The dipsogenic potency of peripheral angiotensin II. *Hormones and Behavior*, 8, 129–140. https://doi.org/10.1016/0018-506X

Hübschle, T., McKinley, M. J., & Oldfield, B. J. (1998). Efferent connections of the lamina terminalis, the preoptic area and the insular cortex to submandibular and sublingual gland of the rat traced with pseudorabies virus. *Brain Research*, 806, 219–231. https://doi.org/10.1016/s0006

Hübschle, T., Mathai, M. L., McKinley, M. J., & Oldfield, B. J. (2001). Multisynaptic neuronal pathways from the submandibular and sublingual glands to the lamina terminalis in the rat: a model for the role of the lamina terminalis in the control of osmo- and thermoregulatory behavior. *Clinical and Experimental Pharmacology and Physiology*, 28, 558–569. https://doi.org/10.1046/j.1440-1681.2001.03487.x

Humphrey, S. P., & Williamson, R. T. (2001). A review of saliva: normal composition, flow, and function. *Journal of Prosthetic Dentistry*, 85, 162–169. https://doi.org/10.1067/mpr.2001.113778

Jalowiec, J. E. (1974). Sodium appetite elicited by furosemide: effects of differential dietary maintenance. *Behavioral Biology*, 10, 313–328. https://doi.org/10.1016/s0091

Jansen, A. S. P., Ter Horst, G. J., Mettenleiter, T. C., & Loewy, A. D. (1992). CNS cell groups projecting to the submandibular parasympathetic preganglionic neurons in the rat: a retrograde transneuronal viral cell labeling study. *Brain Research*, 572, 253–260. https://doi.org/10.1016/0006-8993

Jennings, J. H., Ung, R. L., Otte, S., et al. (2015). Visualizing hypothalamic network dynamics for appetitive and consummatory behaviors. *Cell*, 160, 516–527. https://doi.org/10.1016/j.cell.2014.12.026

Jewell, P. A., & Verney, E. B. (1957). An experimental attempt to determine the site of neurohypophysial osmoreceptors in the dog. *Philosophical Transactions of the Royal Society of London*, 240B, 197–324. https://doi.org/10.1098/RSTB.1957.0002

Johnson, A. K., & Buggy, J. (1978). Periventricular preoptic-hypothalamus is vital for thirst and normal water economy. *American Journal of Physiology: Regulatory, Integrative and Comparative Physiology*, 234, R122–129. https://doi.org/10.1152/ajpregu.1978.234.3.R122

Johnson, A. K., & Epstein, A. N. (1975). The cerebral ventricles as the avenue for the dipsogenic action of intracranial angiotensin. *Brain Research*, 86, 399–418. https://doi.org/10.1016/0006-8993

Johnson, A. K., & Thunhorst, R. L. (1997). The neuroendocrinology of thirst and salt appetite: visceral sensory signals and mechanisms of central integration. *Frontiers in Neuroendocrinology*, 18, 292–353. https://doi.org/10.1006/frne.1997.0153

Johnson, R. F., Beltz, T. G., Thunhorst, R. L., & Johnson, A. K. (2003). Investigations on the physiological controls of water and saline intake in C57BL/6 mice. *American Journal of Physiology: Regulatory, Integrative and Comparative Physiology*, 285, R394–R403. https://doi.org/10.1152/ajpregu.00130.2003

Johnson, R. F., & Johnson, A. K. (1990a). Light/dark cycle modulates food to water intake ratios in rats. *Physiology and Behavior*, 48, 707–711. https://doi.org/10.1016/0031-9384

(1990b). Light-dark cycle modulates drinking to homeostatic challenges. *American Journal of Physiology: Regulatory, Integrative and Comparative Physiology*, 259, R1035–R1042. https://doi.org/10.1152/ajpregu.1990.259.5.R1035

(1991a). Drinking after osmotic challenge depends on circadian phase in rats with free-running rhythms. *American Journal of Physiology: Regulatory, Integrative and Comparative Physiology*, 261, R334–R338. https://doi.org/10.1152/ajpregu.1991.261.2.R334

(1991b). Meal-related and rhythmic drinking: effects of abolition of rat's eating rhythm. *American Journal of Physiology: Regulatory, Integrative and Comparative Physiology*, 261, R14–R19. https://doi.org/10.1152/ajpregu.1991.261.1.R14

Julien, E. A., & Bayer, S. A. (1990). Timetables of cytogenesis in the rat subfornical organ. *Developmental Brain Research*, 56, 169–176. https://doi.org/10.1016/0165-3806

Kahrilas, P. J., & Rogers, R. C. (1984). Rat brainstem neurons responsive to changes in portal blood sodium concentration. *American Journal of Physiology: Regulatory, Integrative and Comparative Physiology*, 247, R792–R799. https://doi.org/10.1152/ajpregu.1984.247.5.R792

Kakolewski, J. W., & Deaux, E. (1970). Initiation of eating as a function of ingestion of hypoosmotic solutions. *American Journal of Physiology*, 218, 590–585. https://doi.org/10.1152/ajplegacy.1970.218.2.590

Kanosue, K., Nakayama, T., Tanaka, H., Yanase, M., & Yasuda, H. (1990). Modes of action of local hypothalamic and skin thermal stimulation on salivary secretion in rats. *Journal of Physiology*, 424, 459–471. https://doi.org/10.1113/jphysiol.1990.sp018077

Kanter, G. S. (1953). Excretion and drinking after salt loading in dogs. *American Journal of Physiology*, 174, 87–94. https://doi.org/10.1152/ajplegacy.1953.174.1.87

Katafuchi, T., Hattori, Y., Nagatomo, I., Koizumi, K., & Silverstein, E. (1991). Involvement of angiotensin II in water intake of genetically polydipsic mice. *American Journal of Physiology: Regulatory, Integrative and Comparative Physiology*, 260, R1152–R1158. https://doi.org/10.1152/ajpregu.1991.260.6.R1152

Katayama, Y., Sakamoto, T., Saito, K., et al. (2018). Drinking by amphibious fish: convergent evolution of thirst mechanisms during vertebrate terrestrialization. *Scientific Reports*, 8, 625. https://doi.org/10.1038/s41598

Kaufman, S. (1981). Control of fluid intake in pregnant and lactating rats. *Journal of Physiology*, 318, 9–16. https://doi.org/10.1113/jphysiol.1981.sp013846

Kemefick, R. W., & Cheuvront, S. N. (2012). Hydration for recreational sport and physical activity. *Nutrition Reviews*, 70(Suppl. 2), S137–S142. https://doi.org/10.1111/j.1753-4887.2012.00523.x

Khan, M. S., Sasidharan, T. O., & Ghosh, P. K. (1979). Water regulation in Barmer goat of the Rajasthan desert. *Experientia*, 35, 1185–1186. https://doi.org/BF01963277

Kiecker, C. (2018). The origins of the circumventricular organs. *Journal of Anatomy*, 232, 540–553. https://doi.org/10.1111/joa.12771

Kim, C. K., Adhikari, A., & Diesseroth, K. (2017). Integration of optogenetics with complementary methodologies in systems neuroscience. *Nature Reviews Neuroscience*, 18, 222–235. https://doi.org/10.1038/nrn.2017.15

King, M. S., & Baertschi, A. J. (1991). Central neural pathway mediating splanchnic osmosensation. Brain Research, 550, 268–278. https://doi.org/10.1016/0006-8993(91)91328-x

Kinsman, B., Cowles, J., Lay, J., Simmonds, S. S., Browning, K. N., & Stocker, S. D. (2014). Osmoregulatory thirst in mice lacking the transient receptor potential vanilloid type 1 (TRPV1) and/or type 4 (TRPV4) receptor. *American Journal of Physiology: Regulatory, Integrative and Comparative Physiology*, 307, R1092–R1100. https://doi.org/10.1152/ajpregu.00102.2014

Kinsman, B. J., Simmonds, S. S., Browning, K. N., & Stocker, S. D. (2017). The organum vasculosum of the lamina terminalis detects NaCl to elevate sympathetic nerve activity and blood pressure. *Hypertension*, 69, 163–170. https://doi.org/10.1161/hypertensionaha.116.08372

Kinsman, B. J., Simmonds, S. S., Browning, K. N., Wenner, M. M., Farquhar, W. B., & Stocker, S. D. (2020). Integration of hypernatremia and angiotensin II by the organum vasculosum of the lamina terminalis regulates thirst. *Journal of Neuroscience*, 40, 2069–2079. https://doi.org/10.1523/JNEUROSCI.2208-19.2020

Kirby, C. R., & Convertino, V. A. (1985). Plasma aldosterone and sweat sodium concentrations after exercise and heat acclimation. *Journal of Applied Physiology*, 61, 967–970. https://doi.org/10.1152/jappl.1986.61.3.967

Kirby, R. F., Novak, C. M., Thunhorst, R. L., & Johnson, A. K. (1994). The role of beta₁ and beta₂ adrenoceptors in isoproterenol-induced drinking. *Brain Research*, 656, 79–84. https://doi.org/10.1016/0006-8993

Kissileff, H. R. (1969a). Food associated drinking in the rat. *Journal of Comparative and Physiological Psychology*, 67, 284–300. https://doi.org/10.1037/h0026773

(1969b). Oropharyngeal control of prandial drinking. *Journal of Comparative and Physiological Psychology*, 67, 309–319. https://doi.org/10.1037/h0026774

(1971). Acquisition of prandial drinking in weanling rats and in rats recovering from lateral hypothalamic lesions. *Journal of Comparative and Physiological Psychology*, 77, 97–109. https://doi.org/10.1037/h0031573

(1973). Nonhomeostatic controls of drinking. In A. N. Epstein, H. R. Kissileff, & E. Stellar, eds., *The neuropsychology of thirst: new findings and advances in concepts*. Washington, DC: Winston-Wiley, pp. 163–198.

Kobashi, M., Ichikawa, H., Sugimoto, T., & Adachi, A. (1993). Response of neurons in the solitary nucleus, area postrema and lateral parabrachial nucleus to gastric load of hypertonic saline. *Neuroscience Letters*, 158, 47–50. https://doi.org/10.1016/0304-3940

Kobayashi, H., Uemura, H., Takei, Y., Itatsu, N., Ozawa, M., & Ichinohe, K. (1983). Drinking induced by angiotensin II in fishes. *General and Comparative Endocrinology*, 49, 295–306. https://doi.org/10.1016/0016-6480(83)90147-8

Kobayashi, H., Uemura, H., Wada, M., & Takei, Y. (1979). Ecological adaptation of angiotensin-induced thirst mechanisms in tetrapods. *General and Comparative Endocrinology*, 38, 93–104. https://doi.org/10.1016/0016-6480

Koga, H., Hori, T., Kiyohara, T., & Nakashima, T. (1987). Responses of preoptic thermosensitive neurons to changes in blood pressure. *Brain Research Bulletin*, 18, 749–755. https://doi.org/10.1016/0361-9230

Kozlowksi, S., & Drzewiecki, K. (1973). The role of osmoreception in portal circulation in control of water intake. *Acta Physiologica Polonia*, 24, 325–330. (PMID 4711431)

Kozlowski, S., & Szczepanska-Sadowska, E. (1975). Mechanisms of hypovolaemic thirst and interactions between hypovolaemia, hyperosmolality and the antidiuretic system. In G. Peters, J. T. Fitzsimons, & L. Peters-Haefeli, eds., *Control mechanisms of drinking*. New York: Springer-Verlag, pp. 25–35.

Kraly, F. S. (1978). Abdominal vagotomy inhibits osmotically induced drinking in the rat. *Journal of Comparative and Physiological Psychology*, 92, 999–1013. https://doi.org/10.1037/h0077517

(1984a). Physiology of drinking elicited by eating. *Psychological Review*, 91, 478–490. (PMID 6390479)

(1984b). Preabsorptive pregastric vagally mediated histaminergic component of drinking elicited by eating in the rat. *Behavioral Neuroscience*, 98, 349–355. https://doi.org/10.1037/0735-7044.98.2.349

Kraly, F. S., & Corneilson, R. (1990). Angiotensin II mediates drinking elicited by eating in the rat. *American Journal of Physiology: Regulatory, Integrative and Comparative Physiology*, 258, R436–R442. https://doi.org/10.1152/ajpregu.1990.258.2.R436

Kraly, F. S., Kim, Y. M., Dunham, L. M., & Tribuzio, R. A. (1995). Drinking after intragastric NaCl without increase in plasma osmolality in rats. *American Journal of Physiology: Regulatory, Integrative and Comparative Physiology*, 269, R1085–R1092. https://doi.org/10.1152/ajpregu.1995.269.5.R1085

Kraly, F. S., & Specht, S. M. (1984). Histamine plays a major role for drinking elicited by spontaneous eating in rats. *Physiology and Behavior*, 33, 611–614. https://doi.org/10.1016/0031-9384

Krause, E. G., de Kloet, A. D., & Sakai, R. R. (2010). Post-ingestive signals and satiation of water and sodium intake of male rats. *Physiology and Behavior*, 99, 657–662. https://doi.org/10.1016/j.physbeh.2010.01.030

Krause, E. G., Melhorn, S. J., Davis, J. F., et al. (2008). Angiotensin type 1 receptors in the subfornical organ mediate the drinking and hypothalamo-pituitary-adrenal responses to systemic isoproterenol. *Endocrinology*, 149, 6416–6424. https://doi.org/10.1210/en.2008-0477

Kreček, J., & Krečkova, J. (1957). The development of the regulation of water metabolism: III. Preference in water and milk solution by young rats. *Physiological Bohemoslovenica*, 6, 14–21. (PMID 13461107)

Kültz, D. (2015). Physiological mechanisms used by fish to cope with salinity stress. *Journal of Experimental Biology*, 218, 1907–1914. https://doi.org/10.1242/jeb.118695

Kutscher, C. L. (1969). Species differences in the interaction of feeding and drinking. *Annals of the New York Academy of Sciences*, 157, 539–552. https://doi.org/10.1111/j.1749-6632.1969.tb12906.x

Latta, T. (1832). Letter from Dr. Latta to the secetary of the Central Board of Health, London, affording a view of the rationale and results of his practice in the treatment of cholera by aqueous and saline injections. *Lancet*, ii, 274–277.

Leenen, F. H., & McDonald, Jr., R. H. (1974). Effect of isoproterenol on blood pressure, plasma renin activity, and water intake in rats. *European Journal of Pharmacology*, 26, 129–135. https://doi.org/10.1016/0014-2999

Leenen, F. H., & Stricker, E. M. (1974). Plasma renin activity and thirst following hypovolemia or caval ligation in rats. *American Journal of Physiology*, 226, 1238–1242. https://doi.org/10.1152/ajplegacy.1974.226.5.1238

Lehr, D., Goldman, H. W., & Casner, P. (1975). Evidence against the postulated role of the renin-angiotensin system in putative renin-dependent drinking responses. In G. Peters, J. T. Fitzsimons, & L. Peters-Haefeli, eds., *Control mechanisms of drinking*. New York: Springer-Verlag, pp. 79–83.

Lehr, D., Mallow, J., & Krukowski, M. (1967). Copious drinking and simultaneous inhibition of urine flow elicited by beta-adrenergic stimulation and contrary effect of alpha-adrenergic stimulation. *Journal of Pharmacology and Experimental Therapeutics*, 158, 150–163. (PMID 6054075)

Leib, D. E., Zimmerman, C. A., Poormoghaddam, A., et al. (2017). The forebrain thirst circuit drives drinking through negative reinforcement. *Neuron*, 96, 1272–1281. https://doi.org/10.1016/j.neuron.2017.11.041

Lepkovsky, S., Lyman, R., Fleming, D., Nagumo, M., & Dimick, M. M. (1957). Gastrointestinal regulation of water and its effect on food intake and rate of digestion. *American Journal of Physiology*, 188, 327–331. https://doi.org/10.1152/ajplegacy.1957.188.2.327

Leschke, E. (1918). Über die Durstempfindung. *Archiv für Psychiatrie und Nervenkrankenheiten, 59,* 773–781.

Leshem, M., Boggan, B., & Epstein, A. N. (1988). The ontogeny of drinking evoked by activation of brain angiotensin in the rat pup. *Developmental Psychobiology, 21,* 63–75. https://doi.org//10.1002/dev.420210105

Leshem, M., & Epstein, A. N. (1988). Thirst-induced anorexias and the ontogeny of thirst in the rat. *Developmental Psychobiology, 21,* 651–662. https://doi.org/10.1002/dev.420210704

Leshem, M., Saaadi, A., Alem, N., & Hendi, K. (2008). Enhanced salt appetite, diet and drinking in traditional Bedouin women in the Negev. *Appetite, 50,* 71–82. https://doi.org/10.1016/j.appet.2007.05.010

Lešnik, A., Piko, N., Železnik, D., & Bevc, S. (2017). Dehydration of older patients in institutional care and the home environment. *Research in Gerontological Nursing, 10,* 260–266. https://doi.org/10.3928/19404921-20171013-03

Levick, J. R., & Michel, C. C. (2010). Microvascular fluid exchange and the revised Starling principle. *Cardiovascular Research, 87,* 198–210. https://doi.org/10.1093/cvr/cvq062

Liedtke, W., & Friedman, J. M. (2003). Abnormal osmotic regulation in *trpv4-/-* mice. *Proceedings of the National Academy of Sciences USA, 100,* 13698–13703. https://doi.org/10.1073/pnas.1735416100

Liljestrand, G., & Zotterman, Y. (1954). The water taste in mammals. *Acta Physiologica Scandinavica, 32,* 291–303. https://doi.org/10.1111/j.1748-1716.1954.tb01177.x

Lillywhite, H. B., Sheehy, C. M., Sandfoss, M. R., et al. (2019). Drinking by sea snakes from oceanic freshwater lenses at first rainfall following seasonal drought. *PLoS One, 14,* e0212099. https://doi.org/10.1371/journal.pone.0212099

Lind, R. W., Thunhorst, R. L., & Johnson, A. K. (1984). The subfornical organ and the integration of multiple factors in thirst. *Physiology and Behavior, 32,* 69–74. https://doi.org/10.1016/0031-9384

Lind, R. W., Van Hoesen, R. W., & Johnson, A. K. (1982). An HRP study of the connections of the subfornical organ in the rat. Journal of Comparative Neurology, 210, 265–277. https://doi.org/10.1002/cne.902100306

Lotter, E. C., McKay, L. D., Mangiapane, M. L., et al. (1980). Intraventricular angiotensin elicits drinking in the baboon. *Proceedings of the Society for Experimental Biology and Medicine, 163,* 48–51. https://doi.org/10.3181/00379727-163-40720

Lucas, G. A., Timberlake, W., & Gawley, D. J. (1989). Learning and meal-associated drinking: meal-related deficits produce adjustments in postprandial drinking. *Physiology and Behavior, 46,* 361–367. https://doi.org/10.1016/0031-9384

Luke, R. G. (1973). Natriuresis and chloruresis during hydrogenia in the rat. *American Journal of Physiology, 224,* 13–20. https://doi.org/10.1152/ajplegacy.1973.224.1.13

Lund, J. P., Barker, J. H., Dellow, P. G., & Stevenson, J. A. F. (1969). Water intake of normal and desalivate rats on exposure to environmental heat.

Canadian Journal of Physiology and Pharmacology, 47, 849–852. https://doi
.org/10.1139/y69

Luo, L., Callaway, E. M., & Svoboda, K. (2018). Genetic dissection of neural
circuits: a decade of progress. *Neuron, 98*, 256–281. https://doi.org/10.1016/j
.neuron.2018.03.040

McCance, R. A. (1948). Renal function in early life. *Physiological Review, 28*,
331–348. https://doi.org/10.1152/physrev.1948.28.3.331

McCleary, R. A. (1953). Taste and post-ingestion factors in specific hunger
behavior. *Journal of Comparative and Physiological Psychology, 46*, 411–421.
https://doi.org/10.1037/h0059419

McDonald, T. J., Li, C., Nijland, M. J., Caston-Balderrama, A., & Ross, M. G.
(1998). Fos response of fetal sheep anterior circumventricular organs to
osmotic challenge in late gestation. *American Journal of Physiology: Heart
and Circulatory Physiology, 275*, H609–H614. https://doi.org/10.1152/
ajpheart.1998.275.2.H609

McGowan, M. K., Brown, B., & Grossman, S. P. (1988). Lesions of the MPO or
AV3V: influences on fluid intake. *Physiology and Behavior, 42*, 331–342.
https://doi.org/10.1016/0031-9384

McIntosh, G. H., Baghurst, K. I., Potter, B. J., & Hetzel, B. S. (1979). Foetal
brain development in the sheep. *Neuropathology and Applied Neurobiology, 5*,
103–114. https://doi.org/10.1111/j.1365-2990.1979.tb00664.x

McKenna, T. M., & Haines, H. (1981). Sodium metabolism during acclimation
to water restriction by wild mice, *Mus musculus. American Journal of
Physiology: Regulatory, Integrative and Comparative Physiology, 240*,
R319–R326. https://doi.org/10.1152/ajpregu.1981.240.5.R319

McKinley, M. J., Badoer, E., & Oldfield, B. J. (1992). Intravenous angiotensin II
induces Fos-immnuno-reactivity in circumventricular organs of the lamina
terminalis. *Brain Research, 594*, 295–300. https://doi.org/10.1016/0006-8993

McKinley, M. J., Cairns, M. J., Denton, D. A., et al. (2004). Physiological and
pathophysiological influences on thirst. *Physiology and Behavior, 81*,
795–803. https://doi.org/10.1016/j.physbeh.2004.04.055

McKinley, M. J., Congiu, M., Denton, D. A., et al. (1984). The anterior wall of
the third cerebral ventricle and homeostatic responses to dehydration.
Journal de Physiologie (Paris), 79, 421–427. (PMID 6536750)

McKinley, M. J., Denton, D. A., Leksell, L. G., et al. (1982). Osmoregulatory
thirst in sheep is disrupted by ablation of the anterior wall of the optic recess.
Brain Research, 236, 210–215. https://doi.org/10.1016/0006-8993

McKinley, M. J., Denton, D. A., Leksell, L. G., Tarjan, E., & Weisinger, R. L. S.
(1980). Evidence for cerebral sodium sensors in water drinking in sheep.
Physiology and Behavior, 25, 501–504. https://doi.org/10.1016/0031-9384

McKinley, M. J., Denton, D. A., Nelson, J. F., & Weisinger, R. S. (1983).
Dehydration induces sodium depletion in rats, rabbits, and sheep.
*American Journal of Physiology: Regulatory, Integrative and Comparative
Physiology, 245*, R287–R292. https://doi.org/10.1152/ajpregu.1983.245.2
.R287

McKinley, M. J., Denton, D. A., Park, R. G., & Weisinger, R. S. (1986).
Ablation of the subfornical organ does not prevent angiotensin-induced

water drinking in sheep. *American Journal of Physiology: Regulatory, Integrative and Comparative Physiology*, 250, R1052–R1059. https://doi.org/10.1152/ajpregu.1986.250.6.R1052

McKinley, M. J., Denton, D. A., Ryan, P. J., Yao, S. T., Stefanidis, A., & Oldfield, B. J. (2019). From sensory circumventricular organs to cerebral cortex: neural pathways controlling thirst and hunger. *Neuroendocrinology*, 31, 12689.https://doi.org/10.1111/jne.12689

McKinley, M. J., Denton, D. A., Thomas, C. J., Woods, R. L., & Mathai, M. L. (2006). Differential effects of aging on fluid intake in response to hypovolemia, hypertonicity, and hormonal stimuli in Munich Wistar rats. Proceedings of the National Academy of Sciences USA, 103, 3450–3455. https://doi.org/10.1073/pnas.0511099103

McKinley, M. J., Denton, D. A., & Weisinger, R. S. (1978). Sensors for antidiuresis and thirst – osmoreceptors or CSF sodium detectors? *Brain Research*, 141, 89–103. https://doi.org/10.1016/0006-8993

McKinley, M. J., Hards, D. K., & Oldfield, B. J. (1994). Identification of neural pathways activated in dehydrated rats by means of Fos-immunohistochemistry and neural tracing. *Brain Research*, 653, 305–314. https://doi.org/10.1016/0006-8993

McKinley, M. J., McAllen, R. M., Whyte, D., & Mathai, M. L. (2008). Central osmoregulatory influences on thermoregulation. *Clinical and Experimental Pharmacology and Physiology*, 35, 701–705. https://doi.org/10.1111/j.1440-1681.2007.04833.x

McKinley, M. J., & Mathai, M. L. (2014). Interdependent preoptic osmoregulatory and thermoregulatory mechanisms influencing body fluid balance and heat defense. In L. A. De Luca, J. V. Menani, & A. K. Johnson, eds., *Neurobiology of body fluid homeostasis*. Boca Raton, FL: CRC Press, pp. 111–121.

McKinley, M. J., Mathai, M. L., Pennington, G., Rundgren, M., & Vivas, L. (1999). Effect of individual or combined ablation of the nuclear groups of the lamina terminalis on water drinking in sheep. *American Journal of Physiology: Regulatory, Integrative and Comparative Physiology*, 276, R673–R683. https://doi.org/10.1152/ajpregu.1999.276.3.R673

McKinley, M. J., Olsson, K., Fyrhquist, F., & Liljekvist, E. (1980). Transient vasopressin release and thirst in response to prolonged intracerebroventricular infusions of hypertonic mannitol in saline. *Acta Physiologica Scandinavica*, 109, 427–431. https://doi.org/10.1111/j.1748-1716.1980.tb06616.x

McKinley, M. J., Walker, L. L., Alexiou, T., et al. (2008). Osmoregulatory fluid intake but not hypovolemic thirst is intact in mice lacking angiotensin. *American Journal of Physiology: Regulatory, Integrative and Comparative Physiology*, 294, R1533–R1543. https://doi.org/10.1152/ajpregu.00848.2007

McKinley, M. J., Weissenborn, F., & Mathai, M. L. (2009). Drinking-induced thermoregulatory panting in rehydrated sheep: influences of oropharyngeal/esophageal signals, core temperature, and thirst satiety. *American Journal of Physiology Regulatory Integrative Comparative Physiology*, 296, R1881–1888. https://doi.org/10.1152/ajpregu.90890.2008

Macchione, A. F., Beas, C., Dadam, F. M., et al. (2015). Early free access to hypertonic NaCl solution induces a long-term effect on drinking, brain cell activity and gene expression of adult rat offspring. *Neuroscience*, 298, 120–136. https://doi.org/10.1016/j.neuroscience.2015.04.004

Mack, G. W., Weseman, C. A., Langhans, G. W., Scherzer, H., Gillen, C. M., & Nadel, E. R. (1994). Body fluid balance in dehydrated healthy older men: thirst and renal osmoregulation. *Journal of Applied Physiology*, 76, 1615–1623. https://doi.org/10.1152/jappl.1994.76.4.1615

Maddison, S., Wood, R. J., Rolls, E. T., Rolls, B. J., & Gibbs J. (1980). Drinking in the rhesus monkey: peripheral factors. *Journal of Comparative and Physiological Psychology*, 94, 365–374. https://doi.org/10.1037/h0077664

Maejima, S., Kunno, N., Matsuda, K., & Uchiyama, M. (2010). Central angiotensin II stimulates cutaneous water intake behavior via an angiotensin II type-1 receptor pathway in the Japanese tree frog *Hyla japonica*. *Hormones and Behavior*, 58, 457–464. https://doi.org/10.1016/j.yhbeh.2010.05.007

Mandelblat-Cerf, Y., Kim, A., Burgess, C. R., et al. (2017). Bidirectional anticipation of future osmotic challenges by vasopressin neurons. *Neuron*, 93, 57–65. https://doi.org/10.1016/j.neuron.2016.11.021

Mangiapane, M. L., & Simpson, J. B. (1980). Subfornical organ lesions reduce the pressor effect of systemic angiotensin II. *Neuroendocrinology*, 31, 380–384. https://doi.org/10.1159/000123107

Mann, J. F. E., Johnson, A. K., & Ganten, D. (1980). Plasma angiotensin II: dipsogenic levels and angiotensin-generating capacity of renin. *American Journal of Physiology: Regulatory, Integrative and Comparative Physiology*, 238, R372–R377. https://doi.org/10.1152/ajpregu.1980.238.5.R372

Marciante, A. B., Wang, L. A., Farmer, G. E., & Cunningham, J. T. (2019). Selectively inhibiting the median preoptic nucleus attenuates angiotensin II and hyperosmotic-induced drinking behavior and vasopressin release in adult male rats. *eNeuro*, 6, e0473–18.2019. https://doi.org/10.1523/ENEURO.0473-18.2019

Marson, O., Chernicky, C. L., Barnes, K. L., Diz, D. I., Slugg, R. M., & Ferrario, C. M. (1985). The anteroventral third ventricle region: participation in the regulation of blood pressure in conscious dogs. *Hypertension*, 7 (Suppl. 1), I-80–I-87. https://doi.org/10.1161/01.hyp.7.3_pt_2.i80

Martin, J. R., Fuchs, A., & Harting, J. (1985). Drinking by senescent and adult rats in response to regulatory challenges. *Neurobiology of Aging*, 6, 57–59. https://doi.org/10.1016/0197-4580

Maruyama, M., Nishi, M., Konishi, M., et al. (2003). Brain regions expressing Fos during thermoregulatory behavior in rats. *American Journal of Physiology: Regulatory, Integrative and Comparative Physiology*, 285, R1116–R1123. https://doi.org/10.1152/ajpregu.00166.2002

Marwine, A., & Collier, G. (1979). The rat at the water hole. *Journal of Comparative and Physiological Psychology*, 93, 391–402. https://doi.org/10.1037/h0077552

Massi, M., DeCaro, G., Mazzarella, L., & Epstein, A. N. (1986). The role of the subfornical organ in the drinking behavior of the pigeon. *Brain Research*, 381, 289–299. https://doi.org/10.1016/0006-8993

Mathai, M. L., Hübschle, T., & McKinley, M. J. (2000). Central angiotensin receptor blockade impairs thermolytic and dipsogenic responses to heat exposure in rats. *American Journal of Physiology: Regulatory, Integrative and Comparative Physiology*, 279, R1821–R1826. https://doi.org/10.1152/ajpregu.2000.279.5.r1821

Matsuda, T., Hiyama, T. Y., Niimura, F., et al. (2017). Distinct neural mechanisms for the control of thirst and sodium appetite in the subfornical organ. *Nature Neuroscience*, 20, 230–241. https://doi.org/10.1038/nn.4463

Mayer, A. (1901). *Essai sur la soif: ses causes et son mécanisme*. Paris: Félix Alcan.

Mecawi, A. S., Macchione, A. F., Nuñez, P., et al. (2015). Developmental programming of thirst and sodium appetite. *Neuroscience and Biobehavioral Reviews*, 51, 1–14. https://doi.org/10.1016/j.neurobiorev.2014.12.012

Mendelsohn, F. A., Quirion, R., Saavedra, J. M., Aguilera, G., & Catt, K. J. (1984). Autoradiographic localization of angiotensin II receptors in rat brain. *Proceedings of the National Academy of Sciences USA*, 81, 1575–1579. https://doi.org/10.1073/pnas.81.5.1575

Metzler, C. H., Thrasher, T. N., Keil, L. C., & Ramsay, D. J. (1986). Endocrine mechanisms regulating sodium excretion during water deprivation in dogs. *American Journal of Physiology: Regulatory, Integrative and Comparative Physiology*, 251, R560–R568. https://doi.org/10.1152/ajpregu.1986.251.3.R560

Miescher, E., & Fortney, S. M. (1989). Responses to dehydration and rehydration during heat exposure in young and older men. *American Journal of Physiology: Regulatory, Integrative and Comparative Physiology*, 257, R1050–R1056. https://doi.org/10.1152/ajpregu.1989.257.5.r1050

Miller, N. E., Sampliner, R. I., & Woodrow, P. (1957). Thirst-reducing effects of water by stomach fistula vs. water by mouth measured by both a consummatory and an instrumental response. *Journal of Comparative and Physiological Psychology*, 50, 1–5. https://doi.org/10.1037/h0046009

Mimee, A., Smith, P. M., & Ferguson, A. V. (2013). Circumventricular organs: targets for integration of circulating fluid and energy balance signals? *Physiology and Behavior*, 121, 96–102.

Miselis, R. R. (1981). The efferent connections of the subfornical organ of the rat: a circumventricular organ within a neural network subserving water balance. *Brain Research*, 230, 1–23. https://doi.org/10.1016/0006-8993

Montain, S. J., & Coyle, E. F. (1992). Influence of graded dehydration on hyperthermia and cardiovascular drift during exercise. *Journal of Applied Physiology*, 73, 1340–1350.

Moore-Gillon, M. J. (1980). Effects of vagotomy on drinking in the rat. *Journal of Physiology*, 308, 417–426.

Morgan, J. I., & Curran, T. (1986). Role of ion flux in the control of c-Fos expression. *Nature*, 322, 552–555. https://doi.org/10.1038/322552a0

Morien, A., Garrard, L., & Rowland, N. E. (1999). Expression of Fos immunoreactivity in rat brain during dehydration: effect of duration and timing of water deprivation. *Brain Research*, 816, 1–7.

Morimoto, T. (1990). Thermoregulation and body fluids: role of blood volume and central venous pressure. *Japanese Journal of Physiology*, 40, 165–179. https://doi.org/10.2170/jjphysiol.40.165

Morita, S., & Miyata, S. (2012). Different vascular permeability between the sensory and secretory circumventricular organs of adult mouse brain. *Cell and Tissue Research*, 349, 589–603. https://doi.org/10.1007/s00441-012-1421-9

Morita, H., Yamashita, Y., Nishida, Y., Tokuda, M., Hatase, O., & Hosomi, H. (1997). Fos induction in rat brain neurons after stimulation of the hepatoportal Na-sensitive mechanism. *American Journal of Physiology: Regulatory, Integrative and Comparative Physiology*, 272, R913–R923. https://doi.org/10.1152/ajpregu.1997.272.3.R913

Moriya, T., Shibasaki, R., Kayano, T., et al. (2015). Full-length transient receptor potential vanilloid 1 channels mediate calcium signals and possibly contribute to osmoreception in vasopressin neurons in the rat supraoptic nucleus. *Cell Calcium*, 11, 003. https://doi.org/10.1016/j.ceca.2014.11.003

Morley, J. E., & Flood, J. F. (1989). The effect of neuropeptide Y on drinking in mice. *Brain Research*, 494, 129–137. https://doi.org/10.1016/0006-8993(89)90151-0.

Morris, P., & Mogenson, G. J. (1980). Dissociation of nocturnal feeding and drinking behavior in the rat. *Behavioral and Neural Biology*, 30, 299–311. https://doi.org/10.1016/s0163

*Molecular Pharmacology*Murphy, M. S., & DeNardo, D. F. (2019). Rattlesnakes must drink: meal consumption does not improve hydration state. *Physiological Biochemistry and Zoology*, 92, 381–385.

Myer, J. S., & Kowell, A. P. (1971). Loss and subsequent recovery of body weight in water-deprived snakes (Elaphe obsoleta obsoleta). *Journal of Comparative and Physiological Psychology*, 75, 5–9. https://doi.org/10.1037/h0030684

Myers, K. P., & Hall, W. G. (2001). Effects of prior experience with dehydration and water on the time course of dehydration-induced drinking in weanling rats. *Developmental Psychobiology*, 38, 145–153. https://doi.org/10.1002/dev.1008

Naeini, R. F., Witty, M.-F., Séguéla, P., & Bourque, C. W. (2006). An N-terminal variant of Trpv1 channel is required for osmosensory transduction. *Nature Neuroscience*, 9, 93–98. https://doi.org/10.1038/nn1614

Nagakura, A., Hiyama, T. Y., & Noda, M. (2010). Na_x-deficient mice show normal vasopressin response to dehydration. *Neuroscience Letters*, 472, 161–165. https://doi.org/10.1016/j.neulet.2010.01.077

Nation, H. L., Nicoleau, M., Kinsman, B. J., Browning, K. N., & Stocker, S. D. (2016). DREADD-induced activation of subfornical organ neurons stimulates thirst and salt appetite. *Journal of Neurophysiology*, 115, 3123–3129. https://doi.org/10.1152/jn.00149.2016

Nehmé, B., Henry, M., Mouginot, D., & Drolet, G. (2012). The expression pattern of the Na+ sensor, Na_x in the hydromineral homeostatic network: a comparative study between the rat and mouse. *Frontiers in Neuroanatomy*, 6, 26. https://doi.org/10.3389/fnana.2012.00026

Nicolaïdis, S. (1969). Early systemic responses to orogastric stimulation in the regulation of food and water balance: functional and electrophysiological data. *Annals of the New York Academy of Sciences*, 157, 1176–1203. https://doi.org/10.1111/j.1749-6632.1969.tb12942.x

Nicolaïdis, S., & El Ghissassi, M. (1991). Angiotensin and sodium interaction in the organum cavum pre-lamina terminalis: electrophysiological and drinking responses. *Brain Research Bulletin*, 27, 469–473. https://doi.org/10.1016/0361-9230

Nicolaïdis, S., & Fitzsimons, J. T. (1975). La dépendence de la prise d'eau induite par l'angiotensine II envers la function vasomotrice cérébrale chez le rat. *Comptes Rendus de l'Académie des Sciences*, 281D, 1417–1420.

Nicolaïdis, S., Galaverna, O., & Metzler, C. H. (1990). Extracellular dehydration during pregnancy increases salt appetite of offspring. *American Journal of Physiology: Regulatory, Integrative and Comparative Physiology*, 258, R281–R283. https://doi.org/ 10.1152/ajpregu.1990.258.1.R281

Nicolaïdis, S., & Rowland, N. (1975). Regulatory drinking in rats with permanent access to a bitter fluid source. *Physiology and Behavior*, 14, 819–824. https://doi.org/10.1016/0031-9384

Nishihara, E., Hiyama, T. Y., & Noda, M. (2011). Osmosensitivity of transient receptor potential vanilloid 1 is synergistically enhanced by distinct activating stimuli such as temperature and protons. *PLoS ONE*, 6, e22246. https://doi.org/10.1371/journal.pone.0022246

Nobata, S., Ando, M., & Takei, Y. (2013). Hormonal control of drinking behavior in teleost fishes: insights from studies using eels. *General and Comparative Endocrinology*, 192, 214–221. https://doi.org/10.1016/j.ygcen.2013.05.009

Nose, H., Morimoto, T., & Ogura, K. (1983). Distribution of water losses among fluid compartments of tissues under thermal dehydration in the rat. *Japanese Journal of Physiology*, 33, 1019–1029. https://doi.org/10.2170/jjphysiol.33.1019

Nose, H., Sugimoto, E., Okuno, T., & Moromoto, T. (1987). Changes in blood volume and plasma sodium concentration after water intake in rats. *American Journal of Physiology: Regulatory, Integrative and Comparative Physiology*, 253, R15–R19. https://doi.org/10.1152/ajpregu.1987.253.1.R15

Nose, H., Yawata, T., & Morimoto, T. (1985). Osmotic factors in restitution from thermal dehydration in rats. *American Journal of Physiology: Regulatory, Integrative and Comparative Physiology*, 249, R166–R171. https://doi.org/10.1152/ajpregu.1985.249.2.R166

Nothnagel, C. W. H. (1881). Durst und polydipsie. *Archiv für Pathologische Anatomie und Physiologie*, 86, 435–447.

Novin, D. (1962). The relation between electrical conductivity of brain tissue and thirst in the rat. *Journal of Comparative and Physiological Psychology*, 55, 145–154. https://doi.org/10.1037/h0044312

Oatley, K. (1964). Changes of blood volume and osmotic pressure in the production of thirst. *Nature*, 202, 1341–1342. https://doi.org/10.1038/2021341a0

   (1967a). Diurnal influences on postdeprivational drinking in rats. *Journal of Comparative and Physiological Psychology*, 64, 183–185. https://doi.org/10.1037/h0024804

   (1967b). Drinking in response to salt injections at different times of day. *Psychonomic Science*, 9, 439–440.

(1971). Dissociation of the circadian drinking pattern from eating. *Nature*, 229, 494–496. https://doi.org/10.1038/229494a0

Oatley, K., & Toates, F. M. (1969). The passage of food through the gut of rats and its uptake of fluid. *Psychonomic Science*, 16, 225–226.

O'Connor, W. J. (1977). Drinking caused by exposing dogs to radiant heat. *Journal of Physiology*, 264, 229–237. https://doi.org/10.1113/jphysiol.1977.sp011665

Oka, Y., Ye, M., & Zuker, C. S. (2015). Thirst driving and suppressing signal encoded by distinct neural populations in the brain. *Nature*, 520, 349–352. https://doi.org/10.1038/nature14108

Oldfield, B. J., Badoer, E., Hards, D. K., & McKinley, M. J. (1994). Fos production in retrogradely labelled neurons of the lamina terminalis following intravenous infusion of either hypertonic saline or angiotensin II. *Neuroscience*, 60, 255–262. https://doi.org/10.1016/0306-4522

Oldfield, B. J., Bicknell, R. J., McAllen, R. M., Weisinger, R. S., & McKinley, M. J. (1991). Intravenous hypertonic saline induced Fos immunoreactivity in neurons throughout the lamina terminalis. *Brain Research*, 561, 151–156. https://doi.org/10.1016/0006-8993(91)90760-S

Oldfield, B. J., Miselis, R. R., & McKinley, M. J. (1991). Median preoptic nucleus projections to vasopressin-containing neurons of the supraoptic nucleus in sheep: a light and electron microscopic study. *Brain Research*, 542, 193–200. https://doi.org/10.1016/0006-8993

Oliet, S. H., & Bourque, C. W. (1992). Properties of supraoptic magnocellular neurons isolated from the adult rat. *Journal of Physiology*, 455, 291–306. https://doi.org/10.1113/jphysiol.1992.sp019302

Olsson, K. (1973). Further evidence for the importance of CSF Na+ concentration in the central control of fluid balance. *Acta Physiologica Scandinavica*, 88, 183–188. https://doi.org/10.1111/j.1748-1716.1973.tb05445.x

Ormerod, J. K., Elliott, T. A., Scheet, V. P., et al. (2003). Drinking behavior and perception of thirst in untrained women during 6 weeks of heat acclimation and outdoor training. *International Journal of Sport Nutrition and Exercise Metabolism*, 13, 15–28. https://doi.org/10.1123/ijsnem.13.1.15

Ortiz, R. M. (2001). Osmoregulation in marine mammals. *Journal of Experimental Biology*, 204, 1831–1844. (PMID 11441026)

Overmann, S. R., & Yang, M. G. (1973). Adaptation to water restriction through dietary selection in weanling rats. *Physiology and Behavior*, 11, 781–786. https://doi.org/10.1016/0031-9384

Paes-Leme, B., Dos-Santos, R. C., Mecawi, A. S., & Ferguson, A. V. (2018). Interaction between angiotensin II and glucose sensing at the subfornical organ. *Journal of Neuroendocrinology*, 30, e12645. https://doi.org/10.1111/jne.12654

Paget, S. (1897). On cases of voracious hunger and thirst from injury or disease of the brain. *Transactions of the Clinical Society of London*, 30, 113–119.

Paque, C. (1980). Sahara Bedouins and the salt water of the Sahara: a model for salt intake. In M. Kare, ed., *Biological and behavioral aspects of salt intake*. Orlando, FL: Academic Press, pp. 31–47.

Patke, A., Young, M. W., & Axelrod, S. (2020). Molecular mechanisms and physiological importance of circadian rhythms. *Nature Reviews Molecular and Cell Biology*, 21, 67–84. https://doi.org/10.1038/s41580

Patronas, P., Horowitz, M., Simon, E., & Gerstberger, R. (1998). Differential stimulation of c-Fos expression in hypothalamic nuclei of the rat brain during short-term heat acclimation and mild dehydration. *Brain Research*, 798, 127–139. https://doi.org/10.1016/s0006

Peck, J. W., & Blass, E. M. (1975). Localization of thirst and antidiuretic osmoreceptors by intracranial injections in rats. *American Journal of Physiology*, 228, 1501–1509. https://doi.org/10.1152/ajplegacy.1975.228.5.1501

Perillan, C., Costales, M., Diaz, F., Vijande, M., & Arguelles, J. (2004). Thirst changes in offspring of hyperreninemic rat dams. *Pharmacology, Biochemistry and Behavior*, 79, 709–713. https://doi.org/10.1016/j.pbb.2004.09.023

Perillan, C., Costales, M., Vijande, M., & Arguelles, J. (2007). Maternal RAS influence on the ontogeny of thirst. *Physiology and Behavior*, 92, 554–559. https://doi.org/10.1016/j.physbeh.2007.04.031

(2008). In utero extracellular dehydration modifies thirst in neonatal rats. *Appetite*, 51, 599–603. https://doi.org/10.1016/j.appet.2008.04.015

Perrier, E. T. (2017). Shifting focus: from hydration for performance to hydration for health. *Annals of Nutrition and Metabolism*, 70(Suppl. 1), 4–12. https://doi.org/10.1159/000462996

Perrier, E., Demazières, A., Girard, N., et al. (2013). Circadian variation and responsiveness of hydration biomarkers to changes in daily water intake. *European Journal of Applied Physiology*, 113, 2143–2151. https://doi.org/10.1007/s00421

Petter, L. P. M., Hourihane, J. O'B., & Rolles, C. J. (1994). Is water out of vogue? A survey of the drinking habits of 2–7 year olds. *Archives of Diseases of Childhood*, 72, 137–140. https://doi.org/10.1136/adc.72.2.137

Phillips, P. A., Bretherton, M., Johnston, C. I., & Gray, L. (1991). Reduced osmotic thirst in healthy elderly men. *American Journal of Physiology: Regulatory, Integrative and Comparative Physiology*, 261, R166–R171. https://doi.org/10.1152/ajpregu.1991.261.1.R166

Phillips, P. A., Bretherton, M., Risvanis, J., Casley, D., Johnston, C., & Gray, L. (1993). Effects of drinking on thirst and vasopressin in dehydrated elderly men. *American Journal of Physiology: Regulatory, Integrative and Comparative Physiology*, 264, R877–R881. https://doi.org/10.1152/ajpregu.1993.264.5.R877

Phillips, P. A., Rolls, B. J., Ledingham, J. G., et al. (1984). Reduced thirst after water deprivation in healthy elderly men. *New England Journal of Medicine*, 311, 753–759. https://doi.org/10.1056/NEJM198409203111202

Phillips, P. A., Rolls, B. J., Ledingham, J. G. G., Forsling, M. L., & Morton, J. J. (1985). Osmotic thirst and vasopressin release in humans: a double-blind crossover study. *American Journal of Physiology: Regulatory, Integrative and Comparative Physiology*, 248, R645–R650. https://doi.org/10.1152/ajpregu.1985.248.6.R645

Phillips, P. A., Rolls, B. J., Ledingham, J. G. G., Morton, J. J., & Forsling, M. L. (1985). Angiotensin II-induced thirst and vasopressin release in man. *Clinical Science*, 68, 669–674. https://doi.org/10.1042/cs0680669

Pitts, G. C., Johnson, R. E., & Consolazio, F. C. (1944). Work in the heat as affected by intake of water, salt, and glucose. *American Journal of Physiology*, 142, 253–259.

Possidente, B., & Birnbaum, S. (1979). Circadian rhythms for food and water consumption in the mouse, *Mus musculus*. *Physiology and Behavior*, 22, 657–660. https://doi.org/10.1016/0031-9384

Prager-Khoutorsky, M., & Bourque C. W. (2015). Anatomical organization of the rat organum vasculosum laminae terminalis. *American Journal of Physiology: Regulatory, Integrative and Comparative Physiology*, 309, R324–R337. https://doi.org/10.1152/ajpregu.00134.2015

Proctor, G. B. (2016). The physiology of salivary secretion. *Periodontology*, 70, 11–25. https://doi.org/10.1111/prd.12116

Propper, C. R., Hillyard, S. D., & Johnson, W. E. (1995). Central angiotensin II induces thirst-related responses in an amphibian. *Hormones and Behavior*, 29, 74–84. https://doi.org.10.1006/hbeh.1995.1006

Purdy, J. (1990). Danger at the water hole. *Journal of General Psychology*, 117, 107–113. https://doi.org/10.1080/00221309.1990.9917778

Rabe, E. F. (1975). Relationship between absolute body-fluid deficits and fluid intake in the rat. *Journal of Comparative and Physiological Psychology*, 89, 468–477. https://doi.org/10.1037/h0077057

Radford, E. P. (1959). Factors modifying water metabolism in rats fed dry diets. *American Journal of Physiology*, 196, 1098–1108. https://doi.org/10.1152/ajplegacy.1959.196.5.1098

Radke, K. J., Willis, L. R., Zimmerman, G. W., Weinberger, M. H., & Selkurt, E. E. (1986). Effects of histamine-receptor antagonists on histamine-stimulated renin secretion. *European Journal of Pharmacology*, 123, 421–426. https://doi.org/10.1016/0014-2999

Ramsay, D. J., & Booth, D. A., eds. (1991). *Thirst: physiological and psychological aspects*. London: Springer-Verlag.

Ramsay, D. J., Rolls, B. J., & Wood, R. J. (1977a). Body fluid changes which influence drinking in the water deprived rat. *Journal of Physiology*, 266, 453–469. https://doi.org/10.1113/jphysiol.1977.sp011777

(1977b). Thirst following water deprivation in dogs. *American Journal of Physiology: Regulatory, Integrative and Comparative Physiology*, 232, R93–R100. https://doi.org/10.1152/ajpregu.1977.232.3.R93

Rand, R. P., Burton, A. C., & Ing, T. (1965). The tail of the rat in temperature regulation and acclimatization. *Canadian Journal of Physiology and Pharmacology*, 43, 257–267. https://doi.org/10.1139/y65

Redman, R. S., & Sweney, L. R. (1976). Changes in diet and patterns of feeding activity of developing rats. *Journal of Nutrition*, 106, 615–626. https://doi.org/10.1093/jn/106.5.615

Rettig, R., Ganten, D., & Johnson, A. K. (1981). Isoproterenol-induced thirst: renal and extrarenal mechanisms. *American Journal of Physiology: Regulatory, Integrative and Comparative Physiology*, 241, R152–R157. https://doi.org/10.1152/ajpregu.1981.241.3.R152

Rinaman, L., Stricker, E. M., Hoffman, G. E., & Verbalis J. G. (1997). Central c-Fos expression in neonatal and adult rats after subcutaneous injection of hypertonic saline. *Neuroscience*, 79, 1165–1175. https://doi.org/10.1016/s0306

Rinaman, L., Vollmer, R. R., Karam, J., Phillips, D., Li, X., & Amico, J. A. (2005). Dehydration anorexia is attenuated in oxytocin-deficient mice. *American Journal of Physiology: Regulatory, Integrative and Comparative Physiology*, 288, R1791–R1799. https://doi.org/10.1152/ajpregu.00860.2004

Ritter, R. C., & Epstein, A. N. (1974). Saliva lost by grooming: a major item in the rat's water economy. *Behavioral Biology*, 11, 581–585. https://doi.org/10 .1016/s0091

Roberts, M. M., Robinson, A. G., Fitzsimmons, M. D., Grant, F., Lee, W. S., & Hoffman, G. E. (1993). C-Fos expression in vasopressin and oxytocin neurons reveals functional heterogeneity within magnocellular neurons. *Neuroendocrinology*, 57, 388–400. https://doi.org/10.1159/000126384

Robinson, M. M., & Evered, M. D. (1983). Effects of systemic and intracranial inhibition of angiotensin-converting enzyme on isoproterenol-induced drinking in the rat. *European Journal of Pharmacology*, 90, 343–348. https:// doi.org/10.1016/0014-2999

(1987). Pressor action of intravenous angiotensin II reduces drinking response in rats. *American Journal of Physiology: Regulatory, Integrative and Comparative Physiology*, 252, R754–R759. https://doi.org/10.1152/ajpregu .1987.252.4.R754

Röcker, L., Kirsch, K., Stoboy, H., Schmidt, H. M., & Wicke, J. (1977). The influence of heat stress on plasma volume and intravascular proteins in sedentary females. *European Journal of Applied Physiology*, 36, 187–192. https://doi.org/10.1007/BF00421749

Rodriguez, M. M., Overshiner, C., Leander, J. D., et al. (2017). Behavioral effects of a novel benzofuranyl-piperazine serotonin-2C receptor agonist suggest a potential therapeutic application in the treatment of obsessive-compulsive disorder. *Frontiers in Psychiatry*, 8, 89. https://doi.org/10.3389/ fpsyt.2017.00089

Rolls, B. J. (1975). Interaction of hunger and thirst in rats with lesions of the preoptic area. *Physiology and Behavior*, 14, 537–543. https://doi.org/10.1016/ 0031-9384

Rolls, B. J., & Rolls, E. T. (1982). *Thirst*. Cambridge: Cambridge University Press.

Rolls, B. J., Wood, R. J., & Rolls, E. T. (1980). Thirst: the initiation, maintenance, and termination of drinking. In J. M. Sprague & A. N. Epstein, eds., *Progress in psychobiology and physiological psychology*. Cambridge: Academic Press, pp. 263–321.

Rosen, A. M., Roussin, A. T., & DiLorenzo, P. M. (2010). Water as an independent taste modality. *Frontiers in Neuroscience*, 4, 175. https://doi.org/10 .3389/fnins.2010.00175

Ross, M. G., Kullama, L. K., Ogundipe, A., Chan, K., & Ervin, M. G. (1985). Central angiotensin II stimulation of ovine fetal swallowing. *Journal of Applied Physiology*, 76, 1340–1345. https://doi.org/10.1152/jappl.1994.76.3 .1340

Ross, M. G., & Nijland, M. J. (1998). Development of ingestive behavior. *American Journal of Physiology: Regulatory, Integrative and Comparative Physiology*, 274, R879–R893. http://doi.org/10.1152/ajpregu.1998.274.4 .R879

Ross, M. G., Sherman, D. J., Ervin, M. G., et al. (1989). Stimuli for fetal swallowing: systemic factors. *American Journal of Obstetrics and Gynecology*, 161, 1559–1565. https://doi.org/10.1016/0002-9378

Ross, M. G., Sherman, D. J., Schreyer, P., et al. (1991). Fetal rehydration via intraamniotic fluid: contribution of fetal swallowing. *Pediatric Research*, 29, 214–217. https://doi.org/10.1203/00006450-199102000-0023

Roth, B. L. (2016). DREADDs for neuroscientists. *Neuron*, 89, 683–694. https://doi.org/10.1016/j.neuron.2016.01.040

Rowe, B. P., Grove, K. L., Saylor, D. L., & Speth, R. C. (1991). Discrimination of angiotensin II receptor subtype distribution in the rat brain using non-peptidic receptor antagonists. *Regulatory Peptides*, 33, 45–53. https://doi.org/10.1016/0167-0115

Rowland, N. E. (1976a). Circadian rhythms and partial recovery of regulatory drinking in rats after lateral hypothalamic lesions. *Journal of Comparative and Physiological Psychology*, 90, 383–393. https://doi.org/10.1016/0031-9384

(1976b). Endogenous circadian rhythms in rats recovered from lateral hypothalamic lesions. *Physiology and Behavior*, 16, 257–266. https://doi.org/10.1016/0031-9384

(1988). Water intake of Djungarian and Syrian hamsters treated with various dipsogenic stimuli. *Physiology and Behavior*, 43, 851–854. https://doi.org/10.1016/0031-9384

(1991). Ontogeny of preference and aversion to salt in Fischer 344 rats and Syrian hamsters. *Developmental Psychobiology*, 24, 211–218. https://doi.org/10.1002/dev.420240306

(1995). Neural activity and meal-associated drinking in rats. *Neuroscience Letters*, 189, 125–127. https://doi.org/10.1016/0304-3940

(1998). Brain mechanisms of mammalian fluid homeostasis: insights from use of immediate early gene mapping. *Neuroscience and Biobehavioral Reviews*, 23, 49–63.

(2020). Thirst. In *Oxford research encyclopedia of psychology*. Oxford: Oxford University Press. https://doi.org/10.1093/acrefore/9780190236557.013.723

Rowland, N. E., Del Bianco, A., & Fregly, M. J. (1996). Age-related decline in thirst and sodium appetite in rats related to kininase II inhibition. *Regulatory Peptides*, 66, 163–167. https://doi.org/10.1016/S0167

Rowland, N. E., Farnbauch, L. J., & Crews, E. C. (2004). Sodium deficiency and salt appetite in ICR:CD1 mice. *Physiology and Behavior*, 80, 629–635. https://doi.org/10.1016/j.physbeh.2003.11.004

Rowland, N. E., & Flamm, C. (1977). Quinine drinking: more regulatory puzzles. *Physiology and Behavior*, 18, 1165–1170. https://doi.org/10.1016/0031-9384

Rowland, N. E., & Fregly, M. J. (1988a). Characteristics of thirst and sodium appetite in mice (*Mus musculus*). *Behavioral Neuroscience*, 102, 969–974. https://doi.org/10.1037/0735-7044.102.6.969

(1988b). Induction of an appetite for sodium in rats that show no spontaneous preference for sodium chloride solution. *Behavioral Neuroscience*, 102, 961–968. https://doi.org/10.1037//0735-7044.102.6.961

(1997). Role of angiotensin in the dipsogenic effect of bradykinin in rats. *Pharmacology, Biochemistry and Behavior*, 57, 699–705. https://doi.org/10.1016/s0091

Rowland, N. E., Fregly, M. J., & Cimmerer, A. L. (1995). Bradykinin-induced water intake and brain Fos-like immunoreactivity in rats. *Brain Research*, 669, 73–78. https://doi.org/10.1016/0006-8993

Rowland, N. E., Fregly, M. J., Li, B., & Smith, G. C. (1994). Action of angiotensin converting enzyme inhibitors in rat brain: interaction with iso-proterenol assessed by Fos immunocytochemistry. *Brain Research*, 654, 34–40. https://doi.org/10.1016/0006-8993

Rowland, N. E., Goldstein, B. E., & Robertson, K. L. (2003). Role of angiotensin in body fluid homeostasis of mice: fluid intake, plasma hormones, and brain Fos. *American Journal of Physiology: Regulatory, Integrative and Comparative Physiology*, 284, R1586–R1594. https://doi.org/10.1152/ajpregu.00730.2002

Rowland, N. E., Grossman, S. P., & Grossman, L. (1979). Zona incerta lesions: regulatory drinking deficits to intravenous NaCl, angiotensin, but not to salt in the food. *Physiology and Behavior*, 23, 745–750. https://doi.org/10.1016/0031-9384

Rowland, N. E., Li, B.-H., Rozelle, A. K., Fregly, M. J., Garcea, M., & Smith, G. C. (1994). Localization of changes in immediate early genes in brain in relation to hydromineral balance: intravenous angiotensin II. *Brain Research Bulletin*, 33, 427–436. https://doi.org/10.1016/0361-9230

Rowland, N. E., Li, B.-H., Rozelle, A. K., & Smith, G. C. (1994). Comparison of Fos-like immunoreactivity induced in rat brain by central injection of angiotensin II and carbachol. *American Journal of Physiology: Regulatory, Integrative and Comparative Physiology*, 267, R792–R798. https://doi.org/10.1152/ajpregu.1994.267.3.R792

Rowland, N. E., Minaya, D. M., Cervantez, M. R., Minervini, V., & Robertson, K. L. (2015). Differences in temporal aspects of food acquisition between rats and two strains of mice in a closed economy. *American Journal of Physiology: Regulatory, Integrative and Comparative Physiology*, 309, R93–R108. https://doi.org/10.1152/ajpregu.00085.2015

Rowland, N. E., & Morian, K. R. (1999). Roles of aldosterone and angiotensin in maturation of sodium appetite in furosemide-treated rats. *American Journal of Physiology: Regulatory, Integrative and Comparative Physiology*, 276, R1453–R1460. https://doi.org/10.1152/ajpregu.1999.276.5.R1453

Rowland, N. E., Morien, A., & Fregly, M. J. (1996). Losartan inhibition of angiotensin-related drinking and Fos-immunoreactivity in hypertensive and hypotensive contexts. *Brain Research*, 742, 253–259. https://doi.org/10.1016/s0006

Rowland, N. E., Morien, A., Garcea, M., & Fregly, M. J. (1997). Aging and fluid homeostasis in rats. *American Journal of Physiology: Regulatory, Integrative and Comparative Physiology*, 273, R1441–R1450. https://doi.org/10.1152/ajpregu.1997.273.4.R1441

Rowland, N. E., & Nicolaïdis, S. (1976). Metering of fluid intake and determinants of ad libitum drinking in rats. *American Journal of Physiology*, 231, 1–8. https://doi.org/10.1152/ajplegacy.1976.231.1.1

Rullier. (1821). Soif. In *Dictionnaire des sciences médicales par une société des médecins et de chirurgiens*. Paris: Panckoucke, pp. 51, 448–490.

Russell, P. J. D., Abdelaal, A. E., & Mogenson, G. J. (1975). Graded levels of hemorrhage, thirst and angiotensin II in the rat. *Physiology and Behavior*, 15, 117–119.

Saker, P., Farrell, M. J., Adib, F. R. M., Egan, G. F., McKinley, M. J., & Denton, D. A. (2014). Regional brain responses associated with drinking water during thirst and after its satiation. *Proceedings of the National Academy of Sciences USA*, 111, 5379–5384. https://doi.org/10.1016/0031-9384

Saker, P., Farrell, M. J., Egan, G. F., McKinley, M. J., & Denton, D. A. (2016). Overdrinking, swallowing inhibition, and regional brain responses prior to swallowing. *Proceedings of the National Academy of Sciences USA*, 113, 12274–12279. https://doi.org/10.1073/pnas.1613929113

(2018). Influence of anterior midcingulate cortex on drinking behavior during thirst and following satiation. *Proceedings of the National Academy of Sciences USA*, 115, 786–791. https://doi.org/10.1073/pnas.1717646115

Sakuta, H., Nishihara, E., Hiyama, T. Y., Lin, C.-H., & Noda, M. (2016). Na$_x$ signaling evoked by an increase in [Na$^+$] in CSF induces water intake via EET-mediated TRPV4 activation. *American Journal of Physiology: Regulatory, Integrative and Comparative Physiology*, 311, R299–R306. https://doi.org/10.1152/ajpregu.00352.2015

Salisbury, J. J., & Rowland, N. E. (1990). Sham drinking in rats: osmotic and volumetric manipulations. *Physiology and Behavior*, 47, 625–630. https://doi.org/10.1016/0031-9384

Sandick, B. L., Engell, D. B., & Maller, O. (1984). Perception of drinking water temperature and effects for humans after exercise. *Physiology and Behavior*, 32, 851–855. https://doi.org/10.1016/0031-9384

Satinoff, E., Liran, J., & Clapman, R. (1982). Aberrations of circadian body temperature rhythms in rats with medial preoptic lesions. *American Journal of Physiology: Regulatory, Integrative and Comparative Physiology*, 242, R352–R357. https://doi.org/10.1152/ajpregu.1982.242.3.R352

Sawka, M. N., Montain, S. J., & Latzka, W. A. (2001). Hydration effects on thermoregulation and performance in the heat. *Comparative Biochemistry and Physiology, Part A*, 128, 670–690. https://doi.org/10.1016/s1095

Schmidt-Nielsen, K., & Schmidt-Nielsen, B. (1952). Water metabolism of desert mammals. *Physiological Review*, 32, 135–166. https://doi.org/10.1152/physrev.1952.32.2.135

Schoorlemmer, G. H. M., & Evered, M. D. (2002). Reduced feeding during water deprivation depends on hydration of the gut. *American Journal of Physiology: Regulatory, Integrative and Comparative Physiology*, 283, R1061–R1069. https://doi.org/10.1152/ajpregu.00236.2002

Schwartz, N. (2003). Self-reports in consumer research: the challenge of comparing cohorts and cultures. *Journal of Consumer Research*, 29, 588–594. https://doi.org/10.1086/346253

Shadt, J. C., & Ludbrook, J. (1991). Hemodynamic and neurohumoral responses to acute hypovolemia in conscious mammals. *American Journal of Physiology: Heart and Circulatory Physiology*, 260, H305–H318. https://doi.org/10.1152/ajpheart.1991.260.2.H305

Sharpe, L. G., & Swanson, L. W. (1974). Drinking induced by injections of angiotensin into forebrain and mid-brain sites of the monkey. *Journal of Physiology*, 239, 595–622. https://doi.org/10.1113/jphysiol.1974.sp010584

Shen, E., Dun, S. L., Ren, C., Bennett-Clarke, C., & Dun, N. J. (1992). Hypotension preferentially induces c-Fos immunoreactivity in supraoptic vasopressin neurons. *Brain Research*, 593, 136–139. https://doi.org/10.1016/0006-8993

Shi, P., Martinez, M. A., Calderon, A. S., Chen, Q., Cunningham, T. J., & Toney, G. M. (2008). Intra-carotid hyperosmotic stimulation increases Fos staining in forebrain organum vasculosum laminae terminalis neurons that project to the hypothalamic paraventricular nucleus. *Journal of Physiology*, 586, 5231–5245. https://doi.org/10.1113/jphysiol.2008.159665

Shinghai, T. (1980). Water fibers in the superior laryngeal nerve of the rat. *Japanese Journal of Physiology*, 30, 305–307. https://doi.org/10.2170/jjphysiol.30.305

Siegel, P. S., & Stuckey, H. L. (1947). The diurnal course of water and food intake in the normal mature rat. *Journal of Comparative and Physiological Psychology*, 40, 365–370. https://doi.org/10.1037/h0062185

Silver, A. J., Flood, J. F., & Morley, J. E. (1991). Effect of aging on fluid ingestion in mice. *Journal of Gerontology*, 46, B117–B121. https://doi.org/10.1093/geronj/46.3.b117

Silver, A. J., Morley, J. E., Ishimaru-Tseng, V., & Morley, P. M. K. (1993). Angiotensin II and fluid ingestion in old rats. *Neurobiology of Aging*, 14, 519–522. https://doi.org/10.1016/0197-4580

Simpkins, J. W., Field, F. P., & Ress, P. J. (1983). Age-related decline in adrenergic responsiveness of the kidney, heart and aorta of male rats. *Neurobiology of Aging*, 4, 233–238. https://doi.org/10.1016/0197-4580

Simpson, J. B., Epstein, A. N., & Camardo, J. S. (1978). Localization of receptors for the dipsogenic action of angiotensin II in the subfornical organ of rat. *Journal of Comparative and Physiological Psychology*, 92, 581–601. https://doi.org/10.1037/h0077503

Simpson, J. B., & Routtenberg, A. (1975). Subfornical organ lesions reduce intravenous angiotensin-induced drinking. *Brain Research*, 88, 154–161. https://doi.org/10.1016/0006-8993

Sinnayah, P., Burns, P., Wade, J. R., Weisinger, R. S., & McKinley, M. J. (1999). Water drinking in rats resulting from intravenous relaxin and its modification by other dipsogenic factors. *Endocrinology*, 140, 5082–5086. https://doi.org/10.1210/endo.140.11.7091

Sladek, C. D., & Johnson, A. K. (1983). Effect of anteroventral third ventricle lesions on vasopressin release by organ-cultured hypothalamo-hypophyseal explants. *Neuroendocrinology*, 37, 78–84. https://doi.org/10.1159/000123519

Smith, D. W., & Day, T. A. (1995). Hypovolaemic and osmotic simuli induce distinct patterns of c-Fos expression in the rat subfornical organ. *Brain Research*, 698, 232–236. https://doi.org/10.1016/0006-8993

Smith, D., Moore, K., Tormey, W., Baylis, P. H., & Thompson, C. J. (2004). Downward resetting of the osmotic threshold for thirst in patients with SIADH. *American Journal of Physiology: Endocrinology and Metabolism*, 287, E1019–E1023. https://doi.org/10.1152/ajpendo.00033.2004

Spiers, D. E., Barney, C. C., & Fregly, M. J. (1981). Thermoregulatory responses of tailed and tailless rats to isoproterenol. *Canadian Journal of Physiology and Pharmacology*, 59, 847–852. https://doi.org/10.1139/y81

Spiteri N. J. (1982). Circadian patterning of feeding, drinking and activity during diurnal food access in rats. *Physiology and Behavior*, 28, 139–147. https://doi.org/10.1016/0031-9384

Stachenfeld, N. S., DiPietro, L., Nadel, E. R., & Mack, G. W. (1997). Mechanism of attenuated thirst in aging. *American Journal of Physiology: Regulatory, Integrative and Comparative Physiology*, 272, R148–R157. https://doi.org/10.1152/ajpregu.1997.272.1.R148.

Stachenfeld, N. S., Mack, G. W., Takamata, A., DiPietro, L., & Nadel, E. R. (1996). Thirst and fluid regulatory responses to hypertonicity in older adults. *American Journal of Physiology: Regulatory, Integrative and Comparative Physiology*, 271, R757–R765. https://doi.org/10.1152/ajpregu.1996.271.3.R757

Stacy, B. D., & Warner, A. C. I. (1966). Balances of water and sodium in the rumen during feeding: osmotic stimulation of sodium absorption. *Quarterly Journal of Experimental Physiology*, 51, 79–93. https://doi.org/10.1113/expphysiol.1966.sp001843

Starbuck, E. M., & Fitts, D. A. (1998). Effects of SFO lesion or captopril on drinking induced by intragastric hypertonic saline. *Brain Research*, 795, 37–43. https://doi.org/10.1016/s0006

(2002). Subfornical organ disconnection and Fos-like immunoreactivity in hypothalamic nuclei after intragastric hypertonic saline. *Brain Research*, 951, 202–208. https://doi.org/10.1016/s0006

Starbuck, E. M., Wilson, W. L., & Fitts, D. A. (2002). Fos-like immunoreactivity and thirst following hyperosmotic loading in rats with subdiaphragmatic vagotomy. *Brain Research*, 931, 159–167. https://doi.org/10.1016/s0006

Stellar, E., Hyman, R., & Samet, S. (1954). Gastric factors controlling water- and salt-solution-drinking. *Journal of Comparative and Physiological Psychology*, 47, 220–226. https://doi.org/10.1037/h0063148

Stephan, F. K., & Zucker, I. (1972a). Circadian rhythms in drinking behavior and locomotor activity of rats are eliminated by hypothalamic lesions. *Proceedings of the National Academy of Sciences USA*, 69, 1583–1586. https://doi.org/10.1073/pnas.69.6.1583

(1972b). Rat drinking rhythms: central visual pathways and endocrine factors mediating responsiveness to environmental illumination. *Physiology and Behavior*, 8, 315–326. https://doi.org/10.1016/0031-9384

Stocker, S. D., Hunwick, K. J., & Toney, G. M. (2005). Hypothalamic paraventricular nucleus differentially supports lumbar and renal sympathetic outflow in water-deprived rats. *Journal of Physiology*, 563, 249–263. https://doi.org/10.1113/jphysiol.2004.076661

Stoynev, A. G., & Ikonomov, O. C. (1983). Effect of constant light and darkness on the circadian rhythms in rats: I. Food and water intake, urine output and electrolyte excretion. *Acta Physiologica Pharmacologica Bulgaria*, 9, 58–64. (PMID 8870837)

Stoynev, A. G., Ikonomov, O. C., & Usunoff, K. G. (1982). Feeding pattern and light-dark variations in water intake and renal excretion after suprachiasmatic nuclei lesions in rats. *Physiology and Behavior*, 29, 35–40. https://doi.org/10.1016/0031-9384

Stricker, E. M. (1971a). Effects of hypovolemia and/or caval ligation on water and NaCl solution drinking by rats. *Physiology and Behavior*, 6, 299–305. https://doi.org/10.1016/0031-9384

  (1971b). Inhibition of thirst in rats following hypovolemia and/or caval ligation. *Physiology and Behavior*, 6, 293–298. https://doi.org/10.1016/0031-9384

Stricker, E. M., Callahan, J. B., Huang, W., & Sved, A. F. (2002). Early osmoregulatory stimulation of neurohypophyseal hormone secretion and thirst after gastric NaCl loads. *American Journal of Physiology: Regulatory, Integrative and Comparative Physiology*, 282, R1710–R1717. https://doi.org/10.1152/ajpregu.00548.2001

Stricker, E. M., & Hainsworth, F. R. (1970a). Evaporative cooling in the rat: effects of hypothalamic lesions and chorda tympani damage. *Canadian Journal of Physiology and Pharmacology*, 48, 11–17. https://doi.org/10.1139/y70

  (1970b). Evaporative cooling in the rat: effects of dehydration. *Canadian Journal of Physiology and Pharmacology*, 48, 18–27. https://doi.org/10.1139/y70

  (1971). Evaporative cooling in the rat: interaction with heat loss from the tail. *Quarterly Journal of Experimental Physiology*, 56, 231–241. https://doi.org/10.1113/expphysiol.1971.sp002124

Summerlee, A. J., & Robertson, G. F. (1995). Central administration of porcine relaxin stimulates drinking behavior in rats: an effect mediated by central angiotensin II. *Endocrine*, 3, 377–381. https://doi.org/10.1007/BF03021422

Sun, Z., Fregly, M. J., Rowland, N. E., & Cade, J. R. (1996). Comparison of changes in blood pressure and dipsogenic responsiveness to angiotensin II in male and female rats chronically exposed to cold. *Physiology and Behavior*, 60, 1543–1549. https://doi.org/10.1016/s0031

Sunn, N., Egli, M., Burazin, T. C. D., et al. (2002). Circulating relaxin acts on subfornical organ neurons to stimulate water drinking in the rat. *Proceedings of the National Academy of Sciences USA*, 99, 1701–1706. https://doi.org/10.1073/pnas.022647699

Sunn, N., McKinley, M. J., & Oldfield, B. J. (2001). Identification of efferent neural pathways from the lamina terminalis activated by blood-borne relaxin. *Journal of Neuroendocrinology*, 13, 432–437. https://doi.org/10.1046/j.1365-2826.2001.00650.x

Symons, J. P., & Sprott, R. L. (1976). Genetic analysis of schedule induced polydipsia. *Physiology and Behavior*, 17, 837–839. https://doi.og/10.1016/0031-9384

Tabarin, A., Diz-Chaves, Y., Consoli, D., et al. (2007). Role of the corticotropin-releasing factor receptor type 2 in the control of food intake in mice: a meal pattern analysis. *European Journal of Neuroscience*, 26, 2303–2314. https://doi.org/10.1111/j.1460-9568.2007.05856.x

Takamata, A., Yoshida, T., Nishida, N., & Morimoto, T. (2001). Relationship of osmotic inhibition in thermoregulatory responses and sweat concentration in humans. *American Journal of Physiology: Regulatory, Integrative and Comparative Physiology*, 280, R623–R629.

Takei, Y. (1977). The role of the subfornical organ in drinking induced by angiotensin in the Japanese quail. *Cell and Tissue Research*, 185, 175–181. https://doi.org/10.1007/BF00220662

(2000). Comparative physiology of body fluid regulation in vertebrates with special reference to thirst regulation. *Japanese Journal of Physiology*, 50, 171–186. https://doi.org/10.2170/jjphysiol.50.171

Takei, Y., Hiroi, J., Takahashi, H., & Sakamoto, T. (2014). Diverse mechanisms for body fluid regulation in teleost fishes. *American Journal of Physiology: Regulatory, Integrative and Comparative Physiology*, 307, R778–R792. https://doi.org/10.1152.ajpregu.00104.2014

Takei, Y., Okawara, Y., & Kobayashi, H. (1988). Drinking induced by cellular dehydration in the quail, *Coturnix coturnix japonica*. *Comparative Biochemistry and Physiology: A Comparative Physiology*, 90, 291–296. https://doi.org.10.1016/0300-9629

Takeuchi, K., Yamakuni, H., Nobuhara, Y., & Okabem S. (1986). Functional and morphological alterations in the rat stomach following exposure to hypertonic NaCl solution. *Japanese Journal of Pharmacology*, 42, 549–560. https://doi.org/10.1254/jjp.42.549

Tanaka, J., Kaba, H., Saito, H., & Seto, K. (1985). Subfornical organ neurons with efferent projections to the hypothalamic paraventricular nucleus: an electrophysiological study in the rat. *Brain Research*, 346, 151–154. https://doi.org/10.1016/0006-8993

Tang, M., & Falk, J. L. (1974). Sar[1]-Ala[8]-angiotensin II blocks renin-angiotensin but not beta-adrenergic dipsogenesis. *Pharmacology, Biochemistry and Behavior*, 2, 401–408. https://doi.org/10.1016/0091-3057

Taylor, A. C., McCarthy, J. J., & Stocker, S. D. (2008). Mice lacking the transient receptor vanilloid potential 1 channel display normal thirst responses and central Fos activation to hypernatremia. *American Journal of Physiology: Regulatory, Integrative and Comparative Physiology*, 294, R1285–R1293. https://doi.org/10.1152/ajpregu.00003.2008

Taylor, C. R. (1970). Strategies of temperature regulation: effect on evaporation in East African ungulates. *American Journal of Physiology*, 219, 1131–1135. https://doi.org/10.1152/ajplegacy.1970.219.4.1131

Taylor, K., Mayer, L. P., & Propper, C. R. (1999). Intra- and extracellular dehydration-induced thirst-related behavior in an amphibian. *Physiology and Behavior*, 65, 717–721. https://doi.org/10.1016/s0031

Thompson, C. J., Edwards, C. R. W., & Baylis, P. H. (1991). Osmotic and non-osmotic regulation of thirst and vasopressin secretion in patients with compulsive water drinking. *Clinical Endocrinology*, 35, 221–228. https://doi.org/10.1111/j.1365-2265.1991.tb03526.x

Thornton, S. N. (1984). A central Na+ receptor and its influence on osmotic and angiotensin II induced drinking in the pigeon *Columba livia*. *Journal of Physiology (Paris)*, 79, 505–510. (PMID 6443127)

(1986). The influence of intracerebroventricular infusions on osmotically induced urine excretion in the pigeon (*Columba livia*). *Physiology and Behavior*, 37, 673–679. https://doi.org/10.1016/0031-9384

Thornton, S. N., & Fitzsimons, J. T. (1995). The effects of centrally administered porcine relaxin on drinking behavior in male and female rats. *Journal of
Neuroendocrinology*, 7, 165–169. https://doi.org/10.1111/j.1365-2826.1995
.tb00743.x

Thrasher, T. N., Brown, C. J., Keil, L. C., & Ramsay, D. J. (1980). Thirst and
vasopressin release in the dog: an osmoreceptor or sodium receptor mechanism? *American Journal of Physiology: Regulatory, Integrative and
Comparative Physiology*, 238, R333–R339. https://doi.org/10.1152/ajpregu
.1980.238.5.R333

Thrasher, T. N., Chen, H. G., & Keil, L. C. (2000). Arterial baroreceptors
control plasma vasopressin responses to graded hypotension in conscious
dogs. *American Journal of Physiology: Regulatory, Integrative and Comparative
Physiology*, 278, R469–R475. https://doi.org/10.1152/ajpregu.2000.278.2
.R469

Thrasher, T. N., Jones, R. G., Keil, L. C., Brown, C. J., & Ramsay, D. J. (1980).
Drinking and vasopressin release during ventricular infusions of hypertonic
solutions. *American Journal of Physiology: Regulatory, Integrative and
Comparative Physiology*, 238, R340–R345. https://doi.org/10.1152/ajpregu
.1980.238.5.R340

Thrasher, T. N., & Keil, L. C. (1987). Regulation of drinking and vasopressin
secretion: role of organum vasculosum laminae terminalis. *American Journal
of Physiology: Regulatory, Integrative and Comparative Physiology*, 253,
R108–R120. https://doi.org/10.1152/ajpregu.1987.253.1.R108

Thrasher, T. N., Keil, L. C., & Ramsay, D. J. (1982). Hemodynamic, hormonal
and drinking responses to reduced venous return in the dog. *American
Journal of Physiology: Regulatory, Integrative and Comparative Physiology*,
243, R354–R62. https://doi.org/10.1152/ajpregu.1982.243.3.R354

Thrasher, T. N., Simpson, J. B., & Ramsay, D. J. (1982). Lesions of the
subfornical organ block angiotensin-induced drinking in the dog.
Neuroendocrinology, 35, 68–72. https://doi.org/10.1159/000123357

Thunhorst, R. L., Beltz, T. N., & Johnson, A. K. (2009). Hypotension- and
osmotically induced thirst in old brown Norway rats. *American Journal of
Physiology: Regulatory, Integrative and Comparative Physiology*, 297,
R149–R157. https://doi.org/10.1152/ajpregu.00118.2009

   (2010). Drinking and arterial blood pressure responses to ANG II in young
and old rats. *American Journal of Physiology: Regulatory, Integrative and
Comparative Physiology*, 299, R1135–R1141. https://doi.org/10.1152/
ajpregu.00360.2010

   (2014). Age-related declines in thirst and salt appetite responses in male
Fischer 344 × brown Norway rats. *Physiology and Behavior*, 135, 180–188.
https://doi.org/10.1016/j.physbeh.2014.06.010

Thunhorst, R. L., Grobe, C. L., Beltz, T. G., & Johnson, A. K. (2011). Effects of
β-adrenergic receptor agonists on drinking and arterial blood pressure in
young and old rats. *American Journal of Physiology: Regulatory, Integrative and
Comparative Physiology*, 300, R1001–R1008. https://doi.org/10.1152/ajpregu
.00737.2010

Thunhorst, R. L., & Johnson, A. K. (2003). Thirst and salt appetite responses in
young and old brown Norway rats. *American Journal of Physiology:*

Regulatory, Integrative and Comparative Physiology, 284, R317–R327. https:// doi.org/10.1152/ajpregu.00368.2002

Toth, D. M. (1973). Temperature regulation and salivation following preoptic lesions in the rat. *Journal of Comparative and Physiological Psychology*, 82, 480–488. https://doi.org/10.1037/h0034118

Towbin, E. J. (1949). Gastric distention as a factor in the satiation of thirst in esophagostomized dogs. *American Journal of Physiology*, 159, 533–541. https://doi.org/10.1152/ajplegacy.1949.159.3.533

(1955). Thirst and hunger behavior in normal dogs and the effects of vagotomy and sympathectomy. *American Journal of Physiology*, 182, 377–382. https:// doi.org/10.1152/ajplegacy.1955.182.2.377

Trimble, M. E. (1970). Renal response to solute loading in infant rats: relation to anatomical development. *American Journal of Physiology*, 291, 1089–1097. https://doi.org/10.1152/ajplegacy.1970.219.4.1089

Tsutsumi, K., & Saavedra, J. M. (1991). Quantitative autoradiography reveals different angiotensin II receptor subtypes in selected rat brain nuclei. *Journal of Neurochemistry*, 56, 348–351. https://doi.org/10.1111/j.1471-4159.1991 .tb02602.x

Uschakov, A., McGinty, D., Szymusiak, R., & McKinley, M. J. (2009). Functional correlates of activity in neurons projecting from the lamina terminalis to the ventrolateral periaqueductal gray. *European Journal of Neuroscience*, 30, 2347–2355. https://doi.org/10.1111/j.1460-9568.2009 .07024.x.

van Belzen, L., Postma, E. M., & Boesveldt, S. (2017). How to quench your thirst: the effect of water-based products varying in temperature and texture, flavor, and sugar content on thirst. *Physiology and Behavior*, 180, 45–52. https://doi.org/10.1016/j.physbeh.2017.08.007

Vokes, T. J., Weiss, N. M., Schreiber, J., Gaskill, M. B., & Robertson, G. L. (1988). Osmoregulation of thirst and vasopressin during normal menstrual cycle. *American Journal of Physiology: Regulatory, Integrative and Comparative Physiology*, 254, R641–R647. https://doi.org/10.1152/ajpregu.1988.254.4.R641

Waldbillig, R. J., & Lynch, W. C. (1979). Oroesophageal factors in the patterning of drinking. *Physiology and Behavior*, 22, 205–209. https://doi.org/10.1016/ 0031-9384

Watanabe, E., Fujikawa, A., Matsunaga, H., et al. (2000). Na$_v$2/NaG channel is involved in control of salt-intake behavior in the CNS. *Journal of Neuroscience*, 20, 7743–7751.

Watanabe, E., Hiyama, T. Y., Shimizu, H., et al. (2006). Sodium-level-sensitive sodium channel nax is expressed in glial laminate processes in the sensory circumventricular organs. *American Journal of Physiology: Regulatory, Integrative and Comparative Physiology*, 290, R568–R576. https://doi.org/10 .1152/ajpregu.00618.2005

Watts, A. G. (1999). Dehydration-associated anorexia: development and rapid reversal. *Physiology and Behavior*, 65, 871–878. https://doi.org/10.1016/s0031

(2001). Neuropeptides and the integration of motor responses to dehydration. *Annual Review of Neuroscience*, 24, 357–384. https://doi.org/10.1146/annurev .neuro.24.1.357

Watts, A. G., & Boyle, C. N. (2010). The functional architecture of dehydration-anorexia. *Physiology and Behavior*, 100, 472–477. https://doi.org/10.1016/j.physbeh.2010.04.010

Weisinger, R. S., Burns, P., Eddie, L. W., & Winotour, E. M. (1993). Relaxin alters the plasma osmolality-arginine vasopressin relationship in the rat. *Journal of Endocrinology*, 137, 505–510. https://doi.org/10.1677/joe.0.1370505

Wettendorff, H. (1901). Modifications du sang sous l'influence de la privation d'eau: contribution à l'étude de la soif. *Travaux du Laboratoire de Physiologie, Instituts Solvay*, 4, 353–484.

Whyte, D. G., Thunhorst, R. L., & Johnson, A. K. (2004). Reduced thirst in old, thermally dehydrated rats. *Physiology and Behavior*, 81, 569–576. https://doi.org/10.1016/j.physbeh.2004.02.030

Wiepkema, P. R., Prins, A. J., & Steffens, A. B. (1972). Gastrointestinal food transport in relation to meal occurrence in rats. *Physiology and Behavior*, 9, 759–763. https://doi.org/10.1016/0031-9384

Wilk, B., & Bar-Or, O. (1996). Effect of drink flavor and NaCl on voluntary drinking and hydration in boys exercising in the heat. *Journal of Applied Physiology*, 80, 1112–1117.

Wilson, J. X. (1984). The renin-angiotensin system in nonmammalian vertebrates. *Endocrine Review*, 5, 41–61. https://doi.org/10.1210/edrv-5-1-45

Wilson, K. M., & Fregly, M. J. (1985). Factors affecting angiotensin II–induced hypothermia in rats. *Peptides*, 6, 695–701. https://doi.org/10.1016/0196-9781

Wilson, L. M., Chan, S.-S. P., Henning, S. J., & Margules, D. M. (1981). Suckling: developmental indicator of genetic obesity in mice. *Developmental Psychobiology*, 14, 67–74. https://doi.org/10.1002/dev.420140109

Wirth, J. B., & Epstein, A. N. (1976). Ontogeny of thirst in the infant rat. *American Journal of Physiology*, 230, 188–198. https://doi.org/10.1152/ajplegacy.1976.230.1.188

Wolf, A. V. (1950). Osmometric analysis of thirst in man and dog. *American Journal of Physiology*, 161, 75–86. https://doi.org/10.1152/ajplegacy.1950.161.1.75
   (1958). *Thirst: physiology of the urge to drink and problems of water lack.* Springfield, IL: C. C. Thomas.

Wong, P. C., Hart, S. D., Zaspel, A. M., et al. (1990). Functional studies of nonpeptide angiotensin II receptor subtype-specific ligands: DuP753 (AII-1) and PD123177 (AII-2). *Journal of Pharmacology and Experimental Therapeutics*, 255, 584–592. (PMID 2243344)

Wood, R. J., Maddison, S., Rolls, E. T., Rolls, B. J., & Gibbs, J. (1980). Drinking in rhesus monkeys: roles of presystemic and systemic factors in control of drinking. *Journal of Comparative and Physiological Psychology*, 94, 1135–1148. https://doi.org/10.1037/h0077745

Wood, R. J., Rolls, E. T., & Rolls, B. J. (1982). Physiological mechanisms for thirst in the nonhuman primate. *American Journal of Physiology: Regulatory, Integrative and Comparative Physiology*, 242, R423–R428. https://doi.org/10.1152/ajpregu.1982.242.5.R423

Wright, J. W., Morseth, S. L., Fairley, P. C., Petersen, E. P., & Harding, J. W. (1986). Angiotensin's contribution to dipsogenic additivity in several rodent species. *Behavioral Neuroscience*, 101, 361–370. https://doi.org/10.1037//0735-7044.101.3.361

Wright, J. W., Morseth, S. L., LaCrosse, E., & Harding, J. W. (1984). Angiotensin III-induced dipsogenic and pressor responses in rodents. *Behavioral Neuroscience*, 98, 640–651. https://doi.org/10.1037//0735-7044.98.4.640

Wright, J. W., Schulz, E. M., & Harding, J. W. (1982). An evaluation of dipsogenic stimuli in the African green monkey. *Journal of Comparative and Physiological Psychology*, 96, 78–88. https://doi.org/10.1037/h0077867

Xu, Z., & Herbert, J. (1996). Effects of unilateral or bilateral lesions within the anteroventral third ventricular region on c-Fos expression induced by dehydration or angiotensin II in the supraoptic and paraventricular nuclei of the hypothalamus. *Brain Research*, 713, 36–43.

Xu, Z., Nijland, M. J. M., & Ross, M. G. (2001). Plasma osmolality dipsogenic thresholds and c-Fos expression in the near-term ovine fetus. Pediatric Research, 49, 678–685.

Yan, J.-J., & Hwang, P.-P. (2019). Novel discoveries in acid-base regulation and osmoregulation: a review of selected hormonal actions in zebrafish and medaka. *General and Comparative Endocrinology*, 277, 20–29. https://doi.org/10.1016/j.ygcen.2019.03.007

Yawata, T., Okuno, T., Nose, H., & Morimoto, T. (1987). Change in salt appetite due to rehydration level in rats. *Physiology and Behavior*, 40, 363–368. https://doi.org/10.1016/0031-9384

Yeomans, M. L., & Savory, C. J. (1988). Intravenous hypertonic saline injections and drinking in domestic fowls. *Physiology and Behavior*, 42, 307–312. https://doi.org/10/1016/0031-9384

(1989). Altered spontaneous and osmotically induced drinking for fowls with permanent access to silute quinine. *Physiology and Behavior*, 46, 917–922. https://doi.org/10.1016/0031-9384

Yoshimura, M., Matsuura, T., Ohkubo, J., et al. (2014). A role of nestafin-1/NucB2 in dehydration-induced anorexia. *American Journal of Physiology: Regulatory, Integrative and Comparative Physiology*, 307, R225–R236. https://doi.org/10.1152/ajpregu.00488.2013

Zerbe, R. L., & Robertson, G. L. (1983). Osmoregulation of thirst and vasopressin secretion in human subjects: effect of various solutes. *American Journal of Physiology: Endocrinology and Metabolism*, 244, E607–E614. https://doi.org/10.1152/ajpendo.1983.244.6.E607

Zhang, H., Fan, Y., Xia, F., et al. (2011). Prenatal water deprivation alters brain angiotensin system and dipsogenic changes in the offspring. *Brain Research*, 1382, 128–136. https://doi.org/10.1016/j.brainres.2011.01.031

Zhao, S., Malmgren, C. H., Shanks, R. D., & Sherwood, O. D. (1995). Monoclonal antibodies specific for rat relaxin. VIII. Passive immunization with monoclonal antibodies throughout the second half of pregnancy reduces water consumption in rats. *Endocrinology*, 136, 1892–1897. https://doi.org/10.1210/endo.136.5.7720635

Zimmerman, C. A., Huey, E. L., Ahn, J. S., et al. (2019). A gut-to-brain signal of fluid osmolality controls thirst satiation. *Nature, 568*, 98–102.

Zimmerman, C. A., Lin, Y.-C., Leib, D. E., et al. (2016). Thirst neurons anticipate the homeostatic consequences of eating and drinking. *Nature, 537*, 680–684.

Zocchi, D., Wennemuth, G., & Oka, Y. (2017). The cellular mechanism for water detection in the mammalian taste system. *Nature Neuroscience, 20*, 927–933. https://doi.org/10.1038/nn.4575

Zorilla, E. P., Inoue, K., Fekete, E. M., et al. (2005). Measuring meals: structure of prandial food and water intake of rats. *American Journal of Physiology: Regulatory, Integrative and Comparative Physiology, 288*, R1450–R1467. https://doi.org/10.1152/ajpregu.00175.2004

Zotterman, Y., & Diamant, H. (1959). Has water a specific taste? *Nature, 183*, 191–192.

Zucker, I. (1971). Light-dark rhythms in rat eating and drinking behavior. *Physiology and Behavior, 6*, 115–126. https://doi.org/10.1016/0031-9384

Index

Lightning Source UK Ltd.
Milton Keynes UK
UKHW020827101222
413700UK00031B/645